The GIANT
Encyclopedia of
Transition
Activities
for Children 3 to 6

Over 600 Activities
Created by Teachers for Teachers

Edited by Kathy Charner
Maureen Murphy, and Jennifer Ford

Illustrated by Kathi Whelan Dery

Gryphon House, Inc.
Beltsville, Maryland

The Giant Encyclopedia of Transition Activities

Edited by Kathy Charner, Maureen Murphy, and Jennifer Ford

© 2005 Gryphon House
Published by Gryphon House, Inc.
PO Box 207, Beltsville, MD 20704
800.638.0928; 301.595.9500; 301.595.0051 (fax)

Visit us on the web at www.gryphonhouse.com

Illustrations: Kathi Whelan Dery

Cover Art: Beverly Hightshoe

Library of Congress Cataloging-in-Publication Data
The giant encyclopedia of transition activities / edited by Kathy Charner, Maureen Murphy, and Jennifer Ford.
   p. cm.
 Includes index.
 Summary: "Resource book with over 600 transition activities for teachers of preschool children ages three to five to use in the classroom"--Provided by publisher.
 Includes index.
 ISBN-13: 978-0-87659-003-4
 ISBN-10: 0-87659-003-2
 1. Education, Preschool--Activity programs--Encyclopedias. I. Charner, Kathy. II. Murphy, Maureen. III. Ford, Jennifer, 1980-
 LB1140.35.C74G55 2005
 372.5--dc22
                                     2005001917

Gryphon House is a member of the Green Press Initiative, a nonprofit program dedicated to supporting publishers in their efforts to reduce their use of fiber sourced forests. For further information visit www.greenpressinitiative.org.

The Giant Encyclopedia of Transition Activities for Children 3 to 6

Table of Contents

Introduction **13**
Anytime Ideas **19**
"5 More Minutes" Sign. 19
A Smile 20
Block Corner Open or Closed 20
The Apple Tree 21
Labels for Us 22
Plastic Letters 23
Books for Transitions 24
Theme Book Basket 24
Popping Up 25
Transition Bag 25
My Own Book 26
All Wrapped Up. 27
Yarn Necklaces 28
Follow the Bubbles 29
Go Ahead and Wiggle. 29
Line Up Here 30
Linked and Lined Up 31
Partner, Please. 32
Photo Lineup. 33
The Name Game. 33
Who's Next? Jar 34
The Sorting Hunt 35
The Train 36
Red Light, Green Light 36
Keep Your Bubbles in Your Mouth . . 37
Look at Me 38
Lost and Found Boxes. 38
Sanding. 39
Sanding Wood Slices 40
Squishy Bags 41
Busy Boxes. 42
My Own Box 43
My Special Box 44
Animal Observation. 45
Water and Clean Plants. 46
The Magic Wand. 46
Hickory, Dickory, Dock. 47
What Time Is It?. 47
Silent Counting. 48

Listen to the Quiet 48
Try to Whisper 49
Look at the Clock 49
Clapping Echo. 50
Clapping Names 51
Clapping Words 51
Are You Ready? 52
Come and Join Me. 52
Stop Song. 53
Rhyming Song. 54
Pocket Full of Fun. 55
Following Directions 56
Shifting Gears 57
Color Bright 57
Color Match. 58
What Am I Wearing Today? 58
Sewing Is Fun 59
Fitting Together 59
How Many Cotton Balls Does It Take to
　　Make a Bunny Tail? 60
Lineup Lengths. 61
Over and Under 62
Happy Birthday. 62
Famous Quotations 64
Fun With Initials 65
Grab Bag Letters 66
I Know My Name 67
"I'm Thinking of…". 67
My Name Has a ___ in It. 68
Poetry Place. 68
Question Cards 69
Rhyming Wheel Game 70
Same and Different 72
Someone Just Like Me 72
Sounds of the Alphabet 73
My Name 74
Under the Sea Wheel 74
Using Foreign Languages 76
Velcro Alphabet 77
Writing Letters. 78
The Opposite Boat. 78
I Can't Make Up My Mind. 79
Did You Know? 80

Arrivals **81**
A Welcome Note 81
Entering School: Extending Children's
    Comfort Zone 82
Hello, How Are You? 82
I'm Glad You Came to School 83
Morning Greeting 84
Sing and Sign 85
Arrival Transitions 87
Arrival Candle 87
Good Morning 88
Good Morning to You! 88
Door Stop Ritual 89
That Awkward Arrival Time 89
Morning Transition Playdough 90
Class Pets 90
Puppet Pals 91
Happy or Sad 92
Feelings 93
Who Is at School Today? 94
Attendance Board 94
Question of the Day 96
Morning Message 97
Morning Transition Journals 97
Name Necklaces and Nametags 98
Sign Your Name 98
Please Sign Up 99
Welcome to Our Zoo 100
Classroom Calendar 101

Art **103**
Personal Art Journals 103
Handy Art Labels 103
Time for Art 104
A Dot Will Do 104
Color Quartet 105
Driftwood Art 106
Create-a-Picture 106
My Own Chalkboard 107
Never-Ending Artwork 108
Picture Starter 109
Squiggles 109
No More Paint or Paper 110
Name the Animal 111
Matching Mittens 112

Shape Up 113
Thinking Caps 114
Stained Glass Window 115

Attention Grabbers **116**
Salami 116
The Cheering Section 116
Get Ready Rhyme 117
Point 117
1, 2, Come Here to Me 118
Catch a Bubble 118
Chant and Clap 119
I Say, You Say 120
Inside Voice 121
It Might Be You 121
May I Have Your Attention, Please? . 122
One, Two, Three, Eyes on Me 122
Quiet Song 123
If You Can Hear Me! 124
Do What I Do and Say What I Say . . 125
Echo-Location 125
Attention Grabbers 126
Pay Attention 126
Visual or Auditory 127
Freeze! 127
Doggie, Doggie 128
Hush 129
My Binoculars 129
Drum Beating 130
Make a Little Rain 131
Make It Magic 131
Guessing Box 132
The Mouse Train 133
Movin' On 134
P-L-A-Y 134
Silly Names 135
Tool Rap 135
Copy Me! 136
Making a List, Checking It Twice . . . 136
Wow Sounds! 137
Take Five 138
Calling All Sailors 139

Cleanup **140**
"If You're Happy" Game 140
Clean Classroom 140
Clean Up Our Work 141
Cleanup Song 141
Clean Up the Room 142
Cleanup Theme Song 143
Cleanup Chant 143
I'll Be Cleanin' Up the Classroom 144
I'm a Little Sweeper 144
On a Bright and Sunny Day 145
On the Floor 146
Pickup Song 146
Pick Up Your Work 147
Picking Up 148
Ten Minutes Left! 149
This Is the Way We Clean
    Our Room 149
We Are Going to Clean Up 150
Zip-a-Dee-Doo-Dah! 150
Thank You 151
Beat the Timer 151
Beat the Music! 152
Clean Up 153
Creature Cleanup 153
I Spy Game 154
Music to Clean By 155
Who Wants to Be a Vacuum
    Cleaner? 156
Pickup Choices 156
Table Toy Time 157
Transition Toys 158
Wash Day 159
Towel Fun 160
Vacuum Cleaners 160
Surprise the Teacher 161
While I'm Not Looking 162
Cleaning Buddies 162
You're In Charge 163

Departure Time **164**
Lucky Leprechaun 164
Another Day 165
Departure Song 165
Goodbye Everybody 166

Goodbye, Little Friend 167
Goodbye Song 168
It's Time to Say Goodbye 168
Time to Leave 169
Tommorrow 170
End-of-the-Day Transition 170
We Had a Ball 171
Rhyming Word Fun 172
Waiting to Go Home 172
After 5 Box 173
Saying Goodbye 174
Going on a Bus Ride 174
Where Did They Go? 175
Be a Friend 176
Reflection Journal 177
Crazy Cube 178
Sweet and Sour 179

Dramatic Play **180**
Let's Be Like . . ." 180
Butterfly Drama 180
Transition Activity With Stuffed
    Animal 181
Winterskoll (Winter Cheer) 182
Lights, Camera, Action! 183
Quiet as Mice 183
Let's Travel Around the
    World/Country/Town 184
Observing X-Rays 186

Fingerplays, Songs, and Poems . . **187**
Move to a Different Area 187
5 Minutes Left 188
A Simple Song 188
"Autumn Leaves" Song 190
"Autumn Leaves" Fingerplay 191
Cats 192
Cleanup Song 193
Five Speckled Frogs 193
Fly Away, All 194
Bored? No Way! 195
Free Time 196
Hands Go Up 196
Hello, Goodnight, Goodbye 197
I'm Ready to Learn 198

Mary Wore a Red Dress............ 198
Pizza Pizzazz 199
Sing Songs 200
Sneaky Black Cat 201
We Know How to Get in Line 201
The Eensy Weensy Spider Game ... 202
Lining Up Rhyme 203
Look at Me! 203
Open Them, Shut Them 204
Please Quiet Down 205
The Listening Position 205
A Knocking at the Door 206
Bendable Me..................... 207
Bingo........................... 207
Can You?........................ 208
Class Song 209
Five Little Snakes 209
Days of the Week 210
Fingerplay Library 211
"Grandma's Glasses" Fingerplay 213
I Am Special..................... 213
Mother Goose Picks a Poem 214
"One Potato, Two Potato"......... 214
Right and Left 215
"The Grand Old Duke of York" 216
Waiting With a Song.............. 216
We're Glad You're Here 217
Whoops, Johnny 218
Wiggle Your Nose................ 218
Exercise Away 219
Follow the Leader 220
If You're Ready to Go Outside...... 221
Marching Song................... 222
The Wiggle Song 222
A Circle Is a Shape 223
If You're Listening................ 224
Flashing Fireflies................. 224
Mother Goose Mix-Up 226
Doggy, Doggy Where's Your Bone? . 227
Thumbelina..................... 228
Nursery Rhymes Are Lots of Fun ... 228
Say Something 231
Sensory Song 232
Cookie Jar....................... 233

Sing a Silly Song.................. 234
Wheelbarrow 236
Ten Little Beavers................. 237
The Alphabet Song 238
Loony Limericks 239
Spelling Numbers 241
Count With the Inchworm........ 242

Games 243
Cookie Jar Name Game 243
"Rig a Jig Jig"................... 244
Birds Fly 244
Clap the Parts 245
"Pass Some Love" Game.......... 245
Dinosaur Game.................. 246
Hula Hoop Sort.................. 246
Letter Game..................... 247
Match-the-Photo Game 248
Name It........................ 248
Me Puzzles...................... 249
Officer, Where Is My Child? 250
Transition Cube 251
Lining Up—Where to Stand 253
Who Am I Thinking Of?........... 254
Around the Room 255
Beginning Sounds Wheel Game ... 255
Button, Button................... 257
Chairs for Bears.................. 258
I Spy! 259
Pass It 259
Putting the Pieces Together 260
The Rhyming Game.............. 261
Sight Word Wheel Game 261
The Listening Game 263
Weather Charades 263
Twenty Questions 264
"What If...?"..................... 265
What's Missing? 265
The Opposite Game 266
Whose Feet? Wheel Game 266
Remote Control 268
My Name Starts With "M"......... 268
Nursery Rhyme Riddles 269
What Am I? 270

Go-Togethers 270
Button Math 271
Find a Match 272
Last Name Game 273
Alphabet Riddles 274

General Tips **275**
Transition Tips and Techniques 275
Developmentally Appropriate
    Changes 276
Be Prepared for Transitions 277
Transition Ideas 277
Transition to Preschool 278
Substitute Teacher Transition 279
It's Time Now 280
Classroom Schedule 281
Daily Schedule Cards 283
Our Daily Activities 284
What Will We Do Next? 286
Job Captains 287
Water Table Dryer 288
Class List at a Glance 289
Inventory Lists 289
Magnetic ID 290
Cubby Photos 291
Photo Groups 291
Self-Managing Areas 292
Bathroom Signs 293
Button Jar Party 293
Partnering With Families 295
Pocket Pack 296
Quick Pick Transitions 297
Routine Songs 297
Storytelling 298
Our Transition Stories 298
The Music Box Trick 299
Reminders Are a Must! 300
Signals 300
Creative Lineups 301
Using the Line Rope 302
Morning Break 303
Jigsaw Puzzle Moments 303
Daisy Wheel 304
Job Visors 305

Get Moving! 306
"K" Transition 306

Gross Motor **308**
Exercise Song 308
Quiet Movements 308
Hop, Skip, or Jump 309
Motor Time 309
Popcorn 310
Easy Hoop Ball 312
Elevator Up and Down 312
Galloping 313
Familiar Games 314
Mirrors and Shadows 315
Pat and Clap 315
Touch the Line 316
What Animals Do 316
Alternating Steps 317
Stretch, Stretch! 318
Wiggle Words 319
Pattern Path 319
Road Trips 320
The Farmer Is Planting
    Some Seeds 321
Alien Spaceships 322
A Rolling Transition 323
Look, I'm a Letter! 324

Group or Circle Time **325**
1, 2, I Love You 325
Call to Circle Time 325
Gathering the Group 326
Get on Board, Little Children 326
Walk to Group Time 327
It's Time to Come to Circle 327
Make a Circle 328
Move It! 328
More Friends 329
Music Box Transitions 330
Super-Bowl Soup 331
Time for Circle 331
Color Muncher 332
Musical Hugs 333
I Can Wait 333

Puppet Songs 334
Watch and Follow 335
What's in the Bag? 335
Willaby Wallaby 336
Interruption Song 338
Greeting 338
Hello! Hello! 339
Microphone 339
Left and Right 340
Song for Walking, Sitting, and Quiet
    Times 340
Show and Tell 341
Field Trip Song 342
Birthday 343
Birthday Boy or Girl 343
Rhyme Time 344
Transition Turns 345
Washing Hands Poem 345
Choose a Friend 346
Bottom of Your Shoes 347
If Your Name Is 347
Roll the Ball 348
Pack-It-Up Suitcase Fun 349
Pull 'n Tell Story 350
Carpet Squares 350
Alphabet Soup 351
Class Calendar 352
The "Because" Book 353
Grocery Cart Game 353
Sharing Clues 354
What's That Sound Coming From
    the Barn? 355
Weather Graph 355
Little Bit of the Old With the New . . 357
Shape Game 358
Winter Words 358
Coins in the Can 359
Create-a-Creature 360
What's in a Name? 361
Writing Numbers 361
Question of the Week 362

Music and Movement **363**
A Walk in Space 363
Animals Walk 364
Copy Me 365
Follow My Rhythm 365
Follow the Wind 366
Galloping Cowpokes 367
Get Moving! 368
How Can We Move Our Bodies? 368
Marching Along 369
Moving Along 370
Musical Circles 370
Musical Moving 371
Music Transitions 372
She'll Be Coming 'Round the
    Corner... 372
The Parachute-Pokey 373
Welcoming a New Day! 374
Yoga Stretches 374
Watch Me! 375
Making Music 375
Using Music 376
Instrumental Changes 377
Michael, Row Your Boat Ashore 378
Mirror Dance 378
Move-Chucka-Lucka-Lucka! 379
Music Hunt 380
Pet Play 380
The Instruments on the Bus 381
Name That Tune 382
Rainbow Hand Jive 382
The Shuffle 383

Outdoor Play **384**
Colored Feet 384
From Inside to Outside 385
Going Outside 385
Meet Me 386
Outdoor Play 386
The Little Red Caboose 387
Tunnel Ball 387
What Will You Do When You Go
    Outside? 388
Weather Buddy 389
Run and Stop 391

The GIANT Encyclopedia of Transition Activities

Too Much Energy! 391
Get Your Drink. 392
The Playground Express. 392
Sardine Squeeze. 393
Target Toss 394
Peanut Butter March. 395
Relax and Unwind 395
Come Form a Line 396
It's Time to Go Inside. 396
Take a Ticket 397
Wind Away. 398
Little Things Count a Lot 398
What's My Shape? 399

Rainy Day Ideas **401**
What to Do on Rainy Days. 401
Breathing Technique. 402
Go Away, Rainy Day 402
Rainy Day Paint With Cattails 403
Tie Dye With Coffee Filters 404
Rainy Day Activities. 405
Raindrop Art 406
Picture-Song Storybooks. 406
Raffi's Rainy Day Songs. 408
Rain Songs. 408
Basket Bounce 411
Rainy Day Obstacles 412
A House Is a House for Me. 412
Visualization Treasures 413
Going to Sleep 414

Rest and Nap Time **415**
Nap Transitions. 415
Nap Time Stories 415
Quiet as a Crab 416
Rag Doll 417
See the Sleeping _____ 417
Sleep Tight. 418
Time for Quiet Time. 419
The Sticker Fairy 419
The Sun Is Sleeping 420
Dinosaur Dreams 421
Sleep Sack 422
Listen to the Seashell 423

When I Was a Child... 423
Put Your Shoes On 424
Read Aloud 425
Sweet Dreams Book 425

Snack and Lunch **427**
Snack Time Sing-Along Song 427
All Sit Down. 428
Snack Time Song 428
Are You Hungry? 429
Are You Ready? 429
Breakfast Break. 430
Healthy Food Fun. 431
What's for Lunch?. 431
Table Setting 432
Table for Two. 433
It's Time to Wash Our Hands 433
Getting Ready for Snack. 434
Soap Dispenser. 435
Edible Ladybugs. 435
Frozen Bananas 437
Birds in the Wilderness 437
Lunch Box Duty 438
Name Cards 439
Napkin Folding 439
Snack Time Math 440
Two Snacks Is Twice the Fun! 441
Shapes and Colors. 441
Snack Bucket. 443
Tasting Booklet. 444
What Kind of Super-Duper
   Sandwich? 445
Lunch Time Foods 445

Social Development **447**
I Can Can 447
Classroom Poster 447
Fostering Friendship. 448
Add It to the "Great Vine!" 449
Good Deed Apple 450
Good Graffiti 451
Say Something Nice 451
Friendship Quilt 452
Who Am I? 452

Whose Family? 453
Island Time. 454
S-T-O-P 455
Time Capsule Envelope 456

Storytime **457**
Interviews. 457
Take a Seat. 458
It's Story Time 458
Time to Sit Down 459
If You're Ready for a Story 460
Talking Stick. 460
A Bounty of Books 461
Story Sounds. 462
Flexible Straw Puppet. 462
Calling All Book Lovers 463
Story Time Present. 464
Let's Tell a Story 465
Author and Illustrator 465
Class Book Reader 466
Goodnight Moon 467
I CAN Tell a Story 467
Puppet Theater. 468
Read Me a Story 469
Song Books 472
Spend Some Time With *The Cat
   in the Hat* 473
Acting Out 474
A Mystery Story 474
What Do You See? 475
From Start to Finish. 476
Mama Don't Allow 477
Queen Forgetta Boutit and
   Concepts of Print 477
Story Leader 478

Indexes **479**
Children's Book Index. 479
Song Index 486
Index. 488

*Introduction**

It's 12:15. Lunch is almost over, except for those two stragglers who spent more time playing than eating. Four children are struggling to make their mats for nap time; three others who should be working on making their mats have decided to empty the block shelves instead. One child can't reach her sheet in her cubby and is calling for help while two others are arguing over the ownership of a brown teddy bear. There are children in both bathrooms while three more are waiting for their turn. Teeth need brushing, dirty dishes need cleaning, tables need wiping and sanitizing, floors need sweeping and, most important of all, children have needs that must be met.

Guess what? It's time for a transition!

And teachers need ideas, guidance, and help! To help the teacher, early childhood professionals have written the activities and ideas in this book. The activities have been tried and tested in classrooms and have proven successful. Any teacher with a classroom full of active, energetic, and lively three- to six-year-olds will find this book an invaluable resource.

A Word About Transitions

Transitions are the moments when children move from one activity or routine to another. Transition times include when children are helping to clean up the classroom; when children are waiting for group time to begin; the times before and after meals; or while children are moving from one place in the building or classroom to another. During these times, children may be unsure of what is expected of them, and they may be anxious about what will happen next.

Transitions can be the most difficult times of a preschooler's day. The difference between chaos and order during this time is the ability to anticipate and avoid problem situations. Teachers must pay close attention to the routine and schedule as well as the activities they plan and the environment they prepare for the children.

While transitional times usually involve groups of children, it is important to remember that each transition is also happening to each individual child. While planning transition activities, take into account not only the group composition but also each child's individuality and temperament.

* This introduction was written by Virginia Jean Herrod of Columbia, SC

The Importance of Room Arrangement, Schedules, and Routines

If calm is to reign during transitions, an orderly and organized environment and schedule must be maintained. Teachers can ease daily transitions, promote independence, and provide many opportunities for learning and decision making by having an organized and accessible room arrangement. The children should know where everything they need is stored. Shelves should be labeled with a photo and the printed name of each item. Items not intended for the children's use should be stored out of sight and out of children's reach.

Plan the daily schedule around the needs of the children. A well-organized schedule offers children the security and consistency they need. Each day should include a balance of active and quiet activities along with time spent in large and small groups. There should also be a balance of teacher- and child-directed activities. An appropriate schedule will also include blocks of time when children can be alone, if they wish.

Establish a routine for each transition and stick with it so the children will know exactly what to do. Doing so reduces opportunities for conflict and gives teachers more time to devote to individual children.

Capture children's attention to make daily transition times go more smoothly. By actively engaging children, teachers eliminate wasted time and provide opportunities for learning.

Developmental Levels and Individuality

While using this book to plan transition activities keep in mind the varying developmental levels of children. In general:

Three-Year-Olds
- Actively explore the world around them
- Imitate adult roles and responsibilities
- Focus on the observable and tangible aspects of events
- Approach new tasks through hands-on trial and error
- Copy others or follow their suggestions
- Assert their own needs and wants
- Begin to negotiate conflict with peers
- Express intense feelings
- Sense others' feelings and show empathy
- Begin to be independent with routine tasks, such as dressing self, using the bathroom and cleaning up after playing or eating
- Can follow two- or three-step directions

Four-Year-Olds

- Actively explore their immediate world
- Begin to show interest in the world beyond home and classroom
- Begin to generate ideas and suggestions about daily events
- Make plans and predictions about what will happen next
- Verbalize their own interpretations of cause and effect
- Begin to play cooperatively
- See "being friends" as important
- Begin willingly to take turns
- May spontaneously offer help, comfort, or objects to others
- Manage routines, such as dressing self, using the bathroom and cleaning up after play, snacks, and meals
- Begin to understand their actions have consequences
- Can follow three- and four-step directions

Five- and Six-Year-Olds

- Demonstrate interest in exploring the world beyond school
- Sustain interest in a task
- Work hard to solve problems independently
- Focus not only on what is observable, but also on what might happen next
- Verbalize their own wants and needs
- Cooperate most of the time in group play and work time
- Use language to express feelings
- Negotiate to resolve disagreements
- Have their own ideas about how to help others
- Manage routines, such as dressing self, using the bathroom and cleaning up after meals, snacks, or play time independently
- Begin to understand consequences of own and others' behavior
- Can follow four- to five-step directions

Allow for individual temperaments when planning transitional times. Give children who find transitions more difficult a longer warning and more guidance. Give more guidance to new children, as they are often unsure about what to do and what comes next.

How to Use This Book

Many activities in this book focus on transitioning children from one time of day to another. Also included are activities that capture children's attention, help children settle down so they are ready for the next activity, make valuable use of wait time, or promote constructive child-to-child interactions. The extended activities in the book turn extra minutes in the day into productive learning times. These extended activities can be a lifesaver during long waits.

This book is organized by activities under specific categories. These categories include:

- Anytime Ideas
- Arrival
- Art
- Attention Grabbers
- Cleanup
- Departure
- Dramatic Play
- Fingerplays, Songs, and Poems
- Games
- General Tips
- Gross Motor
- Group or Circle Time
- Music and Movement
- Outdoor Play
- Rainy Day Ideas
- Rest and Nap Time
- Snack and Lunch
- Social Development
- Story Time

The components of the easy-to-use activities in this book include:

◆ Materials--lists of everything needed to complete the activity. Materials are readily available. Look to neighborhood businesses for sources of free materials. Craft shops, framing shops, carpet and tile stores, paper stores, and lumber yards often have items they are willing to give away. Don't forget about parents. They often have items they can donate.

◆ What to do—easy-to-follow directions in a step-by-step format, making each activity a snap from start to finish. Patterns and illustrations are supplied as needed.

◆ More to do—ideas and extensions to integrate the activity across the curriculum in areas such as math, dramatic play, circle time, blocks, language, snack and cooking.

◆ Related books, poems, and songs—are included for many activities.

Last But Not Least

Remember these tips when planning for transitions:

- ◆ Reduce the number of total transitions in the schedule.
- ◆ Make transitional activities a part of your planning.
- ◆ Prepare activities ahead of time.
- ◆ Warn the children before transitions occur.
- ◆ Use sensory cues, such as ringing a chime or playing a musical instrument, to signal a change in routine. Avoid turning overhead lights on and off as this often excites or upsets children.
- ◆ Announce the next activity; this often motivates the children to move on.
- ◆ Allow one caregiver to start a short transition activity in the target area while one caregiver finishes the previous activity. This will often entice children to join the new activity.
- ◆ Avoid moving children in large groups. Divide large groups if at all possible.
- ◆ Use calming activities in a pre-designated area to settle children.
- ◆ Most important of all, remember to have fun!

"5 More Minutes" Sign

3+

Materials   8" x 12" poster board

What to do

1. Write the words "5 More Minutes" on a piece of poster board to make a sign. Let the children help create and decorate the sign. They may want to write the numeral five all over it, or trace someone's hand on it. Attach a string on it so it can hang over a child's neck.

2. Five minutes prior to a change in activities, select a child to be the "5 More Minutes" sign helper to carry the sign around for the other children to see. The sign helper says to the children, "Five minutes left to play" (or snack, or whatever they are doing), and he makes sure each child sees the sign.

3. Introduce the following song at circle time, letting the children practice the song and words.

   Five More Minutes (Tune: "Skip to My Lou")
   Five more minutes left to play.
   Five more minutes left to play.
   Five more minutes left to play.
   Five more minutes to play.

4. Make up other verses depending on the activity, for example, "five more minutes left for snack," or "five more minutes left to paint."

5. Sing the song while the child carries the sign around the room.

6. As you sing the song, hold up one hand with your five fingers out to show that there are five minutes left of that activity.

★ *Sandra L. Nagel, White Lake, MI*

A Smile

3+

Materials
poster board or card stock
markers
laminator
scissors
pocket chart

What to do
1. Print the following poem on poster board for a pocket chart.
2. Laminate for durability.
3. Cut each line into strips to fit on the pocket chart.

   A Smile
   You cannot give a smile away
   No matter what you do.
   Every time you give me one
   I'll give it back to you.

 Jackie Wright, Enid, OK

Block Corner Open or Closed

3+

Materials
two pieces of poster board or heavy paper

What to do
1. Make two signs, one that says "open" and one that says "closed."
2. Every time you wish to close one area of activity, select a child to hang up the "closed" sign.
3. Select another child to hang up the "open" sign in the area you wish children to play in.

Ingelore Mix, Gainesville, VA

The Apple Tree

Materials
foam board or wood
scissors
construction paper
Velcro

What to do
1. Cut out a heavy-duty tree from foam board or wood.
2. Cut out apples from construction paper and write the alphabet or children's names on each apple. Laminate for durability.
3. Attach Velcro to the back of each apple and to the tree in random spots.
4. Use the apples for recognition activities. When a child recognizes his name, he may place the apple on the tree and then pick an area to play in for free play.
5. Or use alphabet letters and have the children pick a letter and find an object in the classroom that starts with that letter.

★ *Cookie Zingarelli, Columbus, OH*

LAMINATED APPLE
WITH CHILD'S NAME

VELCRO
ON BACK

Labels for Us

3+

Materials   none

What to do

1. During a transition time, peek at the label inside each child's shirt. Never mention which designer/store made the clothes; this conveys improper values to your class and could make some children feel left out.

2. Instead, read the size, the fabric content, or country of manufacture on each label. Often a three-year-old may be wearing a size 4 or 6 shirt. This makes them feel so big! If a three-year-old is wearing a size 3, your comment could be, "This shirt is just the perfect size for you!" or "Shirley also has a size 3 on today!"

3. If you read the fabric content on each label, you could then group the class according fabric (cotton, polyester, and so on). You could discuss the source of various fabrics and how they are produced, and discuss the attributes of each type. For example, cotton breathes, polyester dries quickly and doesn't wrinkle, linen has a pleasant texture, and so on.

4. If you note the country of manufacture, this could lead to geography and economics lessons and map reading.

Author's Note: Once you start doing this activity with your class, most likely they will ask you to do it every day!

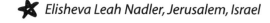 *Elisheva Leah Nadler, Jerusalem, Israel*

Plastic Letters

3+

Materials
plastic gallon milk jug
scissors
letter stencils
marker

What to do
1. Trace letters onto a plastic milk jug and cut them out. Use these for the first letter in each child's name.
2. Hold up the first letter of each child's name and sing the following song to your own tune. Continue until you have mentioned each child's name.

"Z" is for Zachary,
"Z" is for Zachary,
He is one of our friends.
"B" is for Billy,
"B" is for Billy,
He is one of our friends.

3. Use the plastic letters as tracing templates, in the sand and water table, or to help children learn to spell their names.

⭐ *Carrielin Jones, Sheboygan, WI*

Books for Transitions

3+

Materials   books

What to do

1. Books are a great way to settle everyone down and move on to the next activity. Many books lend themselves to gross motor activities.
2. Read *If You Give a Mouse a Cookie* by Laura Joffe Numeroff, *Mouse Paint* by Ellen Stoll Walsh, or *Mouse Count* by Ellen Stoll Walsh and then ask the children to move to the next activity "as quiet as a mouse."
3. After reading a book about trains, such as *Freight Train* by Donald Crews or *The Little Engine That Could* by Watty Piper, ask the children to line up "like a train."
4. Read a story about friendship, such as *Frog and Toad Together* by Arnold Lobel or *Little Blue and Little Yellow* by Leo Lionni, and ask the children to hold hands to go to the next activity.

   Author's Note: The children in my class love to line up chairs like a bus and sing "The Wheels on the Bus." If it is the end of the day, I sing, "The teacher on the bus waves bye-bye." If it is snack time, I sing, "The teacher on the bus says wash your hands." If it is outdoor time, I sing, "The teacher on the bus says get your coat."

★ Audrey Kanoff, Allentown, PA

Theme Book Basket

3+

Materials   basket
assortment of books all related to a theme or topic

What to do

1. In the morning when children are arriving or at the end of lunch, bring out a basket of books for the children to look at as they arrive or finish eating.
2. This is a great extension to a theme or subject that you are studying. For example, if the children are learning about collages in Art, fill the basket with books by Eric Carle. These books are all done in collage art and make a nice impression when they are together for children to see the similarities in the books.
3. Make the books different from the ones on your standard bookshelf.

★ Gail Morris, Kemah, TX

Popping Up

3+

Materials	pop-up books

What to do
1. Children love pop-up or lift-the-flap books, but many are so delicate that you don't want to put them out to be torn. Children love to hear them read over and over and often give their immediate, undivided attention whenever you pull one out.
2. Keep pop-up, lift-the-flap, and turn-the-wheel books on a special shelf near a spot where children may need to wait once in a while (perhaps where they line up). Whenever there is a lull between activities, grab a quick pop-up book to make the most of the moment.
3. There are many pop-up books that feature the alphabet, counting, colors and other themes that you can change to fit your themes through the year.

More to do **Books:** Help the children make their own pop-up books to keep, or make a class pop-up book to keep on the special shelf.

Related books *Alpha Bugs* (and other *Bugs in a Box* books) by David A. Carter
The Honeybee and the Robber by Eric Carle

⭐ *Laura Durbrow, Lake Oswego, OR*

Transition Bag

3+

Materials duffle or any kind of bag
small toys (small Etch-a-Sketches, magic boards, jacks, Legos, tops, Slinkies, tic-tac-toe sets, Colorform sets, small travel games, and so on)

What to do
1. Fill a small bag with a variety of toys.
2. Put this bag out only during transitions times periodically throughout the year.
3. Make several bags with different themes, such as a puzzle bag, a book bag, a felt board bag, and a science bag.

⭐ *Gail Morris, Kemah, TX*

My Own Book

3+

Materials
35 mm or digital camera
card stock paper
glue stick
markers
stickers
hole punch
yarn

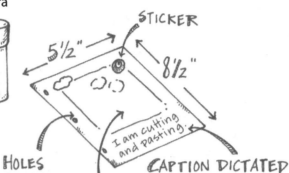

STICKER
5½"
8½"
I am cutting and pasting.
HOLES for BINDING
CAPTION DICTATED BY CHILD
PHOTO
Mike's Book

What to do

1. Children will love looking at a book all about them while they wait for activities to begin or when there are a few extra minutes to fill.
2. Take several photos of each child as he goes about the day. Make sure to take photos of the child interacting with friends and teachers.
3. Print the photos (4" x 6") or have them developed.
4. Give each child a few pieces of card stock. Help them cut the card stock paper in half, creating 8 ½" x 5 ½" pages.
5. Encourage the children to glue their photos on separate pages (one photo per page).
6. Ask each child to dictate a caption for each of their photos. Print the caption under each photo using brightly colored markers.
7. Provide stickers for the children to decorate the pages.
8. Help each child punch three holes on the edge of each page and then bind the pages together using the yarn.
9. The children can store their own books in their cubbies or keep them in a common bin.
10. During difficult transition times, let the children get out their own books to look at and read.

Related books
A My Name Is Alice by Jane Bayer
Anna Banana and Me by Lenore Blegvad
Black Like Kyra, White Like Me by Judith Vigna
A Boy Named Giotto by Paolo Guarnieri

Just Me by Marie Hall Ets
Just You and Me by Sam McBratney
Me & Neesie by Eloise Greenfield
Me First by Helen Lester
Meet M &M by Pat Ross
Play With Me by Marie Hall Ets
The Shape of Me and Other Stuff by Dr. Seuss

★ *Virginia Jean Herrod, Columbia, SC*

All Wrapped Up

3+

Materials	various colors of yarn (one color per child)

What to do

1. Tie the different colors of yarn loosely around items in the room (table and chair legs work well).
2. Assign a color to each child.
3. Ask the children to follow their color around the room, untangling the yarn as they go.
4. Talk about spider webs as they untangle the yarn.

More to do

Art: Give children a simple weaving project to do.
Large and Small Motor: Let the children wrap yarn around the room for others to untangle.

★ *Monica Hay Cook, Tucson, AZ*

Yarn Necklaces

Materials
two large pieces of railroad board
scissors
markers
thick yarn in several different colors
glue
brad fastener

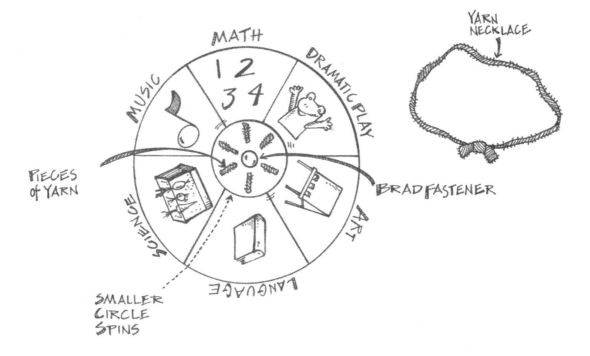

What to do

1. Cut out two large circles from the railroad board, one smaller than the other.
2. Divide the larger circle into parts and either draw pictures of different areas of the room or glue photos of items from each area (such as a painting easel).
3. On the smaller circle, glue colored pieces of yarn; one color for each picture. Attach the small circle on top of the large circle with a brad fastener, so that you can turn the smaller circle (see illustration).
4. Give each child a yarn necklace using the same colors you used on the small circle. Ask them to go to the place in the room that matches their color yarn.

⭐ *Barbara Saul, Eureka, CA*

Follow the Bubbles

3+

Materials   small bottle of bubbles

What to do
1. Line up the children to move to another place in the room or to another room.
2. Hold a bottle of bubbles and blow bubbles as you lead the children to the destination.
3. The children follow the bubbles. The children may quietly pop the bubbles as they walk.
4. Choose a child to lead the group with the bubbles.

More to do   **Outdoors:** Choose a child to be the leader outside. The children follow as the leader blows bubbles and maneuvers around the playground.

Related book   *The Bubble Factory* by Tomie dePaola

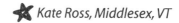 *Kate Ross, Middlesex, VT*

Go Ahead and Wiggle

3+

Materials   carpet square

What to do
1. Place a carpet square in an out-of-the-way area of the classroom.
2. If a child is too active to sit still for an activity, invite him to go to the carpet square to be as active as he needs.
3. The only condition is that he must remain quiet and stay on the carpet square until he is ready to rejoin the class. The carpet square must stay where you put it.

Jackie Wright, Enid, OK

Line Up Here

3+

Materials
markers
8 ½" x 11" card stock
laminator (optional)
contact paper
scissors

What to do
1. Draw the outline of two feet or shoes on a piece of card stock. Laminate for durability, if possible.
2. Place it on the floor where you want a line to start.
3. Place a piece of contact paper over the mat to attach it to the floor.
4. When it is time to move the class from one place to another, instruct the line leader to stand on the mat.
5. This helps the rest of the children get in line in an organized fashion.

⭐ *Jackie Wright, Enid, OK*

Linked and Lined Up

3+

Materials   heavyweight construction paper in a variety of colors
scissors
laminator
Velcro

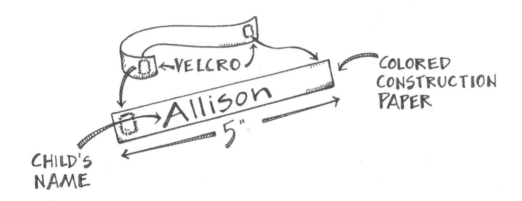

What to do
1. Cut 5" strips of construction paper, write each child's name on a strip (one name per strip), and laminate for durability. Attach Velcro to the strip to make it into a bracelet.
2. When each child arrives in the classroom, fasten a strip to his wrist. Remind him of the color's name, and explain that the bracelet will be used for something later in the day.
3. When it is time to line up, call out colors. "If you have a blue bracelet, you may join the line."
4. As each child joins the line, remove his bracelet. Link the bracelets together and hang it for the children to see.

More to do
Art: Make color strips using only primary or secondary colors, and teach these color concepts.
Math: Count the links in the chain, and then count the number of children in the class to show one-to-one correspondence.
More Math: Count the number of links of each individual color and discuss the concepts of "most" and "least."

⭐ *Karyn F. Everham, Fort Myers, FL*

Partner, Please

3+

Materials   blindfolds

What to do
1. In a large room free of obstacles or an enclosed outdoor area, pair the children.
2. Let each pair pick a sound, such as an animal, bird, or human sound. Make sure each pair has a different sound.
3. Select several pairs to have a turn at the same time. Help them put on blindfolds.
4. The children walk around the room, calling out their special sound, yet pausing to listen for the same call back.
5. When the partners find each other, they take off their blindfolds and sit down away from the children still blindfolded.
6. When all the pairs have found each other, choose several other pairs to have a turn.

More to do   **Science:** Discuss how humans and animals communicate with one another.

Related books   *If Animals Could Talk* by Don Dentinger
Wacky Wild Animals by Angie Sage

⭐ *Monica Hay Cook, Tucson, AZ*

Photo Lineup

3+

Materials	photos of each child's face copier pen

What to do

1. Take photos of each child's face and make photocopies of each face.
2. Tape the pictures of the children on a wall in alphabetical order and write their names beneath.
3. When the children need to line up, ask them to stand next to their picture and name.

More to do

General Tips: Glue the children's pictures and names to 3" x 5" cards. Put the cards in a box and choose one when an individual is needed for a job or to provide an answer.

Math: Use the photo cards for matching and sorting activities. Encourage the children to match the cards to the "photo lineup" on the wall. They can also use the cards to sort by hair color, first name, and so on.

⭐ *Barbara Saul, Eureka, CA*

The Name Game

3+

Materials	none

What to do

1. This activity can be used for lining up, taking attendance, or calling children to a group activity.
2. Call each child's name and then lead the class in clapping the syllables in each name. Announce that everyone whose name has two syllables can line up, then one syllable, three syllables, and so on. Call each child's name slowly.
3. Make a graph displaying the children's names and how many syllables each name has.

⭐ *Kaethe Lewandowski, Centreville, VA*

Who's Next? Jar

3+

Materials large, clean plastic jar, such as a mayonnaise jar
slips of paper or craft sticks
stickers
mailing-size adhesive label

What to do
1. Moving children from a large group time, such as circle time to center time, can be difficult, as each child is anxious start playing. Use the Who's Next? Jar to give the children more control over who goes next.
2. Explain to the children that they will help make a Who's Next? Jar to help them decide in what order they will go to centers.
3. Let them work together to decorate the jar with a variety of colorful stickers.
4. Print "Who's Next?" on the adhesive label and stick it to the jar. Write each child's name on a slip of paper or a craft stick and put them in the jar.
5. Bring out the jar after circle time. Pull out a slip of paper or craft stick and read the name on it. Ask that child which center he would like to go to. After he answers, let him pull the next name out of the jar.
6. Continue until all of the children have had a chance to participate.

More to do **Writing:** Let the children use the Who's Next? Jar at the writing table. Encourage them to pull out the names and copy them on paper or on another craft stick.

Related song **Pull a Name** (Tune: "Twinkle, Twinkle, Little Star")
Let me pull a name and say
Who's the next to go and play?
Is it Sam or is it Joan?
Will they play together or play alone?
Let me pull a name and say
Who's the next to go and play.

Related books *Wait and See* by Robert Munsch
Waiting for Mom by Linda Wagner Tyler
Waiting for Mr. Goose by Laurie Lears
Waiting for the Evening Star by Rosemary Wells
Wilbur Waits by Victoria Sherrow

 Virginia Jean Herrod, Columbia, SC

The Sorting Hunt

3+

Materials   colored construction paper
scissors

What to do

1. In advance, cut out different colored triangles, squares, circles, diamonds, hearts, stars, and other shapes. Make sure to vary the colors so that you have a variety of different colored shapes.
2. Sit down with a child (or children) and review the shapes and colors.
3. Ask the child to hide his eyes while you place the shapes in obvious hiding places (a few on the table, one on the floor in the corner, and so on).
4. Ask the child to find all of one color or all of one shape. For example, encourage him to put all of the stars on the table or put all of the yellow shapes in the kitchen.
5. Give a different direction for each color or shape. This will teach the child to follow directions as well as to sort shapes and colors.

More to do

Art: When finished with the shapes, show the children how to put shapes together to make a picture (e.g., a triangle on top of a square makes a house). Let them glue shapes onto a piece of construction paper to make a collage.
Math: Once the children have learned to sort all the shapes and colors, play pattern games. Lay out a pattern, such as a heart, square, heart, square, heart. Point to the shapes, saying their names in order, and then ask the children if they know what comes next. Keep the patterns fairly simple at first.

Sarah Hartman, Lafayette, LA

The Train

3+

Materials   train whistle
conductor's hat (optional)
red handkerchief (optional)

What to do
1. Tell the children that when they hear you blow the train whistle, it's time for the next activity.
2. Choose one child to be the leader and wear the hat and handkerchief. The other children line up behind the leader and make a train around the room, leading to the next activity.

Related songs   "I've Been Workin' on the Railroad"
"Down by the Station"

Related book   *The Little Engine That Could* by Watty Piper

⭐ *Barbara Saul, Eureka, CA*

Red Light, Green Light

3+

Materials   red, yellow, and green paper
scissors
large black paper rectangle
glue

What to do
1. Cut out a circle from red paper, one from green paper, and one from yellow paper. Glue the circles on the black rectangle to look like a stoplight. Hang it where all the children can see it.
2. Explain what each color means.
3. Use the traffic light to signal that it's time to change activities.

⭐ *Barbara Saul, Eureka, CA*

Keep Your Bubbles in Your Mouth 3+

Materials   none

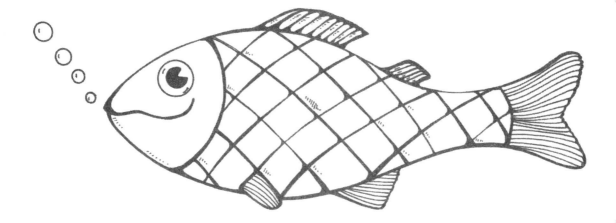

What to do
1. This activity helps during those times when children must be quiet, such as in the halls or on field trips.
2. At the beginning of the year, have a discussion about fish and how they keep air bubbles in their mouths and swim quietly.
3. When the children need to get from place to another, ask them to "keep their bubbles in their mouths" and move quietly like fish.

★ *Jodi Sykes, Lake Worth, FL*

Look at Me

`3+`

Materials

hat
apron
gloves
pillow

What to do

1. Gather different items to signal transition time.
2. To signal going outside, put on a special hat; for lunch or snack, put on a cooking apron; to clean up, put on work gloves; and for rest time, pull out a pillow.
3. After a while, the children will pick up on the visual cues without you saying a word.
4. If desired, let the children take turns putting on the special transition item.

More to do

Social Studies: Go into the community to learn about what kinds of uniforms people need for their jobs.

Related books

Career Day by Anne Rockwell
Community Helpers From A to Z by Bobbie Kalman and Niki Walker
Jobs People Do by Christopher Maynard

★ *Monica Hay Cook, Tucson, AZ*

Lost and Found Boxes

`3+`

Materials

18" x 24" plastic box
permanent marker

What to do

1. Label a box "Lost and Found" or draw a question mark for children who can't recognize the words.
2. When items are found on the floor or in unlikely places, put them in the box.

3. When children have lost something, they should go to the box first before asking a friend or you to help them find it.

4. At the end of the week, before story time, bring the box to circle and hold up the found objects. Ask the children to guess who owns the items before they are claimed.

5. When a child finds an item that belongs to him, he can transition to the next activity.

   Note: Add different items to the box, such as a "mystery object" that is related to the next week's theme or a special item that has "teachable moment" value, such as a telephone (dial 911), a stuffed animal (being a responsible pet owner), or holiday items. You may even add a "message" item, such as a magazine, to remind children to bring in magazines for a cut-and-paste project.

More to do   **Math:** Count and weigh the items.
More Math: Have the children sort the items into categories, such as soft/hard, colors, clothes, toys, or size.

★ Susan R. Forbes, Daytona Beach, FL

Sanding

3+

Materials   sandpaper
wood item to sand (such as cutting board or wooden bowl)
mineral oil

What to do   1. This purposeful activity gives children something to do with their hands, and can be very peaceful and centering. Children can work on it whenever they are waiting for a new activity or for others to finish.

2. Show the child how to sand something, and then always have sandpaper and a purposeful sanding project available.

3. After weeks of making the wood smooth, put some mineral oil on a cloth and let the children rub it into their project.

4. Use the finished pieces in the classroom so the children see their hard work put to good use.

5. You can use any item, such as a table or chair, for a whole-group activity.

★ Susan Rubinoff, Wakefield, RI

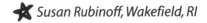

Sanding Wood Slices

3+

Materials   different sizes of wood slices (available from a tree trimmer,
                          carpenter, or fallen trees)
                     sandpaper
                     craft sticks (optional)
                     paint or markers
                     safety glasses (optional)

What to do   1. If possible, obtain sandpaper that has a sticky back. Cut it into pieces and
                      attach to craft sticks to make it easier for children to handle. This is optional;
                      you can also use regular sandpaper.
                   2. Obtain wood slices and make sure they are clean. Local tree trimmers or
                      carpenters are good sources for these.
                   3. During times when children are waiting for an activity or for others to finish,
                      they can sand the wood slices to make them smooth. This may take a few
                      days.
                   4. Discuss how the rings on the tree represent the "age" of the tree.
                   5. Encourage the children to paint or use markers to decorate their slices.

★ *Eileen Lucas, Halifax, Nova Scotia, Canada*

Squishy Bags

3+

Materials quart-size zipper-closure bags (one for each child)
hair gel in fun colors or plain gel and food coloring
disposable spoons and cups
masking tape

What to do

1. Give each child a baggie, a spoon, and a disposable cup filled with hair gel.
2. Ask the children to scoop the hair gel into the baggie until it is about a third full. If using food coloring, let the children squirt a small amount of the color of their choice in the bag.
3. Help the children squeeze most of the air out of their baggie and securely zip their bags shut.
4. Wipe off the edges of the zipper and secure it with masking tape.
5. Let the children squish the bags to distribute the food coloring, if needed.
6. Let the children store their Squishy Bags in their cubbies, if possible, or in a large basket.
7. Bring out the bags whenever the children have to wait for a few moments for others to get ready to transition from one activity to another. The children can squeeze and manipulate the bags, which is very soothing.

More to do **Literacy:** Show the children how to use one fingertip as a pencil and print their names on their Squishy Bags.

⭐ *Virginia Jean Herrod, Columbia, SC*

Busy Boxes

3+

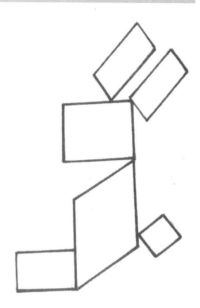

Materials
simple games and puzzles
inexpensive manipulatives (from a dollar store)
1" mosaic tiles
small, flat wooden shapes from a craft shop
stamp pad and rubber stamps
paper
5" x 7" index cards
plastic sandwich bags
small boxes

What to do
1. Separate the materials (tiles, puzzles, manipulatives, and wooden shapes) into plastic bags.
2. Fill at least three boxes with the same activity. Rotate the activities weekly to keep the novelty.

RABBIT

3. Place the lids on the boxes after filling them, and put them on a convenient shelf. Introduce how to use the boxes during morning time.
4. A popular box contains mosaic tile tangrams (a Chinese puzzle in which a square is made out of seven shapes) and index cards. The children can make a design out of the tiles and trace them on the cards. Another favorite box contains rubber stamps and paper for making patterns or holiday cards.
5. The purpose of these boxes is for transition time. The boxes provide children who finish assignments early with an alternative to reading a book while the other children are finishing.

More to do
Manipulatives: Make simple puzzles by drawing a picture of a familiar fun activity on a piece of shirt cardboard and cutting it out with an Ellison punch machine.

★ *Susan R. Forbes, Daytona Beach, FL*

My Own Box

Materials   small boxes (one for each child)
variety of small items to go into the boxes (sorting bears, shapes, numbers, or
letters; travel-size Etch-a-Sketch, small containers of playdough, small pads
of paper and pencils, small boxes of crayons)
markers, crayons, and paints
collage materials
glue

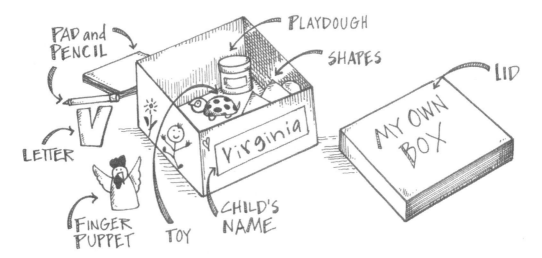

PAD and PENCIL — PLAYDOUGH — SHAPES — LID
LETTER — FINGER PUPPET — TOY — CHILD'S NAME — Virginia — MY OWN BOX

What to do   1. Waiting for others to get ready can be a trying time for young children. Make
a "My Own Box" for each child to use during this difficult transition.

2. Give each child a small box and let him decorate it using items in the art
center. Keep in mind that these boxes will be handled daily so glued-on
items might come off easily.

3. Give the children paper to print their names. Glue each child's name to the
front of his box.

4. Decide where you will store the boxes. If the children's cubbies are large
enough, store them there. Otherwise, store them on a low shelf or in an
easily accessible basket.

5. Fill each child's box with a variety of small toys and activities. You might want
to let the children help fill the boxes so they can choose the items they want.
Or fill them yourself so they will be surprised.

6. When transitioning from one activity to another in a large group, let the
children who are ready early use their boxes.

7. Frequently change the items in the box so the children will not lose inerest.

(continued on the next page)

Related books *Boxes! Boxes!* by Leonard Everett Fisher
The Color Box by Dayle Ann Dodds
Don't Open This Box by James Razzi
The Memory Box by Mary Bahr
Shape Space by Cathryn Falwell
Surprise Box by Nicki Weiss

★ *Virginia Jean Herrod, Columbia, SC*

My Special Box

3+

Materials   box wrapped like a fancy present (optional)

What to do
1. Children love to use their imaginations; this activity helps them develop their creativity.
2. Have the children sit in a circle. Tell them that you received a very special box with something special inside it. Explain that you can't tell them what it is and they won't be able to see it. For older children, use an imaginary box.
3. Think about an object and without telling them what it is, pretend that you are removing it from the box. For example, you might pretend the object is a balloon. Pretend to blow it up and use your hands to show it is getting bigger. Or pretend it is a kitten and cup your hands while making a gentle petting motion.
4. Tell the children that the object is about to change. Using your hands, have the object become something heavy or something very small.
5. Then pass the imaginary object around the circle of children. Ask them to think about what special object they want it to become. Encourage them to use motions to show what the object is, but not to say the name of it out loud.
6. You might want to have other children in the group try to guess what the object has become.

More to do **Dramatic Play:** This activity can extend into the dramatic play area. Encourage the children to take turns acting out animals or community workers and letting the other children guess who or what they are.

⭐ *Michelle Barnea, Millburn, NJ*

Animal Observation

3+

Materials animals of any kind

What to do
1. This is a great idea if you have classroom pets. Children love to observe them.
2. This idea came from the children, because during those hard transition times (such as when only a few are through with lunch or while some are waiting for others to clean up), they started asking if they could go and watch the animals.
3. Observing the animals seems to have a calming effect on the children and they never seem to get bored doing it.
4. If desired, rotate the animals in the classroom, such as according to the theme the children are learning.

⭐ *Wanda Guidroz, Santa Fe, TX*

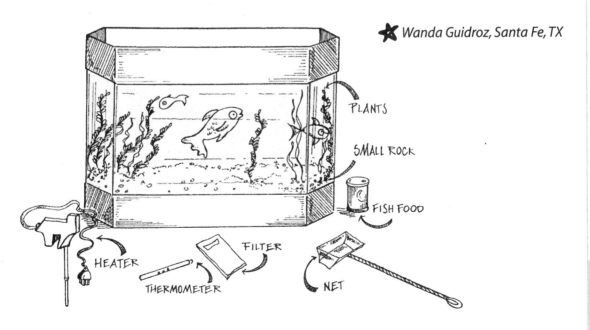

Water and Clean Plants

3+

Materials   spray bottle with water
plant
cloth

What to do

1. When a child must wait for others to finish an activity, lunch, or whatever, ask him to spray the leaves of a plant. (Ivy plants are easy to care for and can get very dusty.)
2. If the child has more time to spare, ask him to wipe the leaves gently with a cloth.
3. This activity is good for developing eye-hand coordination and learning self-control (squirting friends can be very hard to resist!). Children also learn to care for plants.

⭐ *Susan Rubinoff, Wakefield, RI*

The Magic Wand

3+

Materials   magic wand

What to do

1. Find a sparkly and glittery "magic" wand and keep it in a special place. Bring it out only at "magical" (transition) times.
2. In a very special voice, tell the children that you will tap them on their heads with your magic wand one by one, and they will see the most glorious things happen!
3. Whenever the children need to move somewhere or get something, tap them on their heads and ask them to do it. For example, ask them to hop over to get their coats as you tap them on their heads. The "magic" wand truly works wonders and makes transitions fun for the children.
4. This is also great for cleanup, snack, and naptime.

⭐ *Susan Myhre, Bremerton, WA*

Hickory, Dickory, Dock

`3+`

Materials   clock that chimes on the hour

What to do
1. Switch activities every hour when the clock chimes.
2. Teach the children what time it is by counting the chimes.
3. If desired, find a clock that chimes at each quarter hour, or a clock that plays seasonal music, bird songs, or other sounds.

Related book   *Ten Minutes 'Til Bedtime* by Peggy Rathmann

 *Barbara Saul, Eureka, CA*

What Time Is It?

`3+`

Materials   none

What to do
1. Sing the following song to the tune of "The Muffin Man."

   Oh, do you know what time it is,
   What time it is,
   What time it is?
   Oh, do you know what time it is?
   It's time to get your coat.

2. Add other verses depending on the transition, for example, it's time to get your coat, it's almost story time, and so on.

 *Jackie Wright, Enid, OK*

Silent Counting

3+

Materials   none

What to do
1. When transitioning between activities or when you need to quiet down the group, hold up your hands and say, "Let's do silent counting."
2. As the children hold up each finger, they mouth the words instead of speaking, "One, two, three...." This creates instant quiet!
3. You can also have them count backwards silently, sing a familiar song silently, clap silently, or do the movements to a familiar fingerplay silently.

Laura Durbrow, Lake Oswego, OR

Listen to the Quiet

3+

Materials   none

What to do
1. Line up the children before leaving the room or area.
2. Ask them to be very quiet. Explain that they must remain quiet so they can listen for sounds as they walk from one area to the next.
3. Move to the next activity, area or room.
4. Upon arrival, ask what they heard as the transition occurred. Did they hear the heater? Did they hear the scuffle of feet? Did they hear the wind outside?

More to do   Assemble the children in a circle, inside or outside. (You may even want to do this activity inside and outside to compare the results.) Ask the children to lie down on the floor or ground. Encourage them to listen quietly to the sounds in the room or in nature. After a significant amount of time, discuss results.

Related book   *Owl Moon* by Jane Yolen

Kate Ross, Middlesex, VT

Try to Whisper

Materials   none

What to do   1. Sing the following song to remind children that quiet, whispering voices are appreciated. All too often precious time is lost when loud voices interrupt an activity and cause a delay.
2. Sing the song to the tune of "Love Somebody, Yes I Do."

Try to whisper, if you please.
Try to whisper, if you please.
Try to whisper, if you please.
Then we'll move along just like a breeze.

★ *Jackie Wright, Enid, OK*

Look at the Clock

Materials   wall clock

What to do   1. This is a good activity for creating "peace and quiet" after a busy activity such as playtime, or transitioning from outdoor play to indoors.
2. Ask the children to join you on the floor. Turn off the lights and explain that they are going to slow down, unwind, and relax by looking at the second hand on the clock. Remind them not to talk during this time.
3. This calms them down because children are often entranced by clocks.

(continued on the next page)

More to do   **Math:** Ask the children to count how many times the second hand moves from the 1 to the 12. Or, tell them they will move on to the next activity when the little hand reaches 5. Children will soon understand the purpose of the clock. Another way to use the clock is when you are busy with a few children and another child wants you to join him. Say, "I will be with you when the big hand is on the 3!" Children love watching the clock to see if it's time.

Jodi Sykes, Lake Worth, FL

Clapping Echo

3+

Materials   none

What to do

1. This is a simple activity, requiring no materials, and is an excellent way to develop rhythm and listening skills.
2. Have the children sit in a circle on the floor. Clap a pattern for them to repeat, beginning with a simple pattern of one clap, two claps. If the children can do this successfully, clap your hands on the first beat and your knees on the second.
3. Add a third beat and accent the first "one-two-three, one-two-three," clapping your hands on one, and slapping your knees on two and three.
4. You may vary the pattern, increasing the difficulty as the children progress.

More to do   **Language:** For variety, clap the syllables in words and the children's names, letting the rhythm indicate accented syllables. For example, "hi-ber-nate" or "E-liz-a-beth."

Nursery Rhymes: Use clapping to accompany nursery rhymes. For example:

One, two, (clap hands)
Buckle my shoe (slap knees)
Three, four (clap hands)
Shut the door. (slap knees)

Mary Jo Shannon, Roanoke, VA

Clapping Names

3+

Materials   none

What to do
1. While the children are waiting for an activity, have a child say his name. The rest of the children clap the number of syllables in his name.
2. The child then picks a friend, who says his name. The children clap the syllables in his name.
3. Repeat as needed to fill the time or until all of the children have had a turn.

★ Phyllis Esch, Export, PA

Clapping Words

3+

Materials   word charts, chalkboard, or dry-erase board

What to do
1. Write a sentence or a few words on the board. Read the words to the children, one at a time.
2. Have the children repeat each word.
3. If clapping the words in a sentence, say the sentence again and clap each word.
4. For an added challenge, break the words into syllables and clap the syllables.

★ Phyllis Esch, Export, PA

Are You Ready?

`3+`

Materials   none

What to do   1. Prepare the children for a new activity by giving them a cue during an activity in progress and singing the following song.

   Are You Ready? (Tune: "Frere Jacques")
   Are you ready? Are you ready?
   Look at me. Look at me.
   Listening ears are tuned in, faces ready in a grin,
   What comes next? What comes next?

   2. Then tell them what to do, such as walk to the rug, line up at the door, or whatever they are transitioning to.

⭐ *Margery Kranyik Fermino, Hyde Park, MA*

Come and Join Me

`3+`

Materials   none

What to do   Use the following song to call the children to circle time, to line up, or for snack. Sing it to the tune of "London Bridge."

   Come and join me in the circle, (or table, snack)
   In the circle,
   In the circle.
   Come and join me in the circle,
   So we can have some fun.

⭐ *Cookie Zingarelli, Columbus, OH*

Stop Song

3+

Materials none

What to do
1. This is a fun way for children to get their wiggles out just before circle time or whenever they have been sitting a while and are about to move to another activity.
2. Sing the following song to the tune of "Little Red Wagon." Encourage the children to do the actions in the song. When you get to "Stop," the children put up their hands as if to say, "Stop," and freeze in place.
3. Repeat the song, adding another verse and actions. Remind them they need to stay in their given areas on the floor.

Stomp, stomp, stomp, little children,
Stomp, stomp, stomp, little children,
Stomp, stomp, stomp, little children,
While I sing this song.
STOP!

Wiggle your fingers, little children,
Wiggle your fingers, little children,
Wiggle your fingers, little children,
While I sing this song.
STOP!

Cookie Zingarelli, Columbus, OH

Rhyming Song

Materials   file cards
pencil or pen
sticky note pad

What to do

1. Write the verses of the following song on a sticky note. Reach for one any time during the day when the children need to wait a minute or two. Sing the verse with the children.

   Anytime Rhyming Song (Tune: "Farmer in the Dell")
   House rhymes with mouse.
   House rhymes with mouse.
   Hi! Ho! Just listen, oh!
   House rhymes with mouse.

   Wet rhymes with pet.
   Wet rhymes with pet.
   Hi! Ho! Just listen, oh!
   Wet rhymes with pet.

   Additional verses:
   Man rhymes with can…
   Toes rhymes with nose…
   Cat rhymes with bat…
   Snow rhymes with blow…
   Hit rhymes with sit…
   Sun rhymes with run…

2. Write a list of rhyming words on a file card. Add them to the song, checking them off as you use them. Keep adding to the list of rhyming words—the possibilities are endless!
3. Another good transition activity is to name a body part and have the children think of a rhyming word. For example, "hair" rhymes with "chair," and "hand" rhymes with "band."

More to do   **Gross Motor:** Ask the children to do a motion such as kick, and then think of a rhyming word ("thick").
Language: Cut out pictures of rhyming words from a magazine and mount them on oak tag. Show the children one picture, and they choose the rhyming picture.

Books: Read stories with many rhyming words in them. Read one rhyming word and let the children guess (using the sentence context) what the rhyming word might be.

Related book *A Fly Went By* by Mike McClintock

⭐ *Mary Brehm, Aurora, OH*

Pocket Full of Fun

3+

Materials

3" x 5" index cards
loose-leaf ring or key chain ring
apron with pockets

What to do

1. Write a few short games, songs, poems, fingerplays, and jokes on index cards.
2. Punch holes in the cards and hold them together with a ring.
3. Categorize the cards and put them into several groups to switch around so that you only carry several at a time.
4. Keep the cards in the apron pockets so you can take them out quickly when needed.
5. Whenever you transition from one activity to another (especially if it entails lining up or moving with several children at a time), reach into the apron pocket and pull out a card. Introduce a favorite song, joke, and so on so the children can focus on a positive way to move.

More to do

Music: Use interactive songs when possible to keep everyone's attention. For example, sing, "If you are wearing a blue shirt, wave hello!" Continue with other identifiers such as, "If you have a big smile, walk in line."
More Music: Make up songs with familiar tunes. For example, sing, "Mary put some blocks away, blocks away, blocks away, before you come to snack!" (to the tune of "Mary Had a Little Lamb"). The children are much happier to respond to musical requests.

⭐ *Maxine Della Fave, Raleigh, NC*

Following Directions

4+

Materials   none

What to do   1. Explain to the children that there are three steps to following directions:

   ◆ Listen carefully and ask the person to repeat directions, if needed.
   ◆ Understand the steps. If you don't understand, ask for clarification.
   ◆ Remember the steps in order.

2. Choose a child to follow the directions. Start by asking him something simple such as, "Touch your nose."
3. Add another direction as the child is ready, such as, "Stand up, jump two times."
4. Eventually, you will be able to give three or more instructions such as, "Stand up, walk to the door, knock three times."
5. The rest of the class should check that the child followed the directions. They will need to pay close attention to the sequence of actions and number of knocks, jumps, and so on.
6. Encourage the children to ask questions if they do not understand, for example, "Which door should I knock on?" You will be amazed to see how many instructions the children can follow in sequence once they are accustomed to the necessary steps.

Related book   *Amelia Bedelia* by Peggy Parish

★ *Iris Rothstein, New Hyde Park, NY*

Shifting Gears

4+

Materials   none

What to do   1. Talk about driving a car and shifting gears to go slowly, in reverse, or neutral.
2. Establish a "gear-shifting" routine for classroom management. For example, first gear means to line up slowly, neutral gear means to stand still, and reverse gear means to stop and sit down.
3. When necessary, tell children it is time to "shift gears."
4. Create your own gears with moving directions as needed.

 *Margery Kranyik Fermino, Hyde Park, MA*

Color Bright

4+

Materials   box of 8 crayons

What to do   1. While the children are waiting for the next scheduled activity of the day, take out a box of crayons. Ask a child to close his eyes and pick a crayon from the box.
2. Ask everyone wearing that color to stand. Count the children standing before they sit down again. Keep that crayon out of the box.
3. If there is enough time, repeat the activity with another child and another crayon until all the crayons have been chosen. Finally, ask all the children who did not have a matching color to stand up and be counted, too.

Related books   *1 Is One* by Tasha Tudor
Brown Bear, Brown Bear, What Do You See? by Bill Martin, Jr.
Little Blue and Little Yellow by Leo Lionni

Susan Oldham Hill, Lakeland, FL

Color Match

4+

Materials   small items from around the classroom

What to do   1. During transition times, ask a child to name a color. Then ask him to choose two friends to find an item of that color from somewhere in the room.
2. Repeat for other colors.

Related books   *Brown Bear, Brown Bear, What Do You See?* by Bill Martin, Jr.
Little Blue and Little Yellow by Leo Lionni

★ *Susan Oldham Hill, Lakeland, FL*

What Am I Wearing Today?

4+

Materials   color cards (optional)

What to do   1. This is a great transition activity to do when the class is learning colors. Have the children transition to a new activity or line up by calling out colors of clothing. For example, "If you are wearing red, go line up."
2. If children are still learning colors, hold up a color card as a cue.
3. For a more advanced option, call two colors ("If you are wearing blue and green…").
4. Try giving descriptors other than colors, such as stripes, corduroy, short sleeves, turtleneck, sandals, and so on.

Related books   *A Bad Case of Stripes* by David Shannon
Brown Bear, Brown Bear, What Do You See? by Bill Martin, Jr.
Who Said Red? by Mary Serfozo

★ *Sandra Suffoletto Ryan, Buffalo, NY*

Sewing Is Fun

4+

Materials
plastic needle
yarn
plastic window blind strip (Venetian blinds)
hole punch
stapler (optional)

What to do
1. Punch holes along the plastic strips. When you have a few extra moments, have the children thread yarn through the holes.
2. Tie or staple the strips together to make letters and shapes, such as "N," "M," "X," and triangles and squares, and display them around the classroom.

★ *Carrielin Jones, Sheboygan, WI*

Fitting Together

4+

Materials
long piece of butcher paper (approximately 1' wide)
crayons or markers
scissors

What to do
1. Lay out a long sheet of butcher paper and encourage the children to draw pictures and color all over it.
2. Cut the paper into jagged sections, approximately 1' in length.
3. Give one section to each child.
4. Select a child to stand up with his section.
5. Call on children, one at a time, to see if their piece fits with the one of the child standing. If it does, the child remains standing and the children hold their pieces together. If not, that child sits down and another child tries to fit his section with the first piece.
6. Keep going until all the pieces fit together and the children are lined up. They are now ready to go.

(continued on the next page)

More to do

Art: Let children make their own puzzles. Encourage them to draw pictures on paper and mount them on poster board. Then help them cut the picture into pieces. They are now ready for reassembling.

★ *Monica Hay Cook, Tucson, AZ*

How Many Cotton Balls Does It Take to Make a Bunny Tail?

4+

Materials

poster board or stiff cardboard
scissors
marker
laminator
cotton balls

BUNNY CUTOUTS

NUMBER ON TAIL

3

5

BOWL OF COTTON BALLS

1. Cut out at least ten bunnies from poster board or cardboard.
2. Number the bunny tails from one to ten. Laminate the bunnies.
3. Place the bunnies on a table and put cotton balls in a bowl next to the bunnies.

4. Encourage the children to match the number of cotton balls with the number on the tail of each bunny.
5. When each child makes a match, he can move to the next activity.
6. For children who are just learning to count, you might want to use five bunnies instead of ten.

⭐ *Eileen Lucas, Halifax, Nova Scotia, Canada*

Lineup Lengths

4+

Materials   none

What to do
1. This is a centering, calming activity, and is especially good for transitions.
2. Ask the children to line up silently according to height, using body language to communicate.
3. Sometimes vary the sequencing. You may try ordering them from shortest to tallest or from tallest to shortest.

More to do   **Math:** Cut straws (or yarn) in varying lengths. Encourage the children to arrange them in sequence, shortest to longest, and glue them to paper.
Music: Provide xylophones and discuss the order of the keys.
Science: Fill glasses with different amounts of water. Supervise the children as they lightly tap the glass with a spoon and listen to the different tones.

⭐ *Jill Putnam, Wellfleet, MA*

Over and Under

4+

Materials   small lightweight beanbag or stuffed toy

What to do   1. Any time the children are restless and they need to line up, get their
attention by putting an object (beanbag or stuffed toy) in your pocket.
2. Take out the object and ask the children to pass it over their head to the
next child.
3. The next child finds a new way to pass the object, for example, by passing it
through his legs or by turning around. To avoid throwing, remind children
that they cannot let go of the object until the next child is holding it.
4. Vary this by asking the children to balance the object on their shoulder,
head, or another part of their body and see how far they can walk before it
falls. When it falls, the next child has a turn.
5. Children can work in pairs holding the object by walking or standing
together and copying what the other child does. Large motor skills can also
be incorporated by doing movements such as hopping with the object.

⭐ *Maxine Della Fave, Raleigh, NC*

Happy Birthday

4+

Materials   shoebox
wrapping paper
tape
small treats or stickers
birthday hat (optional)

What to do   1. Wrap a shoebox in paper, making sure that the lid can still be removed.
2. Place small treats or stickers inside the box.

3. Play this fun game to help children remember the date of their birthday as well as the months of the year. Have the children sit in a circle and pass the box around as you say this rhyme:

   Birthdays, birthdays, come each year.
   Tell me when your birthday's here.

4. When the rhyme is done, the children stop passing the box. The child holding the box tells the class when his birthday is. If this is difficult, name the months of the year to help.
5. The child then lifts the box lid off, takes a treat, and moves to the next activity.
6. You could also play this game using a birthday hat and no box—just pass around a birthday hat and say the rhyme. This is good when you have no treats.

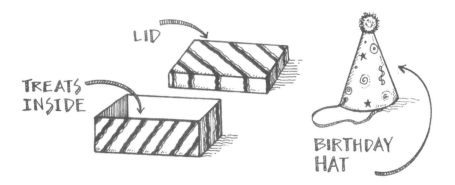

More to do   **Math:** Make a birthday graph by listing children's names and birthdays on a birthday candle shape. If possible, take photos of the children using a camera that takes sticker photos and add them to the candles. Make birthday cakes from construction paper, and write a different month on each one. Talk about who has birthdays in the same month.

Related books   *Birthday Bugs* by David A. Carter
Birthday Monsters! by Sandra Boynton
Clifford's Birthday Party by Norman Bridwell
Happy Birthday to You! by Dr. Seuss
Happy Birthday, Moon by Frank Asch

⭐ *Sue Fleischmann, Sussex, WI*

Famous Quotations

4+

Materials   none

What to do
1. Whenever you have a few minutes to fill, play this memory-stimulating game. First, think of a familiar story or nursery rhyme.
2. Ask, "Who said this?" and then quote a line said by a character in the story or nursery rhyme.
3. Let the children take turns guessing.
4. Following are some sample quotes:

   "Not by the hair of my chinny chinny chin." (The Three Little Pigs)
   "What big eyes you have." (Little Red Riding Hood)
   "Somebody ate my porridge." (The Three Bears)
   "What a good boy am I." (Little Jack Horner)

5. During story time, be sure to read lots of stories over and over again so the children will become familiar with them.

More to do   **Books:** Make a book of famous quotations. Print a quote along the bottom of a piece of art paper. Let the children draw a picture of the character quoted. Repeat for several different quotes. Create a cover and bind the pages together into a book.

Related books   *The Golden Goose* by L. Leslie Brooke
Goldilocks and the Three Bears by Jan Brett
Humpty Dumpty and Other Nursery Rhymes by Lucy Cousins

Virginia Jean Herrod, Columbia, SC

Fun With Initials

4+

Materials   paper letters (optional)

What to do
1. This activity can be used for any transitional time.
2. Sing a song to the tune of "If You're Happy and You Know It." The song starts, "If your name starts with _____" (fill in the blank with an initial). The rest of the song depends on what the children are transitioning to. For example:

    If your name starts with ___, wash your hands…
    If your name starts with ___, get in line…
    If your name starts with ___, choose a center…
    If your name starts with ___, take your jacket…

3. If desired, hold up a paper letter for each initial.

More to do   **Circle Time:** Practice the alphabet by holding up a letter and singing the following song: "If your name starts with 'B,' please stand up." The child whose name begins with "B" stands up and says his name and letter: "Brian, Brian, Brian, starts with 'B'." Give the children their letters and seat them in alphabetical order. Sing the alphabet song with the children. When a child hears his letter, he stands up.

✸ *Deborah Hannes Litfin, Forest Hills, NY*

Grab Bag Letters

4+

Materials
index cards
scissors
marker
paper bag
set of 26 alphabet letter cards
pocket chart or chalkboard

CARDS

GRAB BAG

What to do
1. Cut index cards in half and write one alphabet letter on each half. Put the index cards in a paper bag.

INDEX CARDS CUT IN HALF

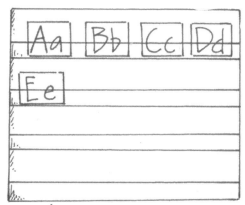

ALPHABET LETTER CARDS

POCKET CHART

2. Place the letter cards in a pocket chart or tape them to a chalkboard.
3. Let the children take turns pulling a card from the bag and matching it to the letter card in the pocket chart or on the board.
4. After each child matches a pair of cards, he moves to a new activity.

More to do
Math: Use numbers or shapes instead of alphabet letters.
Songs: Let the children use the alphabet letters to sing the alphabet song.

Related book   *Chicka Chicka Boom Boom* by Bill Martin, Jr.

⭐ *Martha Myers, Riverside, CA*

I Know My Name

4+

Materials   one piece of 9" x 12" white poster board for each child
black marker

What to do   1. Write the name of each child in bold black letters on a piece of poster board.
2. While the children sit at a table, hold up a name. If the child can read his name, he may put on his jacket, move to the next activity, or do whatever is next.

 Ingelore Mix, Gainesville, VA

"I'm Thinking of..."

4+

Materials   none

What to do   1. This game can be played at any transition time or during snack time. It improves children's memory, can be used to teach important information, and helps children with categorization skills.
2. Say, "I'm thinking of someone who's wearing red!" The children look around and announce who fits into this category. Then switch to a different color.
3. Use other categories, for example, items of clothing ("I'm thinking of someone wearing a sweater") or fabrics ("I'm thinking of someone wearing corduroy"). These categories are great to use when teaching about seasons and how the clothing we wear changes appropriately.
4. If desired, make a list of who fits into what category as you play the game. Post the list in your classroom and review it with the children during a subsequent transition time or snack time.

Related song   "What Are You Wearing?" by Hap Palmer

Elisheva Leah Nadler, Jerusalem, Israel

My Name Has a ____ in It

`4+`

Materials   index cards
pocket chart

What to do

1. Write each child's name on a separate index card.
2. Write the words "My name has a ___ in it" on a sentence or strip of paper and put at the top of the pocket chart. Insert whatever letter the children are learning in the blank space.
3. When lining up or preparing to wash hands, call each child's name and hand him his name card. Have them put their name card in the pocket chart if their name has that letter in it.
4. Find a fun place for children to put their name cards if their name doesn't have the selected letter in it.

 Gail Morris, Kemah, TX

Poetry Place

`4+`

Materials   chart paper
markers

What to do

1. When you have a few extra minutes between activities, choose a topic the children will find appealing, such as balloons or clouds, or a topic you are studying, such as oceans or dinosaurs.
2. Ask the children to finish a simple sentence such as "Balloons are ___." Or "Balloons like to ___." Write their responses on the chart paper, collecting three or four ideas at a time.
3. Over the next day or two, repeat the sentence and encourage them to add to the original responses. Write these on chart paper too.
4. Save the list for a whole-group language activity. Re-read the children's thoughts and ask them to choose the ones that form a picture in their minds.

5. Finally, ask them which sentence would be the best opening line to start a poem and which would be the best closing.
6. Re-copy the poem in the order they choose and title it.

More to do   **Home-to-School Connection:** Duplicate the poem for the children to illustrate and take home.

Related book   *The Random House Book of Poetry for Children* by Jack Prelutsky

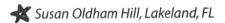 *Susan Oldham Hill, Lakeland, FL*

Question Cards

 4+

Materials   index cards, shaped paper, or die-cut shapes
permanent fine-tip marker
laminator (optional)
container for cards

What to do   1. Write a few questions on index cards, notepad shape paper, or die-cut shapes. Laminate them for durability, if possible.
2. Any simple question will work as long as it is something the children will be able to answer. You can ask simple questions: "How old are you?" "Do you have a pet?" "What did you come to school in?" or more open-ended discussion questions: "Tell us one of your wishes." "What makes you angry?" "What makes you laugh?" "What is your favorite song (or book or color)?"
3. Keep the cards in an interesting container, such as an old jewelry box, sparkly gift bag, or basket.
4. When the children might need to wait for a while or are transitioning between activities, bring out the container and let each child draw a question from it.
5. Read the questions and encourage the children to answer.

Related book   *My Favorite Things* by Richard Rogers

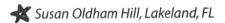 *Laura Durbrow, Lake Oswego, OR*

Rhyming Wheel Game

4+

Materials
pictures of rhyming pairs
card stock or poster board
scissors
glue
two brad paper fasteners

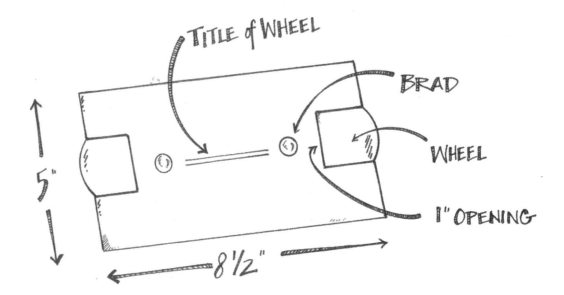

What to do

1. Make your own rhyming wheel game to keep children busy during transition and waiting times.
2. Cut a piece of card stock or poster board into an 8 ½" x 5" rectangle. Cut out a 1" x 1" square from the middle of each 5" side to make "windows" (see illustration).
3. Cut out two 5" circles to make the wheels.
4. Glue one of each rhyming pair on each wheel. Make sure the pictures go in the same direction so that they don't appear upside down in the windows when you turn the wheels.
5. Use brad fasteners to attach the wheels to the back of the main piece so that one picture of each wheel shows through the window as the wheel is turned.
6. The child turns the left and right wheels to match rhyming pictures.

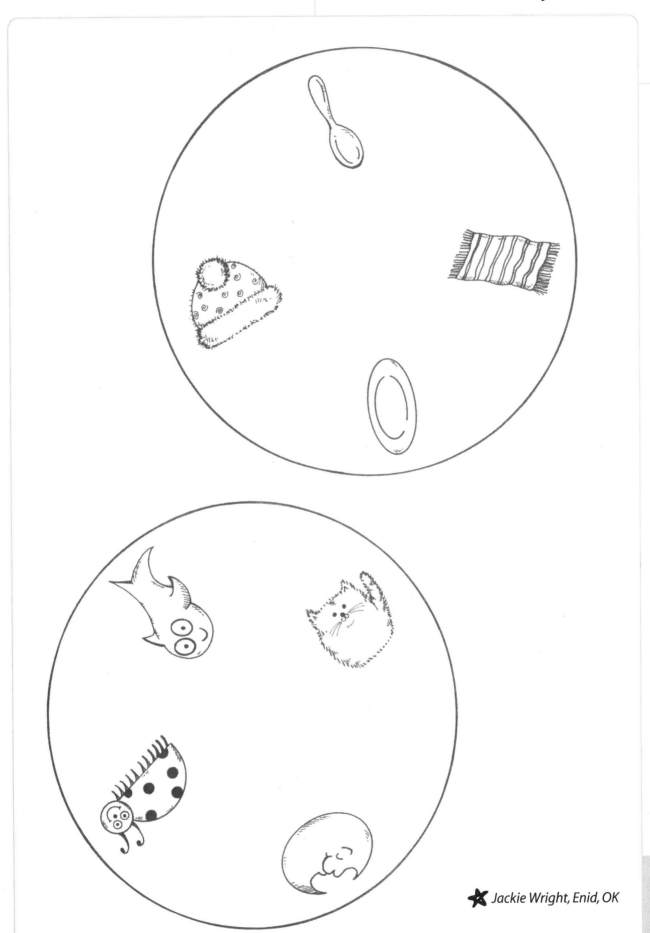

Jackie Wright, Enid, OK

Same and Different

4+

Materials   sets of two objects that have a similarity and a difference

What to do

1. This activity promotes discrimination skills and verbal expression. It is great to use when children are waiting to go somewhere or for a new activity.
2. Show the children two identical objects or pictures and agree that they are the same (two red crayons).
3. Then, show them a pair of objects that are different but have something in common. For example, red and green crayons are both crayons, but are different colors. Other ideas are a toy dog and cat, a book and newspaper, a car and motorcycle, a chair and table, and so on.
4. Encourage the children to tell what is similar and different about each pair. Any logical answer is acceptable.

More to do   **Games:** Ask a child to select two objects from anywhere in the room and see if the class can tell what is the same and what is different about them. The child can confer with you, if necessary. The child who answers correctly has the next turn.

Related book   *Big and Little* by Margaret Miller

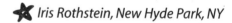 *Iris Rothstein, New Hyde Park, NY*

Someone Just Like Me

4+

Materials   none

What to do

1. When you have a few extra minutes between activities, ask the children to look at their classmates to find things such as hair color or types of clothing that match their own.

2. Use the following simple rhyme, or just ask the children questions such as, "Marcie has a ponytail today. Who can find another friend who is wearing a ponytail?" or "Jason is wearing a shirt with long sleeves. Does anyone else have long sleeves?"

Someone just like me,
I'm wondering if I can see,
Someone, someone just like me.

⭐ *Susan Oldham Hill, Lakeland, FL*

Sounds of the Alphabet 4+

Materials   none

What to do   1. Take advantage of the love children have for rhythm and sound. Use time while you're waiting for everyone to get ready for outdoor play or other group activities to teach the sounds of the letters. (This can, and should, begin long before children are introduced to the symbols.)
2. Use an "echo procedure" for this activity. Say the letter name and the sound it produces using short vowel sounds ("A, /a/"). The children repeat. Then say, "B, /b/," and the children repeat. Continue until you have recited all the letters.
3. Children really enjoy this activity, and when the time comes to show them their first letter flash card, they will automatically attach the sound to the symbol.
Note: Be sure you know the correct sounds and enunciate clearly.

⭐ *Mary Jo Shannon, Roanoke, VA*

My Name

4+

Materials
one piece of 9" x 12" white poster board for each child
black marker

What to do
1. Write the name of each child in bold black letters on a separate piece of poster board.
2. Hold up a name. If the child can read his name, he may do the next activity.
3. For very young children, it is best to begin with just the first letter of the children's names. As time goes on, add letter by letter. This is great incentive for the children to learn to spell their names, and you may ask families to help the children learn, too.

✱ *Ann Scalley, Orleans, MA*

Under the Sea Wheel

4+

Materials
2 sheets of card stock (8 ½" x 11")
scissors
glue
laminator (optional)
pictures of animals found under the sea
brad paper fastener

What to do
1. Cut out two 7" circles from card stock or heavy paper. Cut out a "window" in one of the circles, about halfway from the middle of the circle (see illustration). Cut out another window on the other side of the circle. One window will show the picture of the animal and the other window will show the name of the animal.
2. Write a title on the circle such as "Under the Sea" or glue a picture with an ocean theme on it. This will be the top circle.
3. Glue or draw seven sea animals on the other circle so that when this circle is put directly underneath the top circle, the animal is viewed at the same time as its word when the top wheel is attached and spun around.
4. Laminate both pictures for durability and trim them.

5. Poke a hole in the center of both circles and attach them with the brad fastener.
6. Make this available to children when they have to wait for a turn or when centers are closed. This gives them something constructive to do before the next activity begins.

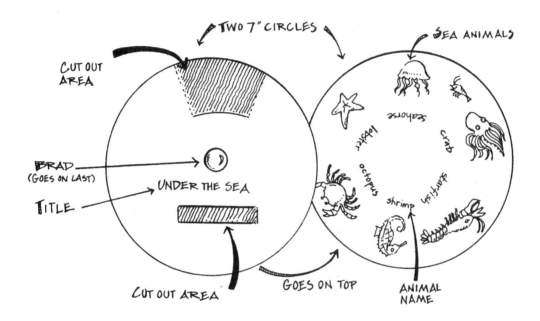

★ *Jackie Wright, Enid, OH*

Using Foreign Languages

4+

Materials   none

What to do
1. Whenever you wish to get the children's attention, start talking in another language. It is recognized that young children learn and pick up foreign languages very easily, and they also enjoy listening to and learning languages.
2. Following are some examples of when to use other languages in the classroom:

   ◆ **Lining Up:** When children line up to move from one location or room to another, you probably count to make sure everyone is accounted for. Besides ensuring that everyone is there, this is also an opportunity to teach counting. To make counting even more fun for the children, count in another language.
   ◆ **Waiting:** When waiting is necessary, children become bored easily. This is a good time to teach another language to children. Teach numbers, the alphabet, or a simple song in another language.
   ◆ **Sitting:** Occasionally children must sit and wait for the rest of the class to finish. Try giving simple directions in another language (such as "sit down, please," and "thank you"). At first they may look at you quizzically. Instead of repeating yourself in English, simply repeat it in the foreign language, but include movements to indicate what the words mean. The children catch on fast and in time try to say it themselves.

Related books   *Abuela* by Arthur Dorros
Knots on a Counting Rope by Bill Martin, Jr. and John Archambault
One Smiling Grandma: A Caribbean Counting Book by Ann Marie Linden
What Is Your Language? by Debra Leventhal

⭐ *Deborah R. Gallagher, Littleton, NH*

Velcro Alphabet

5+

Materials   large piece of cardboard
Velcro strips
thick cardboard, fun foam, or felt in a selection of colors
pencil
scissors
box or container

What to do
1. Hang a large, plain-colored piece of cardboard on a wall of your classroom.
2. Glue Velcro strips to the cardboard.
3. Cut out the letters of the alphabet from cardboard, fun foam, felt, or any other material that will withstand repeated handling. Make several of each letter, especially the more popular ones.
   Author's Note: As a rule of thumb, the lower a letter's Scrabble score, the more you need to make.
4. Stick a piece of Velcro on the back of each letter.
5. Put the letters in a container and let the children pick them out and stick them to the Velcro on the wall to form words. Their names are good to start with, but also encourage them to write words related to the classroom theme.
6. Encourage the children to form words on the wall when they are waiting for a new activity or for others to finish.
7. Another way to use the letters is to hang one letter at a time and let only those children whose name begins with that letter move to the next activity, put on their coat, go outside, and so on.

More to do   **Language:** Instead of using letters, try writing words on narrow strips of cardboard or card stock. Include a good mixture of nouns, verbs, adjectives, and so on, and then ask the children to arrange them into sentences. If they are very ambitious, they could even try arranging the words into a short story!

⭐ *Kirsty Neale, Charleville Circus, London, United Kingdom*

Writing Letters

5+

Materials   none

What to do

1. If the children must line up for an activity, encourage them to practice writing by using their fingers to "write" on the back of the child in front of them. Not only will this give them practice in printing, it will also feel good and calm them down.
2. The child who is first in line will have to write in the air, and the child who is last in line will not have anyone writing on his back. If a child is uncomfortable with being touched, leave him at the end of the line. If not, make sure these two children trade places with two other children after an appropriate time.
3. At other times in the day, have the children pair up and write their name on their partner's back. Each child has a turn to write and be written upon. If possible, play soothing, background music to promote calmness and enjoyment.

★ *Phyllis Esch, Export, PA*

The Opposite Boat

5+

Materials   chairs, pillows, or carpet squares

What to do

1. Line up chairs, pillows, or carpet squares in two rows. These will be the "boat."
2. Ask the children to sit on a chair, pillow, or carpet square. Explain that they are going for a ride in the "opposite boat," and will be traveling to a land where everything is opposite!
3. Begin the journey by telling them that the boat is rocking on the waves. Pretend that the boat is going through a storm and have the children rock back and forth quickly. (This will get them in the spirit of adventure!)
4. Soon, tell them they have arrived at the land of opposites. Ask them if they'd like to get out of the boat for a "swim." Tell them that although people swim under the water, in the land of opposites, where would they swim?

5. Explain that they are "swimming" to the "opposite island." Ask them questions as they walk around the pretend land. What color is the snow on Opposite Island? Do birds swim and fish fly? Do they run slowly and walk quickly? Encourage them to make up their own opposites.

6. Have everyone get back in the boat and travel back to the real world where things are normal.

More to do
Art: Give each child a piece of paper and crayons. Have them draw something from the opposite world. Then, encourage the children to hold up their drawing and tell what is different about their opposite picture.

★ *Sarah Hartman, Lafayette, LA*

I Can't Make Up My Mind   5+

Materials   none

What to do
1. This is great to use when the children seem tired or bored. It is also great for explaining a difficult principle, to "shake up" confused minds and tired bodies.

2. As seriously as possible, ask the class to stand. Then, looking as though you are debating a decision, ask them to sit.

3. Then continue by saying, "Oh, no, I really meant for you to stand!" After they stand up, say, "Actually I think I need you to sit." Continue asking them to sit and stand alternately until they are laughing. This will refresh their bodies and their minds.

4. When first playing this game, the children gradually realize it is a game. Then it becomes a joy to watch them pretending to object to you pretending to forget. This simple brain/body exercise can brighten and enliven those difficult times of the day. It can be as noisy or as quiet as you choose.

★ *Robyn Dalby-Stockwell, Cambridgeshire, United Kingdom*

Did You Know?

5+

Materials   empty can, such as a soup can
construction paper and glue
markers
Popsicle sticks

What to do

1. Decorate the can by covering it with paper and drawing on it.
2. Write different facts on Popsicle sticks about topics either related to the children's interests at the time or any subject. Start each fact with, "Did you know?"
3. Place the sticks in the can.
4. During waiting times, let the children take turns removing one stick at a time. Read the fact to the children and talk about it.

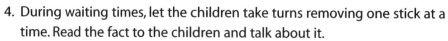

POPSICLE STICK

BRIGHTLY DECORATED SOUP CAN

Was it sweet or sour?

★ *Eileen Lucas, Halifax, Nova Scotia, Canada*

A Welcome Note

3+

Materials envelopes
note cards
stamps

What to do

1. Before school starts for the year, write a short note to each child welcoming her to your classroom.
2. Include in your note what they should expect the first day of school and some of the things the class will be doing.
3. For preschoolers, you might want to include photos of yourself and other staff. Ask parents to review who the people in the photos are before school starts. By the time the child arrives at school, she can already be familiar with the staff and have an increased comfort level.
4. Mail the letters home to each child. Children love receiving letters in the family mailbox.
   Note: You can also use interesting postcards instead. They are less expensive to mail and are still fun for the children.
5. If possible, use interesting stamps.

More to do Follow up with a unit about the post office, letter carriers, and writing letters to someone. Let the children send a note to a friend, family member, or classmate.

⭐ *Sandra Nagel, White Lake, MI*

Entering School: Extending Children's Comfort Zone

`3+`

Materials pictures of the child's family, friends, and pets

What to do

1. Before school begins for the year, send a short note to each family asking them to glue pictures about the child to a square piece of paper and send it in on the first day. Explain that this will increase their child's comfort in the new school environment.
2. Display the pictures on a wall at the children's viewing level.
3. Often, just having a picture of home helps the child feel more comfortable in an unfamiliar environment.
4. Encourage the children to talk about their pictures. It will help them get to know each other and it is a great language activity.

★ *Sandra Nagel, White Lake, MI*

Hello, How Are You?

`3+`

Materials none

What to do

1. Sing the following to the tune of "Skip to My Lou" to greet children in the morning.

   Hello, how are you?
   Hello, how are you?
   Hello, how are you?
   How are you today?

   I'm glad you came, everyone,
   I'm glad you came, everyone,
   I'm glad you came, everyone,
   I'm glad you came today.

2. Sing this third verse and have the children say their names. Pretend you have a microphone and let each child say her name loudly into it.

I'm glad you came, Ann.
I'm glad you came, John.
I'm glad you came, Jill.
I'm glad you came today.

3. Repeat this as many times as necessary so that everyone has a chance to say her name. Don't forget to include yourself.
4. As a variation, use other languages for the word "hello." Following is a list of ways to say hello in other languages.

- ◆ German: Guten Tag or Hallo
- ◆ French: Bonjour
- ◆ Italian: Salve
- ◆ Spanish: Hola
- ◆ Hawaiian: Aloha
- ◆ Hebrew: Shalom

★ *Cookie Zingarelli, Columbus, OH*

I'm Glad You Came to School 3+

Materials   none

What to do   1. Sing the following song to the tune of "The Farmer in the Dell." Substitute the children's names in the second verse and sing until you have named all the children.

I'm glad you came to school,
I'm glad you came to school,
Heigh-ho, the derry-oh,
I'm glad you came to school.

I'm glad to see _____ here.
I'm glad to see _____ here.
Heigh-ho, the derry-oh,
I'm glad to see _____ here.

★ *Jackie Wright, Enid, OK*

Morning Greeting

Materials none

What to do 1. Use the familiar chant "Hello Everybody, Yes Indeed" to turn your morning routine into a learning experience.

Hello, everybody, yes indeed,
Yes indeed, yes indeed,
Hello, everybody, yes indeed,
Yes indeed, my darling.

2. Add more verses related to the day of the week, weather, or class news:

Today is Monday, yes indeed...
The day is sunny, yes indeed...
Today is Stevie's birthday, yes indeed...

3. At departure time, sing:

Goodbye, everybody, yes indeed,
Yes indeed, yes indeed,
Goodbye, everybody, yes indeed,
Yes indeed, my darling.

We'll see you tomorrow, yes indeed,
Yes indeed, yes indeed...

More to do **Language:** This chant lends itself to syllable clapping. Encourage the children to clap the syllables along with the chant. Being able to recognize syllables as parts of words is an important pre-reading skill.

Related book *The Very Hungry Caterpillar* by Eric Carle

⭐ *Iris Rothstein, New Hyde Park, NY*

Sing and Sign

Materials   none

What to do   1. To ease the transition during arrival time, teach the children this song and the sign language to go along with it.

Hello, hello, hello, how are you?
I'm fine, I'm fine, and I hope that you are too.

(continued on the next page)

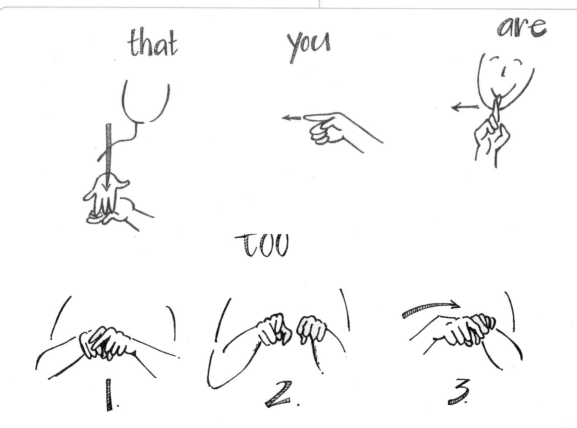

2. Practice the signs until the children are comfortable with them.
3. At arrival time, begin to sing and sign to the children as they enter the room. Encourage any children who are already in the room to join in as you sing and sign together.

More to do   **Home-to-School Connection:** Send a sheet of the signs and song home with the children so their parents can learn the song in sign language also.

Related books   *Handtalk Zoo* by George Ancona and Mary Beth Miller
A Very Special Friend by Dorothy Hoffman Levi
Words in Our Hands by Ada B. Litchfield

★*Virginia Jean Herrod, Columbia, SC*

Arrival Transitions

Materials   none

What to do
1. Make a chart with pictures or photos to help the children with the morning routine. Include such tasks as hanging up their coats, unpacking their backpacks, handing in lunch money, putting away borrowed books, and so on.
2. As the children arrive in the morning, the chart helps them to become more independent as they transition into the classroom.
3. With so many children doing the same routine over and over, it is always helpful to have a picture cue to follow!

⭐ *Tracie O'Hara, Charlotte, NC*

Arrival Candle

3+

Materials   scented candle

What to do
1. When you arrive in the morning, light a scented candle. Nice scents to use are vanilla or cookie dough.
2. Blow out the candle before the children arrive. When they arrive, the room has a very warm and inviting smell.

⭐ *Audrey Kanoff, Allentown, PA*

Good Morning

`3+`

Materials   none

What to do
1. As the children arrive, sing, "Good morning, good morning, and how are you?" to each child. The children can respond by singing, "I'm fine, I'm fine, and I hope you are too!"
2. Sing good morning in different languages. Use body language to greet each other during this song, such as shaking hands, waving, or giving a hug.

⭐ *Kaethe Lewandowski, Centreville, VA*

Good Morning to You!

`3+`

Materials   none

What to do
1. This activity helps children develop self-confidence and poise.
2. At the start of the day, have the children stand in a circle as you move around shaking hands and greeting each child by name.
3. After you say the child's name and shake her hand, she sits down.
4. When all the children have been greeted and are seated, the day is ready to begin.

⭐ *Mary Jo Shannon, Roanoke, VA*

Door Stop Ritual

3+

Materials   none

What to do
1. Stand in front of the door to greet each child in the morning.
2. Create a special handshake or greeting phrase that lets each child knows that she is part of the class. Suggested examples are saying: "Alacazam, ma'am (or sir)!" or making a circle with your hands (Circle of Love).
3. End the day at the door with the same secret handshake, slogan, or ritual.
4. Another idea is to have a special surprise to share with each child related to the theme of the day. For example, hand out a red sticker for "red day," feathers for a bird unit, or a card with the letter of the day on it.

Susan R. Forbes, Daytona Beach, FL

That Awkward Arrival Time

3+

Materials   none

What to do
1. It is not necessary to start each day with the full, undivided attention of the children. Because children often arrive at different times, it is difficult to have circle time early in the day.
2. Try starting the day with organized free play. Contrary to what some may think, this does not necessarily result in chaos.
3. Put out different activities at each table, such as playdough at one table, a teacher-led game at another, and art materials at another. These activities may vary from day to day.
4. Also have the painting easel and sand and water table available.
5. This helps reduce the stress of wanting everyone present for a morning greeting at the very beginning of the day. This also will free you to greet parents and children individually as they arrive. While another teacher watches the children, you can take a minute to talk to parents.
6. If you feel that the children who arrive last are missing out on this opportunity to play, try extending play time.

Deborah R. Gallagher, Littleton, NH

Morning Transition Playdough 3+

Materials   playdough (see recipe below)
cookie cutters
playdough tools

What to do   1. Make playdough beforehand using the following recipe. This recipe is easy to make, and produces a very soft dough that feels good to knead.

1 cup flour
½ cup salt
2 teaspoons cream of tartar
1 cup water
1 tablespoon oil
food coloring or Liquid Watercolor

2. Combine flour, salt, and cream of tartar. Set aside. Bring water, oil, and food coloring to a boil. Pour into the dry mixture. Mix until it is cool enough to knead. Store in an airtight container.
3. Put playdough out on the tables before the children arrive. When the children come in, they can play with the playdough. This is a fun way to start the day as you wait for the entire class to arrive.
4. For variety, make a new color every month or add special touches to the playdough such as glitter, scented oils, or a package of Kool-Aid to engage the senses.

⭐ *Gail Morris, Kemah, TX*

Class Pets 3+

Materials   class pet (mouse, guinea pig, fish)
pet supplies and food

What to do   1. When a child has a hard time separating from a parent in the morning, a class pet really helps.

2. Give the children food to feed the pet when they arrive, such as carrots for a guinea pig.
3. This lets children feel helpful and ready to begin the day.
4. Create a home-school connection by asking the children to bring in food for the class pet.

⭐ *Audrey Kanoff, Allentown, PA*

Puppet Pals

3+

Materials
two puppets
blank cassette tape
cassette tape player

What to do
1. Before children arrive, make a tape using different voices to make it seem like two puppets are talking to each other. Have the puppets explain class rules and consequences. (Keep the list of rules to five or six so the children can remember them.)
2. After children arrive, play the tape and make the puppets "talk."
3. The next day, play a different tape reminding the children what the rules are. Have the puppets ask the children to repeat the rules.
4. Continue until you feel that the children have learned the rules from the puppets.
5. Send a note home to parents explaining the puppets and the class rules.
6. Bring out the puppets to talk whenever there is a special event or just to "talk" to the children.

Related books *Did You Carry the Flag Today, Charley?* by Rebecca Caudill
No, David! by David Shannon
Officer Buckle and Gloria by Peggy Rathmann

⭐ *Barbara Saul, Eureka, CA*

Happy or Sad

Materials   piece of card stock for each child
pens
pocket chart

What to do
1. This is a great activity to do as children arrive in the morning.
2. Draw a happy face on one side and a sad face on the other side of each card. Put a child's name under each face.
3. When the child arrives, let her turn her card in the pocket chart to show whatever she is feeling.
4. Let the children talk about why they are happy or sad, either in a group or individually. Help them express their feelings and learn how they can change their moods.
5. Make graphs with the faces in the pocket chart and see which has the most, happy or sad. Read the graph with the children and let them tell about their feelings.

Related books   *Alexander and the Terrible, Horrible, No Good, Very Bad Day* by Judith Viorst
Angry Arthur by Hiawyn Oram
Goodbye House by Frank Asch
Lilly's Purple Plastic Purse by Kevin Henkes
Today I Feel Silly: And Other Moods That Make My Day by Jamie Lee Curtis
When Sophie Gets Angry—Really, Really, Angry… by Molly Bang

Feelings

Materials
poster board
markers
paper
scissors
container

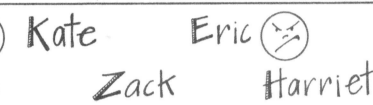

EYE LEVEL POSTER

Matt Kate   Eric
Allie   Zack   Harriet

Happy   Sad   Sleepy   Mad   Excited

What to do

1. Write each child's name on a piece of poster board, leaving a space next to each name. Hang it at children's eye level.
2. Draw and cut out faces expressing happy, sad, sleepy, mad, and excited and put them in a small container.
3. As each child arrives, talk about how she feels and why. Let each child choose a face that depicts her feelings and attach it to the chart by her name with tape.

More to do

Language: During group time, let each child finish a sentence such as, "I feel happy when…" Write their answers on chart paper. Repeat this activity with other emotions.

⭐ *Barb Lindsay, Mason City, IA*

Who Is at School Today?

3+

Materials
photos of each child
laminator (optional)
magnetic tape
magnetic board

What to do
1. Take a photo of each child and laminate it. Put the photos in a basket by the door.
2. As the children arrive, they find their picture and put it on the magnetic board.
3. At circle time, review who is there and who is not (pictures left in the basket).
4. As they begin to recognize their names, switch from pictures to name cards.
5. At the beginning of the year, this helps children learn their classmates' names and helps with the transition of arriving at school.

★ Audrey Kanoff, Allentown, PA

Attendance Board

3+

Materials
mailing labels
markers
large piece of poster-size tagboard
tape
book pockets (the manila envelopes used to hold library cards)

What to do
1. Write each child's name on a mailing label. Affix each label to a book pocket, tape the pockets to the tagboard, and hang in the arrival area.
   Note: Using mailing labels on the pockets allows you to rearrange the names from time to time or to add or delete names as registration changes.
2. Write each child's name on an index card. Let them decorate their name cards with markers or stickers.
3. When each child arrives, she finds her name card and slips it into the corresponding name pocket.

4. This short activity provides the children with something to do while you continue greeting arriving children. The children will quickly recognize the board as a way to determine who is absent.

5. At the end of the day, let the children remove their name as a departure activity.

    Author's Note: You can also use these pockets to hold small notes to be sent home, reminders of who has a library book checked out, or other such notes.

More to do   Instead of index cards, provide the children with cutout shapes that correspond with the seasons (such as leaves in the fall or mittens in the winter) or the weekly activity (such as vehicle shapes during a transportation unit). You can also give them letters of the alphabet that correspond with their names.

Literacy: As the children's abilities increase, encourage them to write their own names on the attendance cards, their age, or other ideas.

⭐ *Lauri Robinson, Big Lake, MN*

Question of the Day

3+

Materials   roll of calculator paper
construction paper
scissors
markers
hole punch
map pins

What to do   1. Make two-sided nametags with both sides different colors. For example, cut out identical red and green apple shapes and glue them together (or use white paper and color each side a different color). You can use any shape you want.
2. Help the children write their names on each side of the nametag.
3. Use map pins to hang each nametag on a bulletin board at children's eye level.
4. Each day before the children arrive, write a question on calculator paper and hang it above the nametags. Examples of questions are: "Did you have fun on the field trip?" "Did you play in the snow?" "Are you wearing red today?"
5. Each child's parent reads the question to his or her child. If the child's answer is yes, the child hangs the apple with the green side showing. If the child's answer is no, the child hangs the apple with the red side showing.

More to do   **Math:** Use the answers to the questions to make a graph. Discuss the results at circle time.

★ *Sandy L. Scott, Vancouver, WA*

Morning Message

4+

Materials   large chart paper or blackboard
pen or chalk

What to do
1. Write a sentence or two on a blackboard or chart before the children arrive. Use this morning message to tell the children about an upcoming event, class projects, or something about individual children.
2. Read the message out loud and then have the children read it with you.
3. To teach letter recognition, call on children to come and circle all the instances of one letter that she sees. Choose a different letter each day.

 Barbara Saul, Eureka, CA

Morning Transition Journals

4+

Materials   one spiral notebook for each child

What to do
1. Write each child's name on a spiral notebook. Show them the notebooks and explain that these are their own personal journals to write or draw in.
2. Explain how to start a journal and tell them that every time they write in it, they should use the next page.
3. Put the notebooks on a table when the children arrive in the morning and let them draw or write whatever they choose.
4. If desired, add the date and the children's own words about their picture to make it a special treasure.
5. Put out the journals periodically. Keep them all year and let the children take them home at the end of the year. They will be very excited to take their journals home after working on them all year, and it may encourage the wonderful habit of journaling.
6. You can use the journals at the end of the year for assessments to see the gradual improvement in writing and art skills.
7. Bring out the journals at other transition times, such as after lunchtime.

 *Gail Morris, Kemah, TX*

Name Necklaces and Nametags 4+

Materials
yarn
paper
markers

What to do
1. Make name necklaces for the children. Write each child's name on a strip of paper, punch a hole in it, and insert it a piece of yarn through the hole. Tie the ends of the yarn together to make a necklace.
2. Place the necklaces on a table or hang them from a display.
3. Greet the children as they arrive and ask them to find their name necklaces. As each child finds her name necklace, she has an opportunity to learn name recognition.
4. At the end of the day, the children hang up their name necklace or put them back on the table.

More to do
More Transitions: Use the name necklaces for other transitions. For example, "If you have the letter 'J' in your name, you may get up and wash your hands." Children will look at their names for the letters you call. This is great letter recognition practice.

★ *Susan Myhre, Bremerton, WA*

Sign Your Name 4+

Materials
construction paper
bingo markers
markers
pencils
modeling clay
liquid starch
tissue paper
non-toxic white glue
glitter

What to do

1. Every day when children arrive, have a different sign-in activity for them to do. Before they arrive, print each child's name on a 12" x 18" piece of construction paper. Have them do the following activities on different days:

   ◆ Use bingo markers to place on the letters of their names.
   ◆ Trace their names with glue and then sprinkle glitter, colored sand, or other material on the glue.
   ◆ Roll softened modeling clay into ropes and place it on each letter.
   ◆ Paint their names with liquid starch and stick small squares of tissue paper on each letter.

2. As the children become more interested in writing their own names, write the letters of their names in dots and have them connect the dots.
3. When they are proficient in this, encourage them to copy their names from an example such as a name card.

Donna Martin, Sonora, CA

Please Sign Up

4+

Materials

daily sign-in sheet
photocopier
laminator or clear contact paper
dry erase pens or crayons

What to do

1. Enlarge your daily sign-in sheet using a photocopier. Laminate each sheet to save paper.
2. Place these large sheets on a low table near the regular sign-in sheet, and let the children sign in and out just like teachers and parents.
3. You will notice less scribbling on the actual sign-in sheet if you try this.
4. Children can also fill out lunch or snack slips in this way.

Linda Ford, Sacramento, CA

Welcome to Our Zoo

4+

Materials
paper plates
scissors
craft sticks
white glue
marker
crayons

What to do

1. This is a fun activity for children to do when they arrive at school. It sets a fun tone, which relieves some of their anxiety at arrival.
2. Make a mask for each child by cutting eye holes in paper plates. Glue each plate to a craft stick. Label the concave side of each plate with the child's name.
3. Tape or staple the masks to a wall outside the classroom for the children to see when they arrive. Be sure their names are visible.
4. Make several sample masks to display on tables in the class, and make one for yourself.
5. Put crayons on the table for children to decorate their masks.
6. Greet the children as they arrive and show them your mask. Invite them to make an animal mask for the "classroom zoo."

Karyn F. Everham, Fort Myers, FL

Classroom Calendar

Materials   large pieces of card stock
scissors
markers
ruler
paper fasteners

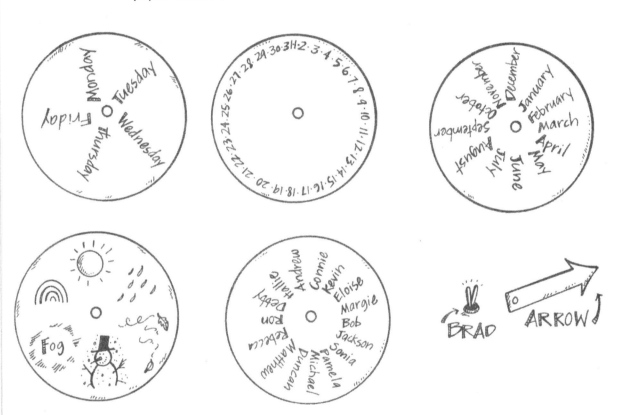

What to do
1. Cut out five large circles from card stock and mark the center of each one.
2. Divide the first circle into five segments. Write the days Monday through Friday in the segments.
3. Divide the second circle into 31 segments and write the numbers 1 through 31 in each one (these are the days of the month). If desired, write the numbers around the circle's edge like a clock face.
4. Mark 12 segments on the third circle and write the name of a month in each one.
5. Circle number four is a weather indicator. Make segments for sunshine, rain, wind, snow, fog, rainbows, or whatever is appropriate to your local climate. Write or draw a picture of each weather condition.

(continued on the next page)

6. Write the names of each child in the class on the fifth circle (make as many segments as needed to fit each name). This will show whose turn it is to change the calendar settings each day. This allows the children to see clearly how long they have to wait for their turn.

7. Make an arrow marker for each circle. Draw these onto a piece of card stock, cut them out, and use a paper fastener to attach each arrow in the center of a circle. These should leave the arrows free to rotate and point in any direction.

8. To help children transition during arrival time, the child whose name is indicated on the fifth circle (with children's names) moves the arrows on each circle to point towards the day, date, month, and weather. Make sure to move the arrow on the fifth circle to the next segment each day so that each child gets a turn.

More to do   **Art:** Ask each child to draw something relating to the calendar, such as a weather scene, flowers, or a holiday design, on a small piece of paper. Join these together to create a border for the class calendar area.

Related books   *Parade Day: Marching Through the Calendar Year* by Bob Barner
The Real Mother Goose by Blanche Fisher Wright
The Story of Clocks and Calendars: Marking a Millennium by Betsy Maestro

Kirsty Neale, Charleville Circus, London, United Kingdom

Personal Art Journals

3+

Materials
drawing paper or construction paper
stapler
crayons or markers
date stamp

What to do

1. At the beginning of the year, make art journals for each child. (Depending on the skill level of the children, you might want to let them create their own journals.)
2. Staple together a lot of paper and add a cover for each book.
3. Encourage the children to decorate and label their book covers.
4. Keep these journals in the art center at all times. The children are free to draw in their journals at any time, especially during transitions.
5. Explain that they are to use the pages in sequence to draw or write anything they would like. Some may want to draw pictures and some may want to practice writing their names or letters.
6. Whenever they finish with a page, they can stamp the date on it.
7. Let the children take their journals home at the end of the year. This is a nice way for parents to see their child's artistic or writing development, and it is all done at the child's pace.

Wanda Guidroz, Santa Fe, TX

Handy Art Labels

3+

Materials
large supply of address labels
computer or markers
date stamp

What to do

1. Using a computer or markers, print many sets of labels for all the children in your class. If there are 16 children in your class, for example, then you would make a sheet of 16 labels, with each child's name on a separate label.

(continued on the next page)

2. Make a lot of these to use throughout the year. These are great to have on hand to label children's work quickly and move to the next activity.

3. When children are painting at the easel or working on a special art project, just stamp the date on the child's label and stick it on the back of the child's paper. This is a great way to see at a glance who has not painted or started a special project.

⭐ *Gail Morris, Kemah, TX*

Time for Art

`3+`

Materials

8 ½" x 11" poster board
markers

What to do

1. Write the following song on a piece of poster board and hang it in the art center.

2. When children are transitioning to the art center and need to put on their smocks (old shirts), sing the song with them.

Time for Art (Tune: "Row, Row, Row Your Boat")
Find, find, find your smock
Help and do your part.
Button, button, button up
Now it's time for art.

⭐ *Jackie Wright, Enid, OK*

A Dot Will Do

`3+`

Materials

poster board or card stock
markers
laminator (optional)
scissors

What to do
1. Print the following poem on poster board. Laminate for durability.
2. Say this poem with children to transition to an activity in which children use glue.

A dot! A dot!
A dot will do!
Any more than that is...
TOO MUCH GLUE!

 Jackie Wright, Enid, OK

Color Quartet

3+

Materials
crayons
rubber bands or masking tape
large sheets of drawing paper

What to do
1. Use full-length crayons that are new or like new for this activity.
2. During a transition time, ask each child to select four colors of crayons. Join them together with a rubber band or masking tape.
3. Encourage them to make fanciful designs using four colors at once.
4. Try joining together four markers. Use these "color quartets" instead of paint at the easel at times when you need easy cleanup.

 Susan Sharkey, La Mesa, CA

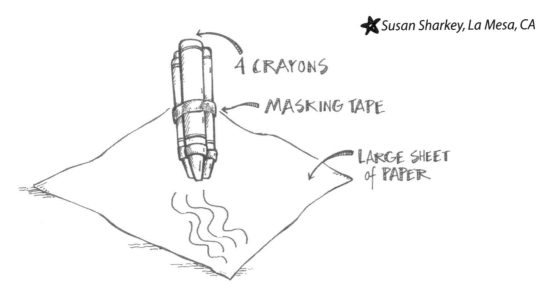

4 CRAYONS
MASKING TAPE
LARGE SHEET of PAPER

Driftwood Art

`3+`

Materials
pieces of driftwood or unusual objects from nature
paint
paintbrushes, sponges, or other painting implements

What to do
1. Grab children's attention by placing pieces of driftwood or other unusual objects in the art center.
2. Encourage the children to paint them.

More to do
Science: Put the objects on the science or discovery table along with paper, pencils, and markers. Encourage the children to name the objects, make up stories about them, or draw pictures of them. Discuss the objects, such as what they think they are, where they came from, or what could be made from them.

★ *Eileen Lucas, Halifax, Nova Scotia, Canada*

Create-a-Picture

`3+`

Materials
markers, colored pens, crayons, paint, and chalk
large piece of paper
easel

What to do
1. Attach a large piece of paper to the easel.
2. Make a line, shape, or simple design on the paper.
3. Ask each child, in turn, to add to the drawing. It will be interesting to see what kind of picture emerges from the collaborative effort.
4. If you want to focus on a theme, start with that idea in mind. You might want to title the project before you begin drawing ("Flowers in My Garden," "Toys in My Room," or "Fun at the Beach").

LINE ADDED
BY TEACHER

5. Use this activity during waiting times.

Note: Large rolls of blueprint paper are great to have on hand for the easel. Seek out a source for this paper, which is often discarded when building projects are complete. It can easily be cut to size.

★ *Judy Fujawa, The Villages, FL*

My Own Chalkboard   3+

Materials
clipboards
chalkboard paint
paintbrush
self-adhesive Velcro
chalk eraser
chunky chalk
cord
hot glue gun (adult only)

What to do
1. Make small chalkboards for each child. Waiting can be fun when you have your own chalkboard to play with!
2. Obtain small clipboards for each child. Paint the front and back of each clipboard with two coats of chalkboard paint.

(continued on the next page)

3. Use hot glue to attach Velcro to the front of the clipboard and to the back of the eraser. Attach the eraser to the clipboard.
4. Tie the cord to the chalk and secure it with hot glue. Tie the other end of the cord to the clipboard.
5. Encourage the children to draw on their own chalkboards during transition times when they must wait for others to get ready or for an activity to begin.

More to do   **Literacy:** Print a vocabulary word or a common shape on a child's clipboard. Challenge the child to read the word or name the shape.

Related book   *The Chalk Doll* by Charlotte Pomerantz

⭐*Virginia Jean Herrod, Columbia, SC*

Never-Ending Artwork   3+

Materials   butcher paper
markers

What to do   1. Cut out long sheets of butcher paper, about 10" wide.
2. Divide the long sheets of paper into 12" sections and mark with a marker.
3. Hang the paper all around the classroom and along the walls of the halls.
4. Children can draw or write on the paper at any transition time.

⭐*Eileen Lucas, Halifax, Nova Scotia, Canada*

Picture Starter

Materials pictures from calendars, magazines, greeting cards, and other sources
11" x 14" drawing paper
glue or tape
markers, colored pens, and crayons

What to do
1. This is a quick art activity to fill a few extra moments until the next activity.
2. Glue or tape pictures from calendars or magazines to pieces of 11" x 14" paper.
3. Invite the children to select a piece of drawing paper with a picture on it. Ask them to use markers, pens, or crayons to add to the picture on the paper, completing it or completing the story that the picture begins.
4. If time allows, write down their comments and descriptions.

Judy Fujawa, The Villages, FL

Squiggles

Materials paper
pencils and markers
photocopier

What to do
1. Draw a curvy line on a piece of paper and photocopy it.
2. During waiting times, give each child a "squiggle." Encourage them to make a picture from the lines.
3. Let the children take turns describing what they made.

Barbara Saul, Eureka, CA

No More Paint or Paper

3+

Materials   five different colors of paint
paintbrushes
easel paper of different shapes and sizes

What to do
1. Put out five different paints and paintbrushes.
2. Clip a large piece of easel paper to the easel.
3. After a short period of time, remove one cup of paint, then another, and so on.
4. Each time you remove a cup of paint, clip a smaller piece of paper to the easel
5. Continue until all the paper and paint is gone.
6. Children love the idea of being the last to paint with only one color on a very small piece of paper.
7. This is a good way to finish in the art center and transition to another activity.

⭐ *Ingelore Mix, Gainesville, VA*

Name the Animal

3+

Materials   none

What to do
1. This is a game that encourages accuracy of description, which is helpful for creative writing, and an imaginative use of color, which is useful in art.
2. Ask the children to think of an animal, including what it looks like, where it lives, what noise it makes, and if possible, what its young are called. Tell them that all the details should be as accurate as possible, except for the animal's color. This should be as strange as the child can make it.
3. Let each child describe his animal to the class, who guess what it is. For example, "My animal is big and says 'moo'. It lives on a farm, gives us milk, and has babies called calves. My animal is sky blue and orange, and sometimes has purple patches."
4. Young children will have quite a laugh over "cherry red" monkeys and "banana yellow" pigs.
5. As a transition, have the children draw pictures of their animals before leaving the art center for other activities.

★*Robyn Dalby-Stockwell, Cambridgeshire, United Kingdom*

Matching Mittens

4+

Materials
construction paper
scissors
mittens, matched and unmatched
art supplies

What to do

1. Before doing this activity, draw the outline of a mitten on construction paper and cut it out. Cut out enough mittens so that each child will get one and put them in the art center.
2. Show the children a variety of real mittens. Talk about the patterns on each mitten that make them the same or different.
3. Let each child choose a mitten and transition to the art center to create a construction paper match to make a pair.
4. Display the construction paper mittens and their matching real mittens on a classroom bulletin board.

MITTENS

CONSTRUCTION PAPER MITTENS

More to do   **Math:** Use the paper mittens for a sorting game.

★ *Barb Lindsay, Mason City, IA*

Shape Up

4+

Materials   large paper
easel
markers or crayons
index cards

What to do
1. This is a good art activity for children to transition from a group activity to the next activity.
2. Tape a large sheet of paper to the easel. Draw a different shape on several cards.
3. Place the cards face down in front of the children, next to the easel.
4. Let the children take turns choosing a marker or crayon and a shape card. The child adds the shape to the paper and then transitions to the next activity. The end result will be a group picture.
5. Several children can go at once to shorten the waiting time.

More to do   **Language:** At some point, bring the group back to the picture and ask them to list items or dictate a story about what they see. Write down what they say and post it next to the picture.

Related book   *The Art Lesson* by Tomie dePaola

Ann Kelly, Johnstown, PA

Thinking Caps

4+

Materials
paper caps
markers
paint
glue
decorations (feathers, pompoms, beads, and so on)

What to do
1. Give a plain paper cap to each child. Encourage them to decorate their hats any way they choose. Tell them they are making "thinking caps."
2. Ask the children to wear their thinking caps each day during difficult classroom activities.
3. You can also make other caps, such as "quiet caps" or "sleeping caps."

Related book *Caps for Sale* by Esphyr Slobodkina

★ Renee Kirchner, Carrollton, TX

Stained Glass Window

5+

Materials
pictures of stained glass windows
paper
pencil
colored markers
tacky craft glue or hot glue gun (adult only)
sheets of transparency (clear) paper

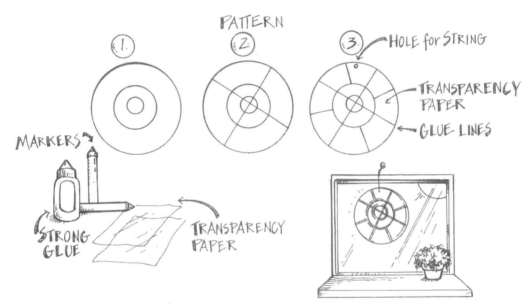

What to do

1. Make "stained glass windows" with the children to hang in the classroom window. Looking at these helps children relax and calm down when transitioning to quiet activities.
2. Show the children pictures of stained glass windows.
3. Demonstrate how to draw the outline of a stained glass window on paper with a pencil. They can draw a closed pattern in any shape (rectangle or circle).
4. Encourage them to connect the interior of the shape with straight or squiggly lines, trying to make patterns.
5. Help the children use tacky glue to trace their pattern on the transparency paper. If using hot glue, an adult must do this step.
6. Let the glue dry for several hours, until no longer tacky. The glue from a glue gun will be ready as soon as it cools.
7. Encourage the children to use markers to color between the lines of glue. Since the glue is raised, it's easy to color between the lines!
8. Attach your creations to the window and wait for the sunshine to stream through.

⭐ *Susan Berk Koch, Mequon, WI*

Salami

`3+`

Materials   none

What to do
1. To get immediate attention from the children, loudly say the word "SALAMI," which is an acronym for "Stop And Look At Me Immediately!"
2. Another way to get their attention is to recite the following "Give Me Five" chant. Hold up one finger as you say each rule.

Eyes are watching,
Ears are listening,
Mouth is quiet,
Hands are to myself,
Hearts are caring.

⭐ *Jackie Wright, Enid, OK*

The Cheering Section

`3+`

Materials   none

What to do
1. Grab the children's attention with the following poem.
2. Recite each line of the poem with the children and together perform the motions.

Give me a one! (hold up one finger)
Give me a two! (hold up two fingers)
Make a loud clap (clap hands)
Shout out "Boo!" (shout "boo!")
Give me a three! (hold up three fingers)
Give me a four! (hold up four fingers)
Slap a high five! (children give a high five to their neighbor)
Ready for more?

⭐ *Karyn F. Everham, Fort Myers, FL*

Get Ready Rhyme

Materials   none

What to do   To get the children's attention, say the following rhyme using appropriate actions. The children repeat the actions.

Clap your hands. (clap three times)
Tap your feet. (tap foot three times)
Now it's time to take a seat. (everyone sits on floor or chairs)
Give your hands one more clap. (clap one time)
Now place them gently on your lap. (hands go to children's laps)

Related books   *Here Are My Hands* by Bill Martin, Jr.
My Father's Hands by Joanne Ryder
My Two Hands/My Two Feet by Rick Walton

⭐ *Christina Chilcote, New Freedom, PA*

Point

Materials   none

What to do   1. When you need to get the children's attention, recite the following rhyme:

Point to the window,
Point to the door,
Point to the ceiling,
And point to the floor.

Point to your elbow,
Point to your knee,
Point to you
And point to me.

(continued on the next page)

2. This is great for labeling parts of the room as well as for talking about body parts.

Related books   *Hooray for Me!* by Remy Charlip
Ruby the Copycat by Peggy Rathmann

⭐ *Sandy L. Scott, Vancouver, WA*

1, 2, Come Here to Me   3+

Materials   none

What to do   Use the following song to get children's attention. Sing it to the tune of "One, Two, Buckle My Shoe."

One, two, come here to me,
Three, four, sit on the floor,
Five, six, sit up straight,
Seven, eight, hands in your lap,
Nine, ten, shh! Let's begin.

⭐ *Cookie Zingarelli, Columbus, OH*

Catch a Bubble   3+

Materials   none

What to do   1. Sing the following song to the tune of "Frère Jacques" to get children's attention when they are playing.
2. If desired, blow real bubbles before and after you sing the song.

Catch a bubble,
Catch a bubble,
1-2-3, look at me.

Catch a bubble,
Catch a bubble,
Look at me.

⭐ *Cookie Zingarelli, Columbus, OH*

Chant and Clap

`3+`

Materials   none

What to do   Use different verses of the following chant to get the children's attention as needed. Repeat each line until all the children are clapping along. Change the chant to fit the transition.

Line up and up and up and up and up!
Line up! (clap twice)
Line up! (clap twice)

Clean up and up and up and up and up!
Clean up! (clap twice)
Clean up! (clap twice)

Listen up…

⭐ *Susan Sharkey, La Mesa, CA*

I Say, You Say

3+

Materials   list of chant words (as suggested below)

What to do   Recite the following chant in a "cheerleading" voice to capture children's attention outdoors or in a noisy room. It has several variations.

> *I say, "Day," you say, "Night."*
> *"Day!" (children reply) "Night!"*
> *"Day!" (children reply) "Night!"*
>
> *I say, "Up," you say, "Down."*
> *"Up!" (children reply) "Down!"*
> *"Up!" (children reply) "Down!"*

Additional verses:
- Opposites: right/left, boy/girl, north/south, east/west
- Go-togethers: ice cream/cake, salt/pepper, ketchup/mustard, peanut butter/jelly
- Spanish words: uno/one, dos/two, hola/hello
- Children's first and last names: Katy/Smith, Tasha/Johnson, Matthew/Curtis

★ *Susan Sharkey, La Mesa, CA*

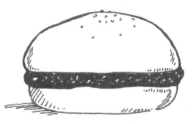

BURGER

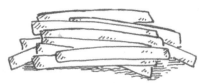

FRIES

Inside Voice

3+

Materials   none

What to do   Sing the following song to the tune of "My Bonnie Lies Over the Ocean" when you need to get the children's attention and quiet them down.

Qui - et, Shh shh!
Oh, use your inside voice for me, for me.
Qui - et, Shh shh!
Oh, use your inside voice for me.

★ *Jackie Wright, Enid, OK*

It Might Be You

3+

Materials   none

What to do   1. To get children's attention and let them know what you want them to do, sing the following song to the tune of the "Oscar Mayer Weiner" theme song.

Oh, I wish that you would (state desired behavior).
That is what I'd love for you to do.
For if you would (state desired behavior).
I will pick someone and it might be you!

2. The desired behaviors might include:

◆ Show me that you're ready.
◆ Sit up tall and straight.
◆ Stand in line quietly.
◆ Finish up your work.
◆ Put away your toys.

3. Recognize those who respond to your request by selecting one child at a time to go outside, line up, or whatever fits your situation.

★ *Jackie Wright, Enid, OK*

May I Have Your Attention, Please?

3+

Materials   none

What to do   Do the following call-and-answer with the children to the tune of "Frère Jacques."

> *Pay attention* (children repeat)
> *Eyes on me* (children repeat)
> *Children, are you listening?* (children repeat)
> *One, two, three.* (point to eyes, ears, and lips, children repeat)

⭐ *Kaethe Lewandowski, Centreville, VA*

One, Two, Three, Eyes on Me

3+

Materials   none

What to do   To get the children's attention say the following chant:

> *Teacher: One, two, three—eyes on me!*
> *Children: One, two—eyes on you!* (children point to the teacher)

⭐ *Jackie Wright, Enid, OK*

Quiet Song

3+

Materials   none

What to do   1. Seat the children in a semicircle and sing the following song:

The Children Are Smiling Now by Mary Brehm
(Tune: "The Wheels on the Bus")
The children in the chairs are smiling now,
Smiling now, smiling now.
The children in the chairs are smiling now,
All around the classroom.

(Say, "Stand up and turn to your neighbor!")

The children shake hands and say, "How do you do?"
"How do you do? How do you do?"
The children shake hands and say, "How do you do?"
To the neighbor next to you.

(Say, "Please sit down!")

The children fold their hands and sit very still,
Sit very still, sit very still,
The children fold their hands and sit very still,
All around the classroom.

2. Use the song as an attention getting by singing different verses throughout the day.

★ *Mary Brehm, Aurora, OH*

If You Can Hear Me!

3+

Materials   none

What to do
1. This activity works for any transition when you need to get the children's attention.
2. Say, "If you can hear me…". Then repeat the phrase. The children respond, "If you can hear me…"
3. Say, "If you can hear me, clap." Clap your hands one time. The children repeat the phrase and clap their hands once.
4. Then say, "If you can hear me, clap." This time, clap your hands two times. The children repeat after you.
5. Continue adding or changing the beat of the claps, or change the motion. ("If you can hear me, put your finger on your lips.") Once you have all the children's attention, proceed with new activity instructions.
6. To quiet the children, say, "If you can hear me, whisper." Repeat as many times as necessary to change the noise level.
7. To line up, whisper, "If you can hear me, tiptoe through the tulips into line." The children tiptoe towards you to the designated line space. This lets children proceed into an orderly line safely while still having fun.
8. Change the activity as needed to get the children's attention, or use it during a period of waiting (such as in a bathroom line). For example, "If you can hear me, snap."
9. Children love the different variations of this activity. As they become more familiar with the activity, you can choose children to lead the activity.

Sarah Murphy, Middleburg Heights, OH

Do What I Do and Say What I Say

3+

Materials   none

What to do
1. To get the children's attention, say, "Do what I do." Do something that catches the children's attention, such as stomping your feet.
2. Then say, "Say what I say." Say something that gets their attention, such as "Yikes!"
3. Repeat the entire sequence.
4. Instruct the children to repeat the sequence with you.
5. Add commands to challenge the children to remember and follow several silly instructions. For example, say, "Do what I do," and stomp, clap, scratch your nose, and so on.

★ *Karyn F. Everham, Fort Myers, FL*

Echo-Location

3+

Materials   none

What to do
1. Explain how bats get their food by sending a voice-sound vibration and waiting for a sound to bounce back to them, like an echo. Tell them bats like to eat moths.
2. When you want to get a child's attention, say "Bat," and the child's name. The child stops what she is doing and responds by saying your name. Then give an instruction to the child.
3. The child will be more attentive and ready to receive direction.

Related books   *Bat Loves the Night* by Nicola Davies
Bats and Their Homes by Deborah Chase Gibson
Stellaluna by Janell Cannon

★ *Jill Putnam, Wellfleet, MA*

Attention Grabbers

3+

Materials

old phone
puppets
shampoo bottle
marbles
quiet bell or chime

What to do

Use the following ideas to get the children's attention and quiet them down.

◆ At circle time, take out an old phone and start talking into it. Children will quiet down to hear what you are saying. Talk about what is going on in the room, for example, "We're going to hear a story, clean up for snack, and go outside."
◆ Use puppets to "whisper" in your ear to quiet the group.
◆ Add a few marbles to a bottle of clear shampoo. Turn the bottle over and see if everyone can sit quietly before the marbles reach the bottom (they move slowly through the shampoo).
◆ Ring a very soft bell or chime and speak in a very soft voice to settle the group down.

★ *Audrey Kanoff, Allentown, PA*

Pay Attention

3+

Materials

What to do

1. When you want to capture the children's attention, begin a motion. For example, tap your head, or touch your finger to your nose.
2. As you make the motion, repeat the phrase, "I know you're paying attention when you're following me."
3. When all of the children are doing the motion, you will have gained their attention in a fun and playful way.

More to do

Gross Motor: Use this activity as a gross motor game outdoors or indoors.

★ *Michelle Barnea, Millburn, NJ*

Visual or Auditory

3+

Materials   small bell
xylophone and other simple musical instruments
light switch
picture cards of different tasks (snack, outdoors, and so on)

What to do   Following are some visual and auditory clues to get the children's attention and signal that it is time to change activities.

- ◆ Ask a "helper" to ring the bell.
- ◆ Play a tune or some simple scales on a xylophone or other instrument.
- ◆ Turn the lights on and off.
- ◆ Hold up a picture card signifying the transition.
- ◆ Hold up your hand.

★ *Sandra Nagel, White Lake, MI*

Freeze!

3+

Materials   none

What to do   1. When children are busy and not listening, say, "One, two, three, freeze!" The children stop what they are doing and "freeze" in whatever funny position they are in.
2. Tell the children the directions you need them to hear and then say, "Unfreeze!" so they may resume what they are doing or follow the direction you gave.

★ *Susan Rubinoff, Wakefield, RI*

Doggie, Doggie

3+

Materials   dog hand puppet (or finger puppet)

What to do   1. When you want to quiet the children and get their attention, put a puppet on your hand and say the following verse to the rhythm of "Teddy Bear, Teddy Bear, Turn Around."

Doggie, Doggie, how quiet are we?
Doggie, Doggie, we will see.
Doggie, Doggie, nod for me. (or child's name)
Doggie, Doggie, 1 -2 - 3!

2. Bend your fingers forward three times on "1 - 2 - 3!"
3. Pass the puppet to a child who is sitting quietly. The child puts the puppet on her hand while the class recites the verse, inserting her name in the third line.
4. She passes it to another quiet classmate.
5. The game continues as the children pass the puppet and recite the poem together until each child has had a turn.

★ *Jackie Wright, Enid, OK*

Hush

Materials   animal puppet

What to do
1. Find an animal puppet and give it a calming name, such as "Hush Puppy" or "Quiet Koala."
2. As the children are transitioning to circle time, bring out your calming puppet.
3. Get the children's attention by telling them that Hush Puppy is very shy. Tell them that they need to be very quiet so the puppet isn't afraid to come out and join them.
4. Have the puppet whisper directions to children who are quiet and they can repeat the directions to the group.

Related book   *Shy Little Moth* by Elizabeth Lawrence

★ *Ann Kelly, Johnstown, PA*

My Binoculars

Materials   none

What to do
1. Whenever you need an attention grabber, reach into your pocket and announce that you are pulling out your "magic binoculars." Use your hands to create imaginary binoculars that you look through.
2. Tell the children that your binoculars are special because they only see children who are sitting quietly and patiently. When you see children doing this, call on them to do whatever activity is next.
3. Use this activity at any time, at a moment's notice!

★ *Susan Myhre, Bremerton, WA*

Drum Beating

3+

Materials   hand drum or one made from a tin can

What to do
1. When you need to get the children's attention, begin to beat the drum.
2. You might want to use a special beat (such as 1 - 2 - 1 - 1) because if you also use the drum during music, it's important that they distinguish the drum beat when you need their attention.

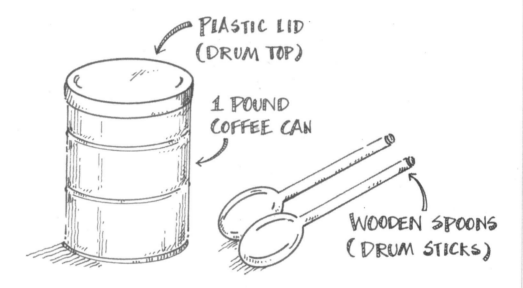

PLASTIC LID
(DRUM TOP)

1 POUND
COFFEE CAN

WOODEN SPOONS
(DRUM STICKS)

More to do   **Music:** Let the children make their own drums using tin cans or plastic containers. Provide wooden spoons for drumsticks and the children can have hours of fun making their own music, concentrating on new beats for patterns.

Eileen Lucas, Halifax, Nova Scotia, Canada

Make a Little Rain

3+

Materials   rain stick (homemade or bought)

What to do

1. When you have to get the children's attention, turn a rain stick upside down until all the children have settled down.
2. When you first start using this method, you may need to turn it over twice to get the children's attention.

⭐ *Eileen Lucas, Halifax, Nova Scotia, Canada*

Make It Magic

3+

Materials   empty clear pepper or sugar shaker
PVA glue
fine glitter
sticky label
colored pens

What to do

1. In advance, brush the inside of an empty sugar or pepper shaker with clear-drying PVA glue and sprinkle a thick layer of glitter inside, shaking to distribute glitter. Allow the glue to dry.
2. Next, design a label for your "magic dust" using colored pens to make it look as magical and mystical as you like. You could name it "magic dust," and maybe add your name ("Ms. Smith's Magic Dust") or give it a special property, for example, "Magic Napping Dust" or "Special Silence Dust."
3. Attach the label to the container and display it somewhere prominent in the classroom, out of the children's reach.

(continued on the next page)

4. When it's naptime, cleanup time, or when children need to be quiet, simply walk around and "sprinkle" everyone very lightly with the magic dust to enchant them. The glitter on the sides of the shaker makes it look full and the glue holds it in place so it doesn't get all over the children.

5. Decide on a special symbol for stopping the "spell," such as a hand clap or magic word. Make sure the children know this before you sprinkle them!

Related books *70 Wonderful Word-Family Poems* by Jennifer Wilen and Beth Handa
Lizards, Frogs and Polliwogs by Douglas Florian

⭐ *Kirsty Neale, Charleville Circus, London, United Kingdom*

Guessing Box

3+

Materials   small classroom object
large shoebox or small packing box
puppet
plastic or cloth drawstring bag

What to do

1. Place a small object or book inside the box. Shake it and give clues as to what is inside. Let the children guess what it is. Then open the box and show them the object to start the lesson.

2. Use a drawstring bag for the same purpose as the box, but let the children reach inside or feel the outside of the bag to help them guess what it is. When you take the object out, let just a small bit show at first to increase suspense.

3. Use a puppet to ask the children questions or bring the new object or book to circle time. The puppet can also make silly assumptions about the topic that the children can correct. The humor and imagination of puppets is a sure attention-getter.

4. When calling a child to a work station, cup your hands around your mouth, face the child, and call her name. The new sound will usually get the child's attention even if the room is noisy.

⭐ *Sandra Gratias, Perkasie, PA*

The Mouse Train

3

Materials
conductor's cap
scissors
poster board
laminator
markers or colored pencils

What to do

1. Cut poster board into rectangles about the size of playing cards. Make one for each child.
2. Draw a simple picture of a train engine on one side of each card. On the other side, write the child's name. Laminate for durability.

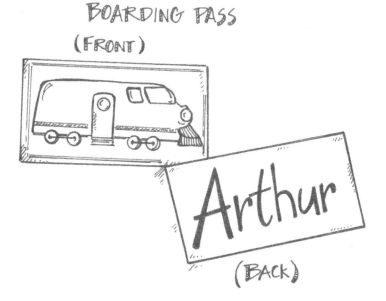

BOARDING PASS
(FRONT)

Arthur
(BACK)

3. Get the children's attention by putting on a conductor's cap and announcing (in a squeaky voice), "Boarding the Mouse Train in five minutes! When you hear your name, you may come get your boarding pass. Be ready to scrunch your nose and swish your tail."
4. Line up the children.
5. For more variety, choose a different animal to study each week. Change the train to match.

Karyn F. Everham, Fort Myers, FL

Movin' On

4+

Materials   none

What to do
1. After the children are comfortable with names of colors and clothing articles, teach them the following chant to get their attention:

   If your name is ____
   And you're wearing the color ____,
   Find a friend who's wearing the color ____
   And walk to the door.

2. If desired, substitute articles of clothing for colors and other parts of the room for "door" (circle time, snack table, and so on).

⭐ *Margery Kranyik Fermino, Hyde Park, MA*

P-L-A-Y

4+

Materials   four pieces of 12" x 15" poster board
scissors
markers or colored pencils
bell

What to do
1. Cut each piece of poster board into the shape of a bell. Write one letter on each bell, to spell the word "play."
2. Just prior to the start of play time, tape the posters to a wall for everyone to see. Explain that the letters spell "play."
3. After about a quarter of play time is over, ring the bell to get the children's attention. Tell them one quarter of playtime is over, and remove the letter "P."
4. Repeat until all of the letters are gone and play time is over.
5. Repeating this activity over many days and weeks will help children grasp the passage of time.

⭐ *Karyn F. Everham, Fort Myers, FL*

Silly Names

4+

Materials   none

What to do
1. Four- and five-year-olds love to make up rhymes—the sillier the better!
2. To get the children's attention, call each child using a rhyme from her name. "This person's name sounds like Bathy. Who is it?" "Kathy!" This gets all the children thinking, and also helps with phonemic awareness.

 Tracie O'Hara, Charlotte, NC

Tool Rap

4+

Materials   poster board
scissors
markers

What to do
1. This song is a great way to capture children's attention.
2. Cut poster board into 8" x 11" rectangles.
3. Draw a simple picture of a tool on each card: a hammer, paintbrush, ruler, and pliers. Print the name of the tool under picture.
4. The following is an echo song. Hold up the card for each verse, chant the lines, and then the children repeat the lines.

Tool Rap
Hammers up, hammers down, (hand actions move up and down)
Tap-tap-tap! Tap-tap-tap! (hand actions taps)

Paintbrush smooth, paintbrush rough, (hand actions smooth and rough)
Slap-slap-slap! Slap-slap-slap! (hand actions do painting movement)

Rulers long, rulers short, (hand actions show long and short)
Inch-inch-inch! Inch-inch-inch! (hand actions show inch length)

(continued on the next page)

Pliers pinch, pliers pull, (hand actions show pinching and pulling)
Twist-twist-twist! Twist-twist-twist! (children twist their whole bodies)

5. Think of other tools to use for the rap, such as wrenches, screwdrivers, or levels.
6. Show the children how real tools work.

⭐ *Jane Cline Rubicini, Kitchener, Ontario, Canada*

Copy Me! 4+

Materials   none

What to do
1. This activity enhances auditory skills. Tell the children that occasionally, if you need to get their attention, you will clap a pattern and they should echo the pattern by clapping the same rhythm.
2. Practice this, and when you need to get the children's attention, start clapping a pattern and watch how they happily respond.

⭐ *Jodi Sykes, Lake Worth, FL*

Making a List, Checking It Twice 4+

Materials   chalkboard, white board, or chart paper
chalk or markers

What to do
1. To get children's attention as they join the group from other activities, use a chalkboard to write the names of the first children to come to the area. Do not read the names out loud as you write. They will eagerly watch for their own names to appear.
2. If time permits, write the names of all the children and ask them to read the names aloud with you.

⭐ *Susan Oldham Hill, Lakeland, FL*

Wow Sounds!

4

Materials variety of objects that produce exciting sounds and/or tape recordings of exciting sounds (a train whistle, dinner bell, foghorn, jackhammer, waterfall, squawking macaw, stadium of people clapping, herd of elephants bellowing, and so on)

What to do
1. Play one of the sounds, making sure it is loud enough to get everyone's attention.
2. Play the sounds again and talk about them because the children will probably be very curious about them.

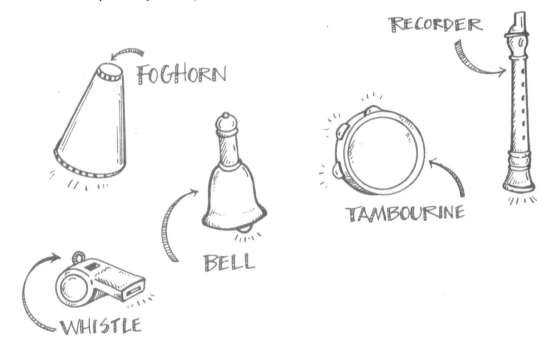

3. Possible discussion questions are:

   ◆ What is making that sound?
   ◆ Where would you hear that sound?
   ◆ Can you make a sound like that?

4. This is a great way to grab children's attention.

⭐ *Karyn F. Everham, Fort Myers, FL*

Take Five

4+

Materials   none

What to do

1. This is a great visual/audio/kinesthetic multiple intelligence approach for getting children in an active listening mode. The visual aspect is the number of fingers held up, the audio is saying the correct number and naming the desired behavior action, and the kinesthetic is the movement that represents the desired behavior.

   ◆ Hold up five fingers and say, "Five" Then say, "Stop," and extend your arm in front of your body, palm facing away.
   ◆ Hold up four fingers and say, "Four." Then say "Look," and move your fingers to your brow, eyes looking out.
   ◆ Hold up three fingers and say, "Three." Then say, "Listen," and cup your fingers behind your ear.
   ◆ Hold up two fingers and say, "Two." Then say, "Shhhh," (or be silent) and rest your index finger on your lips.
   ◆ Hold up one finger and say, "One." Then say, "Think," and tap your temple with one finger.

2. As the children join in counting down from five to one, they will be quiet, have their eyes on you, and be ready to listen.

Jackie Wright, Enid, OK

Calling All Sailors

4+

Materials
scissors
poster board
laminator
markers or colored pencils
sailor's cap

What to do
1. Cut poster board into rectangles about the size of playing cards. Make one for each child.
2. Draw a simple picture of a sailboat on each card. On the other side, write the child's name. Laminate for durability.
3. Prior to changing activities or going somewhere, get the children's attention by putting on a sailor's cap and saying, "Ahoy, mates! We set sail in five minutes! When you hear your name, come get your ticket and I'll show you where to climb aboard!"
4. As you call each child's name, hand her a ticket and call her "Sailor (child's name)."

⭐ *Karyn F. Everham, Fort Myers, FL*

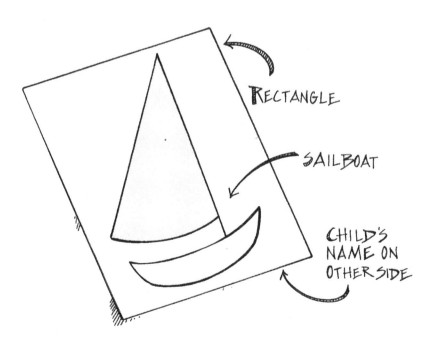

RECTANGLE

SAILBOAT

CHILD'S NAME ON OTHER SIDE

"If You're Happy" Game

Materials   none

What to do   1. At cleanup time, sing the following song with the children to the tune of "If You're Happy and You Know It." Substitute various cleanup tasks and toys to pick up, such as blocks, dolls, and cars for the end of the verse ("clap your hands").

If you're happy and you know it, pick up a block.
If you're happy and you know it, pick up a block.
If you're happy and you know it, and you really want to show it,
If you're happy and you know it, pick up a block.

2. Add children's names, too, for example, "If Jimmy's happy and he knows it, he'll pick up a truck."

⭐ *Cookie Zingarelli, Columbus, OH*

Clean Classroom

Materials   none

What to do   When it is time to clean up, sing the following song to the tune of the Oscar Mayer Weiner theme song.

Oh, I wish that I could see a clean classroom
With everything in the right place!
Oh, I wish that I could see a clean classroom.
Then I would have a smile upon my face!

⭐ *Jackie Wright, Enid, OK*

Clean Up Our Work

3+

Materials   none

What to do

1. Sing this song to the tune of "London Bridge Is Falling Down" as the children clean up.

   We will all clean up our work,
   Up our work, up our work,
   We will all clean up our work,
   Until we're done!

2. Continue singing this song until the children are done.

⭐ *Jackie Wright, Enid, OK*

Cleanup Song

3+

Materials   none

What to do

1. Make up transition songs for cleanup or any other transition. Choose a well-known tune, or make up your own. Songs are easy and get the action started much easier than words alone.
2. Following is an example of a cleanup song. Sing it to the tune of "Mary Had a Little Lamb."

   It's time to put the toys away,
   Toys away, toys away.
   It's time to put the toys away
   And save them for another day!

⭐ *Phyllis Esch, Export, PA*

Clean Up the Room

Materials   none

What to do

1. When it is time to clean up, begin singing this song to the tune of "Skip to My Lou" and encourage the children to join in. Everyone can sing together as they work together putting away materials.

   Clean up, clean up the room.
   Clean up, clean up the room.
   Clean up, clean up the room.
   Clean up the room together.

   Pick up, pick up the blocks
   Pick up, pick up the blocks
   Pick up, pick up the blocks
   And put them in the tub together.

2. Add additional verses as appropriate (pick up carpet squares, clean up snack, and so on).
3. Introduce the song at a circle time so the children can practice it. Use puppets to demonstrate while the group sings the song. The children can take turns making the puppets clean up, such as putting blocks into a tub.
4. Once the children are familiar with the song, you can choose a child to begin the song at cleanup time.

More to do   **Books:** Read cleanup books during circle time and have them available in the reading center.

Related books   *Buggy Bear Cleans Up* by Robert Kraus
Bumble B. Bear Cleans Up by Stephen Cosgrove
Clean-Up Day by Kate Duke
Clifford's Spring Clean-Up by Norman Bridwell
Farm Friends Clean Up by Cristina Garelli
Floppity Pup Cleans Up by Lois Keffer and Kenneth Spingler
Maisy Cleans Up by Lucy Cousins
Max Cleans Up by Rosemary Wells

Sandra L. Nagel, White Lake, MI

Cleanup Theme Song

3+

Materials   none

What to do   Sing this song at cleanup time to encourage the children to put materials away and to remind them of the reasons for helping clean up the room. Sing to the tune of "This Land Is My Land."

> Let's put the blocks back,
> So we can walk here.
> Let's put the paints away,
> To keep our tables clear.
> Let's pick the crayons up,
> So they will not break.
> Look at the difference we can make!

★ Susan Oldham Hill, Lakeland, FL

Cleanup Chant

3+

Materials   none

What to do   1. Sing the following song when it is cleanup time.

> Who is going to pick up the blocks,
> Pick up the blocks, pick up the blocks?
> Who is going to pick up the blocks
> And be a classroom helper?
>
> Stephanie is picking up the blocks
> Picking up the blocks, picking up the blocks.
> Stephanie is picking up the blocks,
> She is a classroom helper.

2. Continue to insert the children's names until everyone has been named.

★ Sandy L. Scott, Vancouver, WA

I'll Be Cleanin' Up the Classroom

3+

Materials   none

What to do   Cue the children that cleanup is about to begin by singing the following song to the tune of "I've Been Workin' on the Railroad."

I'll be cleanin' up the classroom,
All the live long day.
I'll be cleanin' up the classroom,
Just to put the toys away.

★ *Karyn F. Everham, Fort Myers, FL*

I'm a Little Sweeper

3+

Materials   none

What to do   1. Cue the children to perform different cleaning jobs by singing the following song to the tune of "I'm a Little Teapot."

I'm a little sweeper,
Watch me sweep!
Sweepity sweep,
Sweep sweep sweep!

2. Replace "sweep" with other verbs, such as "scrub," "stack," "dust," "wash," "clean," and so on.

★ *Karyn F. Everham, Fort Myers, FL*

On a Bright and Sunny Day 3+

Materials none

What to do 1. When cleanup time begins, sing the following song to the tune of "One Little Elephant Went Out to Play."

On a bright and sunny day
(Your room name) *decided to go out and play.*
When the cleaning up was done,
Everyone went out to have some fun.

2. Ask, "Is the cleaning up done?" If the answer is "yes," then head outdoors. If the answer is "no," sing the song again.
3. Continue until the room is clean.
4. As a variation, encourage individual children by adding their names to the song. For example:

On a bright and sunny day
Sarah decided to go out and play.
When the cleaning up was done,
Sarah went out to have some fun.

Related books *Amelia Bedelia Helps Out* by Peggy Parish
Herman the Helper by Robert Kraus
Hired Help for a Rabbit by Judy Delton
Sophie and Jack Help Out by Judy Taylor
To Hilda for Helping by Margot Zemach

Virginia Jean Herrod, Columbia, SC

On the Floor

Materials   none

What to do

1. Sing the following song to the tune of "Love Somebody (Yes, I Do)." Insert whatever needs to be picked up (crayons, puzzles, paper, crumbs, and so on).

   I see _____
   On the floor.
   I see _____
   On the floor.
   I see _____
   On the floor.
   Someone get the _____
   And I won't say more.

2. Be sure to praise all the helpers.

★ *Jackie Wright, Enid, OK*

Pickup Song

Materials   none

What to do   Sing the following song to the tune of "Twinkle, Twinkle Little Star."

It is time to pick up now,
Pick up, pick up, we know how.
We can pick up; you will see
Just how clean our class can be.
It is time to pick up now,
Pick up, pick up, pick up—wow!

Pick up, pick up, pick up work,
Each and every girl and boy.
Look around and you will see,
All the things that shouldn't be.
Pick up, pick up, pick up work,
Each and every girl and boy.

★ *Jackie Wright, Enid, OK*

Pick Up Your Work

Materials   none

What to do   When it is time to clean up, sing the following songs.

Pick Up Your Work (Tune: "Goodnight, Sweetheart, Goodnight")
Pick up your work, 'cause it's time to go.
Da, da, da, da, da.
Pick up your work, 'cause it's time to go.
Da, da, da, da, da.
I hate to say it, but we really must go.
Pick up your work, pick up.

Put Your Work Away (Tune: "Put Your Little Foot")
Put your work away,
Put your work away,
Put your work away right now,
Put your work away,
Put your work away,
Put your work away right now.

Jackie Wright, Enid, OK

Picking Up

3+

Materials   none

What to do
1. This is a good cleanup song for when a lot of a particular material is being used, such as playdough, paper scraps, or a whole tub of blocks.
2. Introduce the song at circle time and let the children practice the song and words.
3. During cleanup, sing the song and encourage the children to join in. Everyone can sing as they work together putting away materials.

Picking Up (Tune: "Here We Go 'Round the Mulberry Bush")
Picking up blocks, put them in the tub.
Picking up blocks, put them in the tub.
Picking up blocks, put them in the tub.
All the live long day.

Additional verses:
Picking up toys, put them on the shelf…
Picking up placemats, put them on the shelf…
Picking up carpet squares, put them away…

More to do   **Books:** Read some cleanup stories during group time and have them available at the book center.

Related books   *Buggy Bear Cleans Up (Miss Gator's Schoolhouse)* by Robert Kraus
Bumble B. Bear Cleans Up by Stephen Cosgrove
Clean-Up Day by Kate Duke
Clifford's Spring Clean-Up by Norman Bridwell
Farm Friends Clean Up by Cristina Garelli
Floppity Pup Cleans Up by Lois Keffer and Kenneth Spingler
Maisy Cleans Up by Lucy Cousins
Max Cleans Up by Rosemary Wells

⭐ *Sandra Nagel, White Lake, MI*

Ten Minutes Left!

3+

Materials   none

What to do   Smooth the transition from play time to cleanup by singing the following song to the tune of "Twinkle, Twinkle, Little Star."

Ten more minutes left to play,
Then we'll put our toys away.

Five more minutes left to play,
Then we'll put our toys away.

No more minutes left to play,
Time to put our toys away.

⭐ *Karyn F. Everham, Fort Myers, FL*

This Is the Way We Clean Our Room

3+

Materials   none

What to do   1. This song is a good way to help children pick up their toys. Sing to the tune of "This Is the Way We Wash Our Clothes."

This is the way we (or child's name) *pick up our toys,*
Pick up our toys,
Pick up our toys,
This is the way we pick up our toys
So early in the morning. (afternoon, or any other time)

2. Add verses as appropriate, such as pick up blocks, dolls, clay, trains, dishes, housekeeping, art, and so on.

⭐ *Cookie Zingarelli, Columbus, OH*

We Are Going to Clean Up

3+

Materials   none

What to do   Sing the following song as the children clean up.

> **We Are Going to Clean Up** (Tune: "Mary Had a Little Lamb")
> *We are going to clean up*
> *Clean up, clean up.*
> *We are going to clean up*
> *To keep our classroom neat.*
>
> *We will put our work away*
> *Work away, work away.*
> *We will put our work away*
> *To keep our classroom neat.*

⭐*Jackie Wright, Enid, OK*

Zip-a-Dee-Doo-Dah!

3+

Materials   none

What to do   Sing the following song to the tune of "Zip-a-dee-doo-dah!" during cleanup.

> *Zip-a-dee-doo-dah! Zip-a-dee-ay!*
> *It's time to put our work away.*
> *We clean our classroom*
> *Each and every day.*
> *Zip-a-dee-doo-dah! Zip-a-dee-ay!*

⭐*Jackie Wright, Enid, OK*

Thank You

Materials none

What to do
1. When children are cleaning up, begin singing the following song to the tune of "Good Night, Ladies." Insert different names in each space.

   Thank you, (name).
   Thank you, (name).
   Thank you, (name).
   For helping us today.

   Thank you, Sally.
   Thank you, Billy.
   Thank you, Bobby.
   For helping us today.

2. Using children's names in the song encourages more participation and provides positive acknowledgement for most children.

⭐ *Sandra Nagel, White Lake, MI*

Beat the Timer

Materials kitchen timer

What to do
1. Encourage the children to try to "beat the timer" as they clean up the room or a specific area.
2. Set the timer for a reasonable amount of time for the work that needs done; two to five minutes usually works.
3. Say, "Ready, set, go," and start the timer.

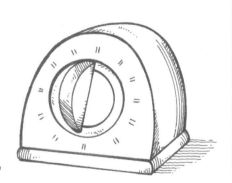

(continued on the next page)

4. Help the children as they clean, reminding them to put things in their proper places.
5. Sing the following song, if desired, to the tune of "Hurry, Hurry, Ring the Firebell."

Hurry, hurry, beat the timer,
Hurry, hurry, beat the timer,
Hurry, hurry, beat the timer,
Ding, ding, ding, ding, ding!

⭐ *Virginia Jean Herrod, Columbia, SC*

Beat the Music!

3+

Materials   cassette or CD with an upbeat tune
cassette or CD player

What to do
1. Cleanup time can be a difficult transition. This fun game helps motivate children to clean. When it's time to clean up, challenge the children to complete cleaning the room before a chosen song ends.
2. Say, "Ready, set, go!" and start the music.
3. Encourage the children to clean quickly but carefully. Help out too!
4. If the children don't finish before the first song is over, give them a second chance by playing another song.
5. Congratulate everyone on their quick and efficient work.

Related books   *Clean Your Room, Harvey Moon!* by Pat Cummings
Jonathan Cleaned Up—Then He Heard a Sound by Robert Munsch

⭐ *Virginia Jean Herrod, Columbia, SC*

Clean Up

3+

Materials   none

What to do

1. Instead of just telling the children to clean up, create a fun story for them to act out as they clean.
2. For example, tell a story about a farmer who had workhorses that were very good helpers around the farm. The children pretend to be the horses. Some of them could get on their hands and knees, and depending on the items being put away, the "farmer" (you or another child) could put things on their backs for them to carry to different parts of the "farm."
3. Sing "Old MacDonald" as the children clean up.
4. Another example is to make up a story about a store with storekeepers who are sitting in different areas of the room, ready to receive different toys. The other children could use chairs as "trucks" by laying them on the floor, putting items on them, and "driving" them to the store. When they are finished, they can "drive" the trucks back to the "garage" (table).

More to do   **More Transitions:** Use this idea for other transitions. For example, tell a story about a restaurant when transitioning to snack or lunch.

⭐ *Susan Rubinoff, Wakefield, RI*

Creature Cleanup

3+

Materials   none

What to do

1. When it's time to clean up, assign each child a different creature or character and ask him to clean up in the style of that creature. Examples of creatures include:

   ◆ Wiggly worm (move in a slinky, wriggling, squirmy way)
   ◆ Rabbit (jump or hop, wrinkling nose)

(continued on the next page)

- ◆ Cat (purr, rub ears, pretend to shake tail)
- ◆ Robot (move in a jerky, robotic fashion)
- ◆ Fish (glide around, open and close mouth silently)
- ◆ Lizard (blink slowly, flick tongue in and out)

2. These are all fairly quiet ideas, so cleanup doesn't turn into a zoo! If noise is not an issue in your classroom, you can assign more vocal creatures.

More to do
More Transitions: Use this idea when moving from the classroom to other areas of the building or outdoors. If the children find it hard to walk without talking, encourage them to move in the style of a quiet creature.

Art: Select the creatures in advance and ask the children to draw or make collage pictures of them on pieces of card stock. Collect the cards and at the beginning of each day or week, hand one to each child randomly. The children become the assigned creature whenever you ask them to during the day or week.

Science and Nature: Talk about the ways different animals move, the sounds they make and why. If it's possible, watching animals in action either on film or an appropriate field trip is the perfect chance for children to observe and use their own words to describe animal behavior.

Related books
Animals on the Move by Pierre De Hugo
Wee Sing Animals, Animals, Animals by Pamela Conn Beall

★ *Kirsty Neale, Charleville Circus, London, United Kingdom*

I Spy Game

3+

Materials
none

What to do
1. Children really enjoy this game of "I Spy." As the children are cleaning up, look for things on the floor that no one has noticed. For example, say, "I spy a book on the floor!"
2. The children have fun looking for the book and putting it quickly back on the shelf. This game lets the children have fun while cleaning the classroom.

★ *Cookie Zingarelli, Columbus, OH*

Music to Clean By

3+

Materials hand bell
record, CD, or cassette player
record, CD, or cassette with lively music

What to do Ring a bell at cleanup time and then sing a cleanup song of your choice. This sets the tone for a pleasant cleanup. The following ideas encourage listening skills and a sense of rhythm. Try any of these during cleanup time:

◆ Play lively music to set the pace. Stop the music at random times and have everyone freeze. The children resume cleaning when the music resumes.
◆ For a change of pace, play slow music and move in slow motion.
◆ Have everyone change places during the music breaks and resume cleaning in another part of the room.
◆ Set a timer and see if the class can beat it!
◆ Sing a song with many verses and challenge the children to get the room clean by the time the song ends.

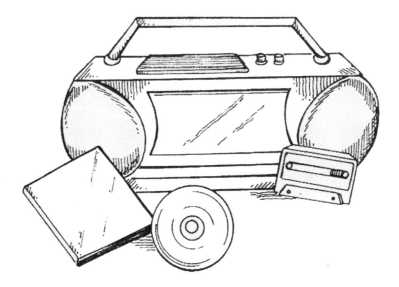

More to do **Movement:** Other ways to reinforce body control are to play freeze tag, red light/green light, or Mother May I?

 *Sandra Gratias, Perkasie, PA*

Who Wants to Be a Vacuum Cleaner?

3+

Materials   none

What to do   1. If you have trouble getting the children to clean up after making a mess in the art center or other area, ask, "Who wants to be a vacuum cleaner?" and they will come running!
2. Pretend to turn them on by flipping a switch on their backs, and then watch them go! The floor and art supplies will be cleaned up in no time.

⭐ *Jodi Sykes, Lake Worth, FL*

Pickup Choices

3+

Materials   one item from each area to be cleaned up or organized (a block from the block area, a book from the book area, a kitchen item, and so on)
basket or container

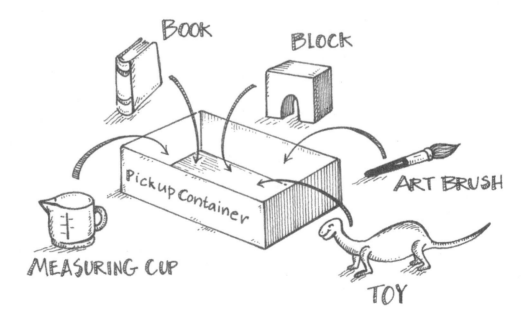

BOOK

BLOCK

Pickup Container

ART BRUSH

MEASURING CUP

TOY

What to do
1. First announce that it will soon be cleanup time.
2. Walk throughout the room and take one item from each of the areas the children are participating in. Place these items in a basket or container.
3. As the children are completing activities, walk through the room a second time. Repeat the announcement that it is now cleanup time.
4. Let each child select an item from the basket or container. This item represents the area in which the child will help clean up.

More to do

Circle Time: At circle time, let the children choose an item from the basket to represent where they will participate during free choice time.

⭐ *Kate Ross, Middlesex, VT*

Table Toy Time

3+

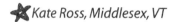

Materials   tables and chairs

What to do
1. Place a variety of quiet activities at a table, such as puzzles, paper, crayons, and other small motor skills toys.
2. At the end of free play time, flash the lights to alert the class to cleanup time.
3. As the children finish cleaning up their areas, let them go to "table toy time." Encourage them to sit at the table and quietly work on the small motor activities. This is a quieting transition activity and not only does it settle the class down before moving on to the rest of the day, but it also gives everyone a chance to work on their small motor skills.
4. Have this transition time last for 10 to 15 minutes before moving on to the next activity.

⭐ *Nancy DeSteno, Andover, MN*

Transition Toys

3+

Material

basket
small, interesting hand-held toys (water or bead maze games, Slinky®, wind-up toys, tops, small party favor games, travel-size Etch-a-Sketches)

What to do

1. It can be a challenge to get a group of preschoolers to clean up and come to circle time. Sometimes an incentive is necessary to help children who have finished to wait patiently and those still cleaning to hurry.

2. Put a variety of small, interesting hand-held toys in a basket. Have several of the same toy in the basket to avoid conflicts. Keep the basket of toys near the circle time area.

3. These toys are only to be used for a few minutes before circle time. The children who clean up quickly can play with the toys as they wait for others to finish. This keeps them busy with a small motor activity. Those still cleaning will want to hurry so they also get a turn.

4. Allot about 4 to 5 minutes for this transition toy time. If any children do not finish in time for the toys, tell them that tomorrow if they clean up a little faster, they will have a turn.

5. Use this transition only when needed. Some days you may need to locate a book for circle, so everyone can play with the toys. Other days only one or two children may be restless, or everyone will finish at the same time and not need it.

6. The toys fulfill many purposes. They get the children to the area, help to quiet and center them after being active, provide practice for fine motor skills, and most importantly, prevent any "dead time" when opportunities arise for misbehavior.

Tracie O'Hara, Charlotte, NC

Wash Day

Materials
lightweight rope or yarn
basket
construction paper
scissors
markers
clothespins

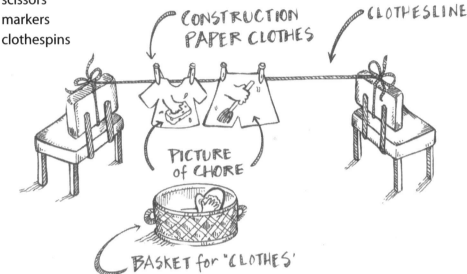

CONSTRUCTION PAPER CLOTHES

CLOTHESLINE

PICTURE of CHORE

BASKET for "CLOTHES"

What to do

1. Do this activity when moving to a new activity such as snack or wash time. String a rope or yarn across a section of the classroom as a "wash line." Be careful that the children do not get tangled in the rope.

2. Beforehand, cut out articles of clothing from construction paper. On each piece, write or place a picture instruction such as washing the snack table. This will be the job that needs to be done. Be sure to keep the instructions short and simple, and remember this is supposed to be fun.

3. Place the construction paper clothing in a basket ("laundry").

4. Let the children take turns choosing an article of clothing from the basket, doing the job written on it, and then hanging it on the string with clothespins.

5. Children then come to snack (or whatever they are transitioning to). Several children can be working at the same time.

More to do

Music: Use some "laundry"-type songs to sing while the children work. For example, "This Is the Way We Wash Our Clothes" or "Hanging Out the Linen Clothes" (from *American Folk Songs for Children* by Ruth C. Seeger).

★ *Maxine Della Fave, Raleigh, NC*

Towel Fun

3+

Materials paper towels

PAPER TOWEL

What to do

1. This is a great way to reinforce hand washing and make potty breaks fun. After each child has washed his hands, pretend a paper towel is a ghost or other appropriate seasonal object and have it "fly" around the child's head until he catches it and dries his hands.

2. Before the child washes his hands, place the towel on his head and ask him to try to balance it while washing, then remove it to use for drying.

3. When the child is ready to dry his hands, hold the towel perpendicular in front of him. Let the child clap his hands on the towel, and look at the wet handprint. Then use the towel to dry.

★ *Sandra Gratias, Perkasie, PA*

Vacuum Cleaners

4+

Materials none

What to do

1. After any messy art activity or when the children have been cutting, pasting, and mounting maps, poems, and so on, the floor will be littered with a pile of debris.

2. Look for a child who has finished the activity and say to him, "I have a job for you to do. But I don't know whether or not you will be able to do it because it's rather difficult. I suppose you might be able to, but then…" By this time you will have the child's full attention and the attention of all around.

3. Appear to make up your mind swiftly and decisively and tell the child that he would make an excellent vacuum cleaner and you would like him to vacuum up all the mess. The child will be very proud and will want to begin immediately.
4. The other children will want to be "vacuum cleaners" too, so let everybody join in when they finish the activity.
5. This creates a spotless classroom, a very proud child who was the "first choice" vacuum cleaner, and a string of others asking whether or not they were good vacuum cleaners.

⭐ *Robyn Dalby-Stockwell, Cambridgeshire, United Kingdom*

Surprise the Teacher

4+

Materials   none

What to do   1. If there are two teachers working in the same classroom, one teacher should leave the room and the other teacher whispers to the children, "Let's get everything picked up and put away before (teacher's name) gets back to surprise her!"
2. The thought that they will surprise their teacher is usually all it takes to get young children motivated. They will work fast, but the teacher who leaves should be sure the children are done before returning.
3. The teacher should walk back in, look surprised, and say, "Oh my goodness! Who did all this work? I can't believe you all did this so fast! Thank you!"
4. The children are delighted to please, and cleanup is done!

⭐ *Susan Myhre, Bremerton, WA*

While I'm Not Looking

4+

Materials   none

What to do
1. Cover your eyes and say, "I'm going to cover my eyes and count to ten and see if the room is cleaned up when I open my eyes."
2. If you do this once in a while, the children will run around cleaning in a hurry.
3. Before you open your eyes, ask if they are done yet. If not, ask what you should count to. You may have to count a few times. (They won't notice if you're peeking at them between your fingers.)
4. You can use this for other situations, too, when you need children to do something quickly. This game also can help relieve the tension in a power struggle with a child.

★ *Laura Durbrow, Lake Oswego, OR*

Cleaning Buddies

4+

Materials   finger puppet for each child and teacher
toy dump truck

What to do
1. Store finger puppets ("cleaning buddies") in a toy truck in a convenient and easily accessible spot.
2. At cleanup time, the children and teachers wear their finger puppets and use them to help in the cleaning process.
3. The children love the thought that the puppets are helping them. After everything is clean, the children put their puppets back in the dump truck until the next cleanup time.

More to do   **Math:** Make a chart with all of the centers on them. The children can record things such as which puppet cleaned the sand area, the dress-up area, and so on. They can also estimate whose puppet will clean the most for a whole week or day.

★ *Eileen Lucas, Halifax, Nova Scotia, Canada*

You're In Charge

4+

Materials   pictures of different areas of your classroom, or a picture of something that represents each area (a block for the block area, plates for the kitchen area, and so on)
laminator
hole punch and string, or safety pins

What to do   1. Laminate the pictures and either punch a hole and string them to make a necklace, or pin safety pins to them. Make enough necklaces for each area and enough for each child.
Author's Note: In our classroom, we have four children clean up the playhouse, art, manipulatives, book, math/science, and games centers; three clean up the writing center; and six to ten clean up the block area. Therefore, we have four necklaces for each of the first centers, three for the writing center, and six to ten necklaces for the blocks.
2. Walk around the room five to ten minutes before cleanup and distribute the necklaces. Tell the children that cleanup time is soon, and give necklaces to children depending on where they spent most of their play time that day. Tell them they are responsible for the area, and give them a corresponding necklace.
3. After the children have cleaned up the area, they return the necklace to a teacher who "checks" and helps children clean the area properly.

Related books   *The Berenstain Bears and the Messy Room* by Stan and Jan Berenstain
Tracy's Mess by Elise Petersen

⭐ *Linda Ford, Sacramento, CA*

Lucky Leprechaun

Materials green paper shamrocks
footprint-shape sponge or rubber stamp

What to do 1. Say this poem during a transition at departure time. Repeat it until the
children know it and can say it with you.

Lucky Leprechaun by Barbara Saul
Away in Ireland
Across the Sea
Lives a Wee Little Man
That no one can see.

He's a wee little man
He's not very big,
He does a dance called an Irish Jig.

He hides behind rainbows
And under a tree.
He'll grant your wishes
1, 2, 3!

But look very closely
Before he is gone,
For that wee little man
Is a leprechaun!

2. After you have done this and the children go home, use the sponge or stamp
to make footprints all around the room. See if the children react the next day
to the footprints.
3. Talk about how the leprechaun might have come to the classroom. Hide little
shamrocks for everyone to find.

More to do **Music and Movement:** Dance to Irish folk music.

⭐ *Barbara Saul, Eureka, CA*

Another Day

3+

Materials   none

What to do   Enjoy this closing song each day of the week by inserting the appropriate day of the week. Sing to the tune of "La Cucaracha."

I'll see you Tuesday.
I'll see you Tuesday.
Then it will be another day.
I'll see you Tuesday.
I'll see you Tuesday.
And we will work, learn, and play.

★ *Jackie Wright. Enid, OK*

Departure Song

3+

Materials   hand puppet (optional)

What to do   1. Sing the song below prior to dismissing the children each day. Have them sit on the floor in a circle with you. Use a hand puppet, if desired.
2. For the second part of the song, insert each child's name and repeat until all are mentioned. As each child's name is called, she stands and gives the puppet a hug and then goes and sits in her chair.

Departure Song by Diane Weiss
(Tune: "Goodnight, Ladies")

So long children,
So long children,
So long children,
School is over today.

(continued on the next page)

Goodbye, (child's name),
Goodbye ,(child's name),
Goodbye, (child's name),
It's time for you to go.

I'll see you tomorrow,
I'll see you tomorrow,
I'll see you tomorrow,
With a great big smile!

⭐ *Diane Weiss, Fairfax, VA*

Goodbye Everybody

`3+`

Materials   puppet

What to do   1. Sing this song as children are getting ready to go home.

Goodbye, everybody, yes indeed,
Yes indeed, yes indeed,
Goodbye, everybody, yes indeed,
See you on (next day) *morning.*

2. Say goodbye in other languages.

⭐ *Kaethe Lewandowski, Centreville, VA*

Goodbye, Little Friend

3+

Materials   none

What to do   1. Sometimes getting the children to leave at the end of the day can be just as hard as getting them to separate from their parents in the morning. Use this song to ease that "going home" transition and remind the children how much you care for them.
2. When the children and their parents head out the door, sing this song to them to the tune of "Goodnight, Sweetheart."

   Goodbye, little friend,
   Oh, it's time for you to go.
   Goodbye, little friend,
   Oh, it's time for you to go.
   I am so glad you had a great time today.
   Come back again tomorrow to play.

3. If the children object to being referred to as a "little friend," you can say "my friend" or use the child's name in the song.

Related books   *Anna's Goodbye Apron* by Julie Brillhart
Goodbye Geese by Nancy White Carlstrom
Goodbye Little Bird by Mischa Damjan
The Goodbye Painting by Linda Berman
I Hate Goodbyes! by Kathleen Szaj
Ira Says Goodbye by Bernard Waber

⭐ *Virginia Jean Herrod, Columbia, SC*

Goodbye Song

3+

Materials   puppet

What to do
1. At the end of the morning (for a morning preschool class) as you gather to wait for pick-up, have a puppet sing the following song:

   Goodbye, (child's name).
   Goodbye, (another child's name),
   It's time to say goodbye.

2. Repeat this for all of the children and have the puppet give them a kiss. Children love this, especially toddlers!

★ *Audrey Kanoff, Allentown, PA*

It's Time to Say Goodbye

3+

Materials   none

What to do
1. When it is time to leave for the day, this cute song helps make departure fun. Sing this to the tune of "The Farmer in the Dell."

   It's time to say goodbye,
   It's time to say goodbye,
   Because we're all going now,
   It's time to say goodbye.

   It's time to say shalom,
   It's time to say shalom,
   Because we're all going now,
   It's time to say shalom.

2. You can substitute other words in other languages for goodbye. See how many ways you can say goodbye. To find other ways to say goodbye using the Internet, try www.ask.com.

- Spanish: Adios
- Italian: Arrivederci
- French: Au revoir
- German: Auf Wiederschen

★ *Cookie Zingarelli, Columbus, OH*

Time to Leave

3+

Materials   none

What to do
1. When it's time to depart, say the following action rhyme and demonstrate the motions for children to imitate.

When it's time to leave,
I turn and wave goodbye. (wave)
We had such a good time,
That I have a smile this wide! (big smile)

I reach out to shake your hand (shake hands)
And tell you my thank you (say thank you loudly)
And say, "I'll come again soon!"
And you say, "Yes, please do." (nod head and/or say yes!)

2. Repeat the rhyme as often as children want.

More to do   **More Transitions:** At each corner of the room, put one of the following pictures: sun and beach, rain and flowers, snow, and a windy scene with leaves blowing. Say various apparel names such as "swimsuit," "sweater," "hat and gloves," "raincoat," "boots," and so on. Children will go to or point to the appropriate weather corner for each. This is a great time-filler as children wait to leave.

Related books   *A Letter to Amy* by Ezra Jack Keats
The Snowy Day by Ezra Jack Keats

★ *Theresa Callahan, Easton, MD*

Tommorrow

`3+`

Materials   none

What to do

1. At the very end of the day, at the end of the final circle time, sing a modified version of the song "Tomorrow" from the musical "Annie." This is great for comforting those children who cry at the end of the day to reassure them that they will be coming back to do it all again.

   Tomorrow, tomorrow
   We'll see you, tomorrow
   It's only a day away!

2. On Friday, sing:

   Monday, Monday,
   We'll see you on Monday,
   It's only three days away.

3. The children love this ritual, and many will not leave until the song is sung, even if it means singing the song in the middle of the day! Little rituals such as this song are sources of comfort for children who use them to feel "at home" at school.

★ *Tracie O'Hara, Charlotte, NC*

End~of~the~Day Transition

`3+`

Materials   *Corner Grocery Store* CD by Raffi

What to do

1. Sing the song "Here Sits a Monkey" by Raffi (*Corner Grocery Store*) and play this game to go along with it.
2. Put a chair in the middle of the circle and choose one child to be the "monkey." When the song says, "Rise up on your feet, greet the first you meet," the "monkey" shakes hands with a friend, who becomes the next monkey.

3. This is a great end-of-the-day transition—as each "monkey" is finished, she goes to her cubby and gets her backpack to prepare for the end of the day and departure. This discourages running to the cubbies and helps avoid confusion.
4. Once they learn the song, you will have to do it again and again to satisfy all the "monkeys!"

Related books *Curious George* books

★ *Tracie O'Hara, Charlotte, NC*

We Had a Ball

`3+`

Materials Koosh ball, nerf ball, pompom, or other soft item that can be tossed

What to do
1. Use a ball to transition children to depart.
2. Toss the ball to a child. The child catches the ball and goes to the cubby area to get her things to go home.
3. When the child comes back, she tosses it back to you so that you can transition the next child.
4. Give each child several tries at catching if she drops the ball.

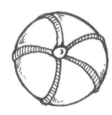  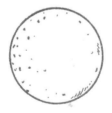 

SOFT BALL POMPOM NERF BALL KOOSH BALL

More to do **Literacy:** Use this activity as a literacy experience by spelling each child's name, stating one letter with each toss.

Related books *A My Name Is Alice* by Jane Bayer
Chrysanthemum by Kevin Henkes

★ *Ann Kelly, Johnstown, PA*

Rhyming Word Fun

3+

Materials   none

What to do
1. Children love rhymes so they will find this departure activity fun.
2. When the children are getting ready to depart, say a word such as "cat." Choose a volunteer to give a rhyming word. If the child is correct, she says a different word and picks the next child to give a rhyme before departing.
3. This goes on until everyone has departed.

⭐ *Eileen Lucas, Halifax, Nova Scotia, Canada*

Waiting to Go Home

3+

Materials   clothesline
scissors

What to do
1. Cut three to five pieces of clothesline long enough so that when you form a circle with a piece, five children can comfortably sit inside. Place the circles on the floor and let the children pretend that they are "birds in a nest."
2. When a parent arrives for pick-up, the "little bird" leaves the nest and flies away.
3. On other days, children can pretend to be ducks that waddle away or bunnies that hop away. You can even have children choose what they want to be.

⭐ *Ingelore Mix, Gainesville, VA*

After 5 Box

3+

Materials   cardboard or plastic box

What to do
1. First determine the best time to do this activity.
   Author's Note: Our center closed at 6, and even when we combined classrooms, most of the children were gone by 5:30. At 5:30, we had ten tired, hungry, cranky children who were anxious to go home, so we made the "after 5 box."
2. Decorate a box in a festive manner.
3. Each morning, stock the box with at least three things for the children to do after 5:00 (or a time when most of the children are gone). Items could include a light snack, some stickers, a board game, a book, a story tape or song, washcloths or wipes for hot and sweaty summer faces, a special project, and so on. The activities don't have to be fancy. You could add a new Frisbee, directions on how to play a new game, or puppets from another classroom.
4. Ask different staff members to be responsible for the box every two weeks. Even the cook and director can stock the box with a surprise! When everyone participates, it doesn't have to be a burden to any one teacher.
5. The box is a good way to introduce new toys, games, or activities to a small group of children, and it helps avoid conflicts when you introduce something new to a larger group.
6. Since there are two or three activities in the box, it is also a good way to use leftover craft supplies. Since the groups of children are smaller, three children could make sock puppets and four could use leftover stickers to make pictures.
7. Ask parents for suggestions or ask the children who stay late to each bring in a game or book from home to put in the box.

Related books   *Everybody Wins* by Jeffrey Sobel
Incredible Indoor Games Book: One Hundred and Sixty Group Projects, Games, and Activities by Bob Gregson
Think of Something Quiet by Clare Cherry

★ *Linda Ford, Sacramento, CA*

Saying Goodbye

4+

Materials   none

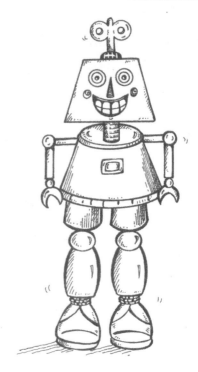

What to do

1. One of our favorite games is taking a pretend phone from the dress-up center and pretend it is a remote control.
2. Have the students lie down and pretend they are robots. Then speak in a computerized voice and command the "robots" to do various things, in a variety of Simon Says. The children love it and request it often. This keeps them busy while they are waiting to go home.

⭐ *Laurel Tuhey, Trumbull, CT*

Going on a Bus Ride

4+

Materials   pictures or models of different kinds of buses
chairs

What to do

1. Show the children pictures or models of different kinds of buses.
2. Encourage them to share their experiences with buses, such as where they've gone and in what kind of bus.
3. Arrange classroom chairs to look like seats in a bus.
4. Talk about going on a "magic bus" ride. The children can choose to go wherever they want.
5. Let the children file onto the "bus," sit in chairs, and put on pretend seat belts.

6. The bus driver (adult or child) discusses the bus rules.
7. The children pretend they are in a moving bus going over bumps and around curves. Sing "The Wheels on the Bus."
8. When you have reached your destination, ask the children to leave the bus in an orderly fashion.
9. This is a good activity to prepare for departure at the end of the day.

More to do   **Field Trip:** This activity provides good practice for children who will be going on a field trip.

Related books   *The Magic School Bus* books by Joanna Cole
School Bus by Donald Crews
The Wheels on the Bus by Paul O. Zelinsky

Monica Hay Cook, Tucson, AZ

Where Did They Go?   4+

Materials   child-made masks or puppets
table

What to do   1. At departure time, seat the children at a table.
2. Distribute the masks or puppets to the children.
3. Instruct the children to hold the masks in front of their faces and pretend to be the character represented in the artwork.
4. When parents arrive, tell them that the children are all gone and "all we have left here are raccoons (or whatever mask they are wearing)." Then say, "You can choose one of them to take home." Children love to think that they are

(continued on the next page)

in on a secret, and they enjoy the anticipation of waiting to be found, as in hide and seek or peek-a-boo.

5. As an alternative, have the children hide under a table and let the parents "find" them.

★ Sandra Gratias, Perkasie, PA

Be a Friend   4+

Materials   none

What to do   1. As you transition to the end of the day, encourage the children to do nice things for each other by singing the following to the tune of "London Bridge."

Who was a friend to you today?
You today, you today?
Who was a friend to you today?
At _____ (school name).

2. The children raise their hands to tell what someone did for them that was nice or helpful.
3. Sing the following for the helpful child.

_____ (helpful child's name) was a friend today,
friend today, friend today.
_____ (helpful child' name) was a friend today,
At _____ (school name).

4. Before singing the song, talk about nice things children do for each other. If you see something especially nice, ring a bell to stop everything and mention what the child has done. This will help children understand what things make someone a good friend.

More to do   **Home-to-School Connection**: If a child has done something especially nice, send a special note home in the mail to her family. Families love this, and it reinforces to the child what a good friend they were.
Author's Note: I try to send a note home about each child at least once a year.

Related books   *Biscuit Finds a Friend* by Alyssa Satin Capucilli
Do You Want to Be My Friend? by Eric Carle
Just My Friend and Me by Mercer Mayer
Where Are Maisy's Friends? by Lucy Cousins

★ *Sue Fleischmann, Sussex, WI*

Reflection Journal   4+

Materials   chart paper
broad multi-colored marker
chart stand
markers or crayons

What to do   1. As part of your closing activity, ask the children, "What went well today?" or "What was your favorite thing we did today?" Record a consensus response on the chart paper.
2. Ask a second question, "What could we do better tomorrow?" or "What did not go well today?" This could be a humorous thing, such as the hamster escaping from her cage, or a mistake, such as not picking up the blocks quietly. Record a consensus response on the chart paper.
3. Date the sheet at the bottom. Ask for a volunteer or select a daily illustrator to draw a picture to go with the two sentences while she is waiting to go home.
4. Periodically, read the journal with the children. This is an excellent activity when there isn't anything exciting to report for the day.

(continued on the next page)

More to do

Art: Let the children design a fancy cover for the chart by tearing pieces of aluminum foil and gluing them on the front and back cover. Cut out the letters for the title ("Reflections") and glue them to the cover.

Books: You could also title the chart "The Daily News" and use pieces of newsprint for the front and back covers. Type up the funniest pages and make miniature versions so that each child gets a copy. After discussing how pictures are used in the regular newspaper, let the children illustrate their own book.

⭐ *Susan R. Forbes, Daytona Beach, FL*

Crazy Cube

4+

Materials

stuffed blocks with plastic sleeve for pictures (teacher-made or purchased)

What to do

1. This is a great end-of-the-day transition activity, when you have five more minutes or the parents or buses are delayed.

2. Put a picture in the pocket on each side of the stuffed "Crazy Cube." The pictures can be children doing an activity, such as

skipping, hopping like a frog, or dancing, or children making a sound, such as yodeling, whistling, crying like a baby, or meowing like a cat.

3. One child rolls the crazy cube, and the rest "read" the picture and act it out.

Author's Note: The commercially made cubes have one side that says "Crazy Cube" on it. When this side is rolled, we either shake all over or make silly noises, and say, "Crazy Cube!" This is a great activity for pre-readers. With older children, use words instead of pictures. My class begs for this activity!

⭐ *Tracie O'Hara, Charlotte, NC*

Sweet and Sour

5+

Materials   small ball, or object that can be easily tossed

What to do
1. This activity is good for the end of the day.
2. Sit in a circle with the children. Toss a small ball or object to a child and say, "Sweet and sour." The child then tells the group something she liked about her day (something sweet) and something she didn't like about her day (something sour).
3. As she talks, give her encouraging remarks such as, "I didn't like that either," or another comment that lets the child know it's okay to show or talk about her emotions.
4. When she is finished, she tosses the ball to another child and says, "Sweet and sour." The new child then takes a turn. Make sure to comment on each child's feelings.
5. Play continues until everyone, including you, has a turn.

Rikki Deal, Beggs, OK

"Let's Be Like..."

3+

Materials   none

What to do
1. During a transition time, choose an animal for children to act like. Encourage the children to make animal sounds and movements.
2. Let the children take turns choosing different animals.
3. Expand on this idea by having the children move like other objects, such as a tree, bulldozer, train, popcorn, and so on.
4. Let the children explore their own ideas as well.

★ *Jodi Sykes, Lake Worth, FL*

Butterfly Drama

3+

Materials   pictures of butterfly life cycle (egg, caterpillar, chrysalis, butterfly)

What to do
1. When children must wait, do the following action rhyme with the children.
2. Say the poem and have the children act out the movements. Provide enough time for children to explore how each stage feels.

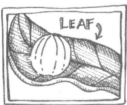  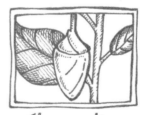 

Egg   Caterpillar   Chrysalis   Butterfly

First a tiny egg, you grow on a leaf (curl body into a ball)
Out you climb—a caterpillar—search for food to eat.
     (crawl around, pretending to eat leaves)
Turn into a chrysalis, relax and close your eyes.
     (wrap arms around body, close eyes)
Finally a butterfly, you fly through the sky. (fly around the room)

More to do   **Art:** Cut out butterflies from construction paper and give one to each child. Show the children how to squirt paint on their butterflies, fold in half, and rub their hands on the paper to move the paint around. When they open the butterfly, encourage them to note the symmetry of colors and patterns.

Related books   *Bugs! Bugs! Bugs!* by Bob Barner
How to Hide a Butterfly and Other Insects by Ruth Heller
The Very Hungry Caterpillar by Eric Carle
Where Does the Butterfly Go When It Rains? by May Garelick

⭐ *Cassandra Reigel Whetstone, San Jose, CA*

Transition Activity With Stuffed Animal

3+

Material   stuffed animal

What to do   1. Choose a favorite stuffed animal for this activity.
2. Tell the children that the animal is asleep on the shelf, so they have to tiptoe very quietly or they will wake him up. Encourage the children to tiptoe around the room, trying to be as quiet as possible.
3. This helps the children be quiet and orderly when moving from place to place to change activities.

More to do   **Games:** When waiting in line to enter a room or place that is not quite ready to enter yet, children often get rowdy. Play this game with them. Ask them to guess answers about your likes and dislikes. Tell them they must raise their hand to be called on. For example:

◆ What is my favorite color?
◆ What kind of pet do I have?
◆ What are my children's names?
◆ What is my favorite food?
◆ What animal am I? (pantomime an animal)

(continued on the next page)

General Tips: When offering an activity for preschoolers to do, never ask if they want to do an activity or if they want to clean up. Their favorite answer at this age will be "No!" Instead, offer them a choice so they can't answer "yes" or "no." For example, ask, "Would you like to go to the blocks or the art center?" or "Would you like to clean up the blocks first or the books first?" Whatever activity you'd really like them to do, say that activity last. Children this age will pay attention to the last item you say and frequently choose that item.

⭐*Teri Phillips, Franklin, TN*

Winterskoll (Winter Cheer) 3+

Materials

plastic snowflake and icicle ornaments
undecorated artificial pine tree
pictures of cold places and animals

What to do

1. To grab the children's attention and help them transition to dramatic play during the winter, decorate the room with artificial pine trees, snowflakes, icicles, and pictures to give the room a wintry feeling. Place mittens, jackets, sweaters, parkas, hats, and other warm clothes in the dress-up area.
2. Show the children pictures of snowy places and animals that live in cold climates (polar bears, penguins). Discuss the pictures.
3. Cut off the sides of a large box. Attach rope to make a handle. Have "pretend sled rides" in the classroom. The cardboard moves easily across bare floors.

More to do

Story Time: Make Eskimo puppets for felt board stories. Cut out a basic person shape, pants, shirts, and mukluks (boots) from felt. Trim the clothes with faux fur. Draw faces with markers and add wiggle eyes. Make felt animals such as polar bears, walruses, seals, snow foxes, and penguins. Make up stories for the felt board.

⭐*Penni Smith, Riverside, CA*

Lights, Camera, Action!

3+

Materials   none

What to do
1. During spare moments, pretend that you are someone or something and ask the children to guess what you are.
2. Your options are limitless! You could pretend to be an animal, a person (such as a firefighter), an object (tea kettle), a weather pattern (wind), and so on.
3. Let the children take turns pretending to be different people or things for the class to guess.
   Note: Some children become anxious when there are too many choices. If this is the case, make suggestions such as "pretend to be an animal that climbs trees."
4. Try using only your body language or your voice and see if children can guess what you are.

Karyn F. Everham, Fort Myers, FL

Quiet as Mice

4+

Materials
paper
markers
scissors
glue
rulers or tongue depressors

What to do
1. Using paper, markers, and scissors, make a mouse mask for each child and teacher. Be sure to cut out eye holes so the children can see clearly through them. Attach the masks to rulers or large tongue depressors.
2. Make a sign that reads, "We are quiet mice. We do not talk."
3. Before leaving the classroom, gather the children and tell them they will pretend to be "quiet mice" as they walk down the hall. Discuss ways they can move quietly. Give each child a mouse mask to wear.

(continued on the next page)

4. Choose a child to hold the sign to alert other teachers and children that you are a group of quiet mice who do not talk.
5. Have fun smiling at everyone in the hallway, but remember no one can talk!
6. This is a great dramatic play activity as well as a way to quietly transition from one part of the school to another.

Related books *Let's Pretend* by Rose Greydanus
Mouse Around by Pat Schories
Sleep Tight, Little Mouse by Mary Morgan
Two Tiny Mice by Alan Baker

★ *Anne Lippincott, New Hartford, CT*

Let's Travel Around the World/Country/Town

4+

Materials large shower curtain
permanent markers
toy ships, planes, cars, buses, and trains
play people
boxes for airport and bus/train stations

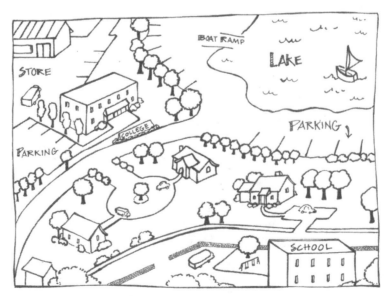

SHOWER CURTAIN

What to do
1. Beforehand, draw a map of the world, country, or town in which the children live on the curtain with permanent markers. Add water areas, islands, and other important details such as airports, train and bus stations, and hospitals. **Note:** You can use the whole curtain to make a large map, or use one large and several small ones (curtain cut in halves or quarters) and draw several different maps on them.
2. Tape the maps securely in an area where children have plenty of space for their travels.
3. During times when children must wait for an activity to start or for others to finish, they can use toy vehicles, play people, and boxes on the maps.

More to do
Math: Children love to compare distances from where they live to where others live. Provide tape measures and rulers and encourage them to measure the distances on a town map. Discuss the words "mile," "meter," "inch," "kilometer," and so on.

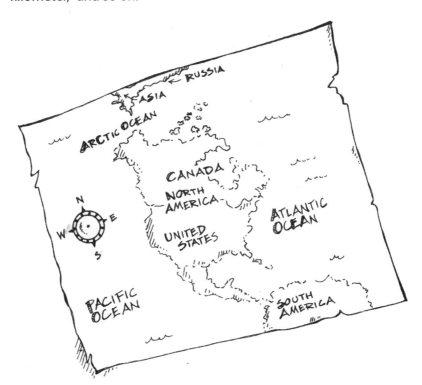

Social Development: Discuss what country the children were born in, who was born in the same country, and how all countries are different. Invite a visitor to come to school to speak about his or her homeland.

 *Eileen Lucas, Halifax, Nova Scotia, Canada*

Observing X-Rays

Materials
x-ray films
transparency sheets
markers

What to do

1. During a transition time, talk about skeletons, bones, and x-rays with the children. Encourage them to pretend to be doctors looking at x-rays.
2. Place a few x-rays in a window low enough for the children to see.
3. After observing the x-rays, encourage the children to draw their own x-rays using transparency sheets and markers.

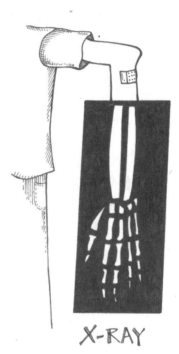

X-RAY

More to do

Science: Put books about skeletons on the discovery table along with real sterilized chicken and turkey bones and heavy cardboard. Encourage the children to glue the bones together on the heavy cardboard to make "bodies" of animals or people.

⭐ *Eileen Lucas, Halifax, Nova Scotia, Canada*

Move to a Different Area 3+

Materials   none

What to do   1. Sing the following to the tune of "Three Blind Mice."

1-2-3, to the chairs, please.
1-2-3, to the chairs, please.
1-2-3, to the chairs, please.

Additional verses:

1-2-3, to the carpets, please…
1-2-3, to the footprints, please…
1-2-3, to the table, please…

2. The song is a repetitive method of informing the children what to do. When the children hear this tune, they know that you are giving them directions about where to go or what to do. Too often children are confused and distracted during transitions. A familiar tune will help them focus on the expected task.
3. When it is time to move to a new area, begin singing the song. Encourage the children to join in and to move to the area in the song.
4. Introduce the song at circle or group time, and ask the children to practice the song and words.
   Author's Note: Use puppets to demonstrate what you want children to do while the group sings the song. The children can also take puppets to the areas and help the puppets follow the directions in the song.

Sandra L. Nagel, White Lake, MI

5 Minutes Left

`3+`

Materials   none

What to do   1. Introduce the song at a circle or group time. Ask the children to practice the song and words.
2. Sing "Five More Minutes" to the tune of "Skip to My Lou" to let the children know about an upcoming transition.

Five more minutes left to play.
Five more minutes left to play.
Five more minutes left to play.
Five more minutes to play.

Additional verses:

Five more minutes left to read…
Five more minutes left to paint…
Five more minutes left to draw…

3. Five minutes prior to a change in activities, begin singing the song. Encourage the children to join in.
4. Sing the song and hold up one hand with the five fingers, showing there are five minutes left of that activity.

Sandra Nagel, White Lake, MI

A Simple Song

`3+`

Materials   none

What to do   1. The children will enjoy hearing you sing whether you think you can sing or not. Whenever you need the children to move from one activity to another, sing your way through the transition.

2. If children become accustomed to this, they will know where to go when they hear a familiar song. The best songs can be the ones you make up on your own.

(Tune: "London Bridge")
It's time to clean up, yes it is,
Yes it is, yes it is,
It's time to clean up, yes it is,
All my little friends.

Thanks for helping
One by one, two by two
And three by three.
Thanks for helping clean the room
All my little friends.

Look how the room looks nice and clean
Nice and clean, nice and clean.
Look how the room looks nice and clean,
All my little friends.

Time to find a place to sit,
Place to sit, place to sit,
Time to find a place to sit,
All my little friends.

(Tune: "Twinkle, Twinkle, Little Star")
Helpers, helpers all around
Look at all the work you found.
Cleaning here and cleaning there,
Cleaning cleaning everywhere.
Helpers, helpers all around
You are the best little helpers in town!

(Tune: "Have You Ever Seen a Lassie?")
It's time for us to clean up   *Put this away and that away,*
To clean up, to clean up.   *Clear this table and that table.*
It's time for us to clean up   *It's time for us to clean up,*
To clean up our room.   *And put all toys away.*

⭐ *Susan Myhre, Bremerton, WA*

"Autumn Leaves" Song

3+

Materials   none

What to do   Sing the following song to the tune of "London Bridge" when moving from one activity to another. The children soon learn the words and sing along.

> Autumn leaves are falling down
> Falling down, falling down.
> Autumn leaves are falling down
> All through the town.
>
> Red, yellow, orange and green
> Orange and green, orange and green.
> Red, yellow, orange and green
> All through the town.

More to do   **Art**: Children can help to collect leaves of a variety of colors to make a class collage. Add these colors of paints to the easel area for the children to make a picture.

Related books   *Red Leaf, Yellow Leaf* by Lois Ehlert
Why Do Leaves Change Color? by Betsy Maestro

Sandy L. Scott, Vancouver, WA

"Autumn Leaves" Fingerplay

3+

Materials   index cards
poster board
markers

What to do   1. Write the fingerplay on index cards and on a poster for the children to see. Teach the children the motions that go with the fingerplay.

Autumn leaves come tumbling down (wiggle fingers downward)
Floating, twirling, twisting to the ground, (twist hands to the ground)
Red, orange, rust, and gold and brown. (wiggle fingers)

Rake them, pile them, crunch them with your shoe. (rake, pile, stomp foot)
See all different shapes come into view, (shield eyes with hand)
Elm leaves, maple leaves, and oak leaves, too.
     (wiggle fingers and move arms for leaves falling)

The wind blows the leaves here and there.
     (move both arms to one side and to the other)
It blows them across the meadow and everywhere.
     (sweep arms across body, then crisscross)
The wind blows them until the trees are bare.
     (hold arms out like tree branches).

2. Tell the children that the wind is blowing them to the next activity.

Related book   *Why Do Leaves Change Color?* by Chris Arvetis and Carole Palmer

★ *Mary Brehm, Aurora, OH*

Cats

3+

Materials   none

What to do   1. Say this poem slowly and have the children pretend they are cats and move as the poem dictates.

CREEPY

Cats by Barbara Saul
Sleepy cats (roll up in a ball on the floor)
Creepy cats (get on all fours and arch backs)
Furry cats (pretend to wash like a cat)
Purry cats (make purring noise)
Huggy cats (hug each other)
Ruggy cats (curl up on rug)

HUGGY

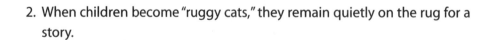

SLEEPY   RUGGY   PURRY   FURRY

2. When children become "ruggy cats," they remain quietly on the rug for a story.

Related books   *Black Cat* by Christopher Myers
Cat Is Sleepy by Satoshi Kitamura
Cat Up a Tree by Ann Hassett
Millions of Cats by Wanda Gag

⭐ *Barbara Saul, Eureka, CA*

Cleanup Song

3+

Materials   none

What to do   1. Announce that it is time to clean up the toys so the children can play with them again the next day.
2. Using the song below assign jobs.

Cleanup Song by Diane Weiss
(Tune: "Here We Go 'Round the Mulberry Bush")
It's time to put our toys away, our toys away, our toys away.
It's time to put our toys away, what job will you get today?
(child's name) *put the* (toy name) *away, the* (toy name) *away,*
   the (toy name) *away.*
(child's name) *put the* (toy name) *away. Who will be done first today?*

3. After singing a verse to assign each child a job, the children can begin their jobs, or give several children a larger job to do together.

More to do   Change the words to the song to fit other group activities.

★ *Diane Weiss, Fairfax, VA*

Five Speckled Frogs

3+

Materials   none

What to do   1. Select five children to be frogs. Teach the children the song "Five Speckled Frogs."
2. One child at a time pretends to jump off the log and into the pool by following the song.
3. If possible, give each child a turn as you transition to another activity.

(continued on the next page)

More to do   Make five frog headbands out of construction paper and staple them to fit a child's head. Make a "speckled log" from construction paper, and a pool out of blue construction paper or blue cloth. Select five children to be frogs. Have each child put on a headband and sit on the log.

Related books   *A Frog's Body* by Joanna Cole
Jump, Frog, Jump by Robert Kalan

★ *Kaethe Lewandowski, Centreville, VA*

Fly Away, All   3+

Materials   none

What to do   1. Teach the children the following fingerplay. As the children are waiting to go out and play, choose five children to stand in a row in front of the group. As they recite the first line of the fingerplay, the first child sinks down, the second child sinks down on line two, and so on. On the last line, they all jump up and twirl back to their seats.
2. Repeat with another group of children as time allows.

1 little leaf,
2 little leaves,
3 little leaves that fall.
4 little leaves,
5 little leaves,
Fly away, fly away, all.

Related books *Red Leaf, Yellow Leaf* by Lois Ehlert
A Tree Is Nice by Janice May Udry
Why Do Leaves Change Color? by Betsy Maestro

⭐ *Susan Oldham Hill, Lakeland, FL*

Bored? No Way!

3+

Materials song (sung to any tune)

What to do 1. Sing the following song with the children and do the actions. This is a great transition for circle or group time or for rainy days.

Bored? No Way!

There's just no way for us to be bored
There's so much we can do,

Like jumping jacks and turning around
And falling to the ground.

We can jump up high and reach for the sky
But sometimes that won't do.

So around the yard we run, run, run
Having lots of fun.

2. Ask the children to suggest additional movements, or mime motions, such as painting pictures, blowing bubbles, sweeping the floor, building with blocks, and so on.

⭐ *Eileen Lucas, Halifax, Nova Scotia, Canada*

Free Time

`3+`

Materials none

What to do Sing the following when it is time to transition to free play time.

>**Free Play** (Tune: "Here We Go 'Round the Mulberry Bush")
>*It's almost time for free time,*
>*Free time, free time.*
>*It's almost time for free time*
>*In (teacher's name) group today.*
>
>*We'll work nicely with our friends,*
>*With our friends, with our friends.*
>*We'll work nicely with our friends,*
>*And share while we play.*

⭐*Jackie Wright, Enid, OK*

Hands Go Up

`3+`

Materials none

What to do During transition times, repeat this rhyme with the children. Add motions to match the words of the rhyme.

>*Hands go up,*   *Hands go high,*
>*Hands go down.*   *Hands go low.*
>*Hands can clap,*   *Hands move fast.*
>*Without a sound.*   *Hands move slow.*

⭐*Susan Oldham Hill, Lakeland, FL*

Hello, Goodnight, Goodbye

Materials   none

What to do   Use the following songs during the appropriate transition times.

Hello Song
Hello, (first child's name).
Hello, (second child's name).
Hello, (third child's name).
We're glad you're here today!

Goodnight Song
Goodnight, (first child's name).
Goodnight, (second child's name).
Goodnight, (third child's name).
It's time to take a nap.

Goodbye Song
Goodbye, (first child's name).
Goodbye, (second child's name).
Goodbye, (third child's name).
We'll see you on (next day).

Related tape/CD Greg and Steve *We All Live Together, Volume 2*

★ *Linda Ford, Sacramento, CA*

I'm Ready to Learn

`3+`

Materials   none

What to do   This is a song to use at the beginning of circle or any time to get everyone settled and ready to listen. As children are starting to sit down for the activity, sing the following to the tune of "I'm a Little Teapot" and do the actions.

> *I am ready to learn at school*
> *'Cause I know a special rule* (shake head yes)
> *Eyes looking up, lips closed, ears listen too* (point to each)
> *Feet and hands still, is what we do.* (fold hands in lap)

Related books   *The Kissing Hand* by Audrey Penn
Mouse's First Day of School by Lauren Thompson
My First Day at Nursery School by Becky Edwards
A Pocket Full of Kisses by Audrey Penn

★ *Sue Fleischmann, Sussex, WI*

Mary Wore a Red Dress

`3+`

Materials   none

What to do   1. While you are transitioning children to another activity, sing or chant the following.

> *Someone's wearing red today, red today, red today,*
> *Someone's wearing red today, go line up!* (or the next activity)

2. Choose a color that a child is wearing and sing that color until all the children have transitioned. If a child cannot recognize colors, add her name to the song. "Karen's wearing blue today" and so on.

More to do Choose an article of clothing instead of color, or you can also choose a pattern such as stripes, flowers, letters, and so on.

Related books *Color Dance* by Ann Jonas
Is It Red? Is It Yellow? Is It Blue? by Tana Hoban
Mouse Paint by Ellen Stoll Walsh
My Crayons Talk by Patricia Hubbard
Red Bear by Bodel Rikys
Red, Blue, Yellow Shoe by Tana Hoban
Who Said Red? by Mary Serfozo

★ Kaethe Lewandowski, Centreville, VA

Pizza Pizzazz

3+

Materials none

What to do When you want to capture the children's attention, recite each line of the following poem. Repeat it with them and together perform the motions.

Stirring sauce! (grip imaginary spoon and mix sauce)
Slicing cheese! (hit edge of palm with other hand)
Pepperoni, if you please (motion as if dealing cards)
A bit of dough that grows and grows (slowly spread hands apart)
Now you know… it's pizza! (take a big bite of imaginary pizza)

★ Karyn F. Everham, Fort Myers, FL

Sing Songs

3+

Materials   none

What to do
1. Make transitions easy by singing through them. Make up songs as you go along. For example, the following is a simple follow-the-leader song that can be used throughout the day:

   Follow the leader
   Follow the leader,
   Follow the leader to the _____ (gym, playground, or any other place)

2. If the children come to school on a school bus, sing this song as they arrive:

   (Tune:"This Is The Way We…")
   The school bus goes to _____ *'s house,* _____ *'s house,*
      _____ *'s house,*
   The school bus goes to _____ *'s house to bring him* (her) *to school.*

3. Adapt this tune for almost any transition task. For example:

   This is the way we pick up our rugs, pick up our rugs, pick up our rugs,
   This is the way we pick up our rugs and put them away.

   This is the way we wash our hands, wash our hands, wash our hands,
   This is the way we wash our hands before we eat our snack.

4. Good waiting songs allow each child to have a turn to add to the song. In the song, "Alligator Pie" (by Dennis Lee), children alternate between slapping their thighs and clapping their hands to create a rhythm. If you don't know the tune, say it as a chant.
5. Repeat, giving each child a chance to sing about their favorite pie or the silliest pie instead of "Alligator" pie.
6. Other good waiting songs incorporate some movement while children are still sitting, such as the following (sung to the tune of "The Farmer in the Dell"). You can call on each child to identify another body part to wiggle:

   I wiggle, I wiggle, my fingers,
   I wiggle, I wiggle, my fingers,
   Hi-ho-the-derrio,
   I wiggle, I wiggle my fingers.

⭐ *Sandra Suffoletto Ryan, Buffalo, NY*

The GIANT Encyclopedia of Transition Activities

Sneaky Black Cat

3+

Materials   none

What to do   1. Children love to pretend to be different characters as they follow you from one activity to another.

Sneaky, sneaky black cat
Sneaky as can be.
Sneaky, sneaky black cat
Won't you follow me?
(Pause)
Quietly as can be!

2. Next time be a scary, scary white ghost!

Jackie Wright, Enid, OK

We Know How to Get in Line

3+

Materials   none

What to do   Make a poster of the following song. In the last line, substitute whatever the next activity is for the word "inside." Sing it to the tune of "Mary Had a Little Lamb."

We know how to get in line,
Get in line, get in line.
We know how to get in line
Every single time!
We face the front and stand up tall,
Stand up tall, stand up tall.
We face the front and stand up tall
So we can go inside!

Jackie Wright, Enid, OK

The Eensy Weensy Spider Game 3+

Materials   none

What to do

1. This game is great when you are trying to transition the children to a quiet time. It also teaches many skills, including listening skills, language acquisition, and how to pay attention.
2. First learn the song and then add the actions.

   The eensy weensy spider went up the water spout.
   (move fingers up like a spider)
   Down came the rain and washed the spider out. (move fingers down like rain)
   Out came the sun and dried up all the rain. (make a big circle with hands)
   And the eensy weensy spider went up the spout again.
   (move fingers up like a spider)

3. After learning the song, hum the tune and use the actions.
4. Next, no singing, only the actions. You'll be amazed at how quiet the children are!

Jackie Wright, Enid, OK

Lining Up Rhyme

3+

What to do   When lining up to go to another room, say the following rhyme to help the children settle down.

Hands up high,
Hands out wide,
By your side.

Inside voices (louder voice but not shouting)
Outside voices (normal)
In the hall
There are no voices (get quieter)
Shhhh… (to reinforce I may say, "Show me what silence sounds like.")

⭐ *Pam Shelest, Prince George, British Columbia, Canada*

Look at Me!

3+

What to do   To help children settle down, say the following rhyme.

Look at Me!
Look at the way I can turn
All the way around. (point to self, then turn around)
I can squat; I can jump. (squat, then jump)
And sit quietly back down. (sit down quietly)

⭐ *Cathy Falk Fort Wayne, IN*

Open Them, Shut Them

3+

Materials   none

What to do   When you want the children's attention or when you want them to settle down, say this poem and do the motions with your hands. Begin when you want the group to quiet down. Say the verse aloud as you move your hands, and the children will follow.

Open them, shut them,
Open them, shut them,
Give a little clap!
Open them, shut them,
Lay them in your lap.

Creep them, crawl them,
Creep them, crawl them,
Right up to your chin.
Open up your little mouth,
But do not let them in!

Open them, shut them,
Open them, shut them,
Make your fingers fly
Then like little birdies
Have them fall down from the sky.
Faster, faster, faster, faster, STOP!

Barbara Saul, Eureka, CA

Please Quiet Down

3+

Materials   none

What to do   1. When you want the children to quiet down, sing the following song.

   Please Quiet Down (Tune: "Are You Sleeping?")
   We are waiting,
   We are waiting,
   For a quiet room,
   For a quiet room.
   We're patiently waiting.
   We're patiently waiting.
   Please quiet down.
   Please quiet down.

   2. Use this song when the noise level in the room gets too high during free time (or any time.) Remember to praise the class when you get the results you want.

Jackie Wright, Enid, OK

The Listening Position

3+

Materials   none

What to do   Recite the following rhyme at transition times. It can also be sung to the tune of "Twinkle, Twinkle, Little Star."

   The listening position has five parts,
   Bottoms on the floor is where it starts.
   Crisscross legs, that's number two,
   I can do it, so can you.
   Opening ears and eyes is three, (point to ears and eyes)

(continued on the next page)

Ready to listen and see.
Hands in your lap is number four.
Now there is just one more. (mime closing mouth)
When all five things have been done,
We're ready to listen and have fun.

⭐ *Barbara Anthony, Wellfleet, MA*

A Knocking at the Door

3+

Materials   none

What to do

1. Say the following rhyme any time during the day when you have a few extra moments.
2. Begin by talking about all the ways children know someone is at the door, including doorbells, door knockers, knocking by hand, or tapping on a door. Also ask how they know who is at the door (peepholes, windows, storm doors, door chains, and so on).
3. Read the following action rhyme, modeling the motions for the children.

There's a knocking at the door (knock on desk)
Who can it be? (shrug shoulders, hold hands up palm face up)
Mom looks through the peephole (curl fingers and look through a peephole)
Who does she see?
A kangaroo hopping big up and downs? (hop)
A skater on ice skates spinning around? (spin)
A woodpecker tapping, rat-a-tat-tat? (clap hands in rhythm)
A tall baseball player swinging his bat? (swinging motion)
The neighbor's little dog, coming to bark? (arf!)
Look, look! It's my friend! We'll play in the park! (cheer)

4. Read the rhyme again so the children can do the motions with you.

More to do   Invite a guest speaker to tell the children about safety and what to do when someone comes to the door.

⭐ *Theresa Callahan, Easton, MD*

Bendable Me

`3+`

What to do   Say the following poem any time during the day when you have a few extra moments

Bendable Me
I bend in the middle, (bow from waist)
I can bend at my knees. (stoop down)
I can bend just about anywhere (bend elbows; rotate head)
That I please. (pat self; smile)

⭐ *Cathy Falk, Fort Wayne, IN*

Bingo

`3+`

Materials   none

What to do   1. At circle or group time, do this activity while the children are waiting for the group to gather. It will help the children recognize and spell their names.

*There was a teacher who had a student
And Maria was her name-oh,
M-A-R-I-A, M-A-R-I-A, M-A-R-I-A, and Maria was her name-oh!*

2. If time allows, sing a verse for each child.

⭐ *Kaethe Lewandowski, Centreville, VA*

Can You?

3+

Materials   none

What to do
1. When you have a few extra moments, read the following poem and have the children do the actions in the poem.

   Can You? by Barbara Saul
   What can I do?
   What can I do?
   I can sing the alphabet song, can you?

   What can I do?
   What can I do?
   I can name the colors, can you?

   What can I do?
   What can I do?
   I can touch my toes, can you?

   What can I do?
   What can I do?
   I can jump up high, can you?

   What can I do?
   What can I do?
   I can comb my hair, can you?

   What can I do?
   What can I do?
   I can brush my teeth, can you?

2. Let the children recite the poem with you and add new activities.

Barbara Saul, Eureka, CA

Class Song

3+

Materials   none

What to do   Whenever the children are waiting for a visitor or on a field trip, or any time they are waiting, it is great to have a class song. This song brings the class into one unit and also focuses their attention on you. If your class is the Kool Koalas, the following is an example of a song that you could use.

> **Class Song**
> *We are the Koalas*
> *The Kool Koalas.*
> *We learn so many*
> *Things here each day.*
> *We laugh and play here.*
> *Let's give a big cheer,*
> *Hip, hip, hooray*
> *For the Kool Koalas.*

> **Note**: You can use common songs, such as the song "Baby Bumblebee" if your class is the Busy Bees.

> *Sandy L. Scott, Vancouver, WA*

Five Little Snakes

3+

Materials   none

What to do   When you have a few extra moments during the day, say the following poem.

> *Five little snakes*
> *Went slithering in the sand.*
> *One caught a fly and said,*
> *"I'm just grand!"*

> *(continued on the next page)*

Four little snakes went
Curling round and round.
One went in a hole
Way deep down in the ground.

Three little snakes
Went out to look for lunch.
One found some bugs and beetles
Gulp, crunch, crunch!

Two little snakes said
"Just hear my hissing sound!"
One slithered away
And no more could be found

One little snake
As alone as he could be
Said, "Come back my brothers
And play with me!"

⭐ *Mary Brehm, Aurora, OH*

Days of the Week

3+

Materials

poster board or card stock
computer and printer (or markers)
laminator (optional)
scissors
pocket chart

What to do

1. Sing the following any time you have a few extra moments.

   Days of the Week (Tune: "We Wish You a Merry Christmas")
   Day one of the week is Sunday.
   Day two of the week is Monday.
   Day three of the week is Tuesday.
   Day four is Wednesday.

   Day five of the week if Thursday.
   Day six of the week is Friday.
   Day seven of the week is Saturday.
   Let's all shout, "Hooray!"

2. Print on poster board for a pocket chart. Laminate for durability. Cut into sentence strips.

⭐ *Jackie Wright, Enid, OK*

Fingerplay Library

3+

Materials

4" x 6" note or index cards
pen or pencil
4" x 6" file card box

What to do

1. The one thing children always have with them is their fingers. Start a Fingerplay Library so at any transition time you will always have a number of fingerplays right at your fingertips!
2. Print a fingerplay on each note or index card.
3. File the cards in the box.
4. Refer to the box whenever you need a quick fingerplay during those busy transition times.
5. Following are some examples.

Two Little Blackbirds
Two little blackbirds (hold up both thumbs, fingers folded)
Sitting on a hill
One named Jack, (raise one thumb)
And one named Jill. (raise the other thumb)
Fly away, Jack. (open fingers and, making a fluttering motion, move one hand behind your back)
Fly away, Jill. (open fingers and, making a fluttering motion, move the other hand behind your back)
Come back, Jack. (open fingers and, making a fluttering motion, move one hand back to the front)
Come back, Jill. (open fingers and, making a fluttering motion, move the other hand back to the front)

(continued on the next page)

Where Is Thumbkin?

Where is Thumbkin? (hide both hands behind your back)
Where is Thumbkin?
Here I am. (move one hand to the front with thumb raised and fingers folded)
Here I am. (move other hand to the front with thumb raised and
    fingers folded)
How are you today, sir? (wiggle one thumb at the other)
Very well, I thank you. (wiggle other thumb at the first)
Run away. (hide one hand behind your back)
Run away. (hide the other hand behind your back)

Continue as above substituting the remaining fingers:
Pointer (index finger)
Middle Man (middle finger)
Ring Man (ring Finger)
Pinky (pinky finger)

After singing a verse about each finger, sing this last verse:
Where is everybody? (hide both hands behind your back)
Where is everybody?
Here we are! (move one hand to the front with fingers in the typical "five" hand)
Here we are! (move other hand to the front with fingers in the
    typical "five" hand)
How are you today, sirs? (wiggle all fingers on one hand at the fingers
    on the other hand)
Very well, we thank you! (wiggle all fingers on the other hand at the
        fingers on the first hand)
Run away. (hide one hand behind your back)
Run away. (hide the other hand behind your back)

Five Little Monkeys

Five little monkeys jumping on the bed (bounce five-hand on outstretched palm)
One fell off and bumped his head. (hold up one finger, then touch
    finger to forehead)
Mama called the doctor and the doctor said, (dial pretend phone or hold
    pretend phone up to ear)
"No more monkeys jumping on the bed!" (waggle one finger in the air)

Four little monkeys…
Three little monkeys…
Two little monkeys…

On the last verse, the last line should be, "Put those monkeys back to bed!"

Virginia Jean Herrod, Columbia, SC

"Grandma's Glasses" Fingerplay `3+`

Materials   none

What to do   Any time you have a few extra moments, say this poem and do the motions with the children.

> **Grandma's Glasses**
> *Here are Grannie's glasses.* (make circles with hands and hold them to eyes like glasses)
> *Here is Grannie's cap.* (hands on head)
> *This is the way she folds them up,* (lock fingers)
> *And puts them in her lap.* (put locked fingers in lap)

⭐ *Barbara Saul, Eureka, CA*

I Am Special `3+`

Materials   none

What to do   When the children are waiting for the next activity, sing this song with them.

> *I am special.*
> *I am special.*
> *I'm a star!*
> *I'm a star!*
> *There's no one quite like me,*
> *There's no one quite like me,*
> *Near or far,*
> *Near or far!*

⭐ *Kaethe Lewandowski, Centreville, VA*

Mother Goose Picks a Poem   3+

Materials   colored index cards
scissors
basket (preferably nest-shaped)
goose puppet (optional)

What to do   1. Cut index cards into egg shapes. On each egg, write one nursery rhyme. Place the "eggs" into a basket.
2. At a transition time, pretend to be Mother Goose (or use the goose puppet) and reach into the basket and pull out an "egg." Share as many rhymes as time allows.
3. Let children pick an egg and recite to the class (with help if necessary).
4. After the children know the rhymes well, teach them to say them using the call-and-response method.
5. Introduce modern nursery rhymes, such as those by Jack Prelutsky and Shel Silverstein.

★ *Karyn F. Everham, Fort Myers, FL*

"One Potato, Two Potato"   3+

Materials   none

What to do   1. When you have a few extra moments, start the "One Potato, Two Potato" rhyme with hand motions (pounding one fist on top of the other right in front of you). Here is the rhyme:

   One potato, two potato, three potato, four.
   Five potato, six potato, seven potato, more.

2. Suggest a few different ways to say the rhyme and do the motions. For example, say the rhyme loudly, say the rhyme softly, say the rhyme with your hands up in the air, say the rhyme with your hands down near the floor, say

the rhyme with both eyes shut, say the rhyme with one eye shut, say the rhyme with a partner, and say the rhyme back to back with a friend.

3. Invite the children to share new and different ideas. Move and grove with this rhyme as time allows.

★ *Judy Fujawa, The Villages, FL*

Right and Left

3+

Materials   none

What to do

1. When you have a few extra moment any time during the day, sing the following to help children learn about right and left.

   Right and Left (Tune: "Mary Had a Little Lamb")
   I want to learn my left from right,
   Left from right, left from right.
   I want to learn my left from right,
   I try with all my might.

   The left hand makes the letter L,
   Letter L, letter L.
   The left hand makes the letter L.
   Hurray! Now I can tell.

2. This is a favorite song to teach children the right and left hand.

★ *Jackie Wright, Enid, OK*

"The Grand Old Duke of York" 3+

Materials   none

What to do
1. Any time you have a few extra minutes, say the following poem.
2. Be sure the children can move around. Say this verse and act it out as you go.

    The Grand Old Duke of York (squat down)
    Had twenty thousand men. (continue squatting)
    He marched them up the hill, (stand)
    And marched them down again. (squat)
    And when they're up they're up. (stand)
    And when they're down they're down. (squat)
    But when they're only halfway up. (squat halfway)
    They're neither up (stand) *nor down!* (squat)

3. Repeat this poem and actions a few times, each time saying and doing the actions faster and faster.

⭐ *Barbara Saul, Eureka, CA*

Waiting With a Song 3+

Materials   none

What to do
1. While waiting for a visitor to arrive or someone to finish a task and join the group, try this sing-song chant. Sway as you say, "Waiting and waiting and waiting and waiting. Waiting for (child's name) to join the group. Waiting and waiting and waiting and waiting." Repeat the chant as many times as necessary.
2. Change the song to express an anticipated event, such as cookies to finish baking, and so on.
3. When the children are sitting at the table waiting for something, play "Johnny Works With One Hammer."

Johnny works with one hammer, one hammer, one hammer,
Johnny works with one hammer (all the while beat one fist on the table in
    rhythm),
Then he works with two.

Johnny works with two hammers, two hammers, two hammers,
Johnny works with two hammers (all the while beat both fists on the table in
    rhythm),
Then he works with three.

Johnny works with three hammers, three hammers, three hammers,
Johnny works with three hammers (all the while use both hands and one foot),
Then he works with four.

Johnny works with four hammers, four hammers, four hammers,
Johnny works with four hammers (all the while tap both fists and both feet),
Then he works with five.

Johnny works with five hammers, five hammers, five hammers,
Johnny works with five hammers (all the while tap both fists and both feet,
    and nod head),
Then he goes to sleep.

★ *Sandra Gratias, Perkasie, PA*

We're Glad You're Here

3+

Materials   none

What to do   As the children arrive at the beginning of the day, for circle or group time, or
any time during the day, sing the following to the tune of "B-I-N-G-O."

There was a class that had a girl (boy).
And (child's name) *was her* (his) *name-o,*
Jump, jump, (child's name).
Jump, jump, (child's name).
Jump, jump, (child's name).
We're glad you're here today.

★ *Jackie Wright, Enid, OK*

Whoops, Johnny

`3+`

Materials   none

What to do
1. This is a great fingerplay to say any time the children are waiting.
2. Hold up your left hand, palm facing the children.
3. Using the index finger of your right hand, start saying "Johnny" while tapping the top of the pinky of the left hand. Say, "Johnny" while tapping the ring, middle, and index finger of the left hand. Slide the right index finger from the top of the left index finger down along the curve to the thumb, saying "Whoops." Say, "Johnny" as you tap the top of the thumb.
4. Now repeat backwards. Slide your right index finger back down and up the curve of the left hand saying, "Whoops" until you touch the tip of the left index finger. Say, "Johnny" while tapping the tip of the left index finger. Say, "Johnny" while tapping the middle, ring, and pinky (one "Johnny" for each finger).
5. Children are fascinated by this ancient fingerplay. Try substituting the names of the children in your group for "Johnny."

Jackie Wright, Enid, OK

Wiggle Your Nose

`3+`

Materials   none

What to do   To pass the time between activities or help children settle down for a quiet activity, try the following rhyme. Teach the children the simple motions that go along with the words.

Eyes open, (open eyes wide)
Eyes closed. (close eyes tight)
Wiggle your fingers. (hold hands up and wiggle fingers)
Wiggle your nose. (wiggle nose)
Thumbs up. (make fists, holding thumbs up)
Thumbs down. (make fists, pointing thumbs down)

Make a little smile. (grin broadly)
Make a little frown. (frown sadly)
Wiggle, clap. (first wiggle fingers, then clap hands)
Wiggle, snap. (wiggle fingers, then snap fingers)
Let them fly (wiggle fingers high above head)
Right to your lap. (flutter fingers slowly into lap).

⭐ *Susan Oldham Hill, Lakeland, FL*

Exercise Away
3+

Materials   none

What to do
1. On the way inside or outside keep the children singing and exercising.
2. Sing the following to the tune of "Mary Had a Little Lamb."

   Merrily we hop along,
   Hop along,
   Hop along,
   Merrily we hop along,
   On our way inside.

3. The word "inside" can be changed to "outside" when going outdoors.
4. Other movements include clapping, shrugging, wiggling, jumping, marching, and reaching.

More to do   **Language**: Children can make up their own verses to "Mary Had a Little Lamb."

Related books   Mother Goose rhyme books, such as the *Best Mother Goose Ever!* by Richard Scarry, *Black Mother Goose Book* by Elizabeth M. Oliver, *The Real Mother Goose* by Blanche Fisher Wright, and *My Very First Mother Goose* by Iona Archibald Opie

⭐ *Monica Hay Cook, Tucson, AZ*

Follow the Leader

3+

Materials   none

What to do

1. It can be a distracting and chaotic time simply moving children down a hallway from one activity to another. Teach them this simple song to help them keep their minds on what they are doing.
2. One day, as you are walking in the hallway, begin to sing this simple song.

   Follow the Leader
   Hanna (or another child's name) *is our leader, our leader, our leader.*
   Hanna is our leader, our leader today.
   Let's follow Hanna, Hanna, Hanna.
   Let's follow Hanna, follow Hanna today.

3. Use the Leader of the Day's name in the song.
4. Choose any familiar tune that you think will fit the words, or make up a tune of your own.
5. If your walk is particularly long, you can add a verse that says something about your destination.

   We're going to the playground, the playground, the playground.
   We're going to the playground, the playground today.

6. Add a fun and spontaneous verse as you go along. For example, if you pass by a room where younger children are playing you can sing:

   Wave to the babies, the babies, the babies.
   Wave to the babies, the babies today.

7. Celebrate your arrival at your destination by adding one last verse:

   We made it to the playground, the playground, the playground
   We made it to the playground, now let's go play!

Related books   *The Boy Who Was Followed Home* by Margaret Mahy
    Follow Me! by Nancy Tafuri

★ *Virginia Jean Herrod, Columbia, SC*

If You're Ready to Go Outside 3+

Materials   none

What to do
1. Sing this to the tune of "If You're Happy and You Know It." It helps children focus by having to repeat your actions, reinforces children's ability to name and identify their body parts, and also refines eye-hand coordination.
2. Adapt the verses to meet the transition time and the developmental needs of the children in your class. Have a child head the group after the class is familiar with the song.

   If you're ready to go outside, tap your head.
   If you're ready to go outside, tap your head.
   If you're ready to go outside, and run and play and hide,
   If you're ready to go outside, tap your head.

   If you're ready to go outside, rub your belly.
   If you're ready to go outside, rub your belly.
   If you're ready to go outside, and run and play and hide,
   If you're ready to go outside, rub your belly.

   If you're ready to go outside, follow me.
   If you're ready to go outside, follow me.
   If you're ready to go outside, and run and play and hide,
   If you're ready to go outside, follow me.

3. Apply this song to different aspects of your curriculum by prompting the children during different transitions throughout the day. For example:

   If you're ready to go eat lunch, _____.
   If you're ready to go eat lunch, _____.
   If you're ready to go eat lunch, and fill your bellies up,
   If you're ready to go eat lunch, _____.

   ★ *Steve Rubin, Waldorf, MD*

Marching Song

3+

Materials   removable colorful dot stickers (optional)

What to do

1. If children are still learning to distinguish their left foot from their right foot, try this song any time you have a few extra moments.
2. Place a removable colored dot sticker on each child's left shoe. Have children line up and practice marching, starting with their left foot.
3. Sing any marching song, such as "When Johnny Comes Marching Home" or "The Ants Go Marching."
4. March to outdoor playtime, around the gym, or between the desks in the classroom.

More to do   **Music and Movement**: Sing and dance "The Hokey Pokey" to practice more left foot-right foot movements.

★ *Christina Chilcote, New Freedom, PA*

The Wiggle Song

3+

Materials   none

What to do

1. To help children settle down, sing the following to the tune of "The Bear Went Over the Mountain."

My fingers are starting to wiggle.
My fingers are starting to wiggle.
My fingers are starting to wiggle
Around, around, around.

My hands are starting to wiggle.
My hands are starting to wiggle.
My hands are starting to wiggle
Around, around, around.

2. Ask the children to name as other parts of the body (in addition to fingers and hands) that come in "pairs," then use the named parts in the song. Continue singing additional verses substituting different body parts for the underlined words. Sing a verse for each "pair" mentioned.

⭐ *Jackie Wright, Enid, OK*

A Circle Is a Shape

3+

Materials   ball
small block
book

What to do   1. Sing this song at group or circle time when you have a few extra moments. It teaches children about shapes.
2. Sit on the floor and begin singing the first verse to let children know it is time to learn shapes!

A Circle Is a Shape (Tune: "The Wheels on the Bus")
The shape of a ball is a big circle (hold up ball)
A big circle, a big circle.
The shape of a ball is a big circle
A circle is a shape.

The shape of a block is a small square, (hold up block)
A small square, a small square.
The shape of a block is a small square,
A square is a shape.

The shape of a book is a rectangle (hold up book)
A rectangle, a rectangle.
The shape of a book is a rectangle.
A rectangle is a shape.

More to do   **Games:** Have the children go on a scavenger hunt for shapes in the classroom. Start with circles, then squares, and so on.

Related book   *Pancakes, Crackers, and Pizza: A Book of Shapes* by Marjorie Eberts and Margaret Gisler

⭐ *Renee Kirchner, Carrollton, TX*

If You're Listening

4+

Materials   none

What to do   1. To capture the children's attention, sing the following song until all the children are playing along.

If you're listening to me touch your head.
If you're listening to me touch your head, touch your foot.
If you're listening to me touch your head, touch your foot, touch your tummy.

2. Continue to add another body part until all children are participating in the song. The children will notice what their friends are doing.
3. This is great to use when talking about the parts of the body or studying senses.

Related books *I Can Tell by Touching* by Carolyn Otto
My Five Senses by Aliki

★ *Sandy L. Scott, Vancouver, WA*

Flashing Fireflies

4+

Materials   5 working flashlights or one flashlight per child
The Very Lonely Firefly by Eric Carle

What to do   1. Talk about how fireflies flash their lights at night.
2. Read *The Very Lonely Firefly* by Eric Carle.
3. Play this subtraction rhyme to transition the children to the next activity. Have each child (or five children at a time) dance with a flashlight.
4. As you say the following rhyme, turn off the lights and invite each child to turn on her flashlight and dance around. When the rhyme is done, touch one dancing firefly. That child stops dancing, turns off the flashlight, and moves on to the next activity.

5. As you finish the rhyme, all children should have transitioned.

Five little fireflies
Dancing in the night.
One went to bed and
Out went the light.

More to do   **Art**: Make fireflies out of construction paper. Use wax paper for the wings and gold glitter for the firefly light, or glow in the dark paint. Do not use glow sticks because they can be dangerous.
Math: After each firefly leaves, count how many are left.
Story Time: Use this rhyme with flannel board fireflies or stick puppets instead.

Related song   (Tune: "I'm a Little Teapot")
I'm a little firefly in the night,
On my back is a special light.
At night I flash my light to say,
"Other fireflies come and play."

Related books   *Daddies Are for Catching Fireflies* by Harriet Ziefert
Sam and Gus Light Up the Night! by P.D. Eastman

⭐ *Sue Fleischmann, Sussex, WI*

Mother Goose Mix-Up

4+

Materials   Mother Goose rhymes

What to do
1. Tell the children that you are going to say a sentence from a Mother Goose rhyme, but one of the words in the rhyme has been switched.
2. After you read the sentence, call on someone to change the word back to the way Mother Goose said it.
3. The child changes the word to fix the rhyme. Then that child can line up for the next activity.
4. Do this until all the children have had a turn.

Mixed-up rhymes:
◆ Old Mac Donald had a ranch.
◆ Mary had a little goat.
◆ This is the house George built.
◆ Rub-a-dub-dub three men in a puddle.
◆ Here we go round the brambleberry bush.
◆ Pat-a-cake, pat-a-cake, shoemaker's son!
◆ This little donkey went to market.
◆ Little Miss Muffet sat on a buffet.

More to do   **Story Time**: Recite the entire rhymes with the children. Try this with fairy tales as well. Children can make up their own rhymes and mixed-up rhymes too.

Related books   Books of Mother Goose rhymes and books of fairy tales (many versions are available)

★ *Monica Hay Cook, Tucson, AZ*

Doggy, Doggy Where's Your Bone?

4+

Materials   large dog biscuit shaped like a bone

What to do
1. Rely on this favorite old children's rhyme to get you through some tough transition times. Have the children sit in a circle with one child in the middle.
2. Place the bone-shaped dog biscuit in front of the child in the middle. Have that child close her eyes.
3. The children chant the following poem.

   Doggy, doggy, where's your bone?
   Somebody's stole it from your home.
   Guess who!
   It might be you!
   It might be monkey from the zoo!

4. While the children are chanting, one child steals the doggy bone from the child in the middle. Have that child conceal the bone somewhere on their person, such as in pant's pocket or under them.
5. On the last line of the poem, the child in the middle opens her eyes. This child has three tries to guess who has the bone.
6. The child with the bone then goes to the middle.
7. Continue until your next activity is ready or it's time to go.

Related books   *The Amazing Bone* by William Steig
Jack, Skinny Bones, and the Golden Pancakes by Marie-Clare Helldorfer

 Virginia Jean Herrod, Columbia, SC

Thumbelina

4+

Materials   washable pens

What to do   1. When you have a few extra moments, draw a tiny face on each child's thumb. Make tiny faces by drawing dots for eyes and nose and a line for a smile.
2. Say or sing the "Thumbelina" song and have the children use their thumb to act out the words.

Related book   *Thumbelina* by Hans Christian Anderson

★ *Barbara Saul, Eureka, CA*

Nursery Rhymes Are Lots of Fun

4+

Materials   none

What to do   1. To capture children's attention, sing the following to the tune of "London Bridge."

Nursery rhymes are lots of fun,
Lots of fun, lots of fun.
Nursery rhymes are lots of fun.
Try to answer.

2. Sing additional verses as long as the children are interested. With each verse, ask the children to wait until you finish the verse and then ask, "Can you tell me?" before they raise their hand to answer.
Note: All verses are written by Jackie Wright.

Additional verses (Tune: "London Bridges"):
Nursery rhymes are lots of fun,
Lots of fun, lots of fun.
Nursery rhymes are lots of fun.
Try to answer.

Who followed her to school one day
School one day, school one day?
Who followed her to school one day?
Can you tell me?
(Mary Had a Little Lamb)

Who jumps over the candlestick,
Candlestick, candlestick?
Who jumps over the candlestick?
Can you tell me?
(Jack Be Nimble)

Who kissed the girls and made them cry
Made them cry, made them cry?
Who kissed the girls and made them cry?
Can you tell me?
(Georgy Porgy)

Who had a wife but couldn't keep her
Couldn't keep her, couldn't keep her
Who had a wife but couldn't keep her
Can you tell me?
(Peter, Peter, Pumpkin-eater)

Who had a great fall off the wall
Off the wall, off the wall?
Who had a great fall off the wall?
Can you tell me?
(Humpty Dumpty)

Who is under the haystack fast asleep
Fast asleep, fast asleep?
Who is under the haystack fast asleep?
Can you tell me?
(Little Boy Blue)

(continued on the next page)

Who lost her sheep and can't find them
Can't find them, can't find them?
Who lost her sheep and can't find them?
Can you tell me?
(Little Bo-Peep)

Who went for water but falls down the hill
Down the hill, down the hill?
Who went for water but falls down the hill?
Can you tell me?
(Jack and Jill)

What is like a diamond in the sky
In the sky, in the sky?
What is like a diamond in the sky?
Can you tell me?
(Twinkle, Twinkle, Little Star)

Who lost their mittens and began to cry
Began to cry, began to cry?
Who lost their mittens and began to cry?
Can you tell me?
(Three Little Kittens)

Who went to town riding on a pony
Riding on a pony, riding on a pony?
Who went to town riding on a pony?
Can you tell me?
(Yankee Doodle)

Whom do you know who's a merry old soul
Merry old soul, merry old soul?
Whom do you know who's a merry old soul?
Can you tell me?
(Old King Cole)

Who met a pieman going to the fair
To the fair, to the fair?
Who met a pieman going to the fair?
Can you tell me?
(Simple Simon)

The GIANT Encyclopedia of Transition Activities

Who lived in a shoe and didn't know what to do
What to do, what to do?
Who lived in a shoe and didn't know what to do?
Can you tell me?
(There Was an Old Woman)

More to do   Work with the children to make up additional verses to the song.

Jackie Wright, Enid, OK

Say Something   4+

Materials   none

What to do
1. Use this transition activity any time you have a few minutes. It's great for developing language skills.
2. Say the following rhyme like you would say the rhyme "Eeny, Meeny, Miney, Moe."

   Eeny, meeny, miney, moe,
   Let's all say something about Joe

3. As you say the rhyme point to each child in turn. When the rhyme ends, make sure you are pointing to the child whose name you used.
4. Have the children take turns saying something about the child.
   Note: Some children might have a hard time thinking of something to say. If a child hesitates, offer a gentle suggestion, such as. "Look at Joe's shirt. What color is it?" When the child says "red," you can say, "So, you can say 'Joe has on a red shirt.'" Never force a child to say something. If a child is too shy to participate, then offer a comment yourself and continue with the game.
5. Say the rhyme again using another child's name. For example:

   Eeny, meeny, miney, mane,
   Let's all say something about Jane

(continued on the next page)

6. Continue until all children have had a turn or you run out of time.

7. If you have a little extra time, sing this familiar song for each child.

Joe has on a red shirt, a red shirt, a red shirt
Joe has on a red shirt, all day long.

Related books *How Do You Say It Today, Jesse Bear?* by Nancy White Carlstrom
Ruby Mae Has Something to Say by David Small
What Do I Say? by Norma Simon

⭐ *Virginia Jean Herrod, Columbia, SC*

Sensory Song

4+

Materials   none

What to do   Between activities, teach the children this simple song to the tune of the Oscar Meyer Weiner song. They can touch their eyes and feet, and wiggle their noses as they sing about the five senses and the parts of their bodies.

Oh, I'm glad I have two eyes for seeing,
Two ears for hearing lots and lots of sounds.
A nose for sniffing and for smelling,
And feet for walking, walking on the ground.

Oh, I'm glad I have two hands for feeling,
Things that are so smooth for me to touch.
And I'm glad I have a mouth for singing,
All about the things I love so much.

⭐ *Susan Oldham Hill, Lakeland, FL*

Cookie Jar

4+

Materials   alphabet cookies (optional)

What to do   1. when you have a few extra moments between activities, have the children sit in a circle. Show them how to pat their thighs and clap their hands. Repeat until they are able to do this. Start the patting rhythm and say the chant.

Teacher: *Who stole the cookie from the cookie jar?*
Teacher: (child's name) *stole the cookie from the cookie jar!*
Child: *Who, me?*
Group: *Yes, you!*
Child: *Couldn't be!*
Group: *Then who?*
Child: (another child's name) *stole the cookie from the cookie jar!*

2. Repeat this until it is time for the next activity, or until everyone has had a turn. When done give children a handful of alphabet crackers to eat.

More to do   **Writing**: Ask children to write their names with alphabet cookies, exchanging letters when necessary.

Related books   *The Doorbell Rang* by Pat Hutchins
If You Give a Mouse a Cookie by Laura Joffe Numeroff

⭐ *Barbara Saul, Eureka, CA*

Sing a Silly Song

4+

Materials   none

What to do   1. If you find yourself waiting as you transition from one activity to another, challenge the children to help you make up some silly songs to familiar tunes.

2. Start by singing something silly to a tune you are sure the children know. For example, sing this song to the tune "Twinkle, Twinkle, Little Star."

   Sprinkle, sprinkle, little rain
   I can't find the mud again.
   I thought it was here and I thought it was there.
   Turns out it's not anywhere.
   Sprinkle, sprinkle, little rain
   Help me find the mud again.

3. Sing the tune again and pause at certain points. Ask the children to fill in where you pause. For example:

   Sprinkle, sprinkle, little rain
   I can't find the (pause)

4. Ask the children to name something to fill in the blank.

5. Continue the song using what the children have suggested. For example:

   I can't find the CHEESE again.
   I thought it was here and I thought it was there
   Turns out it's not anywhere
   Sprinkle, sprinkle, little rain
   Help me find the cheese again

6. Continue until you run out of time or all the children dissolve into a fit of giggles.

7. Additional examples of silly songs are:

   (Tune: "Mary Had a Little Lamb")
   Janie had a little shoe, little shoe, little shoe.
   Janie had a little shoe and didn't know what to do.
   She took it off and put it on, put it on, put it on.
   She took it off and put it on, then threw it on the lawn.

(Tune: "BINGO")
There was a child who liked to sing and SINGO was his name-o
S-I-N-G-O,
S -I-N-G-O,
S -I-N-G-O.
And SINGO was his name-o.
(Or substitute a child's name in this song)

More to do   Choose a familiar tune and sing nonsense words to it. Don't try to sing actual words, just make up sounds to fit the tune. The children will enjoy trying to keep up with you and it will be great fun for all.
Music and Movement: Record your new song and put the tape in the music area of the classroom.
More Music and Movement: Make up a little dance to go along with your song. Everybody dance together!
Story Time: Ask the children to draw illustrations for the songs. Print the words under the pictures. Create a front and back cover and bind the pages together into a cute little book. Use a copier to make a copy for each child.

Related books   *The Cat Who Loved to Sing* by Nonny Hogrogian
The First Song Ever Sung by Laura Krauss Melmed
Foxie the Singing Dog by Ingri D'Aulaire
The Frog Who Wanted to Be a Singer by Linda Goss
Gabriella's Song by Candace Fleming
A Long Long Song by Etienne Delessert
Mama Rocks, Papa Sings by Nancy Van Laan
My Mama Sings by Jeanne Whitehouse Peterson
Roses Sing on New Snow by Paul Yee
Sing, Pierrot, Sing by Tomie dePaola
Song and Dance Man by Karen Ackerman
A Summertime Song by Irene Haas
Waiting to Sing by Howard Kaplan

Virginia Jean Herrod, Columbia, SC

Wheelbarrow

Materials   none

What to do   1. Any time you have a few extra minutes, sing the following to the tune of "The Wheels on the Bus."

The wheel on the wheelbarrow goes round and round,
Round and round, round and round,
The wheel on the wheelbarrow goes round and round,
All around the yard.

Put some dirt in the wheelbarrow
In the wheelbarrow, in the wheelbarrow,
Put some dirt in the wheelbarrow
And push it to the garden.

Pull out weeds and put them in the wheelbarrow,
Put them in the wheelbarrow, put them in the wheelbarrow,
Pull out weeds and put them in the wheelbarrow,
All around the yard.

2. Or, sing this song to the tune of "Frère Jacques."

Push the Wheelbarrow
Push the wheelbarrow, push the wheelbarrow,
Around the yard, around the yard.
Fill it with some dirt now, fill it with some dirt now,
For the garden, for the garden.

Fill the wheelbarrow, fill the wheelbarrow,
Fill it with flowers, fill it with flowers.
Push it to the garden now, push it to the garden now,
Plant, plant, plant. Plant, plant, plant.

Climb in the wheelbarrow, climb in the wheelbarrow,
Can I have a ride? Can I have a ride?
I will sit so still. I will sit so still.
Yes I will. Yes I will.

★ *Mary Brehm, Aurora, OH*

Ten Little Beavers

4+

Materials   paper
markers

What to do   1. This fingerplay is great to use any time you have a few extra minutes.
2. Write the fingerplay on file cards and on a poster for the children to see.
3. Teach the children the motions that go with the fingerplay. Teach them one or two verses a day until they have learned them all.

One little beaver swam near his home.
He dove in the water and called his brother to come.

Two little beavers swam around and around.
They went inside their lodge and another was found.

Three little beavers swimming near the shore,
Another one came and that made four.

Four little beavers jumped in the water for a dive.
Another beaver joined them and that made five.

Five little beavers chewed on some tender sticks.
Another one was behind a tree and that made six.

Six little beavers went swimming once again.
One more was behind a rock and that made seven.

(continued on the next page)

Seven little beavers were feeling just great.
Then another one joined them and that made eight.

Eight little beavers were swimming in a line.
A little baby beaver came and that made nine

Nine little beavers were chewing on a log, and then
Another one splashed the water and that made ten

Ten little beavers swimming and diving in the sun.
They all swam inside their home and that left none.

Related book   *The Beaver at Long Pond* by Lindsay Barrett George

★ *Mary Brehm, Aurora, OH*

The Alphabet Song

4+

Materials   laminated letters of the alphabet

What to do
1. Children enjoy "being the alphabet" as they wait to go somewhere. Give each child a laminated alphabet card. Keep the leftover letters.
2. Have the children sing the alphabet song slowly as they line up with their letters.
3. Be sure to hand out the letters randomly so no one child leads the line every day.

Related songs   "Alphardy" by Dr. Jean, *Sing to Learn* CD
"Boom Chica Boom" by Dr. Jean, *Keep on Singing and Dancing* CD
"ABC Rock" by Greg and Steve, *We All Live Together* Vol. 1
"Marching Around the Alphabet" by Hap Palmer, *Learning Basic Skills Through Music*

Related books   *26 Letters and 99 Cents* by Tana Hoban
Albert's Alphabet by Leslie Tryon
Anno's Alphabet by Mitsumaso Anno

Black and White Rabbit's ABC by Alan Baker
Chicka Chicka Boom Boom by Bill Martin, Jr.
Curious George ABC by H.A. Rey
Farm Alphabet Book by Jane Miller
Victoria's ABC Adventure by Cathy Warren

★ Kaethe Lewandowski, Centreville, VA

Loony Limericks

5+

Materials   none

What to do   Say these limericks when you have a moment with the children. (All limericks are written by Penni L. Smith.)

A cocky cucumber named Billy
Bragged to a cute radish named Millie,
"I'll soon be the star
Of a big pickle jar.
'Cause Farmer thinks I'm just dilly!"

There was a Princess named Dee
Who was no bigger than a flea.
Her prince on the other hand
Was enormous and grand,
And sat on her 'cause she was too tiny to see!

There once was a ghost named Boo
He haunted his house for a shoe.
He would bellow and cry,
But didn't know why
'Cause he never walked, he flew!

(continued on the next page)

There was a girl named Heather,
Who hated the windy weather.
Where e'er it did blow,
Away she would go!
'Cause she was as light as a feather!

There was a robot named Hymie,
Who was British and nicknamed "Lymie."
He was caught in a flood
Got covered with mud,
And now Hymie is all grimy!

There once was a candle named Max
Who believed in facing the facts.
As his time came near,
He cried tear after tear,
Until he was reduced to a pool of wax!

A nincompoop called Nurp
Sat at the table to slurp.
He was served a bird.
No burping was heard,
Now all he can do is chirp!

There once was a bee named Bo
On vacation he decided to go.
He went to Barcelona
Where he met Ramona
A cute little bug with a glow.

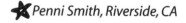 Penni Smith, Riverside, CA

Spelling Numbers

5+

Materials   none

What to do   Sing the following any time you have a few extra minutes to the tune of "The Farmer in the Dell."

O-n-e spells one.
O-n-e spells one.
Heigh-ho, did you know?
O-n-e spells one.

T-w-o spells two.
T-w-o spells two.
Heigh-ho, did you know?
T-w-o spells two.

T-h-r-e-e spells three.
T-h-r-e-e spells three.
Heigh-ho, did you know?
T-h-r-e-e spells three.

F-o-u-r spells four.
F-o-u-r spells four.
Heigh-ho, did you know?
F-o-u-r spells four.

F-i-v-e spells five.
F-i-v-e spells five.
Heigh-ho, did you know?
F-i-v-e spells five.

S-i-x spells six.
S-i-x spells six.
Heigh-ho, did you know?
S-i-x spells six.

S-e-v-e-n spells seven.
S-e-v-e-n spells seven.
Heigh-ho, did you know?
S-e-v-e-n spells seven.

E-i-g-h-t spells eight.
E-i-g-h-t spells eight.
Heigh-ho, did you know?
E-i-g-h-t spells eight.

N-i-n-e spells nine.
N-i-n-e spells nine.
Heigh-ho, did you know?
N-i-n-e spells nine.

T-e-n spells ten.
T-e-n spells ten.
Heigh-ho, did you know?
T-e-n spells ten.

More to do   **Story Time:** Make a class big book using the above song as the text.

⭐ *Jackie Wright, Enid, OK*

Count With the Inchworm

5+

Materials washable fine-point markers or ballpoint pens

What to do

Author's Note: If you do not know the words to the song, "Inchworm," they are available on the Internet.

1. Try this activity any time during the day when you have a few extra minutes.
2. The children can use markers or pens to draw a simple smiley face on the tip of their index finger.
3. Use the beginning of the song to do actual simple math problems, for example, 1+1=2, 1+2=3, 1+3=4, and other simple problems, using visuals such as a blackboard, flashcards, and other props.
4. The children follow your example and crawl their "inchworm" (their index finger) over various parts of their body (hand, wrist, arm elbow, shoulder)

More to do **Dramatic Play**: Children can use cut-off glove fingers and felt-tipped markers to make an inchworm finger puppet.

More to do *The Very Hungry Caterpillar* by Eric Carle
The Very Quiet Cricket by Eric Carle

★ *Christina Chilcote, New Freedom, PA*

Cookie Jar Name Game

3+

Materials   *Who Stole the Cookie From the Cookie Jar?* (use your favorite version)

What to do

1. When you have to wait for a few minutes, have the children sit in a circle. Read the book to the children and teach them the following chant.

Who stole the cookies from the cookie jar?
(name) stole the cookies from the cookie jar!
Who me?
Yes, you!
Couldn't be!
Then who?

2. Start the chant by naming one child in the circle. That child answers the question, "Then who?" by naming the child next to him.
3. Begin the chant again with that child's name, and he supplies the name of the next child, and so on.
4. At the end of the chant, have the guilty cookie stealer be you, the class pet, or a puppet.

More to do   **Cooking:** Bake cookies with the class.
Games: Play the popcorn name game. In a singsong chant, say, "(child's name) pop up, (child's name) pop down." Everyone claps on the syllables "pop up" and "pop down." Use each child's name.
Math: Make a chart of the children's favorite cookies.

Sandra Gratias, Perkasie, PA

"Rig a Jig Jig"

3+

Materials   none

What to do
1. Have the class sit in a circle on the floor. Choose one child to walk around the circle.
2. That child walks around the circle and then chooses a friend to skip around the circle with as everyone sings the following song, "Rig a Jig Jig."

   As_____ was walking down the street, down the street, down the street,
   A friend of his he chanced to meet, hi ho hi ho hi ho!
   Rig a jig jig and away they go, away they go, away they go,
   Rig a jig jig and away they go, hi ho hi ho hi ho!

3. After the song, the first child sits down and the second walks around the circle once, and then chooses a friend to skip around the circle while you all sing the song.
4. Continue until it is time for the next activity or until everyone has had a turn.

★ *Jackie Wright, Enid, OK*

Birds Fly

3+

Materials   none

What to do
1. When the children are waiting for the next activity, try this game to help pass the time.
2. Ask the children to stand and face you. Show them how to flap their arms at their sides like wings. Tell them to listen carefully to your words. If you name something that can fly, they should flap their wings. If you name something that cannot fly, they should keep their arms still.
3. If desired, play a variation called "Fish Swim," using a swimming motion. For example, say, "Dolphins swim (yes), kangaroos swim (not), goldfish swim (yes), whales swim (yes), sharks swim (yes), pigs swim (no), manatees swim (yes), jellyfish swim (yes), cows swim (no), and so on.

More to do **Books:** Read a picture book about birds or fish.

Susan A. Sharkey, La Mesa, CA

Clap the Parts 3+

Materials colored pictures of familiar objects, labeled

What to do
1. Hold up a picture and ask the class to clap the parts (syllables) in each picture. Sort the pictures by one, two, three, and four syllables.
   Author's Note: Two wonderful sources of colored pictures on the Internet are www.Kidzclub.com and www.PBS.org.
2. This excellent transition activity can be done at circle or group time, or any time during the day. If pictures aren't available, simply say the words aloud and have the children clap the syllables.

Jackie Wright, Enid, OK

"Pass Some Love" Game 3+

Materials paper heart

What to do
1. Play this short-but-sweet transition game on Valentine's Day or any time.
2. Sit in a circle with the children.
3. Hold up a paper heart and say, "I love (child sitting next to you) because..." and say something nice about him.
4. Pass the heart to that child, who does the same. Continue until everyone has said something caring and nice about the person next to him.

Jackie Wright, Enid, OK

Dinosaur Game

3+

Materials   dinosaur counters, one less than the number of children in the class

What to do
1. Any time you have a few extra moments, try the following game.
2. Seat the children in a circle on the floor. Select one child to be a dinosaur who marches around the outside of the circle.
3. Pass out dinosaur counters to the seated children. Ask the children to put the dinosaur counters on the floor behind them. The "dinosaur" marches around clockwise, and everyone sings the following to the tune of "This Old Man."

   Dinosaurs, they had fun.
   They made footprints one by one.
   With a boom-boom-boom and a stomp-stomp-stomp
   They all marched around the swamp!

4. The dinosaur picks a dinosaur counter behind one of the children. The chosen child marches around the circle behind the "dinosaur" to catch him before he reaches the empty spot in the circle, like the game "Duck, Duck, Goose."
5. If he doesn't catch the "dinosaur," the game continues. If he does, he becomes the "dinosaur."
6. Continue as time permits until each child has a turn as the "dinosaur."

 *Jackie Wright, Enid, OK*

Hula Hoop Sort

3+

Materials   2 hula hoops

What to do
1. Put two hula hoops on the ground.
2. Tell the children what the sorting rule is. "This hoop is for children with white shoes. This hoop is for children with black shoes."

3. Have all of the children with white shoes stand in the white shoe hoop. All the children with black shoes stand in the other hoop. If there are too many children to fit into the hoop, have them stand with one foot inside the hoop.
4. Sort children by other characteristics, such as age, color or style of clothing, types of shoes, hairstyles, types of pets, and brothers or sisters.
5. Overlap the hoops to make a third category for those who meet both criteria.
6. Dismiss the children in one hoop to go to the next activity.

More to do **Art**: Give each child two paper plates. Let them decorate the plates with sorted colors or shapes.
Math: Play "Guess the Rule." Sort children into groups and let them guess the sorting rule.

Related books *Alligator Shoes* by Arthur Dorros
The Button Box by Margaret S. Reid
Sorting by Henry Pluckrose

★*Cassandra Reigel Whetstone, San Jose, CA*

Letter Game

3+

Materials envelopes
set of alphabet cards (one per envelope)

What to do 1. To prepare, write one child's name on each envelope, and put one alphabet letter card in each envelope.
2. To fill a few extra moments, or any time during the day, sing or chant, "_____'s got a letter, a letter, a letter. _____'s has a letter, I wonder what it is."
3. The child you named comes up for his envelope and opens it to show and name the letter.

★*Regina Smith, Charlotte, NC*

Match-the-Photo Game

3+

Materials photographs of the children

What to do
1. Develop double prints of photographs of the children in various activities indoors and outdoors.
2. Play this transition game any time during the day.
3. Place the photographs face down on the floor in a grid pattern.
4. The children take turns turning over two photographs at a time, looking for a match. If they do not match, they place them back face down in the same place. Continue to do this until all photographs are matched up.

More to do Attach Velcro to the backs of the photographs. Attach one set of photographs to a wall, easel, or game board with Velcro. Place the second set in a folder, box, or apron pockets. The children take turns pulling out a photo and matching it to the ones displayed. The children enjoy seeing themselves in the photographs and recalling the various activities.

★ *Judy Fujawa, The Villages, FL*

Name It

3+

Materials whiteboard and marker, chalkboard and chalk, or easel paper and marker

What to do
1. Try this quick-and-easy transition activity any time you have a few extra minutes to fill.
2. Name a category, such as animals, books, or cereal.
3. Tell the children to call out the names of things that belong in the category. Mark a tally on the board for each different item they identified.
4. At the end of the game, count the tallies. Print and circle the total number on the board and praise them for their score.

★ *Susan A. Sharkey, La Mesa, CA*

Me Puzzles

3+

Materials
35 mm or digital camera
computer and printer or access to a photo developer
card stock paper
glue stick and scissors
quart-size zipper-closure bags
permanent markers

PHOTO PRINTED ON CARDSTOCK

LARGE PUZZLE PIECES

ZIP BAG

Abbie

CHILD'S NAME

PUZZLE PIECES

What to do
1. Take a photo of each child alone. Print the photos on card stock paper or have them developed in 8" x 10" size. If using developed photos, glue them to the card stock paper.
2. Cut the photos apart into puzzle-type pieces. Remember to keep the pieces large so the puzzle is easy to do.
3. Print the child's name on the zippered bag. Store each Me Puzzle in a separate bag.
4. Give the puzzles to the children whenever they need to keep busy for a few minutes.

(continued on the next page)

Black, White, Just Right! by Marguerite Davol
Luap by June Rachuy Brindel
A Rainbow of Friends by P.K. Hallinan
What Am I? by N.N. Charles
Which Is Willy? by Robert Bright

Related song   **I'm Glad I'm Me!** (Tune: "If You're Happy and You Know It")
I'm glad I'm me, so I'll clap my hands!
I'm glad I'm me, so I'll clap my hands!
I'm so glad to be the one and only me!
I'm glad I'm me, so I'll clap my hands!

I'm glad I'm me, so I'll stomp my feet!
I'm glad I'm me, so I'll stomp my feet!
I'm so glad to be the one and only me!
I'm glad I'm me, so I'll stomp my feet!

⭐*Virginia Jean Herrod, Columbia, SC*

Officer, Where Is My Child?   3+

Materials   none

What to do
1. This reinforces critical thinking and the importance of learning classmates' names. Gather children on the floor.
2. Have one child stand next to you and pretend to be the police officer.
3. Pretend you are a parent who cannot find your child. Say, "Officer, can you help me? I was at the playground playing with my child and now I can't find him!"
4. Give a description of a child in the classroom. Let the "officer" try to identify this child by name, or introduce the child after he is found. When a child is "found," dismiss that child to the next activity.
5. If time allows, let the "found" child have a turn at being the "officer." Play until all the children have had a turn. Let the last person be the co-teacher or aide instead of a child.
   Note: When describing where the child got "lost," vary the location (taking a

walk, playing in the yard, visiting the zoo, playing at a park, swimming at the pool, shopping at the store, and so on).

More to do   **Home-to-School Connection:** Send a letter home to parents asking them to teach their children their address and phone number. Create a bulletin board with large pictures of a phone and a house. Write the names of the children inside the phone button spaces and house windows as they learn this information.
Social Development: Discuss stranger safety and the importance of going to a safe person for help.
Story Time: Look at pictures and read books about police officers.

⭐ *Sandra Gratias, Perkasie, PA*

Transition Cube

3+

Materials   milk or juice cartons
scissors
paper or packing material
tape, preferable masking tape
markers

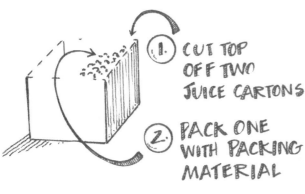

1. CUT TOP OFF TWO JUICE CARTONS
2. PACK ONE WITH PACKING MATERIAL
3. SLIDE SECOND CARTON DOWN OVER TOP

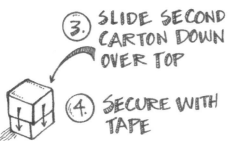

4. SECURE WITH TAPE

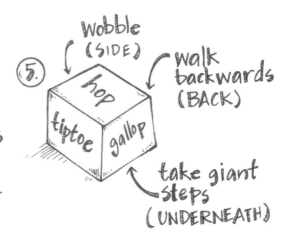

5.
Wobble (SIDE)
walk backwards (BACK)
hop
tiptoe
gallop
take giant steps (UNDERNEATH)

(continued on the next page)

What to do

1. For this activity make one or more cubes, each with six activities or participation options.

2. Start with clean, dry milk or juice cartons. You will need two cartons of the same size for each cube. Cut the cartons to make them as square as possible and the same size. Pack one carton with paper or packing materials to give it greater strength and stability. Then, slide the other carton over the top of the first carton. This will create a six-sided cube. Secure the cartons with tape, covering the writing on the cartons. Attach stickers with activities or write on the sides with markers.

3. On one cube write or draw ways to move from one location to another, such as tiptoe, wobble, hop, gallop, walk backwards, and take giant steps. Roll this cube and the children move that way to the next activity.

4. On another cube, put one color of paper (or write a color word) on each side of the cube, and use it to practice colors as the children transition to another activity. If a red is rolled, all the children wearing red go to the next activity.

5. Make a set of two cubes, one with numbers and another with specific activities. If you need a transition activity during circle time, roll the dice (two cubes) and the child (or children) must do a simple task a certain number of times. For example, if the number cube has the numbers 6 through 11, and the other cube has six movements—snap your fingers, clap your hands, tap the floor with your right hand, tap the floor with the left hand, make two fists and pound them together, and touch your elbows to the floor. Roll both cubes to determine a movement and the number of repetitions.

6. You can make a cube that has the classroom centers on it. The children roll the cube to determine where they go next.

7. Use another cube to select fingerplays, or songs for the group to enjoy.
   Author's Note: Having several cubes with a variety of activities will enable you to use this idea throughout your program. Consider how it could be used to direct children as they head outside to explore the play area, as a group transition, or as a way to redirect a wandering child. Other cubes might contain job duties, cleanup direction, or motor activities.

Bev Schumacher, Racine, WI

Lining Up—Where to Stand

3+

Materials   colorful plastic electrical tape
clear contact paper
paper and scissors or pre-cut shapes

What to do
1. While waiting for a drink at the water fountain: Place a line of tape 10" to 12" from the water fountain and continue placing the strips of tape at approximately 10" intervals. It may require more or less space between the lines depending on the space available and the number of children in your class. The children line up on the tape lines, one child on each tape line. This helps them organize their bodies in the space.
2. While waiting to leave the room: Place cutouts of footprints on a tiled flooring area. (It helps to put a little glue on the back of the footprints to hold them in place.) Unroll a length of clear contact paper and place it over the footprints and the space. (Make sure the flooring is as clean as possible prior to placing down the contact paper. It helps to have two people place the contact paper down to avoid air bubbles.)
Note: A simple version is to place a wide strip of tape on the floor. Place stickers where the children can stand. Or use name tag stickers on a tile floor.

More to do
Art: Have the children make footprints by painting their feet with fingerpaint and making prints of their feet. Make two sets of prints, one to keep and put down on the classroom floor and one for the child to take home. It is fun to use a variety of colors. Cut them out and place them on the floor with the contact paper.
Literacy: Read *The Line Up Book* by Marisabina Russo, and then let the children practice lining up toy figures.
Math: Print numerals on the footprint sets for number recognition practice. The children can say, "I am standing on the red feet." "I am standing on number 4." This encourages cognitive skills as well as language and communication skills.

⭐ *Sandra Nagel, White Lake, MI*

Who Am I Thinking Of?

`3+`

Materials   none

What to do
1. During those inevitable times when waiting is necessary, play this simple game.
2. Tell the children that you are thinking about one of them and want them to guess who.
3. Give hints about the child you are thinking of. For instance, you can say, "I'm thinking of a person who has brown hair" or "This person likes to play with the trucks in the block area."
4. Give the children time to guess who you are thinking about. Congratulate the children on their great deductive skills.
5. Continue until all children have had a turn or it's time to move on to your next activity.

More to do   For older children, make the game more difficult by giving more abstract hints such as "This person's mother's name is _____."
Art and Language: Ask the children make a self-portrait and then ask them to describe themselves. Print what they say on a separate paper and display with the pictures.

Related books   *A My Name Is Alice* by Jane Bayer
Julius, the Baby of the World by Kevin Henkes
Just Me by Marie Hall Ets

⭐*Virginia Jean Herrod, Columbia, SC*

Around the Room

4+

Materials

shape, color, number, or alphabet cards or wall displays

What to do

1. To help pass time when children are waiting for the next activity, try this activity.
2. Choose a concept to practice identifying (shape, color, number, or letter).
3. Take turns calling each child's name and pointing to or holding up a flash card of the shape (or color, etc.) for him to identify. If time allows, continue until each child has had a few turns.

More to do

Expand the concepts as the year progresses by adding more challenging concepts, such as reciting nursery rhymes using pictures or counting items and finding the corresponding number. Or, choose a child to call names and point to the shapes.

★ *Donna Austin, Leighton, PA*

Beginning Sounds Wheel Game

4+

Materials

pictures of objects depicting beginning sounds
markers
card stock or poster board
scissors
glue
two brad paper fasteners

What to do

1. Make this beginning sounds wheel game to keep children busy during transition and waiting times.
2. Cut a piece of card stock or poster board into an 8 ½" x 5" rectangle. Cut out a 1" x 1" square from the middle of each 5" side to make "windows" (see illustration on the next page).

(continued on the next page)

3. Cut out two 5" circles to make the wheels.
4. Be sure to attach pictures to the wheel going in the right direction, or they could appear upside down.
5. Use a marker to write the sounds of the letters on the second wheel.
6. Attach the wheels to the front with brads so that the pictures are exposed one at a time as the wheel is turned.
7. The child turns the left and right wheels to match the picture to the correct letter.

★Jackie Wright, Enid, OK

Button, Button

4+

Materials   assorted buttons

What to do   1. Practice describing items by showing the children how to tell the object's size, color, shape, texture, material, thickness, use, and any other attributes.
2. When there is a little time between activities, teach the children this simple rhyme.

Button, button, in my hand,
How do you look?
I'll tell you if I can!

3. Give the children a button to pass around from child to child while the group repeats the button rhyme. When the rhyme ends, ask the person holding the button to describe one attribute of the button, such as, "It's round," or, "It's blue."
4. Repeat the rhyme as the children continue passing the button around the group. When the chanting stops again, ask that child to give a different attribute to describe the button.
5. Continue until most of the describing words have been used. Then choose a different button to pass around.

Related books   *Corduroy* by Don Freeman
My Five Senses by Aliki

★Susan Oldham Hill, Lakeland, FL

Chairs for Bears

4+

Materials

10" x 15" box lid

20 bottle caps (from soda or water bottles), five each of the following colors: green, yellow, blue, and red

20 plastic sorting bears, five each of the following colors: green, yellow, blue, and red

hot glue gun (adult only)

gallon-size zipper-closure bag

What to do

1. Any time you have a few minutes to spare is a good time for this interesting matching game.
2. Prepare this game by attaching a set of 20 bottle caps to the box lid using the hot glue gun (adult only). Choose random placement or make a pattern. The box lids become the chairs for the plastic bears. Place a box lid and twenty plastic sorting bears in the gallon-size plastic zippered bag. (Make one for the class or one for each child.)
3. During transition times when you need to occupy little minds, give a child the bag with the Chairs for Bears activity inside.
4. Encourage the child to explore the materials on his own. Encourage the child to match the bears to the same colored chair.
5. The children can sort the bears by colors or make a pattern by lining them up on a table.

Related books *Bears in Pairs* by Niki Yektai

Do Baby Bears Sit in Chairs? by Ethel Kessler

Teddy Bears 1 to 10 by Susanna Gretz

When the Teddy Bears Came by Martin Waddell

Related song **Ten Little Teddy Bears** (Tune: "Little Red Wagon")

One little, two little, three little teddy bears

Four little, five little, six little teddy bears,

Seven little, eight little, nine little teddy bears

Ten teddy bears all sitting in chairs.

⭐ *Virginia Jean Herrod, Columbia, SC*

I Spy!

Materials   farm animal play pieces
graph mat
binoculars or magnifying glass

What to do
1. Try this quick-and-easy transition activity any time during the day when you have a few extra moments.
2. Gather some farm animal play pieces, a pair of child's binoculars or a magnifying glass, and a graph mat.
3. Ask children to find animals and place them on the graph mat. The children take turns "spying" an animal with the binoculars or magnifying glass and placing it on the graph mat.
4. Talk about how many are in each column or row.
5. This activity helps with categorization, taking turns, and graphing, and it is fun at the same time.
   Author's Note: You can make your own graph on a computer by creating a table of the desired size and printing it on poster board.

⭐ *Jackie Wright, Enid, OK*

Pass It

Materials   basket of selected items (see below)

What to do
1. Play this game when you have a few extra moments any time during the day.
2. Select an assortment of objects that have specific qualities. For example, choose a river rock (smooth), an ice cube (cold), silly putty (squishy), an aluminum foil ball (shiny), and an apple (red). Place them in a basket.
3. Give the children one object, for example, the river rock, and ask them to pass it around. Say, "Can you name something else that is smooth?"
4. The children pass the object around the circle and name items that have the same quality as the one they are holding.

(continued on the next page)

5. A variation is to name objects in the room that have the same characteristics as the one being passed around.

⭐ *Susan A. Sharkey, La Mesa, CA*

Putting the Pieces Together   4+

Materials   large floor puzzle

What to do
1. Try this game for transitions when you have some extra time to fill between group time and another activity.
2. Talk to the children about the importance of working together and cooperating.
3. Introduce the floor puzzle. Look at the picture of the puzzle, what colors are together, and the shape of the puzzle.
4. Give each child a piece. Ask each child to study his piece and think about where it might go. For example, does the puzzle piece have a flat side? Then it may go on the outside edge of the puzzle. Encourage the children to compare with each other and talk about their piece
5. Start by putting down two or more pieces, seeing if they match, and talking again abut the color, shape, and so on.
6. Look at the box picture. Ask, "Where do you think this piece fits?" Call for certain pieces. "Who has a piece with letters on it?" Invite that child to try his piece. After starting, sit back and let the children interact and do the puzzle, commenting and helping when needed to keep the activity going. "You knew the flat side was for the outside part." "Turn it around and try again." "You worked hard to find the right spot!"

Author's Note: I find more children choose puzzles after working them cooperatively (Vygotsky's theory on Zone of Proximal Development is at work here!). This activity also fills some time on a slow or rainy day.

Related book   *The Crayon Box That Talked* by Shane Derolf

⭐ *Tracie O'Hara, Charlotte, NC*

The Rhyming Game

4+

Materials   card stock or poster board
markers
laminator, optional
scissors
container

What to do
1. Make up riddles for a rhyming game to use when you are between activities or have to wait.
2. Start each riddle with "It rhymes with _____." Give a short clue. For example, "It rhymes with sunny. When something makes you laugh, it is _____."
3. Print these on card stock or poster board.
4. Laminate each riddle card for durability, if desired.
5. Trim the cards and place them in an appropriate container.
6. To play, select a card, read it aloud, and choose a child to give an answer.

 *Jackie Wright, Enid, OK*

Sight Word Wheel Game

4+

Materials   pictures of simple sight word objects
marker
card stock or poster board
scissors
glue
2 brad paper fasteners

What to do
1. Make your own sight word wheel game to keep children busy during transition and waiting times.
2. Make an 8 ½" x 5" shape from paper, and cut a 1" x 1" area from the middle of each 5" side. Make two 5" diameter circle "wheels" from paper (see page 64).
3. Attach the pictures on one wheel and write words on the other so that they will appear right-side-up in the windows as the children turn the wheels.

(continued on the next page)

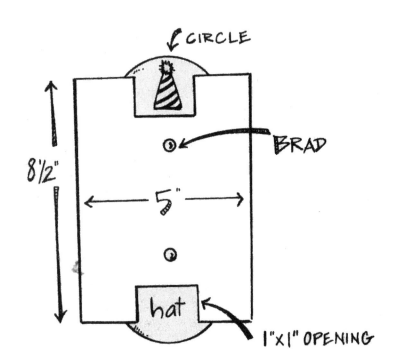

4. Attach the wheels to the back with the brads so that the pictures are exposed one at a time as the wheel is turned.

5. The child turns the left and right wheels and matches the sight words to their picture.

⭐ *Jackie Wright, Enid, OK*

The Listening Game

Materials none

What to do
1. This is a good five-minute time filler that also strengthens children's listening skills.
2. While sitting together on the floor, choose one child to be the first "contestant."
3. Give him a three-step instruction. As the year progresses, add additional steps depending on the children's skills. An example of a four-step instruction: "Susie, I want you to go get a baby doll. Then I want you to give it to Jose, and then you can get an orange crayon from the art center, and sit down."
4. This continues for as long as the children are interested, or until it is time for the next activity.

★ *Jodi Sykes, Lake Worth, FL*

Weather Charades

Materials pictures of different types of weather
glue
poster board
laminator or clear contact paper
container for cards

What to do
1. Locate pictures of different types of weather. Sources include magazines, catalogs, and the Internet.
2. Glue the weather pictures on poster board. Laminate for durability.
3. Cut around the cards and store in an appropriate container.
4. When you have a few extra moments any time during the day, play the game. Place the cards face down on the floor.
5. Have one child draw a card and act out how he would react in that type of weather, or he may pretend to be the weather. This child is not allowed to talk or give hints.

(continued on the next page)

6. The other children guess the weather from the child's actions.
7. Continue the game until it is time for the next activity, or until all children have had a turn.

⭐ *Jackie Wright, Enid, OK*

Twenty Questions

4+

Materials

box with a lid
wrapping paper
tape
small item

WRAPPED LID and BOX

LITTLE PUMPKIN INSIDE

What to do

1. Use this activity whenever you have a few extra minutes before the next activity.
2. To prepare, wrap a box and lid separately so the box can be used again.
3. Put a small item in the box. This might be seasonal item, such as a leaf or an apple.
4. Tell the children that they have twenty questions to ask that will help them figure out what is in the box. Whether or not the children guess the item, take it out of the box after the 20 questions.
5. Pick a child each week to find something to put in the box, and that child can lead the 20 questions.

More to do

Literacy: Ask children to bring something in that starts with a particular letter of the alphabet to put in the box.

⭐ *Barbara Saul, Eureka, CA*

"What If...?"

4+

Materials   none

What to do
1. Play this game.
2. Start by sharing a few examples:

   ◆ What if it rained marshmallows?
   ◆ What if lemonade came out of your faucets?
   ◆ What if peanut butter oozed out of toothpaste tubes?
   ◆ What if cereal danced in your breakfast bowl?

3. Try these "silly starters." Encourage the children to be creative, inventive, and unique in the ideas that they share. If time allows, the children could make drawings of their ideas.

★ *Judy Fujawa, The Villages, FL*

What's Missing?

4+

Materials   four or five different small toys
handkerchief or bandana

What to do
1. Here's a quick and fun game that you can play any time you find yourself waiting for a few minutes.
2. Line the small toys up on a table.
3. Give the children time to look at the toys and then cover the toys with the handkerchief or bandana.
4. Without the children seeing, remove one toy from the group and hide it.
5. Lift the handkerchief or bandana. Ask the children which toy is missing.
6. Offer hints if the children have difficulty guessing.

★ *Virginia Jean Herrod, Columbia, SC*

The Opposite Game

4+

Materials   none

What to do
1. Tell the children that you are going to give directions and they must do the opposite of what you say. Some examples of this are: stand/sit, pat top of the head\pat feet, hold up left hand/hold up right hand, pat your tummy/pat your back, touch the front of your hand/touch the back of your hand.
2. Use this game whenever there are a few free minutes in the day.

Barbara Saul, Eureka, CA

Whose Feet? Wheel Game

4+

Materials   pictures of animal faces and their feet
card stock or poster board
scissors
glue
2 brad paper fasteners

What to do
1. Make a "Whose Feet?" wheel to keep children busy during transition and waiting times.
2. Make an 8 ½" x 5" shape from paper, and cut a 1" x 1" area from the middle of each 5" side. Make two 5" diameter circle "wheels" from paper.
3. Attach animal pictures around one wheel, and the foot pictures on the other. Use the brads to attach the wheels to the back of the main piece of paper, so that a picture is visible in the cutout area on each side. The children can spin the wheels, look at the animals and feet that they see in the 1" x 1" cutout on each side, and match the animals to their feet.

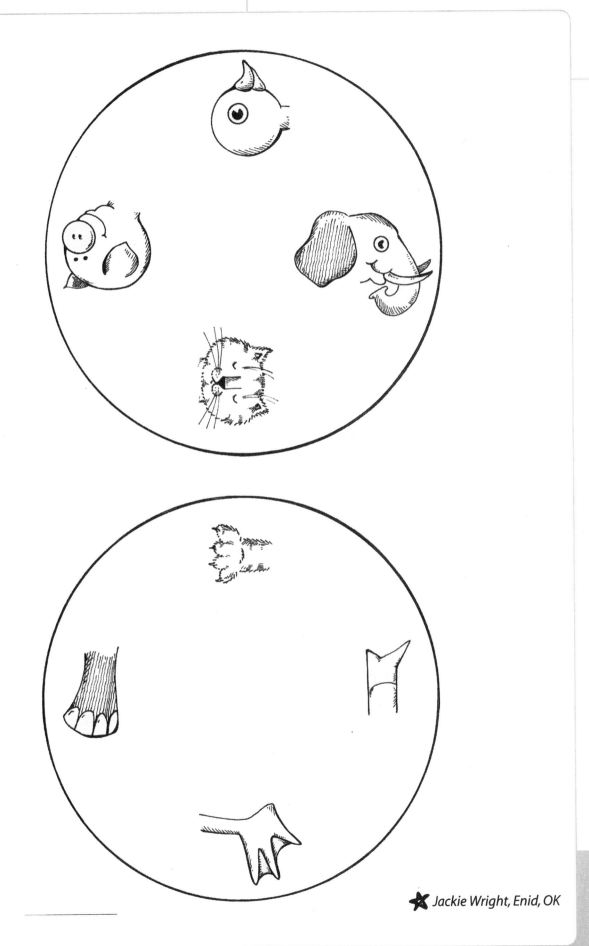

⭐ *Jackie Wright, Enid, OK*

Remote Control

4+

Materials
remote control (actual device or imaginary one, such as a block or a chalkboard eraser)

What to do

1. This is a great game to play when children have been sitting for a while and they need to spend some energy. Ask the children to stand and stretch. Point the remote toward the children, press a button and begin calling out the following commands.
2. Say, "Play" and the children walk around the room. Say, "Fast forward" and the children move quickly. Say, "Pause" and the children freeze in place. Say, "Rewind" and the children walk backwards. Say, "Stop" and the game ends, and the children go to a new activity or return to the original activity.

More to do
Gross Motor: Make this game more challenging by assigning numbers to different movements and "changing channels." Demonstrate and practice matching the numbers and movements with the children. For example, 2: stretch arms outward and twist from side to side; 4: hop on one foot; 6: touch toes; 8: jumping jacks; 10: squat thrusts. Then, change the channels between commands. For example, "Play! Channel 10! Pause! Channel 2! Channel 6! Rewind! Channel 4! Pause! Channel 8! Stop!"

★ *Susan A. Sharkey, La Mesa, CA*

My Name Starts With "M"

4+

Materials
alphabet cards
container

What to do

1. Place alphabet cards in a container. When there is time before lunch or outdoor play, ask a child to draw an alphabet card from the container. Then, ask all the children whose names begin with that letter to stand up. Count the ones who are standing and ask them to sit down again.

2. Repeat with other letters as time allows. Point out that for some letters, no children will stand because there are no children in the class whose names begin with that letter. Discuss the meaning of zero. Chart your results.

More to do   **Math:** Bring out numeral cards and match the numeral to the number of children standing. Chart the results.

Related book   *Dr. Seuss's ABC* by Dr. Seuss

⭐ *Susan Oldham Hill, Lakeland, FL*

Nursery Rhyme Riddles   4+

Materials
card stock
markers
laminator, optional
scissors
container for cards

What to do
1. Make a set of cards (or print out a set from a computer) with riddles about various nursery rhyme characters. For example, write, "I went to school, and my lamb followed me. Who am I?" (Mary). Or, "We went to fetch water and fell down the hill. Who are we?" (Jack and Jill).
2. Laminate the cards for durability, if desired.
3. Cut around the cards and place them in a suitable container.
4. When you are ready for group play, select one card and read it to the children.
5. Ask the children to stand up if they know the answer, and then dismiss them to the next activity.

⭐ *Jackie Wright, Enid, OK*

What Am I?

4+

Materials

card stock
markers
laminator, optional
scissors
container for cards

What to do

1. Write "What Am I?" cards with facts or riddles about different animals. For example, one might read, "I am big and heavy. I have a long nose that I use to pick up food. What am I?" (an elephant). Animal riddles can be found in books and on the Internet.
2. Laminate the cards for durability, if possible.
3. Cut around the cards and place them in a suitable container.
4. Ask the children to raise their hand if they know the answer. After they answer, dismiss them to the next activity.

More to do

Literacy: Read *Walk the Dog* by Bob Barner. The colorful collage illustrations show dogs for each letter of the alphabet. Facts about the breeds are listed in the back of the book. You can make "What Am I?" cards using these facts.

★ *Jackie Wright, Enid, OK*

Go-Togethers

4+

Materials

catalogs and magazines
scissors
construction paper
glue
hole punch
yarn

What to do

1. This quiet activity is great for any transition time during the day.
2. Explain to the children they are to look for items that go together, such as

toothbrush and toothpaste, paintbrush and can of paint, comb and hairbrush, umbrella and rain boots.

3. Give the children catalogs and magazines to look for pictures that go together.
4. Ask them to cut the pictures out and glue each separate picture on a piece of construction paper.
5. Punch a hole in the top two corners of the paper. Cut string or yarn to length. String the yarn through each hole and tie a knot.
6. Each child gets one picture to hang around his neck.
7. Have the children move around the room. When they find the item that goes with theirs, they partner up.
8. Partners move together to next activity.

★ *Monica Hay Cook, Tucson, AZ*

Button Math

4+

Materials
1 plastic lid from a five-gallon ice cream container
8 plastic lids from yogurt snacks
1 small plastic cup
plastic stick-on numbers (1 to 8)
hot glue gun (adult only)
36 assorted buttons
gallon-size zipper-closure bag

What to do
1. Here's an easy activity that you can bring out at any time to enrich children's minds and entertain hands for a few minutes.
2. Hot glue (adult only) the small lids around the inside edge of the large lid. Hot glue (adult only) the small cup to the center of the large lid.
3. Place one number on each small lid, placing the 1 at the top of the circle of lids and continuing clockwise from there. Store everything in a plastic bag.
4. When there are times the children must wait, bring out these bags and some buttons. Give one bag to each child. Let the children experiment with the materials in the bag.
5. Point out the numbers on each lid. Ask the child, "What number do you think this is?"
6. After the child answers, say "So, how many buttons do you think you should put in this lid?"

(continued on the next page)

More to do   Let the children use their Button Math Bags during center time.

Related books   *Buster Loves Buttons!* by Fran Manushkin
Buttons by Brock Cole
Half a Button by Lyn Littlefield Hoopes
I Like Your Buttons! by Sarah Marwil Lamstein

Related song   **Little Buttons Song** (Tune: "Little Red Wagon")
One little, two little, three little buttons
Four little, Five little, round little buttons
Six little, Seven little, cute little buttons
Eight buttons in a row.

★*Virginia Jean Herrod, Columbia, SC*

Find a Match

5+

Materials   small pieces of paper
pen or pencil
safety pins

What to do   1. When you have a few extra moments or when you want to create pairs of children for an activity, try the following game.
2. In advance, separate pieces of paper into two equal piles. Write a different word on each piece of paper in the first pile. These could be words relating to a specific subject, words from a theme selected at random, or maybe words from a story the class has read.
3. Write the same words on the paper in the second pile.
4. Have the children line up or stand where they are and keep their eyes tightly shut. Pin a piece of paper to each child's chest.
5. Ask the class to open their eyes and when you give the signal ("go"), they try and find the other person in the class whose word is the same as theirs.
6. As a variation, you could use numbers or pictures instead of words. Again, these could relate to other subjects or themes appropriate to your group.

More to do **Social Development:** This game is a great way of getting the children into pairs for other activities, especially if you want them to mix with classmates they wouldn't elect to partner if choosing for themselves. You can engineer the pairings within a class; for example, partnering a child who's very physically able with one less confident for a gym activity.

Related book *The Scrambled States of America* by Laurie Keller

★ *Kirsty Neale, Charleville Circus, London, United Kingdom*

Last Name Game

5+

Materials word card or small seasonal shape with each child's first and last name on it, in a pocket chart or on the classroom wall

What to do
1. This silly transition activity helps children learn they have a first and last name. Knowing this is extremely important. Print children's names on a seasonal shape and tape it on the class tree. This activity can be done with the children's names on word cards in a pocket chart too. On the other side, print the name again with photo of child so they can practice any time or learn the names of the children.
   Note: Children can learn to say both first and last names, but when recognizing it in print, start with only the first name.
2. Sit by the tree or pocket chart. As you say a child's first name in the first line of the rhyme below, invite the child to try to remember his last name when you say the second line. After you say the entire rhyme, invite the child to find and point to his name on the shape on the tree or chart and move onto the next activity.

   _____ *is my first name,*
   _____ *is my last.*
   I can find my name
   Very, very fast.

   (continued on the next page)

More to do   **Writing:** invite the child to trace over his name with wipe-off crayon on a laminated word card in the writing center. Use the name cards to help children print their name. Start with only the first name. Use magnetic letters, playdough, sticker alphabet letters, letter stamps, or felt letters.

Related books   *ABC, a Family Alphabet Book* by Bobbie Combs
The Alphabet Room by Sarah Pinto
Chicka Chicka Boom Boom by Bill Martin, Jr.

 Sue Fleischmann, Sussex, WI

Alphabet Riddles   5+

Materials   colored pictures (one for each letter of the alphabet) or computer and printer
4" x 6" index cards
poster board
scissors
laminator
pocket chart, optional

What to do
1. Using a computer program that allows you to create frames or borders, make the desired size to create your own cards to cut out.
   Author's Note: I chose to make two on a page in portrait view. This gave me ample room for the text that follows.
2. Type a riddle for each letter of the alphabet on a separate card. Each riddle has four lines.
3. Save 13 pages of riddles on your computer.
4. Print the riddles on 4" x 6" index cards by changing properties to *scale to fit* and *scale to fit paper in device*. Remember to change the placement from *as is* to *fit to page* just before printing.
5. Print out a picture for each riddle on poster board.
6. Laminate the riddle cards and pictures for durability. Display all the pictures in a pocket chart.
7. Whenever you have a few extra moments during a transition, read the riddle cards and ask for volunteers to answer using the pictures for reference.
   Note: Riddles and many alphabet activities can be found at www.hummingbirded.com in the *ABCs* and *emergent reading* section.

 Jackie Wright, Enid, OK

Transition Tips and Techniques 3+

Materials   none

What to do

1. The most important thing to remember about transitions is "the fewer the better." Check your daily schedule and count the transitions. If you have more than ten transitions daily, consider revising the schedule to reduce the number of transitions.

2. Sing! Sing! Sing! A simple song can help children transition from one activity to another; clean the room; make up their mats for nap time; deal with boo-boos and small social offenses, and a million other things throughout the day. Make up your own songs to familiar tunes or use one of the many songbooks available.

3. Make sure the children are thoroughly familiar with the daily schedule and keep to the schedule. A familiar routine is extremely important for young children.

4. Make your room arrangement conducive to comfortable, active play. Get down on your knees and check out your room from a child's perspective. Are the centers easily identifiable? Is there room for the children to move around without running into each other? Are the materials accessible and arranged in an inviting manner? Make sure you don't crowd the room with lots of furniture. Children need a good amount of floor space for their active little bodies.

5. Label everything that doesn't move! Each toy, puzzle, or item that the children use daily should have its own special spot on the shelves and that spot should be labeled with a picture of the item and the item's name. This is invaluable during cleanup time. It's much easier for children to help put things away when they don't have to ask you where everything goes. Change the labels as needed.

6. Give children lots of responsibility. Let them know you expect them to clean up after themselves and put things away when they are done with them. If tables need to be cleaned, let the children help clean them. If the floor needs to be swept, hand the broom and dustpan to a willing helper. Instead of children standing idly by waiting for you to finish cleaning, let them lend a hand. They love to help! Be a good example for the children. If you drop a box of chalk and it scatters all over the floor, get down and pick them up instead of asking a child to do it for you.

7. Separate large groups of children. If you have a large group and two or more teachers in the room, break the group into smaller ones. Rotate the groups, such as one group on the playground, one group participating in centers, to

(continued on the next page)

give all the children a chance to participate in all the activities planned for the day. This technique requires some juggling of the daily schedule but it can be done!

8. Last, but certainly not least, let the children know that you care about them. Tell them and show them each day how very much they mean to you.

Virginia Jean Herrod, Columbia, SC

Developmentally Appropriate Changes

3+

Materials   none

What to do   Some children do not deal well with transitions (changes) in the classroom. Here are some ideas to help.

- Tell the children to point to where they will go next.
- Ask the children to walk like animals, walk tall, walk short, and so on, to go to the next place.
- Ring a bell or make another sound to tell them where to go next.
- Ask a more experienced child to show the new child where to go.
- Let the children have a special place to go to if they do not want to go to the next activity. This place should be near the new activity, so the children can hear what the other children are doing. This place could be a book corner or drawing corner, as long as it is self-directed. They may rejoin the group at any time.

Barbara Saul, Eureka, CA

Be Prepared for Transitions

Materials   none

What to do   Be prepared for transitions. Keep the following in mind:

- ◆ Always have materials ready.
- ◆ Aim to begin activities without long initial waiting periods.
- ◆ Plan realistically for the group's attention span.
- ◆ Begin whole-group activities with a few children, while enticing the rest of the group with an engaging activity.
- ◆ Keep the routine the same. Children like the predictability of having a daily group time routine that begins and ends the same way each day.
- ◆ Try new and creative transitions to see which they enjoy, and repeat those often. Whenever possible, make them educational and always make them fun.

⭐ *Jackie Wright, Enid, OK*

Transition Ideas

Materials   none

What to do   The most important thing to remember when working with young children is to be flexible and to take advantage of teachable moments. Transition time can be boring or frustrating to some preschoolers. You have children who listen and follow directions very well, and children who don't listen to directions for any number of reasons. Try some of the following ideas for specific transitions:

- ◆ **Two- and One-Minute Warnings:** One of the most important lessons is dealing with transitions. Children need a warning system to prepare them. Though children don't necessarily understand what a minute is, say, "Two minutes to cleanup!" After about a minute, say, "One minute to cleanup!"

(continued on the next page)

When that minute is up, sing a clean-up song or do another transition to cleanup. Work with them so they know where things belong. By the end of the year, they may do this themselves.

◆ **Cleanup Song:** Adapt the words of this song to a tune you know:

It's cleanup time in the school,
Time for girls and boys,
To stop what they are doing,
And put away the toys.

◆ **Lining Up:** Even this can be fun. Call, "Line-up time!" and start counting down as the children run to you and help you count. Encourage them to be in line before you get to zero!

◆ **Standing in Line:** It is important to make this fun. One way is to sing a fun song, such as "The Wheels on the Bus," or another that the children love. You might also try counting the children in a different language. This makes them all feel important, and exposes them to another language at the same time. Children will like to count with you. Another line-up tactic is to remind the children of three hallway rules: walking feet, quiet voices, and hands to your sides or in your pockets. Remind them that these rules are meant to keep them safe. You may want to discuss what might happen if they did not follow these rules, so they appreciate their value.

★ *Deborah Gallagher, Littleton, NH*

Transition to Preschool

3+

Materials   none

What to do
1. Invite the child and her family to come to school for a brief visit before school begins, such as when you are working on bulletin boards and preparing the classroom.
2. Send welcome postcards to the children.
3. On the first day, have a partial day. The children can make name tags, learn where their cubby is located, and participate in a shortened circle time.
4. In the evening, hold an orientation for the parents, without the children.
5. This routine will help children and parents make the transition to school with few tears, and help children have ownership in their classroom.

★ *Sandy L. Scott, Vancouver, WA*

Substitute Teacher Transition   3+

Materials   three-ring binder with dividers
                    typing paper
                    computer or typewriter
                    small photo of each child
                    glue stick

What to do 1. It's always hard on children when their familiar teacher is unexpectedly
                   absent. You can help ease this transition by creating a handbook for the
                   substitute teacher.
                2. Use the dividers to divide the handbook into the following categories.

   ◆ **All About Us**: In this section, paste a small photo of each child to the
     pages. Next to the child's picture, write important information about that
     child, such as known allergies, pertinent family information, or comments
     about the child's temperament or behavior. Keep your comments as
     positive as possible in order to avoid the substitute pre-judging the
     child's behavior.
   ◆ **Our Daily Schedule**: In this area put a copy of your daily schedule with
     detailed explanations as to what activities take place at certain times of
     the day. Also include notes about daily forms, if any, that need to be filled
     out on each child.
   ◆ **"Where Is It?"**: In this area make notes about where important items are
     stored in your classroom, such as emergency contact information, first aid
     kit, teacher supplies (glue, scissors, tape, and so on), and lesson plan
     resource books.
   ◆ **What Do I Do If…?**: In this area make notes about the procedure to be
     followed in certain situations. Some examples are: 1) If the fire alarm rings;
     2) If we have to evacuate due to weather or other conditions; 3) If a child
     is injured; 4) If a child becomes ill; and 5) If a child needs medicine given
     at school.
   ◆ **Important Forms**: In this area place copies of forms frequently needed,
     such as Sick Child; Accident/Incident; Medication Dispensation; and
     Daily Notes.
   ◆ **Help**: In this area include information about the organizational structure
     of your school or center. Include the name and phone number (or
     intercom number) of the director and assistant director. Also, include
     information about teachers or caregivers in nearby classrooms your
     substitute can call on for assistance.

   (continued on the next page)

3. At the end of the handbook, write a nice letter to your substitute thanking her or him for helping out when needed. This letter, since written in advance, will have to be "generic" but it will be a nice touch and greatly appreciated by whoever takes your place as you recover.

More to do   If you are ill, as soon as you are able, write a letter to the children telling them how much you miss them. Mention the substitute and encourage the children to listen to her or him while you are gone.
Literacy: Make sure you have a good supply of "new teacher" books that show the new teacher in a positive light. Ask your substitute to read these books with the children.

Related books   *The Day the Teacher Went Bananas* by James Howe
Ethan's Favorite Teacher by Hila Colman
It's Hard to Share My Teacher by Joan Singleton Prestine
Miss Nelson Is Missing! by Harry G. Allard
Teacher's Pet by Miska Miles
The Teeny Tiny Teacher by Stephanie Calmenson
Where Does the Teacher Live? by Paula Kurzband Feder

⭐ *Virginia Jean Herrod, Columbia, SC*

It's Time Now

3+

Materials   camera   film   scissors
poster board   glue   masking tape
clothespins

What to do   1. Take photographs of the children as they are involved in daily classroom activities and develop them into 4" x 6" prints.
2. Cut each piece of poster board into four sections.
3. Glue one photo on each card and label the activity under the photograph.
4. Connect the squares in a timeline in chronological order horizontally. Attach the squares together with masking tape.
5. Attach the timeline to the wall at the children's eye level. (Good places would be under the chalkboard, or where circle time is conducted.)

6. Cut out a 4" cardboard star and write "now" on it. Attach it to a clothespin.
7. Select a helper to move the clothespins from square to square as the day progresses.
8. Take opportunities to refer to the timeline during the day and talk about past, present, and future.
9. If a special event is planned for the day, such as a visitor, project, or trip, write the word on a sticky note and cover the picture. Or, write the word "special" on a cardboard star and glue it to a clothespin. This helps reduce repeated questions about when a daily special activity will take place.

More to do **Home-to-School Connection:** Make two copies of the photographs and send one copy home to parents so they can see their child interacting in the classroom.

Math: For older children, write the time each activity occurs on the cards. Discussion can lead to opportunities to learn the concept of time. Add a moveable clock to help this skill.

★ *Susan R. Forbes, Daytona Beach, FL*

Classroom Schedule 3+

Materials

train pattern
scissors
pictures of daily activities
   (use digital camera if available)
one red and one green circle shape

construction paper
markers
glue
small stick-on plastic hooks
yarn

(continued on the next page)

What to do

1. Cut out an engine shape and write the name of your classroom on it.
2. Cut out enough train car shapes to correspond with each activity of the day. Make each car a different color. On each car write one daily activity and its time slot, for example, 10:30-10:45 circle time, and then glue the corresponding picture on to the car. Make the caboose the departure car.
3. Under each picture adhere one small plastic hook, and hang at children's level on a wall that is easily accessible.
4. Punch a hole in each red and green circle shape. Attach a loop of yarn to each circle.
   Note: Laminate the train cars and circle for durability.
5. Throughout the day, hang the green and red circles to indicate which activity is ending or over with the red circle and which is current with the green.
6. If desired, let different children be in charge of changing the colored circles from activity to activity. A yellow circle can also be used to provide a warning time of the change of activities.

More to do

Create additional cars for special activities that can be added or removed throughout the year. Two trains can be created to distinguish the morning classroom from the afternoon. Instead of writing the time, draw a clock face to correspond with the time slots. Use other shapes, such as a caterpillar or a roller coaster to depict the schedule. Or, if wall space is an issue, use a flip chart.

⭐*Lauri Robinson, Big Lake, MN*

Daily Schedule Cards

Materials   card stock and markers
hook or easel

What to do
1. Make cards that show each part of the daily schedule, such as lunch, outside time, center time, group time, and so on. Use words with a picture cue for emergent readers. Hang these on a hook at the children's level, or place them on the chalk tray, on an easel, or hang from a suction hook on a white board.
2. Make "schedule changer" a job, like "line leader" or "snack helper" on your helper chart, or select a changer for each transition.
3. When a transition comes, the schedule changer gets the cards, finds the one with the appropriate activity, and places it on the hook. This gives the children experience with "reading" a schedule, and helps children learn organization.

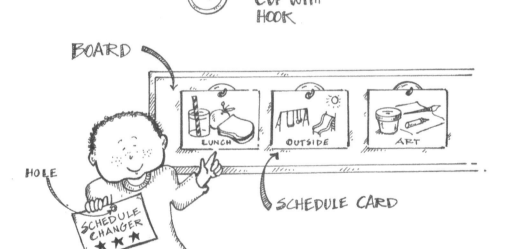

Author's Note: When getting used to a new schedule, I often look it over several times throughout the day to make sure I'm following what needs to happen next. This allows pre- and emerging readers to do the same. It gives me the opportunity to see who is paying attention to what happens next, and who is able to use pictures to "read" cues. With older children, replace the cues with words only. My class loved the responsibility of changing the cards, and in that special way preschoolers think, they sometimes wondered if the next activity

(continued on the next page)

would not happen if the card was not changed. They saw that it would, and the "changer" would be reminded to do her job!

Additional Note From the Author: I made my cards on the computer, using a program with a postcard program and clip art. This made an easy-to handle and easy-to-read card, and made two exactly alike at a time, which is good for matching games. You can also make the cards taking pictures, cutting pictures from magazines, or drawing cues to go with the word.

Related books   *Carl Goes to Daycare* by Alexandra Day
Friends at School by Rochelle Bunnett
Hurry Up! by Bernette Ford
Ricardo's Day by George Ancona

Tracie O'Hara, Charlotte, NC

Our Daily Activities
3+

Materials   digital or 35 mm camera
poster board
glue stick
markers
computer and printer or access to a photo processor

What to do

1. Take a photo of the children as they are engaged in each step of your daily schedule.
2. Develop or print the photos. Size them according to how large you want your chart to be (4" x 6" or 5" x 7" work well).
3. Using the glue stick, arrange the photos on the poster board to show the progression of your day. You can make the chart linear (working left to right from the top of the poster board to the bottom) or vertical (a straight line from the top of the poster board to the bottom). Leave room at the top of the poster board for the header: Our Daily Activities.
4. Use markers to create a caption under each photo. For example, under the photo of children eating breakfast, simply print "breakfast." Under the photo of children engaged in center time activities, print "centers."
5. Show the children how to refer to the activity chart throughout the day. When a child asks "When is center time?" instead of answering the question, take the child to the chart and help her to interpret the photo sequence and determine when center time is during the day.

More to do
Literacy: Make a Daily Activities Book for each child. Print a picture of each daily activity for each child or simply copy them in black and white on a copier. Give the photos to the children and have them paste each photo on a half sheet of construction paper. Help the children print captions under each photo. Let each child create an individual front and back cover. Punch holes along the edge of each sheet of paper and use yarn to bind the pages together.

More Literacy: Make an Our Daily Activities big book for class use. Print the photos out in 8" x 10" size and use the glue stick to affix each photo to a piece of 11 x 15 inch poster board. Instead of a simple caption under each photo, work together with the children to create a story about their day. Print the story under the photos. Let the children create a front and back cover. Punch holes along the edge of each piece of poster board. Use yarn to bind the pages together.

Math: Print a copy of each photo, use the glue stick to affix each one to a 4 x 6 inch card and laminate them for durability. Let the children use them as a sequencing activity.

Home-to-School Connection: Make one special Our Daily Activities book for the parents. Follow the instructions for making a book for each child. However, under each photo print a comment about what the children are learning through participating in the activity. For example, under the photo of the children eating breakfast you could print: "When the children serve themselves, they are developing important skills, such as independence and self-reliance. When they pour milk from a pitcher, they are using their fine motor skills and developing eye-hand coordination. When they sit together in a small group and eat they are developing good social skills." Let the children take turns taking the book home to read with their parents.

Related books
All in a Day by Mitsumasa Anno
The Backward Day by Ruth Krauss
The Best Time of Day by Valerie Flournoy
Carl Goes to Daycare by Alexandra Day
Digby and Kate and the Beautiful Day by Barbara Baker
Dustin's Big School Day by Alden R. Carter
Jamal's Busy Day by Wade Hudson
Just Another Ordinary Day by Rod Clement
Lucy and Tom's Day by Shirley Hughes
One Fine Day by Molly Bang
School Days by B.G. Hennessy
The Sun's Day by Mordicai Gerstein

Virginia Jean Herrod, Columbia, SC

What Will We Do Next?

Materials
poster board
marker or pencil
scissors
two-sided tape
flannel board story board

What to do

1. Outline simple shapes onto the poster board (pail, shovel, oven, chef's hat, spoon, bowl, cake, ball, cups, crackers, books, and so on).
2. Cut them out and put a piece of two-sided tape on the back.
3. Place one item that identifies the next classroom activity onto the storyboard.
4. Let the children guess with each item until they have solved the puzzle and know what comes next in the daily schedule. For instance, a chef hat, bowl, spoon, cake, and coat could mean baking and snack, then outdoor time.

★ *Ingelore Mix, Gainesville, VA*

Job Captains

Materials
poster board (22" x 28"), several pieces
scissors
markers
wooden clothespins
yardstick
pencil
masking or duct tape

What to do

1. Create a Job Captain Chart by cutting each piece of poster board into quarters. Write classroom job titles on each piece of poster board. Classroom jobs include:

   ◆ **Morning Captain** (makes sure cubbies are straight, sharpens pencils, and prepares anything not ready for the day).
   ◆ **Teacher Assistant** (makes sure the small group instruction table is straightened before and after instruction).
   ◆ **Paper Captain** (passes out notes and folders).
   ◆ **Line Captain** (leads the line).
   ◆ **Table Captains** (four people—make sure each table has work materials and clean up after the activity is finished).
   ◆ **Center Captains** (two people—check to make sure each center is neat after activity time).
   ◆ **Story Captain** (checks the classroom library for neatness and selects story to be read at story time).
   ◆ **Sink Captain** (checks the sink area to be sure it is clean and passes out paper towels for lunch preparation).
   ◆ **Rest Captain** (picks the music, wakes children gently with a "magic wand," makes sure mats are stored properly). Rest Captain has the option of sitting in a rocking chair during rest.
   ◆ **Snack Captain** (helps prepare snacks and pass them out, helps clean up).
   ◆ **Outdoor Captains** (two people—make sure play equipment is set out and cleaned up afterward).
   ◆ **Afternoon Captain** (checks the condition of the room and hands out stray objects from Lost and Found during the ending group activity).
   ◆ **Calendar Captain** (marks the day on the classroom calendar).
   ◆ **Flag Captain** (holds the flag during the salute).
   ◆ **Attendance/Lunch Count Captains** (two people—take paper slips to the office and cafeteria).

(continued on the next page)

2. Label clothespins with the words "morning," "teacher," "paper," "line," "table," and so on. Color-coding the chart and clothespins helps with organization. Clip clothespins to the chart in each category.
3. After the morning opening, place the clothespins on the sleeves of the captains. At the end of the day, the children return the pins to the chart.
4. Begin with one or two job captains at the beginning of the year, leaving room on the chart to expand as children mature and are trained. It is important to train the most able and interested children first so they can become Captain Trainers. The sequence is as follows: an adult trains a child, the child does the job for a week, and then the child becomes trainer for next child who does job for the next week.

⭐ *Susan R. Forbes, Daytona Beach, FL*

Water Table Dryer

3+

What to do

1. One way to handle transitions, especially cleanup time, is to find task that children love to do. For example, as much as some children love to play and explore with the items in the water table they love to be the one to clean it up even more. Therefore, one cleanup job is the table dryer.
2. After you have emptied the table, the child whose job it is to dry the table picks a friend to help. The two children use paper towels or cloth towels and completely dry the table inside and out.

Author's Note: I have never had a problem with this job in my room. The water table is usually spotless when they are finished. A lot of the time the children will ask if this can be their job for the day.

⭐ *Wanda Guidroz, Santa Fe, TX*

Class List at a Glance

3+

Materials   paper
marker

What to do

1. Write all the children's names on a sheet of paper (or a half sheet of paper). Make a lot of copies of the class list and keep them in an easy-to-reach place.
2. Whenever you need to keep track of children that have finished a project, or if there is a very popular center or one that all the children need to go to, grab a class list. As each child completes the task, check off her name.
3. This is also great to use when collecting money or items from parents. As you receive items, just check off the child's name.

⭐ *Gail Morris, Kemah, TX*

Inventory Lists

3+

Materials   paper
computer or pen

What to do

1. At the end of the year as you are cleaning your room, make a list of all your supplies. Make a separate list for each cabinet, shelf, or closet and be as specific as you can about each item on the list.
2. Type or hand write the list and make a copy to have at home as well as at school.
3. This is great for lesson planning. You can see at a glance what items you already have to use for different themes.
4. Whenever you put an item out, write the date next to the item on the list. This will help with your rotation of supplies.
5. If you do this on the computer, save it in a file so you can easily make changes as you add or delete supplies.

⭐ *Gail Morris, Kemah, TX*

Magnetic ID

3+

Materials

camera and film
2" x 2" cardboard squares
scissors
glue
laminator
magnetic stripping
glue gun
colored electronic tape

What to do

1. Take headshots of the children and get the film developed.
2. Cut out each photograph and glue it to a cardboard square.
3. Laminate the picture cards, trim the edges, and attach a 2" strip of magnetic tape to the back with a glue gun (adult only).
4. Display the IDs on a magnetic surface, such as a chalkboard, storage cabinet, or file cabinet.
5. The IDs may be used for many purposes, such as identifying children's lunch choices, graphing choices, work groups, daily helpers, and for taking attendance.
6. Use them for transitions to centers by cutting colored electrical tape into squares and labeling them with classroom centers (blocks, art, and so on). Put the squares on whatever magnetic surface the IDs are sticking to. When the children move to a new center, put their ID next to the corresponding label.

More to do

General Tips: Develop a second set of photographs, glue them to rounded squares, write children's names on the squares, laminate, punch a hole in the top, and string a piece of yarn through the hole. These make great ID necklaces for substitutes and guest speakers to learn the children's names.

⭐ *Susan R. Forbes, Daytona Beach, FL*

Cubby Photos

Materials   camera, film, contact paper

What to do
1. As they transition to school at the beginning of the year, some children have trouble recognizing their names.
2. The first week of school take a close-up picture of each child.
3. Attach the child's picture to her cubby and cover with contact paper.
4. When you ask the child to put items, such as artwork, notes, and other things, in her cubby, it will be easier for the child.
   Note: This is especially helpful if you have children with the same name.

⭐ *Sandy L. Scott, Vancouver, WA*

Photo Groups

Materials   copied picture of each child
scissors
card stock
glue
pen

What to do
1. When arranging groups, cut and paste the children's photos and glue them onto card stock according to which group you want them to be in.
2. Put each photo-card at the place you want that group to go, and they can easily find their picture and go there.

⭐ *Barbara Saul, Eureka, CA*

Self-Managing Areas

3+

Materials   self-managing props (see activity)

What to do

1. Make transitions smooth and develop children's independence by putting self-managing props for each area or activity in the classroom. For example, if you have a rocking boat, find child-size life vests for the children to use while playing in the boat. Limiting the number of life vests will naturally limit the number who can safely play in the boat together. In addition, if life vests are only worn in the boat, as children move on to another activity and leave the life vest in the boat, they are indicating they are done and another child can have a turn.

2. Other examples of self-managing props are safety glasses at the workbench, inexpensive nail aprons from the local hardware to transport art items from a shelf to the table, paint shirts at the easels, and protective plastic aprons at the water table.

3. Create a prominent place for every self-managing prop within the play area. When a self-managing prop is returned to its appropriate place, this is a clear indication to the next child that the area is open for new people, and this also encourages the departing child to think about and plan their transition.

4. Let children create props if none are easily available; make life vests out of grocery bags, or necklaces from yarn and paper for the home living area.

★ *Lauri Robinson, Big Lake, MN*

Bathroom Signs

Materials
2 sheets of card stock
marker
hole punch
yarn

What to do
1. Draw a child's face on one piece of card stock and write "boys" under it.
2. Draw a child's face on the other piece of card stock and write "girls" under it.
3. On the back of each, write, "Please Wait."
4. Punch two holes in the top of each and tie yarn through to make a handle to hang the sign.
5. Hang the signs on the correct door and tell children to flip the sign over to "Please Wait" when they go into the bathroom, and flip it back to the face when they come out. Children will know to wait when another child is in the bathroom.

★ *Barbara Saul, Eureka, CA*

Button Jar Party

Materials
two identical clear plastic containers, preferably with a wide mouth
buttons
ribbon
large stickers, optional

What to do
1. Put a ribbon around the mouth of one jar, and put all the buttons in the other jar. Each time a child transitions smoothly to an activity, follows directions, or does something nice, they may take a button from one jar and put it in the jar with the ribbon.
2. All the children cooperate to fill the ribbon jar, and when it is full, have a button jar party with ice cream, popcorn, or cookies.

(continued on the next page)

3. Reward for:
   ◆ Helping with cleanup
   ◆ Walking quietly in the hall
   ◆ Listening quietly at circle or group time
   ◆ Helping to sing songs
   ◆ Eating a healthful snack or lunch
   ◆ Identifying the correct number or letter
   ◆ Using good manners

WIDE OPENING

RIBBON

4. Several children can put buttons in the jar for the same behavior. It should take about a month to fill the jar and have a party.

Related book   *Raggedy Ann: A Thank You, Please, and I Love You Book* by Norah Smaridge

Related poem   **Good Manners** by Mary Brehm
Using good manners is a nice thing to do
Like remembering to say please, and thank you, too.
I never talk when my mouth is full of food.
Then I pass the dish politely, don't interrupt, or be rude.
I shake someone's hand as I say, "How do you do?"
Won't you please remember to use good manners, too?

★ *Mary Brehm, Aurora, OH*

Partnering With Families

3+

Materials paper

What to do
1. Build a partnership with families so they can help their children transition to school on a daily basis.
2. Post a guideline for families on the door of your classroom. This will inform them of activities for the week or month. By doing this, the parent will know what the child is doing without having to ask. Below is a sample of a weekly/monthly learning activity plan:

For the week/month of ____, we'll be learning about:
Colors: red, green, yellow, blue, and orange
Number: 5
Farm Animals: cow, pig, and horse
Art: mixing colors, red and yellow, blue and yellow
Story Time: relating colors to farm animals. We are reading:
   ◆ *Blueberries for Sal* by Robert McCloskey
   ◆ *One Fish Two Fish Red Fish Blue Fish* by Dr. Suess
Baking: baking orange cookies
Fingerplay: "I Have Five Fingers"
Music: "The Farmer in the Dell," "5 Is Such a Pretty Number"
Special Day: Next Monday is "Green Day." Wear or bring something green to school.

⭐ *Ingelore Mix, Gainesville, VA*

Pocket Pack

3+

Materials   index cards
zipper-closure bag
pen

What to do   1. Unexpected transitions can really put you on the spot. Sometimes it's difficult to respond effectively. With a little preparation, you can easily fill those awkward empty spaces that interfere with the flow of your daily routine. You can make your own "pocket pack" of "transition survival cards." Here's how.

2. Write each of the following topics on a separate index card: songs, stories, fingerplays/rhymes/chants, indoor games, and outdoor games.
3. On each card, write the titles of the activities you know by heart, such as:
   Songs: BINGO, Wheels on the Bus, Old MacDonald
   Stories: Three Little Pigs, Goldilocks and the Three Bears, Little Red Riding Hood
   Fingerplays/rhymes/chants: Where Is Thumbkin?; Open, Shut Them; Grandma's Glasses
   Indoor games: I Spy, Hot Potato, Guess What's Missing
   Outdoor games: Duck, Duck, Goose; Red Light, Green Light; Mother May I?
4. Add to your lists as you learn new activities.

⭐ *Susan A. Sharkey, La Mesa, CA*

Quick Pick Transitions

3+

Materials   index cards
pen
hole punch
string or heavy rubber band

What to do   1. Be prepared to transition at any moment by keeping on hand a stack of index cards with your favorite on-the-spot transition activities written on them.
2. After writing down the activity on the card, punch a hole on one end, and attach it to a string for hanging on a wall, or to a rubber band for carrying on your wrist.

★*Karyn F. Everham, Fort Myers, FL*

Routine Songs

3+

Materials   CD or cassette tape
computer, CD player, or tape recorder
tapes and/or CDs with the songs you use daily

What to do   1. Gather songs or music that you use daily or frequently.
2. Transfer the songs to the tape or CD in order of their use. For example, songs could include those that are related to cleanup, arrival, welcome, good morning or good afternoon song, get to know ourselves, movement, calendar or weather songs, and quiet music.
3. Make different sets for themes; group monthly activities; morning and afternoon sessions; for group skill practice, such as movement, cognition, and following directions.
Author's Note: This can help with organizing the music so it is easier to make use of. It can save wear and tear on your purchased CDs and tapes. This way you always have a backup for your songs and music.

★*Sandra Nagel, White Lake, MI*

Storytelling

Materials   very short stories, including Aesop's fables, fairy tales, *One Minute Stories* by Shari Lewis, and *A Piece of the Wind and Other Stories to Tell* by Ruthilde Kronberg and Patricia McKissack

What to do
1. Resolve to learn one very short story to tell children each week. The above suggestions are only a few of the many stories available to tell children.
2. Tell the story at transition times. Not only will this take the anxiety out of transitions, it will also make transitions something children will look forward to Repeat the story several times in the week. You will find your skill and ability to remember stories will improve, and young children love to hear stories repeated.
3. Toward the end of the week, invite the children to participate in telling the story. They will love it!

More to do   Storytelling with children opens many doors to activities involving dramatic play, art, and music. The children can tell the story in pictures, act out the story with or without puppets or other playthings, and experiment with musical accompaniment.

★ *Karyn F. Everham, Fort Myers, FL*

Our Transition Stories

Materials   crayons or markers   heavy paper
photos of the transition, if possible   stapler

What to do
1. Write a story about a transition. For example:

When it is time to eat snack, I line up in front of the sink to wash my hands. I put soap on my hands and rub my hands together under the water. I take one or two pieces of paper towel to dry my hands. When my hands are dry, I put the paper towel into the trash can. Then I walk over to the table and sit in my chair.

2. Transfer the words to pieces of heavy paper, one line on each page.
3. Ask the children to illustrate the words (and glue photos if you have them).
4. Staple the pieces of paper together to make a book.

   Note: Encourage the children to look at photographs of themselves doing classroom activities. Photographs increase the children's interest in these transition books.

5. Make a variety of books for different daily transitions, such as cleanup, using the bathroom, arriving and separating from family members, snack time, putting coats and boots on, playing outside, meeting someone new, or taking field trips.

More to do   **Language:** Have the children dictate a transition story as you write it onto chart paper. Review and edit it with the children. Transfer it to the writing paper with space for the pictures.

Literacy: Place these transition books in the reading center. Read them to the group at reading time or circle time.

⭐ *Sandra Nagel, White Lake, MI*

The Music Box Trick   3+

Materials   wind-up musical jewelry box

What to do
1. Use this activity when children need to transition to circle time or to a quiet activity. Show them the music box and say, "I am going to fill this box with music to remind you to listen quietly." Wind the box several times.
2. "When I hear too much talking, I'll let some music out of the box." Open the box to play music. "As soon as your voices are quiet again, I'll close the box to save the music." Close the box.
3. Let the children know when you open the box, "Uh oh, the music is escaping!" The children will have to stop talking to hear the music. Once they catch on, you can open the box silently and wait for them to remind each other!
4. You might also use this during rest and nap time.

⭐ *Susan A. Sharkey, La Mesa, CA*

Reminders Are a Must!

3+

Materials   none

What to do
1. When young children are engaged in playing and a transition time is nearing, it is important to give them a warning. This can be a simple verbal reminder or something more interesting such as flicking the lights on and off or ringing a bell, or using a puppet to tell the children what comes next.
2. Give children a few directions for each transition. Young children need to know what comes next and they need those gentle reminders every day. This helps smooth out transitions when everyone, including staff, knows what to expect next.

★ *Sue Myhre, Bremerton, WA*

Signals

3+

Materials   none

What to do
1. Let children know ahead of time when a transition is coming. "In five minutes we will be cleaning up!"
2. Children can take turns ringing a big ship bell that signals time to clean up.
3. Try to make cleanup fun. Pretend to be vacuum cleaners and clean up dirt, touch children's noses to turn on the "cleanup robot," or challenge the children to finish before a teacher returns to the room.

★ *Ann Scalley, Orleans, MA*

Creative Lineups

Materials   none

What to do   These techniques will help children wait for the next activity or line up. The techniques move the children in small groups and mix them with different children. They also involve such concepts as grouping, categorizing, noticing details, and reviewing concepts.

- ◆ Call out a color. Everyone wearing that color gets in line. Then call another color.
- ◆ Instead of a color, call out a type of clothing, type of shoe, or clothing feature such as flowers, buttons, stripes, and so on.
- ◆ Call out eye color, or hair color or length and combine this with a discussion about how everyone has similarities and differences but is special in her own way.
- ◆ Spell first names. Call out the first letters in names. Call out initials. When first names are too easy, switch to last names. Choose a letter from anywhere in a name or call children with five, six, or seven letters in her name. Try clapping numbers of syllables.
- ◆ Teach the sign language alphabet and fingerspell their names, or sign the first letter of their names.
- ◆ Whisper each child's name. This helps to quiet everyone down on especially loud or exciting days. Children have to be quiet so everyone can hear the names.
- ◆ Ask children if they remember something about what they did that day, for example, "If your butterfly had blue wings, go wash your hands."

More to do   **Language:** Learn sign language for words like "please," "thank you," "yes," and "no" for use at snack time.
Math: Count the number of children in each category.
More Math: Create charts of the groups in a category, such as types of pants and compare them to the counts the next day. Let the line leader choose a category.

★ *Sandra Gratias, Perkasie, PA*

Using the Line Rope

Materials a length of rope with handles

What to do
1. Take a clothesline rope and make small handles or loops about every 10 to 12 inches. Loops at each end provide places for the teachers. Whenever children must line up to go somewhere, have them hold onto a loop of the rope.
2. The rope helps children stay in line and with the group.
   Author's Note: The rope has been helpful in situations where we must wait for children arriving or being picked up. Also, when we walk down the halls where others are moving in the same hallways, it helps keep the young children safe and traffic patterns running more smoothly. I have used the "Line Rope" for years. I was amused when traveling and I observed preschool teachers in England and Russia using similar "Line Ropes" with preschoolers on outings.
3. With older children, they can take turns as the "front and back helpers" or the line "engine" and "caboose," rather than adults holding the lead and end handles.
4. Sing the following to the tune of "Are You Sleeping?" to help young children remember to hold on to the handles.

   I am walking, I am walking,
   On the rope, On the rope.
   Yes I am walking, yes I am walking,
   With my friends, with my friends.

Related book *The Line Up Book* by Marisabina Russo

★ *Sandra L. Nagel, White Lake, MI*

Morning Break

Materials   none

What to do   After the children have had a quiet period, let them have a morning (or afternoon) break for five minutes. During that time, they can get a drink or go to the bathroom before the next activity starts.

★ *Barbara Saul, Eureka, CA*

Jigsaw Puzzle Moments

Materials   jigsaw puzzle
                     markers

What to do   1. Try the following when you have a few extra moments.
                     2. Have the children number their jigsaw puzzle box, then take out the pieces and number each piece the same number as the box.
                     3. All that is necessary is to match the puzzle piece with the number on the box.
                     Author's Note: This saves time when two or three puzzles are mixed up and it's difficult to find the correct pieces.

More to do   When puzzle boxes are damaged, cut out the picture on the front cover and place it in a large zipper-closure bag with the puzzle pieces. Mark the name of the puzzle on the bag with permanent marker.

★ *Eileen Lucas, Halifax, Nova Scotia, Canada*

Daisy Wheel

4

Materials
foam board or cardboard
scissors
acrylic paint
Velcro

What to do
1. Make two daisies out of foam board or cardboard. Have detachable petals for the second daisy. Each petal can have an area in which the children can choose to play during free play.
2. Let the children choose an area and then place the petal next to the center

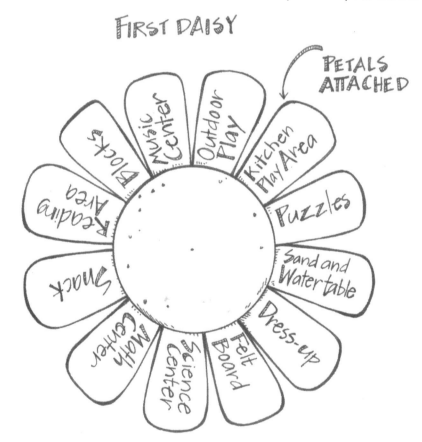

FIRST DAISY

PETALS ATTACHED

EXTRA FLOWER MIDDLES for DIFFERENT CENTERS

SECOND DAISY

DETACHABLE PETALS

of the daisy to form a daisy. You can use this for name recognition with the children.

3. Use this for easy transitions and for job helpers, games, cleanup, snack, or lining up to go outside.
   Note: You need a blank daisy at each center so the child can put her petal on the daisy. When that daisy is full, the child knows that she must find another center to play in.

⭐ *Cookie Zingarelli, Columbus, OH*

Job Visors

4+

Materials   plastic children's visors in different colors
sharpie pens

What to do   1. Use this activity to help with the transition to cleanup time and other times during the day.
2. Use the pens to mark the classroom jobs on the visors. For example, on the red visor write, "Line Leader," on the yellow visor write, "Pick Up Papers," and continue until all of the jobs have a visor. You may want to glue pictures (perhaps from a school supply catalog) to the visors to help pre-readers.
3. Give each child a visor to wear during cleanup. If more than one child does the job, be sure that the other job visors are the same color.

More to do   **General Tips:** Use visors for special occasions, such as birthdays, or any activity that is special to a child.
More General Tips: Give each learning group the same color visors. When it is time to transition to another activity, put a yellow paper where the yellow visors are to go, a red paper where the reds should go, and so on.

⭐ *Barbara Saul, Eureka, CA*

Get Moving!

4+

Materials   none

What to do

1. These transition ideas make the time spent moving from one room activity to another as opportunities to problem solve, use imagination, and get in some gross motor activity. To ensure variety, if you choose the movement on the way to the next place, the line leader can choose the movement on the way back.
2. Ask everyone to move like a character from a recent story or like a favorite animal.
3. Make patterns with children, such as arms up, arms down, arms up, arms down, and so on.
4. Try different types of walks, such as giant steps, baby steps, hop on one or two feet, walk backwards.
5. For quiet walking, think of animals that don't make sounds and imitate them. Some ideas are butterfly, fish, or caterpillar.
6. Pretend to be a person with a job such as a hunter, ballerina, fire fighter, motorcyclist, and so on.
7. Think of a novel situation to imitate such as walking on peanut butter or floating on a cloud.

★ *Sandra Gratias, Perkasie, PA*

"K" Transition

4+

Materials   none

What to do

Author's Note: Each year after spring break, we send our older preschool children to visit the kindergarten class across the hall. We first check with the kindergarten staff to see what time is convenient for their schedule. We then check with families to see if their child will be attending our school for kindergarten and if they are planning on requesting a particular teacher.

1. Take your list of kindergarten-bound children and match them up with parent-requested teachers, so the children become familiar with who they will see the next year.
2. Send children to the kindergarten room in pairs. Try to pair up children who have similar interests so they will get along well.
3. On days that a partner is absent or doesn't want to go to the kindergarten room, allow the other child to pick a new partner. This is when children who aren't attending your school's kindergarten would visit.
4. If this starts in the spring, there should be plenty of time for all of the children to visit.
5. If children visit the kindergarten class and they will not be going to that class, be sure to let them know that they will be going somewhere else for kindergarten.

More to do   **General Tips:** Plan field trips, parties, or shared playground time with the kindergarten class. Some years you may have more outgoing children and you can take a song (such as Greg and Steve's "Chicken Dance") or a book, or short skit (such as "The Three Little Pigs" or "The Billy Goats Gruff") for the children to share with the kindergarten class.

More General Tips: Also, ask the kindergarten teachers to take "shortcuts" through your classroom when they walk around school. This allows the children to become familiar with the teachers in a secure setting.

Related books   *Kindergarten ABC* by Jacqueline Rogers
Miss Bindergarten Gets Ready for Kindergarten by Joseph Slate
The Night Before Kindergarten by Natasha Wing

★*Linda Ford, Sacramento, CA*

Exercise Song

3+

Materials   none

What to do   1. Teach the children the following song and use it for any transition time.

   Exercise, Exercise
   Come on everybody, do your exercise.
   Hands on hips, (put hands on hips)
   Fingers on toes. (put hands on toes)
   (name of child), *show me how your exercise goes?* (select a child to choose an exercise and have the group copy it together)

2. If there is time, give each child a turn.
3. This is great for getting the wiggles out too!

Gail Morris, Kemah, TX

Quiet Movements

3+

Materials   none

What to do   1. When going to the playground or another part of the building, and you want the children to be quiet as you walk through the halls, tell them to copy your quiet movements.
2. The challenge is to move quietly while hopping, skipping, jumping, zigzagging, and other movements.
3. Before you start remind the children that being quiet is one way to be respectful of the other classes.

Cookie Zingarelli, Columbus, OH

Hop, Skip, or Jump

3+

Materials   none

What to do
1. When it is time for a transition, give the children a choice of how they want to move to the new activity.
2. Choose a child and say, "Would you like to hop, skip, or jump to (the next activity)?"
3. When the child decides what he is going to do, chant "hop, hop, hop," "skip, skip, skip," or "jump, jump, jump" as the child moves to the next activity.

More to do   For older children, challenge them to jump to your clapped rhythm as they move to the chosen center.

Related books *Ginger Jumps* by Lisa Campbell Ernst
Hop Jump by Ellen Stoll Walsh
Hop on Pop by Dr. Seuss
Jump, Frog, Jump! by Robert Kalan
Norma Jean, Jumping Bean by Joanna Cole
One Two Three Jump! by Penelope Lively
Skip to My Lou by Robert Quackenbush

⭐*Virginia Jean Herrod, Columbia, SC*

Motor Time

3+

Materials   crawl tunnel
balance beam, piece of wood, or ribbon or tape

What to do
1. As children transition from one area to another, use props as challenges along the way.
2. In a hallway or between classrooms, put out a crawl tunnel so children have to crawl through to the new area.

(continued on the next page)

3. Place a balance beam along a travel path so children have to use it to get to the next area. One day they might walk with their left foot on the beam and their right foot on the floor. Another day the right foot can walk up high while the left foot stays on the floor. Depending on the height of the beam, the children can straddle the beam and walk with their feet on either side.

4. If you do not have a balance beam, you can substitute with a piece of wood, or put a ribbon or piece of tape on the floor.

Bev Schumacher, Racine, WI

Popcorn

3+

Materials   fabric squares in solid colors, one for each child (use at least four colors and make an extra set for you)
container, carton, or basket
carpet squares

What to do

1. Try this activity when it's time to transition to circle or group time, or any time you want to gather the class or capture their attention.

2. Call children to the group area. As children arrive, hand them a square of bright fabric in one solid color. Ask them to crouch down on floor.

3. Hold up a square of fabric or a color. The children who hold that color fabric square spring up like a kernel of popcorn popping and then crouch down again. Repeat showing a second color, and watch the popcorn pop.

4. As more children arrive, hand out more squares of fabric.

5. Continue showing colors by holding up a different color or the same one. Children pop up whenever their color is shown.

6. When more and more children gather, go faster, so that more children are popping up and down.
   Note: It's a good idea for each child to have his own square of carpet as a starting place as well as a place to return.

7. Slow the popping down, and ask all the colors of popcorn to sit on their own carpet squares.

8. If desired, chant the following poem while doing the transition activity.

Popcorn by MaryAnn Kohl
Pop. Pop. Pop. Pop. (normal voice)
Popping, popping.
Popping, popping,
Never stopping.

Pop. Pop. Very slow. (whispering voice, slower)
Popping, popping
Pop and go
Very slow.

Pop. Pop. (loud voice)
Everyone pop.
Popping, popping
Giant popping.

Pop. Pop. (tiny voice)
Baby pop.
Popping, popping
Tiny popping.

Pop. Pop. (ending, quiet voice)
Bye-bye popping.
Popcorn's ready,
We are stopping,
No more popping.

Related books   *Popcorn* by Alex Moran
The Popcorn Book by Tomie dePaola
Sing a Song of Popcorn by Beatrice Shenk De Regniers

⭐ *MaryAnn Kohl, Bellingham, WA*

Easy Hoop Ball

3+

Materials   plastic containers (ice cream containers) and scissors, or old boxes
old newspaper
masking tape

What to do
1. When you have a few extra moments, try this activity.
2. If possible, before beginning this activity, cut the bottom from the containers and attach them to a wall at a level that is appropriate for the children in your class.
3. The children roll pieces of newspaper into the shape of small balls that easily fit into their hands. Use masking tape to hold the balls in one piece.
4. Get ready for the fun! The children throw the balls in the plastic hoops or old boxes.

More to do
Math: Children can use this as a counting game, counting how many balls they can put in the hoop. They can also use distance, how far away can they be from the hoop but still put the balls in. They can then measure the distance or have another child (or the teacher) record the measurements for them.
Outdoors: Take this activity outside and attach the hoops to a fence.

⭐ *Eileen Lucas, Halifax, Nova Scotia, Canada*

Elevator Up and Down

What to do
1. Use this opportunity for exercise when children are waiting for the next activity. It helps relieve the tension of waiting and prevents unwanted fidgeting and children bothering each other.
2. Say, "Let's pretend we are elevators. Let's go up, up, up as high as we can!" (Children and leader stretch arms upward and rise as high as possible on tiptoes.) Now let's go down to the first floor. (Lower arms and come down to standing position.) Going down to the basement! (Bend knees and squat, arms extended forward to keep balance.) Going up to the first floor! (Rise slowly, stopping in standing position. Repeat as often as desired.)

Related poem **Elevator** by Mary Jo Shannon
I'm an elevator! Watch me rise so high!
I can almost touch the sky!
But I find I have to stop
When I reach the very top.
Now there's nowhere else to go
But down, down, down to the floors below.

⭐*Mary Jo Shannon, Roanoke, VA*

Galloping

3+

Materials   song

What to do   Use this song to allow children to get up and move around after sitting for a while. Have them gallop around the room to the tune of the music on the first two lines, then sing slower and slower to the end of the song. If you have a piano or xylophone, you can pick out a descending scale using the keys DBGDBG repeatedly for "galloping."

Galloping (Tune: "Pony Song")
Galloping, galloping, galloping,
How fast my pony can go,
When he's tired we'll come home,
Slow, slow, slow,
Slow, slow, slow.

⭐*Jackie Wright, Enid, OK*

Familiar Games

3+

Materials   none

What to do

1. Try this activity when you have a few extra moments, or any time when the children need to get up and move.
2. Sing "Here We Go 'Round the Mulberry Bush" and change the lyrics to go with different gross motor actions.
3. Ideas for movement include skipping around, riding a bike, flying like a bird, jumping up and down, swinging on a swing, climbing some rocks, galloping like a horse, kicking a ball, hopping like a rabbit, walking on tiptoe, bending and stretching, and marching in a parade.
4. Use these actions in other games, such as "Simon Says," "Mother May I," or "Duck, Duck Goose."

   Note: If necessary, write gross motor actions on file cards, as reminders.

   Here We Go 'Round the Mulberry Bush
   Here we go 'round the mulberry bush,
   Mulberry bush, mulberry bush,
   Here we go 'round the mulberry bush,
   On a bright and sunny day.

   This is the way we hop up and down,
   Hop up and down, hop up and down,
   This is the way we hop up and down,
   On a bright and sunny day.

More to do   **Gross Motor:** Try doing two activities at the same time, such as clapping and jumping. Try doing activities with eyes closed. This is challenging!
More Gross Motor: Have the children do motions of things they do when they get up, such as wash their face.
Math: Count the actions done.

Related book   *Norma Jean, Jumping Bean* by Joanna Cole

⭐ *Mary Brehm, Aurora, OH*

Mirrors and Shadows

3+

Materials   none

What to do

1. These are great games to play when children are waiting.

   ◆ **Shadows:** The first child in a line takes a step forward. He makes movements for the children behind him to copy.
   ◆ **Mirrors:** The first child turns to face other children. He makes movements for the other children to copy.

2. Move each child to the end of the line after he has had a turn as the leader.

More to do   **Dramatic Play**: Use a flashlight to create shadows and full-length mirror to reflect movements to extend the fun.

★ *Susan A. Sharkey, La Mesa, CA*

Pat and Clap

3+

Materials   none

What to do

1. Try the following when children are waiting for the next activity.
2. Sit in a group and begin a pattern of patting legs and clapping hands together. For example, clap, clap, pat, clap, clap, pat...
3. As soon as the children figure out the pattern, they join in, continuing until the entire group can do the pattern.
4. If there is still time, stop the first pattern and begin another. Continue in this fashion.
5. Let children take turns doing a pattern and having other children copy it.

★ *Barbara Saul, Eureka, CA*

Touch the Line

`3+`

Materials   colored tape

What to do
1. When you have a few extra moments before the next activity, gather the children in a group and try the following.
2. Make a large circle with tape on the floor.
3. Have everyone gather around and take turns telling each other what part of the body to touch the tape with.

★ *Jackie Wright, Enid, OK*

What Animals Do

`3+`

Materials   none

What to do
1. When you have a few spare moments to fill, talk to the children about animals and the movements each one makes.
2. Demonstrate or invite a child to pretend to be an animal and make its movements.
3. Invite the children to do the actions as you say the rhyme below. This rhyme is very simple and repetitive, so they children may be able to repeat it with you. Wait several minutes between each animal, so the children have time to do the actions.

Elephant, elephant, in the zoo,
Swing your trunk just like you do.

Lion, lion in the zoo,
Roar very loud just like you do.

Monkey, monkey, in the zoo,
Jump very high just like you do.

Flamingo, flamingo, in the zoo,
Balance on one foot just like you do.

Zebra, zebra, in the zoo,
Gallop very fast just like you do.

Penguin, penguin, in the zoo,
Waddle around just like you do.

Related books *1, 2, 3 to the Zoo* by Eric Carle
Color Zoo by Lois Ehlert
Good Night, Gorilla by Peggy Rathmann
Inside a Zoo in the City by Alyssa Satin Capucilli
Zoo Do's and Don'ts by Todd Parr

Sue Fleischmann, Sussex, WI

Alternating Steps

3+

Materials construction paper
scissors
contact paper

What to do 1. This is a great way to help children learn to alternate their feet on steps.
2. Cut out footprints from construction paper. Put one footprint on each step, where children's feet will go. Cover the footprints with contact paper.
   Note: You may want to continue the footprints past the steps for fun or to support the moving in a line concept. This also helps children stay in a line while walking on the steps.
3. If there is a waiting area, you might choose to put right and left footprints in pairs to mark where the children should stand. Allow ample space between these waiting feet.

Bev Schumacher, Racine, WI

Stretch, Stretch!

3+

Materials none

What to do
1. Try this activity during transition times or as a refresher break during circle or group time if you notice the group becoming restless. It can also be played while waiting for outdoor time or any other activity to start, or at pick-up time.
2. The children can sit down or stand up. Model the stretching exercises. Stretch arms way up as you say, "Stretch, stretch, stretch…!", and then "Over, over, over down to the floor," as you reach for the floor. Repeat twice and then change hand motions to first stretching up and then slowly lowering hands to your lap. Or turn hands around as you say, "Around and around and around—down to your lap." Add new things to suit your class or as suggested by the children.
3. If there is time, move on to stretching legs and feet. If children are seated, stretch feet out and then, say, "Under, under, under…," as you tuck feet under your chair. If children are standing, extend one foot and then the other to practice balancing.
4. Two or three rounds of arm and leg stretches are a refreshing break for everyone!

More to do
Gross Motor: Stretch right and left sides separately to help children learn the right and left sides of their bodies.
More Gross Motor: Add props for children to hold while stretching, such as small balls, beanbags, or stuffed animals.

⭐ *Elisheva Leah Nadler, Jerusalem, Israel*

Wiggle Words

3+

Materials   none

What to do
1. This is a great exercise to do when children have been sitting for a while, or have just come in from outdoor play.
2. Announce, "It's time to get the wiggles out." Sit in a group, and then one at a time, call on each child to stand and imitate the "wiggle" word. Wiggle words include:

- jiggle
- squirm
- twitch
- shake
- jerk
- writhe
- rattle

- wag
- quiver
- wriggle
- waggle
- quiver
- wobble

3. At a more active time, replace these wiggle words with bouncing words.

⭐ *Dotti Enderle, Richmond, TX*

Pattern Path

4+

Materials   3 colors of construction paper
crayons or markers
scissors
large circular items to trace around

What to do
1. Using a crayon, help the children trace around a circular item onto a piece of construction paper and then cut out the circles.
2. Select three children with different colored circles to put their circles in a line on the floor.

(continued on the next page)

3. Talk about the different colors. Tell the children they will be repeating the pattern. Ask the children what color would go next to follow the pattern and have that color added to the line.
4. Keep following the pattern using all the circles the children have cut out.
5. The circles can lead the children to where they need to go next.

More to do   **Gross Motor:** Add more colors to make this activity more difficult.
Math: Make the patterns more challenging for the children.

Monica Hay Cook, Tucson, AZ

Road Trips

4+

Materials   paper
markers
tape

What to do
1. Children cut out long strips of paper to use as road strips.
2. Talk about the different kinds of road signs the children might see as they ride around, such as stop, yield, mph, school, and railroad crossings.
3. Help the children make the signs.
4. Lay out the strips of paper to make roads. Tape the traffic signs around the room.
5. At any transition time, children pretend they are cars going along the road and they must obey the traffic signs along the way.

More to do   **Safety:** Provides a good opportunity to talk about safety when out walking and learning what signs mean.

Related books   *The Car Trip* by Helen Oxenbury
I Read Signs by Tana Hoban
When I Cross the Street by Dorthy Chlad

Monica Hay Cook, Tucson, AZ

The Farmer Is Planting Some Seeds

4+

Materials   ball or beanbag

What to do

1. When you have an extra moment any time during the day, try the following activity.
2. To help the children learn how to catch, gather them in a semicircle in front of you. Tell them you want to grow vegetables for a tasty soup (or fruit for a fruit salad, and so on).
3. Ask children what kinds of seeds they want to plant. The first child says the name of a vegetable, at which point you throw him a ball or beanbag. The child throws it back to you and says, "Here are the ___ seeds."
4. Move on to the next child, who throws the ball back to give you the seeds. Continue until all of the children have given you seeds.

More to do

Outdoors: Create a long obstacle course where the children need to wiggle like a worm on the ground, climb the jungle gym like a spider, or walk on a balance beam "bridge" to the garden.

⭐ *Susan Rubinoff, Wakefield, RI*

Alien Spaceships

4+

Materials
discarded CDs (music, software, or blank)
solid-colored contact paper and scissors, optional
permanent felt-tipped markers in many colors
blue masking tape
variety of "targets" (scatter rug, hula hoop, milk crate, and so on)
    depending on age and abilities of children

What to do

1. When you have an extra moment, try the following activity.
2. Read *Alistair in Outer Space* by Marilyn Sadler or another book about outer space, or talk with the children about outer space.
3. Give each child a CD to decorate as a "flying saucer" with permanent markers. Make sure the child's name is on the bottom side of the "saucer." **Note**: If CDs have designs already on them, cover them with the solid-colored contact paper first. Prepare this ahead of time and trim excess contact paper.
4. After decorating the saucers, move to the "test flight area." Children may test their saucers individually or as teams. Children stand behind the blue masking tape starting line and take turns launching (Frisbee style) their saucers.
5. Start with a large target (scatter rug or hula hoop). Two points are awarded for every saucer inside the target. One point is given for every saucer touching the edge of the target.
6. After everyone has had a turn if there is still time, make the target smaller (milk crate) and everyone tries again.

More to do
Use this activity on a rainy afternoon (near end of day), as a follow-up to a discussion of space, as an art activity, or as a math activity (adding scores).

Related song
"Twinkle, Twinkle, Little Star"

⭐ *Christina Chilcote, New Freedom, PA*

A Rolling Transition

4+

Materials   2 square boxes
newspaper, optional
tape
paper
scissors
markers or crayons
contact paper

What to do
1. Tape the boxes closed to make cubes or dice. (Before taping, stuff the boxes with newspaper to make the boxes sturdier.)
2. Cut pieces of paper to fit each side of the box. Make one set of papers for each box.
3. Make a number die with one cube. Write the numbers 1 to 6 on each piece of paper (one number per piece), tape one number to each side of the cube, and cover each side of the box with contact paper.
4. Make an "action die" with the other cube. Draw six different icons for actions (jump, hop, jumping jack, clap, blink, and so on) that the children can accomplish on the remaining pieces of paper (one action per sheet).
5. Tape an action icon to each side of the remaining box and cover it with contact paper.
6. When transitioning to another activity, have two children each roll one of the dice. They then do the number of actions shown on the dice (three blinks, two hops, four jumping jacks) before moving to the next activity. Try to allow each child to have a turn to roll a die.
7. If you are rushed for time, have two children roll the dice for a small group of children to perform. Repeat this transition activity (throughout the day, if necessary) to give each child an opportunity to roll a die.

More to do   Replace the numbers with dots so that the child has to count to figure out how many actions to perform.

Related books   *Barn Cat* by Carol Saul
Olivia Counts by Ian Falconer
Wacky Flips: Counting Critters by Peggy Tagel

★ *Ann Kelly, Johnstown, PA*

Look, I'm a Letter!

5+

Materials   none

What to do
1. Try the following activity when you have a few extra moments.
2. Have the children make letters with their bodies. This can be done standing or lying on the floor.
3. Start with simple letters, like "I," "C," and "L."
4. If there is time, try more complex letters. The children pick partners so they can work together to make their bodies into letters. Let partners take turns calling out letters for children to make.

Related books   *Ashanti to Zulu* by Margaret Musgrove
Chicka Chicka Boom Boom by Bill Martin, Jr.
Jambo Means Hello by Muriel J. Feelings
On Market Street by Anita and Arnold Lobel

⭐ *Barbara Saul, Eureka, CA*

1, 2, I Love You

3+

Materials
poster board
markers

What to do
Use this poem as a transition to group or circle time. Write it on a poster and hang it near your circle time area.

> 1, 2, I love you.
> 3, 4, come sit on the floor.
> 5, 6, get your body fixed.
> 7, 8, sit up straight.
> 9, 10, time to begin.

⭐ Jackie Wright, Enid, OK

Call to Circle Time

3+

Materials
paper
markers

What to do
Make a poster out of the following rhyme and hang it near your circle area.

> 1, 2, 3, 4,
> Put your bottom on the floor!
> 5, 6, 7, 8,
> Eyes forward, backs straight!

⭐ Jackie Wright, Enid, OK

Gathering the Group

3+

Materials   none

What to do
1. Chant the following verse to the children. Guide them to where you want to assemble for group or circle time.
2. Encourage them to sing the appropriate days of the week.

   Today is (day of the week).
   Yesterday was _____.
   Tomorrow is _____.
   All you happy children, sit right down.

⭐ *Margery Kranyik Fermino, Hyde Park, MA*

Get on Board, Little Children

3+

Materials   none

What to do
1. When transitioning from centers or cleanup to group or circle time, sing this song until every child meets you in the circle.

   Come on board, little children,
   Come on board, little children,
   Come on board, little children
   There's room for plenty of more.

2. If there are particular children who are not at circle, substitute their name instead of "children."

   Come on board, little Christa.

Related books   *Freight Train* by Donald Crews
The Little Engine That Could by Watty Piper
Trains by Byron Barton

⭐ *Kaethe Lewandowski, Centreville, VA*

Walk to Group Time

3+

Materials   none

What to do   To transition the children to group or circle time, sing the following to the tune of "Here We Go 'Round the Mulberry Bush." You may substitute "circle time," "music time," "lunch time," and so on for "group time."

Here I walk to group time,
Group time, group time.
Here I walk to group time,
With very quiet feet.

I'll raise my hand so I can talk,
So I can talk, so I can talk.
I'll raise my hand so I can talk,
And check my hands and feet.

⭐ *Jackie Wright, Enid, OK*

It's Time to Come to Circle

3+

Materials   card for each child, labeled with her name

What to do   1. To transition children to group or circle time, sing the following to the tune of "Did You Ever See a Lassie?"

It's time to come to circle,
To circle, to circle,
It's time to come to circle,
To circle right now.
There's (child's name) and (child's name),
And (child's name) and (child's name).
It's time to come to circle,
To circle right now.

(continued on the next page)

Additional verse:
We're sitting in a circle... right here on the floor.

2. Use the children's names in the song. For practice with reading names, hold up the name cards at the appropriate times.

⭐ *Jackie Wright, Enid, OK*

Make a Circle   3+

Materials   none

What to do   To transition the children to group or circle time, sing the following to the tune of "Frère Jacques."

Make a circle,
Make a circle,
Big and round,
Big and round,
Everybody join hands,
Everybody join hands,
Without a sound,
Without a sound.

⭐ *Jackie Wright, Enid, OK*

Move It!   3+

Materials   none

What to do   1. Sing the song on the following page to the tune of "Buffalo Gals" to transition children to circle time.

Children, children, jump up and down
Jump up and down, jump up and down.
Children, children, jump up and down
Until I say "STOP!" (children stop and freeze)

2. If desired, change "jump up and down" to other actions such as clap your hands, stomp your feet, and spin around. Also change the word "children" to a child's name in the class. The rest of the children can gather in a circle and the one child being sung about can follow directions for the song. You can also change "until I say STOP" to "go sit at the table" or "wait at the door" if you are doing one child at a time.

⭐ *Shelley Hoster, Norcross, GA*

More Friends

3+

Materials   none

What to do
1. Use this activity to transition to circle or group time.
2. Ask one child to sit on the floor. Say the rhyme to this child who picks another child to come and sit down.

   One little child
   Sitting on the floor.
   He wanted a friend,
   So he called one more.

3. The second child sits with the first. Count the number of children together. Say the rhyme again, and ask the second child to pick a friend.

   Two little children
   Sitting on the floor.
   They wanted a friend,
   So they called one more.

4. Always count the number of children out loud before going on. Continue until all the children are sitting.

(continued on the next page)

More to do   Adapt this idea to any theme. Change "child" to duck, bunny, dinosaur, dog, cat, and so on.

Math: This activity can also be modified for older children by asking for two children at a time and counting by twos.

Related books   *Counting Kisses: A Kiss and Read Book* by Karen Katz
Fish Eyes: A Book You Can Count On by Lois Ehlert
Olivia Counts by Ian Falconer

⭐ *Sue Fleischmann, Sussex, WI*

Music Box Transitions   3+

Materials   recordings of familiar songs
CD or tape player

What to do   While children are cleaning up and returning to the rug for a large group activity, try these musical transition activities.

◆ Play a short snippet of a familiar song. Ask a child to identify the song and invite everyone to sing along.

◆ Ask a child to name a favorite tune and stand up to lead the group in singing it.

◆ Keep a bag with song titles written on sturdy cards. Let one child draw a card and sing the song alone, with friends, or lead the whole group.

◆ Play part of a melody and ask the children to pat their legs fast or slowly, depending on the rhythm.

⭐ *Susan Oldham Hill, Lakeland, FL*

Super-Bowl Soup

3+

Materials   large soup tureen
large ladle

What to do
1. To draw the children's attention and transition them to group or circle time, start stirring the ladle in a large soup tureen.
2. Sit in a circle around the tureen and say the following sing-song rhyme:

    Potatoes and carrots, oop, oop, oop!
    What did the cook put into the soup?

3. Go around the circle and give each child a turn to name something that they would put into the Super-Bowl Soup. Some of their ideas may be outlandish and that's the fun of it! Continue as time allows.

More to do   **Literacy:** To emphasize the printed word, write down their ideas on a piece of paper shaped like a potato or carrot and let them add that paper to the tureen.
Music: To emphasize rhythm, invite hand-clapping, finger snapping, and toe tapping motions.

★ *Judy Fujawa, The Villages, FL*

Time for Circle

3+

Materials   none

What to do   To transition children to group or circle time, teach the following to the tune of "Frère Jacques."

    Time for circle, time for circle,
    Sit right down, sit right down.
    We are all together, we are all together,
    Sitting down, sitting down.

(continued on the next page)

More to do Substitute story, singing, or any activity that is preceded by sitting in a group for circle.

★ *Margery Kranyik Fermino, Hyde Park, MA*

Color Muncher

3+

Materials empty tissue box
construction paper in color of the week
wiggle eye
tape
markers

What to do
1. This is a great activity to transition to group or circle time.
2. Before group or circle time, make a "Color Muncher" for each color week (decorate a tissue box). Send home a note to the parents explaining the "Color Muncher" and that it "eats" the color of the week. Ask the parent to send items with their child that is the color of the week such as pieces of fabric, ribbon, balloons, and other appropriately colored items.
3. Use the "Color Muncher" to collect items from each child at the beginning of group or circle time
4. Keep it visible in the classroom throughout the day

More to do Use the "Color Muncher" to introduce the color of the week and explain the colors of the rainbow. You can also have two "Color Munchers"

Related books *Growing Colors* by Bruce McMillan
Little Blue and Little Yellow by Leo Lionni
Planting a Rainbow by Lois Ehlert

★ *Sandy L. Scott, Vancouver, WA*

Musical Hugs

`3+`

Materials record, cassette, or CD player
recording of song with lots of rhythm

What to do
1. This activity is a fun way to transition to group or circle time.
2. Choose upbeat music that everyone likes.
3. Explain that in this game the children put their arms around each other's shoulders and link up in a line. The children must keep time to the music with some sort of action, not necessarily all the same, but they must remain linked and moving to the music.
4. Play music, and after a few minutes, stop the music. Tell everyone to find someone to hug. They stay connected and dance until the game ends.
5. Start the music, and after a few minutes, stop the music again. Tell the partners to find another pair to link to. Now you have groups of four children linked together in a line, moving to the beat of the music.
6. Start the music. Continue as before until you have one giant hug by forming a circle with each person's arm around the shoulder of the person on either side of him.

Jackie Wright, Enid, OK

I Can Wait

`3+`

Materials books or theme-related item

What to do
1. To help children wait while everyone is coming to group or circle time, place a book at each child's spot to look at while they're waiting for the others to join the group.
2. Or, when the children take their spots, give them a theme-related item that will lead into the group lesson. Let children guess what the item is about. The following items would be perfect: cardboard shape, letter or numeral, feather, rock, piece of string or cloth, seashell, ribbon, or a large item to pass around.

(continued on the next page)

3. The first person seated in the "ready to learn" position can be the holder of a special object, stuffed animal, puppet, or magic rock.

More to do If you prefer not to have a permanent large group configuration, invest in carpet squares for "sit-upons," which are 12" x 18" vinyl pads. Place the labeled pads in the group arrangement you need for particular activity. Hiding a piece of tape or card under the pad serves the purpose of choosing who will go first, who is the leader, or who has a special job for the selected activity.

★ *Susan R. Forbes, Daytona Beach, FL*

Puppet Songs

3+

Materials puppets

What to do
1. When some children are waiting for group or circle time to begin, grab your box of puppets and let a child come up and choose one to hold.
2. They may want a friend to come up and join them with a puppet if they like less attention on themselves.
3. The child (or children) can choose a song to sing for the group, or sing with the group. If you have enough puppets, the children who are waiting can each have a puppet to help the group sing songs together.

Related books *The Book of Kids Songs* by Nancy and John Cassidy
If You Give a Moose a Muffin by Laura Joffe Numeroff
Louie by Ezra Jack Keats

★ *Laura Durbrow, Lake Oswego, OR*

Watch and Follow

Materials   none

What to do
1. To grab children's attention when it is time for group or circle time, begin reciting favorite fingerplays, after announcing that it is time to gather on the rug, or for children to take their seats.
2. Begin saying the poems in the normal voice with appropriate gestures.
3. Continue reviewing familiar fingerplays, lowering your voice until you are just humming tune or word syllables. As the children continue to follow your lead, "say" the last familiar or favorite fingerplays, using only gestures.
4. End the ritual with a silent clap, by hugging yourself, or by pointing to your eyes and ears to signal "watch and listen."
5. If the child is not "showing you her eyes," whisper her name, and point to your eyes and ears.

More to do   Using hand signs to communicate is extremely effective for young children. They like the mystery involved with knowing a secret sign. Recommended signs include ones for stop, dangerous, listen, thank you, and take your seats.

Susan R. Forbes, Daytona Beach, FL

What's in the Bag?

Materials   any large bag (fabric, paper, plastic)
tactile object

What to do
1. This is a lovely calming transition activity and a great way to grab children's attention. If you sit alone in a quiet area of the classroom with the bag in front of you, their curiosity will be piqued. With any luck, they'll make their way over one at a time to investigate what's happening and you'll have them hooked until the secret is revealed!

(continued on the next page)

2. In advance, place a tactile object at the bottom of the bag and close the top or make the opening of the bag as small as possible.

3. Have the children gather around you. Sit with the bag on your lap or a table and invite each child in turn to come and put her hand inside to feel the object. The further they have to bury their arm into the bag to reach the "secret" inside, the better!

4. Ask the child for one word to describe the object, such as squashy, smooth, scratchy, furry, cold, small anything, but they mustn't say what they think it is just yet.

5. Keep going until everyone has had a chance to feel what's in the bag, getting each child in turn to use a different descriptive word.

6. When everyone's had their turn, ask for guesses as to what is hidden in the bag.

More to do   **Science:** Write down the words the children used to describe the object when they felt it, and then write a separate list of words which describe it now they can see it. Discuss the five senses and how we use them to identify things. If possible, have a selection of objects (they don't all need to go in the bag) for the children to look at, listen to, touch, smell and taste.

Related books   *My Five Senses* by Aliki
You Can't Taste a Pickle With Your Ear by Harriet Ziefert

⭐ *Kirsty Neale, Charleville Circus, London, United Kingdom*

Willaby Wallaby   3+

Materials   stuffed animals

What to do   1. To grab the children's attention at group or circle time, bring out stuffed animals and tell the children how happy they are to be at school today. Tell them one of the animals has a very funny name, Willaby Wallaby, and he loves sitting on top of people! Start with yourself and say the following rhyme (if your name is Ann!).

Willaby wallaby **wan**,
An elephant sat on **Ann**. (have an elephant sit on top of your head)

2. Move around the circle and let each child have a turn holding the elephant on top of her head, while you say (if the child's name is Jacob), "Willaby wallaby wakened, an elephant sat on Jacob." Then the child can go wash his hands for snack, or do whatever transition is next.

3. With older children, do the first part of the rhyme and see if they can guess whose name it rhymes with and then hand that child the elephant.

4. Instead of an elephant, you can say other names: Willaby wallaby wan, a monkey sat on Ann.

More to do   **Gross Motor**: Read books about elephant or animals. *Elmer* by David McKee is a good book for moving like different animals. Act out "Elephants Went Out to Play." One child sits in the middle of the circle and is the elephant and puts extended arms together to pretend it is the trunk and swings it.

Related song   **One Elephant** (traditional)
One elephant went out to play,
On a spider's web one day.
He had such enormous fun,
That he called for another elephant to come. (Call for elephant.)

A child picks another child to join her in the middle of the circle. At the end, say the following verse:

15 (or the number of children in your class) *elephants went out to play,*
On a spider's web one day.
They had such enormous fun
That their moms all said they had to go home.

Say, "Go home elephant, go home elephant!" And all the elephants (children) return to their seats in the circle.

⭐*Ann Scalley, Orleans, MA*

Interruption Song

3+

Materials   none

What to do   To transition children to group or circle time and help them learn the rules, sing the following to the tune of "Lazy Mary, Will You Get Up?"

Only one can talk at a time,
So this is what I'll try to do.
I'll be as quiet as a mouse,
'Til other folks are through.

★ *Jackie Wright, Enid, OK*

Greeting

3+

Materials   none

What to do   1. To transition to group or circle time, have each child turn to her neighbor and sing this song to the tune of "The Farmer in the Dell."

When I shake your hand,
It means I want to say,
Hi (child's name) *how are you?*
And have a happy day!

2. Instead of shaking hands, you might also wave, give a hug, or say hello.

★ *Kaethe Lewandowski, Centreville, VA*

Hello! Hello!

Materials   none

What to do   Transition children to group or circle time by welcoming each child with the following rhyme.

Hello! Hello!
What do you say?
We're so glad to have _____ (insert child's name) here today!

More to do   **Language**: Replace "hello" with the French "bonjour" or the Spanish "hola."

★ Karyn F. Everham, Fort Myers, FL

Microphone

Materials   microphone with a speaker attached

What to do   1. When you want to get the children's attention during group or circle time, take out a microphone.
2. Let children use it to answer questions related to your theme. For example, for Animals week, you could ask, "What animal would you like to be?" Children love to answer the questions and hear their voice through a microphone.

More to do   Use the microphone for Show and Tell or during daily New Reports from the children. It is a great group or circle time addition to many activities.

★ Gail Morris, Kemah, TX

Left and Right

3+

Materials   none

What to do
1. To transition children to group or circle time, say the following chant.
2. Children will participate quickly when they are included in movements. This also helps with learning the right and left hands.

   This is my left hand la la la la (hold left hand in the air)
   This is my right hand la la la la (hold right hand in the air)
   That is the reason I'm so happy with delight (put both hands down at sides)
   I know my left hand from my right!

   ★ *Sandy L. Scott, Vancouver, WA*

Song for Walking, Sitting, and Quiet Times

3+

Materials   none

What to do
1. Sing this song to transition to circle time.

   We Are Walking (Tune: "Frère Jacques")
   We are walking, we are walking,
   To our seat, to our seat.
   We walk with quiet feet; we walk with quiet feet.
   Yes we will, yes we will.

   We sit so still, we sit so still,
   Hands in our laps, hands in our laps.
   We are very quiet; we are very quiet.
   Shh, shh, shh! Shh, shh, shh! (put finger to lips)

2. Sing other verses for cleanup, music activities, and gross motor activities.

We are cleaning... we like to have our room clean... yes we do.
We are marching... with our instruments... we can make music... as we march.
We are kicking... with our feet... we can kick high... kick, kick, kick.

★ *Mary Brehm, Aurora, OH*

Show and Tell

3+

Materials   none

What to do   To transition to Show and Tell, sing the following to the tune of "The Farmer in the Dell." Substitute another child's name in the second verse each time you sing the song.

> *It's time for show and tell,*
> *It's time for show and tell,*
> *Sit right down and listen well,*
> *It's time for show and tell.*
>
> (Child's name), *it's your turn,*
> (Child's name), *it's your turn,*
> *We'll listen well so we can learn,*
> (Child's name), *it's your turn.*

★ *Jackie Wright, Enid, OK*

Field Trip Song

3+

Materials   none

What to do
1. To help the children transition from group time to a field trip, try this idea.
2. Encourage the children to tell you what they think they might see on the trip. Adapt the tune "Going on a Picnic" on Raffi's *Corner Grocery Store* album to fit the words. Repeat as many times as there are ideas for what they will see.

Going on a field trip,
Leaving right away.
If we could, we would stay all day.

Going to the (destination).
What will we see?
Use your imagination;
You tell me.

Ready for a field trip,
Here we go.

We might see a _____
And we might see a _____
And we might see a _____
And we might see a _____
We might see a _____
And we might see a _____
And we might see a _____
And we might see a _____
And a _____.

⭐ *Jackie Wright, Enid, OK*

Birthday

3+

Materials   computer
color printer or markers
8 ½" x 11" poster board

What to do

1. Use this idea to call roll or dismiss students by having them recite their birthdays.
2. Print out a poster that reads:

   Apples, pears, peaches, plums,
   Tell me when your birthday comes!

3. Point to one child and say the rhyme. After that child says when her birthday is, record them as present, tell her to go wash her hands, go to the snack table, or any other transition.

⭐ *Jackie Wright, Enid, OK*

Birthday Boy or Girl

3+

Materials   none

What to do   On days when a child in your class has a birthday, transition the child (and the rest of the class) to group or circle time by singing the following to the tune of "Do You Know the Muffin Man?"

Oh, (child's name) is the birthday boy (or girl),
The birthday boy, the birthday boy,
Oh, (child's name) is the birthday boy,
On (date of birthday).

(continued on the next page)

We all know how old he (or she) is,
How old he is, how old he is.
We all know how old he is,
He is (number) years old.

Yay! (child's name)! (clap the same number of times as the child is old)

More to do   **Literacy**: Make a class book titled, "What Did You Do on Your Birthday?" Each child can illustrate something she did on her birthday. Take dictation using the child's own words.

⭐ *Jackie Wright, Enid, OK*

Rhyme Time

3+

Materials   none

What to do
1. When you are working on rhymes and you have a few extra moments at circle time, play this simple and fun game.
2. Ask the children to stand up and get ready to listen for rhymes.
3. When you say, "Go!" the children jump up and down. They continue jumping if they hear you say words that rhyme and stop if they hear one word that doesn't rhyme.
4. Say, "Go!" While the children are jumping, call out three to four words that rhyme, such as "cake," "rake," "snake," and "lake," and then call out one that doesn't rhyme, such as "dog." They should stop jumping.
5. Say, "Go!" again and use another rhyming family such as words that end in "all." Keep going until the children get the hang of listening for the words that do not rhyme. Use real and nonsense words for more fun. The point here is for the children to develop their listening skills for rhyming.

Related song   "Rhyme Time" by Greg and Steve

Related books   *Hop on Pop* by Dr. Seuss
There's a Wocket in My Pocket! by Dr. Seuss

⭐ *Shelley Hoster, Norcross, GA*

Transition Turns

3+

Materials   props (puppets or small stuffed animals) for songs "I Know an Old Lady"
                  and "Old MacDonald" (optional)

What to do   1. To facilitate the end of circle in an orderly fashion, sing a song that will give
                     each child a turn. At the end of her turn, the child leaves the group to wash
                     hands and line up. This cuts down on the crowd at the sink!
                     Author's Note: This will work if there is only one teacher in the class, but is
                     even better if there is another adult to facilitate progress.
                  2. With "I Know an Old Lady" use a puppet or a paper bag puppet of the "Old
                     Lady." As each animal is sung about, place the puppets in the Old Lady's
                     tummy. You can sing the song more than once, or the child putting the
                     animal in the "Old Lady" can pick a friend to go with them. Different animals
                     and verses of the song can be created to increase the number of turns so
                     everyone gets a chance.
                  3. With "Old MacDonald" fill a bag with farm animals. Each child has a turn naming
                     the farm animal they want the class to sing about, or they draw an animal from
                     the bag. After their verse, the child goes to wash hands and line up.

★Tracie O'Hara, Charlotte, NC

Washing Hands Poem

3+

Materials   none

What to do   1. Give each child a squirt of liquid soap and say the following poem.

This little hand is a good little hand.
This little hand is his brother.
Together they wash and they wash and they wash.
One hand washes the other.

2. Dismiss the children one at a time or in pairs to wash off the soap.

★Kaethe Lewandowski, Centreville, VA

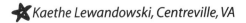

Choose a Friend

3+

Materials none

What to do When moving from circle time to center time, use this social skills activity.
1. When circle time is over, ask the children to stand in a circle.
2. Have one child stand on the outside of the circle. As the children sing the following simple song, the child marches around the outside of the circle. When the song ends, the child chooses a friend.

Choose a Friend (Tune: "Mary Had a Little Lamb")
(Child) *needs to choose a friend,*
Choose a friend, choose a friend.
(Child) *needs to choose a friend,*
A friend to go and play.

3. The first child chooses a center to play in. The children sing the song as the chosen friend marches around the circle. The new child chooses another friend at the end of the song, and then goes to a center.
4. Continue until all the children have been chosen and released to center time.
5. Use this activity in a variety of circumstances. When washing hands for meals, call one child to wash and then ask that child to call another child. Continue until all the children have been called.

Related books *Do You Want to Be My Friend?* by Eric Carle
Everett Anderson's Friend by Lucille Clifton
A Friend Is Someone Who Likes You by Joan Walsh Anglund
Make Friends, Zachary! by Muriel Blaustein
May I Bring a Friend? by Beatrice Schenk de Regniers
My Friends by Taro Gomi
A Rainbow of Friends by P.K. Halliman
Two Good Friends by Judy Delton
We Are Best Friends by Aliki

★ *Virginia Jean Herrod, Columbia, SC*

Bottom of Your Shoes

3+

Materials   shoes

What to do
1. At group or circle time, have the children take a look at the bottom of their shoes and then put their feet out straight so they can see everyone's shoes.
2. Use this to transition gradually from group or circle to washing hands for snack. Say, "If you have black on the bottom of your shoes, you can go wash your hands for snack." Or, "If you have the number 1 on the bottom of your shoe…" or "If you have a flower on the bottom of your shoe…"
3. Say silly things such as, "If you have played on the bottom of your shoes, you can wash your hands for snack."

   Author's Note: The children in my class are so used to this transition activity, sometimes they sit down and start looking at the bottom of their shoes.

More to do   **Literacy**: Create a class "Whose Shoes?" Take pictures of each child from the knees down of their shoes. Make this into a book and guess whose shoes are on each page. The next page could be a picture or name of child whose shoes are on the previous page.

★ *Ann Scalley, Orleans, MA*

If Your Name Is…

3+

Materials   none

What to do
1. Use this activity when dismissing children from group or circle time. Sing to the tune of "If You're Happy and You Know It."

   If your name is _____, wash your hands…

2. You can also sing this song for each child saying something that makes her happy, and then leaving the circle.

★ *Kaethe Lewandowski, Centreville, VA*

Roll the Ball

Materials   any ball

What to do   1. When group or circle time is over and it is time to move to a new area, dismiss the children by singing the following song (Tune: "This Old Man"). When the child rolls the ball back to you, she can move to the next activity.
2. Introduce the song at a group or circle time. Have the children practice the song and words.

Roll the ball, play the game.
When you get the ball you say your name.

Additions:
Roll the bus…
Toss the sponge…
Tell your favorite color…
Toss the beanbag…
Say your age…
Tell where you live…

Sandra Nagel, White Lake, MI

Pack-It-Up Suitcase Fun 4+

Materials   suitcase (decorated, colorful, unique, unusual, or just plain)
colorful pictures of a variety of destinations

What to do   1. Before group or circle time, place colorful pictures of a variety of destinations inside the suitcase. Examples of destinations include campground, mountains, beach, desert, safari, horse ranch, Washington DC, cruise, Disneyland, and the North Pole.

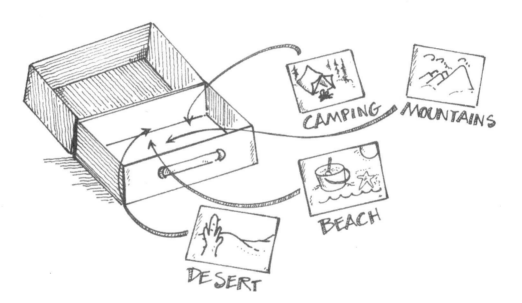

2. When you have a few extra moments, select a child to open the suitcase and take out one of the pictures. Go around the circle asking each child to list an item they would pack for the trip. Continue as time allows.

⭐ *Judy Fujawa, The Villages, FL*

Pull 'n Tell Story

4+

Materials   decorative bag, colorful box, an unusual container, or a plain paper grocery bag
items to put into the bag (see the activity for suggestions).

What to do
1. Before circle or group time, place a variety of items in the bag or box.
   Examples include keys, necklace, crayon, scarf, whistle, glove, shoe, puppet,
   flower, stuffed animal, magnifying glass, cookie cutter, play cell phone, video
   tape, musical tape, map, sunglasses, golf ball, block, and any other item that
   you think will spark the children's imagination.
2. When you have a few extra moments at group or circle time, invite the
   children to create a story, perhaps beginning with "Once Upon a Time…"
3. Pass the bag around the circle. As each child pulls out an item, ask them to
   incorporate that item into the story, weaving a unique tale.

More to do   Change the items in the bag or box on a regular basis. Items can reflect on a
certain "theme" such as an adventure, a mystery, a funny story, a book, a
classroom theme, or the time or season of the year.

★ *Judy Fujawa, The Villages, FL*

Carpet Squares

4+

Materials   carpet sample for each child
3" masking tape
permanent marker

What to do
1. Use this activity to help children transition to group or circle time.
2. Put a strip of tape across one of the short sides of the carpet sample.
3. Write the children's first name so that when they are sitting on the carpet,
   they can read their name.
4. The carpet samples allow the children to have a space that is their own while
   they are waiting for the group or circle time to begin.

5. The carpet sample also gives children a defined area for their hands and feet It is easier for children to sit if others are not in their space.

⭐ *Sandy L. Scott, Vancouver, WA*

Alphabet Soup

4+

Materials   large cooking pot
letters of the alphabet cut from construction paper

What to do   1. When you have a few extra minutes at group or circle time, try this activity.
2. Place the cooking pot in the middle of the floor or on a table. Give each child in the room a letter from the alphabet.
3. Say the first part of the poem:

   Alphabet soup, in the pot
   Stir it up, until it's hot
   Add a letter,
   Make it better,
   Say the word,
   Like B for BIRD.

4. Ask each child, in turn, to bring up her letter. Show it to the class and say a word that starts with that letter. The child places her letter in the pot.
5. When all the children have placed their letter in the pot, say the second part of the poem:

   All those words should taste just fine.
   Let's taste the soup, and try to rhyme.
   Like C for CAT or T for TIME.
   Find a W to WASH the dishes.
   Find a D to yell DELICIOUS!

(continued on the next page)

6. Each child takes a letter from the pot. As they take a letter, they say a word that starts with that letter. If they find the W, they must wash the dishes (that means collect all the letters at the end of the game and clear the pot away). If they find the letter D, they have to yell "Delicious!"

More to do   Talk about food groups and what nutritious foods could be put into a soup that begins with the letters C for Carrot or M for Macaroni.

 Amelia K. Griffin, Ontario, Canada

Class Calendar

4+

Materials   large calendar with no numbers
two sets of calendar numbers

What to do
1. When you have a few moments during group or circle time, do the following activity.
2. Have the children sit in an area close to the calendar. Begin by using one of the calendar numbers.
3. The next day, use a number from the second set of numbers. Continue until the end of the month. Ask who can see the pattern of the numbers and repeat them every day. For example, if you used two Halloween theme calendar numbers, they may see that you used a ghost-witch-ghost-witch pattern.

Related book   *Chicken Soup With Rice* by Maurice Sendak

Barbara Saul, Eureka, CA

The "Because" Book

4+

Materials drawing paper
colored pens
markers, crayons, and pencils

What to do

1. When you have an extra moment during group or circle time, select a topic for a book. Some examples include:

   ◆ My mother is like a doctor because…!
   ◆ My friend is like Curious George because…!
   ◆ My grandpa is like a police officer because…!

2. Go around the circle and ask the children to complete the sentences.

More to do **Books:** If time allows, ask the children draw a picture of their answer. Then write their answers on the drawing paper. This is guaranteed to create an endearing and amusing book.

⭐ *Judy Fujawa, The Villages, FL*

Grocery Cart Game

4+

Materials child-sized grocery cart

What to do

1. When you have a few extra moments at group or circle time, try the following activity.
2. Place a child-sized grocery cart in the middle of the circle.
3. Talk about the different departments in a supermarket, such as frozen foods, canned goods, produce, bakery, deli, and flowers. You might want to make a list of all of the different aisles and departments.

(continued on the next page)

4. Start the game with this simple rhyme:

   I went to the supermarket and this is what I bought…

5. Give each child a turn to name the item they bought, "shopping" in one department at a time. Continue as time allows.

More to do   **Literacy**: Focus on the printed word by writing down the names of the items that they bought in each department.

⭐ *Judy Fujawa, The Villages, FL*

Sharing Clues   4+

Materials   item from home and paper with clues about the item (parents help children with the clues)

What to do
1. Try this activity, which is a variation of Show and Tell, when you have a few extra minutes during group or circle time.
2. Instead of having the children simply show their item to the class, have them place it in a bag and bring clues written on paper (parents help with this).
3. Have three clues about the item. The rest of the class tries to guess what the item is that the child brought to share.
4. The child can call on her classmates to see what they think she brought to school. The clues can include things such as the item's color, whether it is an animal or not, its name, what you can do with the item, and so on.
5. The clues keep all the children involved in the sharing and guessing process.

⭐ *Sandy L. Scott, Vancouver, WA*

What's That Sound Coming From the Barn?

`4+`

Materials   toy barn (or a picture or model of a barn)

What to Do
1. Place a toy barn, or a picture or model of a barn, in the middle of the circle.
2. When you have a few extra moments during group or circle time, say this sing-song rhyme:

   Here we are visiting the farm.
   What's that sound coming from the barn?

3. Go around the circle and give each child a turn to name a sound coming from the barn. Repeat the rhyme after each child's idea is shared. Continue as time allows.

★ *Judy Fujawa, The Villages, FL*

Weather Graph

`4+`

Materials   blank graph with four columns (sample graph on the next page)
markers

What to do
1. Prepare the blank graph ahead of time.
2. At the bottom of the graph, put pictures of the sun, rain, clouds, and snow. Laminate the chart so it can be used for each new month. Pick a child each day to color in a portion of the graph above the weather picture.
3. Use the graph to interest the children in group or circle time. Talk about which picture has the most, least, or none at all. As the month progresses, count the graph segments aloud each day. Use the graph to predict what the weather will be like tomorrow. At the end of the month, the graphs can be cleaned off to use again or they can be saved and put up in the room. As each graph is added, talk about which month had the most rain, and so on.

(continued on the next page)

	Sun	Rain	Clouds	Snow
15				
14				
13				
12				
11				
10				
9				
8				
7				
6				
5				
4				
3				
2				
1				

Related books *Come On, Rain!* by Karen Hesse
Rain by Peter Spier
Snowflake Bently by Jacqueline Briggs Martin
The Snowman by Raymond Briggs
The Snowy Day by Ezra Jack Keats

⭐*Barbara Saul, Eureka, CA*

Little Bit of the Old With the New

4+

Materials appropriate materials to match the circumstance

What to do

1. Transitions are often the most difficult of life's lessons. A positive approach is to provide strategies to guide children through transitions. Start a brief discussion about transitions at a group or circle time activity. Discussion starters include:

   ◆ How do you feel when your mom tells you it's time to go to bed?
   ◆ How do you feel when you have to give up a toy to your brother or sister?
   ◆ What do you do to help you get to sleep at night?
   ◆ What do you do if there is a thunderstorm outside while you're sleeping and you're afraid to get out of bed?
   ◆ How do you feel at childcare or preschool when the teacher tells you it's time to clean up, but you don't feel ready to stop playing yet?

2. Listen for possible answers to the above questions that might spark further ideas.
3. Provide strategies for transitioning comfortably from activity to activity or room to room. For example, perhaps the children could take a bit of the "old" activity with them to the new activity (they could take a block to the kitchen area to now represent food instead of a building block). Perhaps a parent could stay just long enough for a child to feel comfortable playing at a new activity.

More to do As children sit during group or circle time activities, distribute beeswax or small "fidgety-type toys" to them to quietly keep their hands busy while listening. Some children need to have an object or maybe even three objects in their hands at all times. As long as this is not disruptive, it is best to allow it to happen. It likely will help to calm this particular child.

★ *Kate Ross, Middlesex, VT*

Shape Game

4+

Materials   foam core
scissors
container or pocket chart

What to do
1. Ahead of time, cut foam core into shapes and print one child's name or initials on one side of each shape.
2. Hold up a shape. When a child recognizes her name or initials, she gets the shape.
3. When all the children have their shape, call out a shape and the children holding that shape place it on the pocket chart or container and move to the next activity.

BACK OF SHAPES

Terri   Aaron   Amanda   Dennis

★ Regina Smith, Charlotte, NC

Winter Words

4+

Materials   laminated pictures depicting seasons (calendars work well)
easel
chart paper
marker

What to do
1. If it is winter time, focus on winter scenes. To transition the children from group time to the next activity, ask one child to tell you a word describing winter objects, activities, or events (snow, cold, snowman, cocoa, mittens, ice skates, boots, skiing, and so on).
2. After the child has said a winter word, that child can go to the next activity.
3. Write their words on the easel. Give children hints as necessary so everyone is successful.

More to do   **Fine Motor**: Cut the laminated seasonal photos into two to five pieces to make puzzles. Put each puzzle into a zipper-closure bag and place them on the tables so children can practice putting them back together.

Related book   *The Snowy Day* by Ezra Jack Keats

★ *Barb Lindsay, Mason City, IA*

Coins in the Can

Materials   potato chip or nut can (container with a plastic lid and a metal bottom)
duct tape, if necessary
scissors or knife (adult only)
coins—pennies, dimes, nickels, quarters

What to do
1. Use this activity to dismiss each child to the next area.
2. Beforehand, clean out the inside of the can. Make sure there are no sharp edges. Cover any sharp edges with duct tape. Use the scissors or a knife to cut a rectangular slit in the middle of the plastic lid (adult only).

(continued on the next page)

3. At group or circle time, talk about money. Focus on the vocabulary—money, coins, pennies, dimes, nickels, and quarters.

4. Hold up a coin. State what it is called. Place the coin in the slit. The coin will make a sound when it hits the bottom. The sound is often reinforcing for the children and makes them eager to participate.

5. Explain that each child will have a turn to put a coin in to the container. Hand each child a coin.
   Note: When this is a new activity it helps to state what coin the child it receiving.

6. Each child takes a turn saying what coin she has and drops it in to the can. Then dismiss the child to the next activity.

7. To begin, use just two types of coins and then add another coin as the group's skills improve.

More to do   **Literacy:** Use this activity to learn the names of colors by using colored buttons, or learn the name of a picture or what letter it begins with by using metal juice can lids (from frozen juice) with stickers on them. The child must say what the picture is; the beginning sound; the letter or numeral that is printed on the lid.

★ Sandra L. Nagel, White Lake, MI

Create-a-Creature   4+

Materials   drawing paper
markers, crayons, colored pencils

What to do

1. At the end of circle or group time, to help the children transition to the next activity, ask one child at a time to start describing an imaginary creature, one feature at a time.

2. Encourage the use of descriptive words. For example, long curly hair, big buggy eyes, small pointed ears, crooked stumpy legs, and missing teeth.

3. Each child has a piece of drawing paper and adds to their creature as each child shares her suggestion. Remember: NO PEEKING! It will be great fun to see the variety of creatures created.

4. As each child shows her creature, dismiss her to the next area.

More to do   **Literacy**: To focus on the written word, write down each of the descriptive features. Read all of the descriptive words after the drawings are complete and display them for all to see and enjoy.

 Judy Fujawa, The Villages, FL

What's in a Name?

5+

Materials   card stock name cards for the group, approximately 4" x 9"
container the cards will fit into

What to do
1. To encourage children to return to their places after a small group activity, place the name cards out on the rug so all the children can see them.
2. As the children return, ask them to place their name cards in the container.
3. While they wait, the children can read the name cards that are on the rug.

More to do   **Writing**: To motivate good handwriting skills, ask each child to use her best handwriting to make her own name cards for the activity.

Susan Oldham Hill, Lakeland, FL

Writing Numbers

5+

Materials   none

What to do
1. Have children imitate writing a number in the air as they are dismissed.
2. The children should use their arms and hands to imitate your demonstration.
3. Describe the motion while demonstrating the action.
4. Face the same direction as the children or demonstrate the number backwards so the children practice the motion in the correct direction.

Barb Lindsay, Mason City, IA

Question of the Week

5+

Materials

pocket chart
sentence strips
markers
cards with one child's name on each

What to do

1. Brainstorm questions that go with the theme for each week. They can be yes-or-no questions or multiple-choice questions. Write the question on a sentence strip and put it at the top of a pocket chart.
2. Write the possible answers to the questions on smaller pieces of sentence strips and add them under the question.
3. As a transition to leaving group or circle time, read the question and possible answers. One by one, as the children leave group or circle time, go up and put their name card under the answer they choose.
4. After everyone has a turn or later in the day, take a minute to count the responses. Which answer had the most names? Which ones had the least? This is a great math and graphing activity to use regularly in your classroom.

More to do

Literacy: It is helpful to add picture clues next to the answers. This helps with pre-reading skills. If your answers are "yes" or "no," you could add a smile face next to yes and a sad face next to no. Keep the pictures simple. Teachers can add their names to the questions of the week too.

Gail Morris, Kemah, TX

A Walk in Space

3+

Materials   pictures showing outer space, astronauts, and spaceships
chairs

What to do
1. Use this activity for any transition time during the day.
2. Talk about space, gravity, and how astronauts move in space (very slowly).
3. Set up chairs in a circle facing outward.
4. Have the children pretend they are putting on a helmet and space suit. The children sit in their chairs and pretend to strap themselves in to get ready for take off. Together, count down "10, 9, 8, 7, 6, 5, 4, 3, 2, 1. Lift off!"
5. Children pretend they are being "whooshed" up into space. Ask them to look out the windows of the spaceship and describe what they see.
6. Prepare for the landing. Is it a hard or soft landing? Take off seat belts.
7. Encourage them to get up slowly and move around "space," taking large slow steps.
8. When they are finished walking, it is time to reverse the steps to go back to "earth."
9. When you land on earth, tell the children what the next activity is.

More to do   **Science:** Follow up with a unit on the solar system.

Related books   *I Want to Be an Astronaut* by Byron Barton
Moog-Moog, Space Barber by Mark Teague
Regards to the Man in the Moon by Ezra Jack Keats

⭐ *Monica Hay Cook, Tucson, AZ*

Animals Walk

3+

Materials   none

What to do

1. As the children line up and get ready to transition or move from one room or area to another, ask them to think about animals that do not make any sounds, such as insects, worms, lobsters, spiders, rabbit, deer, and fish.

2. Tell the children to pretend to become one of those animals. The whole group can pretend to become one of the animals or each child can choose a different animal. The point is to choose a silent animal so that the children will transition quietly.

3. When the children arrive at the new destination ask them how they moved. Might there be different ways of moving the next time the same animal is chosen? How did they feel becoming that animal? Did the animal have a name? If each child chose a different animal, how did the children feel with other animals close by?

More to do   Instead of animals, the children could pretend to be vehicles. Making a train could be accomplished by putting hands on the shoulders of the person directly in front. A ship or boat could sway quietly on the waves. An airplane can soar quietly through the air.

Related books   *Flying* by Donald Crews
From Head to Toe by Eric Carle
Swimmy by Leo Lionni

★ *Kate Ross, Middlesex, VT*

Copy Me

Materials   none

What to do
1. When moving from one center to another, or when settling into a group time with several children together, have the children copy each other or you. This works especially well with younger preschoolers.
2. Choose one child to suggest what he would like to be or do. For example, he could be a train conductor or a firefighter (or you can choose what to do).
3. Have the child show the other children what the engineer does and the others can follow. They can proceed to "chug, chug, chug, down the tracks" or "drive the fire truck" while moving along. Or just make up silly movements or faces to imitate.
4. If desired, play music or sing songs as you move along. Made-up words and tunes work fine.

More to do   Use a thematic instrument to get or keep the children's attention, such as a train whistle, "fire" bell, cow bell, bicycle horn (some sound like ducks), and so on. Additional ideas include "cowpokes on horses" (galloping), waddling like ducklings, and skating like skaters.

Maxine Della Fave, Raleigh, NC

Follow My Rhythm

Materials   none

What to do
1. Children learn so much more when they use their bodies. This activity can be done at any time of the day as you transition from one activity to another. It will also help children develop the skill of pattern making.
2. Clap a short rhythm with your hands. Repeat the rhythm three times for the children to hear. Then ask them to clap the rhythm with you. For example, clap two times fast and two times slowly, or clap three times fast and two times slowly.

(continued on the next page)

3. After the children have demonstrated that they can correctly clap the rhythm, ask them to walk around the circle to the beat of the rhythm. (If you clapped two times fast and two times slowly, have the children take two quick steps followed by two slow steps.)

4. Have the children move their bodies to the rhythm. For example, have them stand on their tiptoes two times and then bend their knees and bounce on their legs two times. Or, have them put their hands up in the air two times and then touch their knees two times.

More to do   **Math:** The children can repeat the patterns that they have heard and then create the same patterns with manipulatives. For instance, they can assemble the blocks in the same pattern they were clapping—two big blocks, two small blocks, or two blue blocks, then two red blocks, and so on.

 Michelle Barnea, Millburn, NJ

Follow the Wind

3+

Materials   none

What to do

1. The children assemble or form a line to transition to another room or area. Explain that they will pretend to be the wind as they move.

2. Tell the children whether it is a very windy day or a light breezy day, and they move according to this "windy" announcement. For example, they move fast for a very windy day and slowly for a light breezy day.

More to do   The children could pretend to walk like the rain falls, sometimes a fast downpour and sometimes just a light drizzle.

Science: Talk about the wind. Ask the children questions, such as:

◆ What is a hurricane?
◆ What is a tornado?
◆ What are some good things about wind?
◆ What are some difficult circumstances that happen because of wind?
◆ What do you like to do on a windy day?

More Science: The children could make a list of objects that might blow in the wind versus those that might stay put. They could also make a list of animals or insects that might blow in the wind versus those that aren't affected.

Related books *Mirandy and Brother Wind* by Patricia C. McKissack
Rain by Robert Kalan

Kate Ross, Middlesex, VT

Galloping Cowpokes

3+

Materials paper bag horse head on top of a broom handle, cowboy hats, blocks (optional)

What to do
1. This is a transition to use while practicing the difficult skill of galloping. Children stand in a large circle, with or without homemade hobby horses.
2. Demonstrate how to gallop very slowly, and then invite them to gallop slowly around the circle.
3. Sing the song below to the tune of "I'm a Little Teapot" as the class gallops around the circle. Invite the children to sing with you.

I'm a cowpoke on my horse
Doing lots of tricks, of course.
We can gallop fast; we can gallop slow.
'Round the circle, here we go.

4. Gallop to the next transition.
5. As the children improve at galloping, try variations such as setting up small block fences to jump over.

(continued on the next page)

More to do   **Dramatic Play:** Set up blocks and red and yellow tissue paper to have a pretend campfire. Sit around the campfire for songs and stories.

Related books *Buckaroo Baby* by Libby Ellis
Cowboy Bunnies by Christine Loomis
Cowboys Can Do Amazing Things, Too! by Kelly Stuart
A Wild Cowboy by Dana Kessimakis Smith

⭐*Sue Fleischmann, Sussex, WI*

Get Moving!   3+

Materials   none

What to do   1. When it is time to change to a new activity, create a time for singing and dancing. Put on some music and have fun!
2. Choose a new child every day to pick the music and the movements. Allow five to ten minutes before starting the next activity.

⭐*Barbara Saul, Eureka, CA*

How Can We Move Our Bodies?   3+

Materials   none

What to do   1. Have children transition from one activity to another by moving a certain way, for example, jumping, hopping, skipping, walking backwards, or tiptoeing.

2. Try one of the following:

- ◆ Start by telling the children how to move and then demonstrating the movement.
- ◆ Later have children take turns deciding how to move.
- ◆ Have one child choose a movement and the others follow.
- ◆ Try moving in twos with children holding hands and doing the movement.
- ◆ Try adding a second component to the movement, for example, tiptoeing and patting your head.

Related book   *This Is My Body* by Gina and Mercer Mayer

★ *Sandra Suffoletto Ryan, Buffalo, NY*

Marching Along   3+

Materials   CD or tape player
recordings of marching music

What to do   1. Prepare children to listen to marching music.
2. Play a march as children line up to go from one place to the next.
3. Invite children to march to the next activity.

Related book   *Thump, Thump, Rat-a-Tat-Tat* by Gene Baer

★ *Margery Kranyik Fermino, Hyde Park, MA*

Moving Along

3+

Materials   none

What to do   1. To move to the next activity, have the children follow a movement course. At each station they will stop and do the activity. For example, the children will:

- ◆ Flap and flutter with a breeze;
- ◆ Leap like frogs onto a lily pad;
- ◆ Swing like monkeys from branches;
- ◆ Gallop like horses;
- ◆ Swirl like a dust devil; and
- ◆ Slither like a snake.

2. Other movements could be walking, running, jumping, skipping, climbing and crawling.
3. As a variation, children can come up with their own ways to move.

Related book   *From Head to Toe* by Eric Carle

★ *Monica Hay Cook, Tucson, AZ*

Musical Circles

3+

Materials   construction paper
6" circle pattern
scissors
laminator
tape and cassette player, or CD and CD player

What to do   1. Cut out 6" circles in a variety of colors and laminate them for durability. Arrange the circles on the floor 12" apart in a circle shape, large enough for each child to have room to stand on one circle.

2. When the music starts, the children walk from circle to circle. As the music is playing, the teacher picks up one of the circles. When the music stops, each child stops on the nearest circle.
3. The child without a circle to stand on leaves the circle to go to the next activity. Continue the song until all the circles have been picked up.
4. This is a wonderful time to introduce children to a variety of music, such as classical or folk. As each child leaves the circle, they can choose or be given an alternate way to exit, such as, "Wow, Andy doesn't have a circle, he gets to tiptoe all the way to the door" or "Krissy, would you like to hop or crawl over to get your back pack?" By giving children choices for how they leave the circle, no one is a "winner" or a "loser."
5. To save time, you can have more than one child leave at a time. For example, let everyone standing on a red circle leave for the next activity. Instead of circles, use various shapes and allow everyone on a square to leave the circle, everyone on a triangle, and so on. Use numbers or letters and allow the children whose name or age corresponds with the number or letter to leave.

Lauri Robinson, Big Lake, MN

Musical Moving

3+

Materials   xylophone

What to do

1. Use the xylophone as a signal for the children to do the next activity. For example, when the children hear the xylophone, they know it is time to clean up.
2. Play simple tunes, such as the "Alphabet Song," and the children can sing as they proceed to the next activity.
3. Put the xylophone in a music center and let the children experiment with making music.

Barbara Saul, Eureka, CA

Music Transitions

3+

Material
scarves
Greg and Steve CD's
marching or dancing music

What to do

1. In your lesson plans, create a list of quick transition ideas that can be used any time, or that a substitute teacher can use.
2. Greg and Steve have great ideas for this! The song "Popcorn" is easy to start, and the minute the children hear the first few notes, they know what to do. "The Freeze" is another easy-to-do, under-five-minutes transition game.
3. For variety, play some favorite dance tunes and provide a basket of scarves for some quick movement activities. A rousing John Philip Sousa march, with or without instruments, gets children moving toward the door, or just through the room on a rainy day.

⭐ *Tracie O'Hara, Charlotte, NC*

She'll Be Coming 'Round the Corner...

3+

Materials
none

What to do

1. Use this song for any transition time. Sing the following to the tune of "She'll Be Coming 'Round the Mountain."

She'll be coming 'round the corner when she comes, "Hi, kids!" (wave hello)
She'll be coming 'round the corner when she comes, "Hi, kids!" (wave hello)
She'll be coming 'round the corner, she'll be coming around the corner,
She'll be coming 'round the corner when she comes, "Hi, kids!" (wave hello)

Additional verses:

Oh, we'll all go out to recess when she comes. (pretend to bounce a ball)

Oh, we'll all eat our snack when she comes. (pretend to eat)

2. Ask the children to make up additional verses for activities that are special to your group.

⭐ *Barbara Saul, Eureka, CA*

The Parachute-Pokey   3+

Materials   parachute (commercial or homemade using a bed sheet)

What to do

1. When it is time to transition to a parachute activity, sing the following to the tune of "The Hokey Pokey:"

   You move the parachute up,
   You move the parachute down.
   You move the parachute up,
   And you shake it all around.
   You shake it to the left,
   You shake it to the right,
   It's called the parachute flight.

2. Add variety by suggesting some of the following ideas:

   ◆ Keep your arms straight
   ◆ Cross your arms
   ◆ Hold the parachute with one hand (or two hands)
   ◆ Move it while standing up (or kneeling down)
   ◆ Sing with your eyes open (or shut)
   ◆ Sing softly (or loudly)
   ◆ Just the boys (or girls) sing

3. Encourage the children to contribute their ideas. Continue as time allows.
4. Add scarves, feathers, foam pieces, balloons, and other objects to the tossing fun.

⭐ *Judy Fujawa, The Villages, FL*

Welcoming a New Day!

3+

Materials   CD or tape player
recordings of classical or cultural music

What to do
1. Tell the children that they will hear music as they clean up from play time and prepare for group time.
2. Display the name of the music, performer, or country of origin.
3. Initiate discussion about the music as children prepare for group time.
4. Encourage families of different cultures to supply a favorite family recording to play and help with discussion.

★ *Margery Kranyik Fermino, Hyde Park, MA*

Yoga Stretches

3+

Materials   none

What to do
1. Yoga is great for children and adults, especially those children who want to move all the time. Yoga helps children learn body awareness, regulation, and self-control. And it feels great!
2. You can work yoga into your schedule at many transition points during the day, or use it as a stand-alone activity.
   Author's Note: I always teach my class at the beginning of the year to take "big, deep breaths." This helps their bodies to calm down and provides more oxygen to help their brains.
3. At the beginning of circle time, stop to take some relaxing breaths. Before rest time, do "animal stretches" from a yoga workout. You can also stop children who are upset, angry, or out of control in the classroom and ask them to breathe deeply with you, so they can think more clearly.
4. If continued, yoga can be a useful tool in helping children to prepare for tests or studying, or before public speaking to calm down. There are many yoga books, card decks with pictures of poses, and videos that can help you prepare to do a little yoga with your class.

Author's Note: My favorite is the video "Yoga Kids" with Marcia Wenig as the host by Gaiam Living Arts.

🌟 *Tracie O'Hara, Charlotte, NC*

Watch Me!

3+

Materials   none

What to do   1. Ask the group, "Who's watching?" One or two children will watch and copy your actions, such as waving hands, putting their hands on their heads, clapping, and so on.
2. The rest of the children will see this and be inspired to join in.
3. Continue until everyone in the group is copying your actions and paying attention. Then give instructions for the next activity.

🌟 *Barbara Saul, Eureka, CA*

Making Music

3+

Materials   rain stick
hand-shaped castanets
tambourine
jingle bells

What to do   1. Whenever you need to get the attention of the whole group, grab one of the instruments listed above and shake, rattle, or drum it.
2. The children will be sure to look at you. When you have their attention, tell them what you need to say.

(continued on the next page)

More to do   **Music:** Give each child something to shake or bang and make some music together.
More Music: Hold the instrument out of sight from the children when you shake or bang it. Ask the children to identify which instrument you used.

Related books   *Georgia Music* by Helen V. Griffith
Geraldine, the Music Mouse by Leo Lionni
The Music in Derrick's Heart by Gwendolyn Battle-Lavert
Pages of Music by Tony Johnston

★*Virginia Jean Herrod, Columbia, SC*

Using Music

3+

Materials   none

What to do
1. The best way to get children's attention is through music. Children love music and anything can be made into a song. You don't have to be a writer or a musician—all you have to do is put what you want to say into a tune.
2. You can make up your own tune, or simply pick a familiar tune such as "London Bridge," and sing it!
3. Here are a few transition songs:

Find Your Mat (or Sit-Upon) (Tune: "London Bridge")
Find your mat and have a seat,
Have a seat, have a seat.
Find your mat and have a seat,
It is story (or other) time.

(Tune: "If You're Happy and You Know It")
Find your mat and have a seat, have a seat.
Find your mat and have a seat, have a seat.
Find your mat and have a seat,
On your bottom, not your feet.
Find your mat and have a seat, have a seat.

Walking Feet (Tune: "Rock Around the Clock")
Walking feet, walking feet,
We must use our walking feet,
We've got to walk, walk, walk, down the hall,
Walking feet so we won't fall,
Walking feet, down the hall we go!

⭐ *Deborah R. Gallagher, Littleton, NH*

Instrumental Changes

3+

Materials   instrument, such as a plastic guitar
recorded music

What to do
1. When you have a few extra moments, play an instrument or put on some music to play a game similar to hot potato.
2. Have the children pass the instrument as the music plays. The child holding it when the music stops gets to choose the next song for the group to sing.

More to do   **Literacy:** Prepare a song chart with titles and icons that are familiar to the children. Use this to provide a choice of songs. Have the lyrics of these songs written out on large sheets of paper and use a pointer to follow the words of the song as the group sings.

Related books   *Down by the Bay* by Henrick Drescher
Shake My Sillies Out by Raffi
Spider on the Floor by Raffi
Sunshine on My Shoulders adapted by Christopher Canyon

⭐ *Ann Kelly, Johnstown, PA*

Michael, Row Your Boat Ashore 3+

Materials   pictures, books, and models of a variety of boats

What to do
1. When you have a few extra moments, look at pictures of boats and talk about the many different kinds of boats.
2. Ask each child to name his favorite boat, and then sing about each child's boat.
3. If time allows, ask each child to draw a picture of his favorite boat. Again, as you display each drawing, add their name and the kind of boat into each verse. For example:

Mary's boat is a sailboat, Allelujah. (repeat)
Billy's boat is a tug boat, Allelujah. (repeat)
Peggy's boat is a motor boat, Allelujah. (repeat)
Denny's boat is a submarine boat, Allelujah. (repeat)

⭐ *Judy Fujawa, The Villages, FL*

Mirror Dance 3+

Materials   tambourine

What to do
1. This activity is great to do when you have a few extra moments any time during the day.
2. Divide the group into sets of partners. Have the children face their partners and hold hands.
3. Tell the children what actions to do, such as sliding, gliding, skipping, galloping, and leaping.
4. When the children hear the tambourine, they change partners.
5. As a variation, when the children hear the tambourine, they take turns coming up with actions for their partner to imitate.

More to do   **Science**: Children experiment with mirrors, such as writing on a piece of paper and holding it up to a mirror to see what happens.

⭐ *Monica Hay Cook, Tucson, AZ*

Move~Chucka~Lucka~Lucka! 3+

Materials   none

What to do
1. When you have a few spare moments during circle time (or any time), start saying this sing-song rhyme to get the children in a rhythmic mood:

   Move chucka-lucka-lucka,
   Groove chucka-lucka-lucka.

2. While sitting in a circle, add some simple hand motions to get into the spirit of the rhythm. Then, stand up and start adding body parts to the rhyme, for example:

   Head chucka-lucka-lucka!
   Hips chucka-lucka-lucka!
   Knees chucka-lucka-lucka!

3. These body parts will be the moving parts that are emphasized as you say each rhyme (two or three times).
4. Give as many children as possible a chance to choose a body part to do the chucka-lucka-lucka! Encourage both "silly" and "sane" movements.
5. Continue as time allows.

⭐ *Judy Fujawa, The Villages, FL*

Music Hunt

3+

Materials   classroom items

What to do

1. When you have a few extra moments, try this activity.
2. Several children at a time look around the room for something that makes music.
3. When those children come back to the circle, several other children look for items that make music.
4. When every child has had a turn, the children take turns showing how their item makes music.
5. All the children play their item to make music together.

More to do   **Science:** Look for nature items outside that make music. Have an outside nature band.

Related book   *In All Kinds of Weather, Kids Make Music!* by Lynn Kleiner

⭐ *Monica Hay Cook, Tucson, AZ*

Pet Play

3+

Materials   string
pet toys

What to do

1. Try this transition activity when you have a few extra moments.
2. Talk about pets and how pets move.
3. The group chooses a pet to imitate. One example would be a cat. All the children pretend to be a cat. The children curl up like a sleeping cat. They arch their backs and stretch out their legs when they wake up. They walk and purr like a cat. They clean their ears, slink, and creep. They lie on their backs and bat at toys and string. Ask, "How does a cat act when it's angry?"
4. Repeat the activity, pretending to be a dog, horse, or hamster.

More to do   **Science:** Talk with the children about pet care.

Related books   *I'll Teach My Dog a Lot of Words* by Michael Frith
Kitten Care for Children by Grace McHattie & Gordon McHattie

 Monica Hay Cook, Tucson, AZ

The Instruments on the Bus   3+

Materials   musical instruments

What to do   1. When you have a few extra moments, sing "The Wheels on the Bus." Add new ideas and verses to the original song by asking the children, "What's your idea?" Some of their ideas might include:

- ◆ "The seats on the bus go squeak, squeak, squeak…"
- ◆ "The hubcaps on the bus go clatter, clatter, clatter…"
- ◆ "The mirror on the bus goes wiggle, wiggle, wiggle…"
- ◆ "The windows on the bus go rattle, rattle, rattle…"
- ◆ "The floor mats on the bus go squish, squish, squish…"

2. Pass out instruments and encourage the children to play them in turn (or all together). Examples include "The bells on the bus go jingle, jingle, jingle…," "The rhythm sticks on the bus go tap, tap, tap…," and "The sand blocks on the bus go brusha, brusha, brusha…"

More to do   Consider changing the song to "The Animals on the Farm,""The Children at the Park,""The Cars on the Road," or "The Noises in the House."

 Judy Fujawa, The Villages, FL

Name That Tune

4+

Materials   xylophone

XYLOPHONE

What to do
1. To have a smooth busy-to-quiet transition, ask one child to hit two notes on the xylophone.
2. Ask for a volunteer to duplicate the pattern.
3. Repeat as time permits. When children are good at listening and repeating two notes, ask the first child to hit a series of three notes instead.

Related book   *Polar Bear, Polar Bear, What Do You Hear?* by Bill Martin, Jr.

⭐ *Susan Oldham Hill, Lakeland, FL*

Rainbow Hand Jive

4+

Materials   popular CD or tape with a good beat
CD or tape player

What to do
1. Any time during the day, teach the children the simplest version of the Hand Jive (moving your hands to the rhythm of the song):

    ◆ Tap your thighs (twice)
    ◆ Clap your hands (twice)
    ◆ Pass right hand over left hand in front of you (twice)
    ◆ Pass left hand over right hand in from of you (twice)

2. Suggest different body positions (stand up, kneel down, or lie on your back), different formats (in a circle, in a line, back to back, with a partner, or in a group of three), or body movements (while walking, dancing, or skipping).
3. Encourage the children to make up different hand motions.

More to do   Give children colorful gloves to wear. The children will enjoy the colorful array as they make the motions. Mix and match the gloves.

★ *Judy Fujawa, The Villages, FL*

The Shuffle

Materials   cardboard
scissors
shoelaces
pencil

What to do
1. Help the children cut pieces of cardboard approximately 6" x 12". Each child will need two pieces.
2. Have the children step on their pieces of cardboard. Mark the cardboard on each side of a child's foot across the arches.
3. Adult pokes a circular hole through each mark with a scissors. String the shoelace through the holes.
4. Have the children step on each piece of cardboard. Help the children tie a bow across the arches of their feet.
5. Now the children can shuffle around in the shoes. They can shuffle right on to their next activity.

More to do   **Outdoors:** You can even have shuffle-shoe races. Divide the children into teams. "On your mark, get set, go!"

★ *Monica Hay Cook, Tucson, AZ*

Colored Feet

Materials

construction paper
scissors
markers
laminator or clear
contact paper

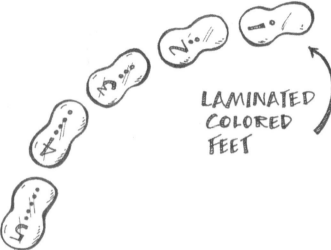

LAMINATED COLORED FEET

What to do

1. At the beginning of the year cut out feet in different colors and laminate them. Attach them to the floor using contact paper.
2. Put dots or numbers on them and write the number word underneath.
3. When going outside (or another place in the building), let the children pick a pair of feet on which to stand.
4. They can choose whatever color they like. This is a good way to teach color and number concepts. It also teaches the children to recognize written numbers.

More to do

Use shapes, letters, animals, and even animal feet to help children with transitions.

✦ *Cookie Zingarelli, Columbus, OH*

From Inside to Outside

Materials   small outside toys, such as shovels, pails, and small sand trucks

What to do
1. Use this activity to transition to the outside.
2. Hand one toy to each child to carry outside.
3. Have the children line up, and sing the following song as you proceed to the playground. Add verses, and sing about things you do outside.

   Heigh ho, heigh ho,
   And off to play we go,
   Pail and shovel in our hand,
   Heigh ho, heigh ho!

⭐ *Ingelore Mix, Gainesville, VA*

Going Outside

Materials   none

What to do   Moving children in an orderly manner can be very challenging. Try to keep it fun and easy. Chants, such as the one below, are great for this situation.

   Zipper up my coat, put my mittens on,
   I am going to play outside.
   It is cold everywhere,
   Better cover up my hair,
   Open up the door,
   Step into the cold,
   I am going outside... goodbye!

⭐ *Kaethe Lewandowski, Centreville, VA*

Meet Me...

Materials   none

What to do
1. When transitioning, it is important that children know where they are supposed to be. Try to avoid putting very young children "in line" as it is not always developmentally appropriate.
2. Instead, have a "meeting carpet" for children to go to during transitions.
3. As you get ready for outside play, one of the children (possibly the helper for the day) chooses who should get ready to go.
4. When you have three or four children at the door, begin slowly walking the children outside. This keeps children moving but allows others to catch up.
5. The children may tiptoe, walk backwards, walk sideways, or "fly" out to the playground.
6. When transitioning back inside, children know to meet at the picnic table. Other meeting areas for outside may be a circle painted on the playground or around a tree.

★ Linda Ford, Sacramento, CA

Outdoor Play

3+

Materials   sand tools, such as shovels and buckets

What to do   Transition to the outside by giving children sand tools to hold. When everyone has a sand tool, begin walking outside.

More to do   **Sand Play:** Sand and children are a perfect combination. Every year, try to have sand delivered to the school so the children can dig tunnels, create rivers, ponds, castles, and more.
More Sand Play: Create a rain barrel out of a plastic barrel. Install a faucet 6" from the bottom, and put it under a rain gutter so it will collect water. While some children are digging, others can fill buckets with water and carry them to the building site.

Author's Note: I supply fewer shovels than there are children to encourage sharing, and it is safer, too.

⭐ *Susan Rubinoff, Wakefield, RI*

The Little Red Caboose

3+

Materials   none

What to do   Help the children transition to the playground by pretending to be a train and singing this traditional song.

> *Little red caboose, chug, chug, chug.*
> *Little red caboose, chug, chug, chug.*
> *Little red caboose behind the train, train, train, train.*
> *Smoke stack on its back, back, back, back.*
> *Hurrying down the track, track, track, track.*
> *Little red caboose behind the train.*

⭐ *Cookie Zingarelli, Columbus, OH*

Tunnel Ball

3+

Materials   8" to 10" playground ball

What to do
1. This is a great game to play as the children are waiting to go outside. Ask the children to spread their feet apart to form a "tunnel."
2. Give the ball to the first child in line to shoot through the tunnel behind her. She should bend over to roll the ball between the other players' feet, and then run to the end of the line to catch it.

(continued on the next page)

3. Once this player catches the ball, ask the children to face in the opposite direction so the ball can be rolled back through the tunnel. Now the first player in line takes her turn.

4. Continue until all players have had a turn.

More to do   **Dramatic Play:** The children can construct tunnels out of blocks and roll small rubber balls through their structures.
Gross Motor: Play this game as a relay race.

⭐ *Susan A. Sharkey, La Mesa, CA*

What Will You Do When You Go Outside?

`3+`

Materials   none

What to do   Have the children chant this song as they wait to go outside. This is a traditional country song. As you repeat the verse, give each child a chance to say what she would like to do when she goes outside to play.

> *What will you do when you go outside,*
> *Go outside, go outside?*
> *What will you do when you go outside,*
> *When you go outside to play?*
>
> *(Harry) wants to play in the sandbox,*
> *In the sandbox, in the sandbox.*
> *(Harry) wants to play in the sandbox,*
> *When we all go out to play.*
>
> *(Mary) wants to swim when we go outside,*
> *Go outside, go outside,*
> *(Mary) wants to swim when we go outside,*
> *When we all go out to play.*

⭐ *Cookie Zingarelli, Columbus, OH*

Weather Buddy

Materials
stuffed bear or doll
doll clothing (or infant-sized regular clothes) for a variety of weather conditions
(raincoat, boots, hat, scarf, mittens, shorts, T-shirt, sunglasses, and so on)

What to do

1. Getting ready to go outside can be a difficult transition as children and teachers try to figure out what to wear. This activity lets the children decide ahead of time what the weather conditions are and ends last-minute decisions.
2. Show the stuffed bear or doll to the children. Let them touch and explore it as you tell them about the activity.
3. Tell them you have noticed that they often wonder what to wear when going outside. Explain that the doll or bear is your new "Weather Buddy." Explain that each morning, one child will be chosen to dress the bear in clothing that is suitable for that day's weather.
4. Show the children the clothing. Hold up each piece and talk about it. Ask questions about each piece, such as, "When would you wear this sweater?" Say, "If it was very cold and snowy outside right now, what would our Weather Buddy wear?" Let the children pick out the appropriate clothing and help dress the bear.
5. After the bear is dressed, ask the children if they think it would be okay for the buddy to go outside in the cold and snow.

DOLL CLOTHING

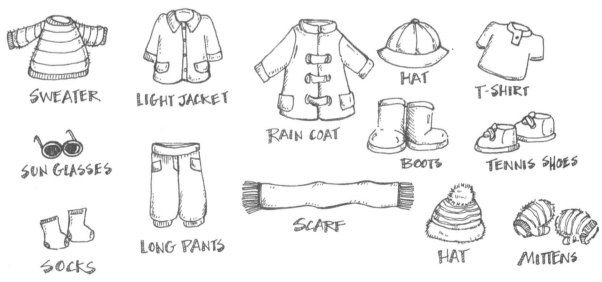

SWEATER   LIGHT JACKET   RAIN COAT   HAT   T-SHIRT

SUN GLASSES   LONG PANTS   BOOTS   TENNIS SHOES

SOCKS   SCARF   HAT   MITTENS

(continued on the next page)

6. Repeat step 4 for another weather condition. Continue until you are sure the children grasp the idea of the Weather Buddy.
7. Remind the children that you will assign a child to dress the Weather Buddy each morning. Make sure they know they will all get a turn.
8. When ready to go outside, ask the children to go and look at the Weather Buddy to check and see what kind of clothing they need to wear.

More to do   **Art**: Let each child make her own Weather Buddy paper doll. Take a photo of the Weather Buddy dressed in shorts and a T-shirt. Print one photo for each child on 8 ½" x 11" card stock paper. Help them cut out the photo. The children can then make clothes for their doll or cut out clothes from magazines. They can pretend to dress their own Weather Buddy by taping or gluing the clothes on.

Related song   **Let's Go Outside** (Tune: "The Farmer in the Dell")
Let's go outside in the snow,
Let's go outside in the snow,
Hi ho the derry oh,
Let's go outside in the snow.

We need to wear a coat,
We need to wear a coat,
Hi ho the derry oh,
Let's go outside in the snow.

We need to wear some mittens,
We need to wear some mittens,
Hi ho the derry oh,
Let's go outside in the snow.
(Change the weather condition and clothing to suit your current weather)

Related books   *Boot Weather* by Judith Vigna
First Comes Spring by Anne F. Rockwell
Forecast by Malcolm Hall
One Hot Summer Day by Nina Crews
Sail Away by Donald Crews
Thunderstorm! by Nathaniel Tripp

⭐*Virginia Jean Herrod, Columbia, SC*

Run and Stop

Materials   indoor or outdoor area large enough to permit running

What to do
1. This simple activity is especially good for helping children develop reflexes. It also requires them to pay attention and stay alert.
2. When outdoors with the child, or indoors in a large area, give them a signal (whistle, bell or simply verbal command) to run. They stop when they hear the signal again.
   Note: Vary the time they run. It's easy to develop a pattern so that children anticipate stopping time. The goal is to respond to the signal.
3. This is a great activity to do at the end of outdoor time.

More to do   Indoors or outdoors, try other activities, such as clapping, stamping feet, swinging arms, clicking tongues (great exercise to improve speech skills) or humming.

⭐ *Mary Jo Shannon, Roanoke, VA*

Too Much Energy!

Materials   none

What to do
1. There are days when children just need to run and spend their extra energy. Rainy days are most often the culprit, followed closely by too much sugar at someone's birthday celebration! On these days, whether you go outside or to an indoor all-purpose room, the first thing to do is tell the children to just run.
2. Sometimes you may want to let them run until they are almost worn out. Other times, play "Red Light, Yellow Light, Green Light," in which red means "stop," yellow means "walk," and green means "run." Sometimes the lights can mean running or walking like a certain animal.
3. Once the children run off their excess steam, their free time play can continue as usual.

⭐ *Deborah R. Gallagher, Littleton, NH*

Get Your Drink

3+

Materials

camera
cardboard
glue
laminator

What to do

1. Take a photo of the class getting a drink at the outdoor water fountain.
2. Enlarge the photo to 8 ½" x 11" and mount it on cardboard. Laminate it.
3. This activity will help stagger the number of children who go for a drink at the fountain so they won't all want to go at once.
4. Make this into a job for the children. Each morning let each child choose a job for the day, one job being "Teacher's Helper."
5. About ten minutes before it is time to go inside, the helper will hold up the sign and walk around the playground. The child will remind the other children that it is almost time to go inside and that they should go get a drink if they would like one.
6. You can also do this activity indoors as a transition to circle time.

Linda Ford, Sacramento, CA

The Playground Express

3+

Materials

train whistle

What to do

1. Give the children a five-minute warning for the end of outdoor play. Explain that the "Playground Express" will be pulling up to the station and that everyone will need to climb aboard.
2. After five minutes, blow the train whistle and start chugging around the playground calling, "All aboard."
3. Snake the train around the playground so that everyone has a chance to chug and whistle.
4. If you need to collect materials, allow children who wish to help pick up toys to "unload" from the train. Be sure to circle around and pick them up in a few minutes. (Being a caboose might be an incentive for some children to help their friends clean up.)

The GIANT Encyclopedia of Transition Activities

Related books   *The Big Book of Trains* by Christine Heap
Maisey's Train by Lucy Cousins
Trains by Byron Barton

★ *Ann Kelly, Johnstown PA*

Sardine Squeeze

3+

Materials   chalk

What to do
1. When you have a few extra moments outdoors, try this game.
2. Draw a chalk shape on the pavement, such a 3' square.
3. Ask the children to guess how many players could fit inside the shape without touching the lines. Write their guesses outside the shape.
4. Call the children by name to stand inside. Stop when the shape is "full." Count the children inside the shape and compare this number with their guesses.
5. Change the shape and size of the chalk drawings to continue the game as long as the children are interested.
6. On rainy days, you can play this game inside by using masking tape to create shapes on the floor.

More to do   **Math**: Use paper, crayons, and counters (poker or bingo disks, teddy bears, or other small objects) to create a tabletop version of this game. "How many teddy bears do you think will fit inside this circle?"

★ *Susan A. Sharkey, La Mesa, CA*

Target Toss

3+

Materials   chalk
sponges
water bucket

What to do

1. This is a great activity when you have a few extra moments outdoors on a hot and sunny day. Use chalk to draw a target on a cement or stucco wall.
2. Place a start line on the pavement.
3. Place a bucket of wet sponges next to the start line.
4. Form a line and encourage the children to take turns tossing the sponges towards the target.

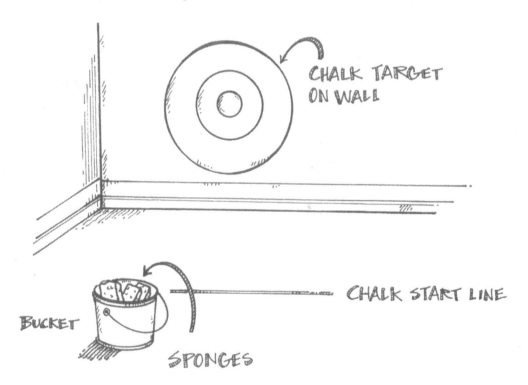

CHALK TARGET ON WALL

CHALK START LINE

BUCKET

SPONGES

More to do

Art: Use paintbrushes dipped in water to make designs on the wall and pavement. Talk about how the sunshine causes the designs to evaporate.

⭐ *Susan A. Sharkey, La Mesa, CA*

Peanut Butter March

Materials   none

What to do
1. This activity enables children to transition from outdoors to indoors. Have the children pretend to spread peanut butter on the soles of their shoes before starting this activity.
2. Chant verse one while the children march along, following you.
3. The children enjoy dramatizing lifting their feet as if they were stuck to the ground.
4. Continue the first verse until the class reaches the door to the building. Chant verse two in repetition until all of the children are inside.
5. The visual imagery of sticking to the floor helps slow down the children who tend to run. Conversely, the rhythmic pattern helps prevent children who tend to straggle from behind from doing so.

   Verse 1: *Hut, two, three, four, peanut butter on the floor!*
   Verse 2: *Hut, two, three, four, wipe the butter on the door!*

More to do   Put a picture on the wall of an entryway that rhymes with "door." The children can wipe their "peanut butter" off on that item. For example, they could wipe their feet on a store, an apple core, or a boar.

⭐ *Steve Rubin, Waldorf, MD*

Relax and Unwind

Materials   quiet instrumental music

What to do
1. This is a great transitional activity after outdoor play. Turn off the lights and tell the children it is time to relax and loosen their muscles.
2. Turn on music and have the children join you on the floor.
3. Show them some quiet, relaxing movements, such as slowly raising your arms over your head, stretching, and moving your fingers slowly.

(continued on the next page)

4. Turn your head around slowly in circles, raise and lower your shoulders, stretch your legs out in front of you, flex your toes, do ankle rolls. Try to emphasize doing this slowly!

5. Once your class has had a few chances to try this activity, encourage them to move their bodies in this quiet, slow, relaxing way on their own.

6. Point out different ways the children are moving, such as, "I see that Johnny is slowly raising her hands above her head and then slowly putting them on her shoulders." The children love this activity and it makes smooth transitions.

★ *Jodi Sykes, Lake Worth, FL*

Come Form a Line   3+

Materials   none

What to do   When you want to transition back to the classroom, sing the following to the tune of "Shortenin' Bread." Substitute your name in the last line.

> *Come form a line, boys and girls,*
> *Come form a line, boys and girls,*
> *One foot on the cement,*
> *One foot on the grass,*
> *Come form a line for (teacher's name)'s class.*

★ *Jackie Wright, Enid, OK*

It's Time to Go Inside   3+

Materials   none

What to do   When it is time to transition from the outside to the inside, sing the song on the following page to the tune of "Oh, Come on, Playmate."

Oh, come on children,
It's time to go inside.
So we can start our day,
And learn in every way.
Come find your places,
And sit down on the floor,
So we can eat our snack,
And much, much more!

⭐ *Jackie Wright, Enid, OK*

Take a Ticket

3+

Materials   objects that relate to the next activity, or tickets with pictures of
the places children are to go next

What to do
1. Use this activity to transition from outside to small group. Have the children
   meet at a designated outdoor place, such as a picnic table.
2. Send the children into the classroom in groups of five to six at a time.
3. One teacher escorts the group into the room for a self-directed activity, such
   as coloring, journals, or playdough. If they are coloring, give each child a
   piece of paper; if they are journaling, have them carry their journals into the
   room.
4. Then send in a group to work with that teacher, also carrying something that
   represents what they are to do (a piece of a puzzle, a bingo game card, or
   small copies of a book they are to read with the teacher inside).
5. The last group will go to the classroom with you, usually doing a gross motor
   skill. You can sing, "Heigh-ho, heigh-ho, it's off to work we go!"

⭐ *Linda Ford, Sacramento, CA*

Wind Away

4+

Materials
crepe paper strips
scissors
pictures of wind-related items, such as kites, weather vanes, and windmills
pictures showing the effects of wind, such as tornados, hurricanes,
    and dust devils
scissors

What to do

1. This is a great activity to transition the children to outdoors.
2. Show the children pictures of wind and its effects. Talk about breezes versus tornadoes and hurricanes.
3. Help each child cut a strip of crepe paper approximately 4" x 24".
4. The children move around the room. They can start by imitating a light breeze and move slowly from side to side. Then the wind gets stronger and moves faster. They can imitate tornadoes and dust devils that go around.
5. The wind just blew the children down the hall and outdoors.

More to do
Science: Discuss how wind can be utilized to provide power. Talk about how various aspects of weather help us.

Related book
Winnie the Pooh and the Blustery Day by Teddy Slater, et al.

 Monica Hay Cook, Tucson, AZ

Little Things Count a Lot

4+

Materials
numeral cards
container for the cards

What to do

1. To transition from inside to outside, ask a child to choose a numeral card from the container. If she draws a four, for example, she selects four friends to get in line.

2. Repeat this until all of the children are ready to go.

Related books   *1 Is One* by Tasha Tudor
Count and See by Tana Hoban

⭐*Susan Oldham Hill, Lakeland, FL*

What's My Shape?

4+

Materials   several shoeboxes with lids
scissors
large heavy-duty rubber bands, two per box
matte board
sandbox

SHOEBOX LID — 3" CIRCLE — RUBBER BANDS

MATTE BOARD SHAPES
SQUARE   CIRCLE   OVAL   RECTANGLE   TRIANGLE

What to do
1. Cut a 3" circle from the middle of each shoebox lid.
2. Put the lid on the box and secure with two rubber bands.
3. Cut matte board into a variety of shapes—a square, rectangle, triangle, circle, oval, and star. (Matte board can be found at craft stores.) The shapes should be big enough for a child to hold easily in her hand, and fit through the hole in the box. Prepare a set of shapes for each box.

(continued on the next page)

SAND

RECTANGLE OUTLINE IN SAND

4. Before you introduce the game, put one cutout shape in each box.
5. After boisterous outdoor play, transition to something quieter with this activity. Invite the children to the sandbox and ask each child to put one hand into the box and touch the item inside. Remind them not to peek or take the item out.
6. Suggest that they examine the item carefully with their fingers. Tell them to imagine their fingers have eyes.
7. Instruct the children to remove their hand and leave the item in the box.
8. Tell the children to try to draw the object in the sand with their fingers. Then they may remove the item and compare it to the sand drawing.

More to do   Increase complexity by putting more than one item in the box.
Replace cutout shapes with numbers and letters.
Use blocks, instead of cutouts, to increase awareness of three-dimensional objects.

★ *Karyn F. Everham, Fort Myers, FL*

What to Do on Rainy Days

3+

Materials   costumes and accessories

What to do
1. Collect and store a large variety of costumes and accessories to use on rainy days, windy days, smoggy days, or on days when you must be inside and have extra time to fill.
2. To begin collecting, post a sign for parents to read. List your needs, and be specific, such as Halloween costumes. Encourage them to donate accessories too, such as shoes, necklaces, rings, hats, gloves, purses, and so on.

3. Check your school's lost and found box for items as well. (Make sure the items are unwanted.)
4. Seek out dresses, skirts, shawls, hats of all types, jewelry, play crowns, wedding veils, flower ringlets, and wands.
5. Keep these on hand and when the weather is bad, bring them out and encourage children to use their imaginations!

More to do   Also use these costumes whenever they coincide with the theme you are working on. Children love to play dress-up!

Penni Smith, Riverside, CA

Breathing Technique

3+

Materials   none

What to do   To prepare children for a quiet activity on a rainy day (or any day), try this deep breathing technique with them. It not only gives them a break from sitting but also is quite relaxing.

Pretend to be a tree.
Slowly raise your arms up to be the branches. (slowly take in a deep breath)
Hold it for a few seconds,
And relax. (blow air out completely and go limp)

★ *Jackie Wright, Enid, OK*

Go Away, Rainy Day

3+

Materials   poster paints in a selection of colors
liquid soap
small containers or palette for mixing
paintbrushes

What to do
1. When you have a few extra moments on a rainy day, try this special activity.
2. Add equal amounts of poster paint and liquid soap to a container or palette and mix together thoroughly.
3. Be sure children are wearing art aprons, as this could be messy!
4. Let children paint cheerful scenes on the classroom windows. Bright, sunny days, seaside images, and springtime flowers or trees work especially well.
5. Let the art dry.
6. When the children have gone home, the liquid soap in the paint makes it simple to wipe off with a damp, soapy cloth. If the children are upset to see their creations gone in the morning, remind them that they can have fun again on the next rainy day.

Author's Note: If painting on the windows is impractical for your class, have them add their designs to sheets of clear plastic or acetate instead. Use sticky tac or tape to attach the plastic or acetate to your classroom windows.

More to do   **Language**: Ask the children how many different kinds of weather and words associated with weather they can think of. Write the children's word(s) on a piece of paper, then stick them all together to make a weather-word collage.
Science: Talk about why and how the weather changes and what effect it has on our environment, for example, temperate conditions helping plants to grow, lack of rain causing drought or arid landscapes, flooding, and so on.

Related books   *Sunshine Makes the Seasons* by Franklyn M. Branley
Weather Words and What They Mean by Gail Gibbons
What Will the Weather Be? by Lynda DeWitt

★ *Kirsty Neale, London, United Kingdom*

Rainy Day Paint With Cattails   3+

Materials   shellac (adult only)
cattails
tempera paint
paper

What to do
1. Before doing this activity, make sure to spray cattails with shellac (adult only) to keep them from breaking open. Let them dry.
2. On a rainy day when you have a few extra moments, encourage the children to roll the cattails in tempera paint and create designs with them on paper. You will be amazed at the children's creativity.
3. After the project, wash the cattails immediately and let them dry to use on another day.
4. Use other materials such as pinecones, toilet paper tubes, or rolling pins if you cannot use cattails.

(continued on the next page)

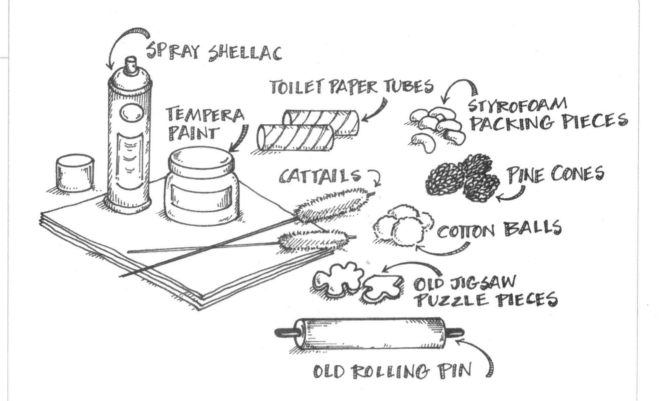

SPRAY SHELLAC

TEMPERA PAINT

TOILET PAPER TUBES

STYROFOAM PACKING PIECES

PINE CONES

CATTAILS

COTTON BALLS

OLD JIGSAW PUZZLE PIECES

OLD ROLLING PIN

More to do **Holidays:** Do this activity around the 4th of July using red and blue paint. Children can make "fireworks" with them and add glitter to enhance this effect.

★ *Cookie Zingarelli, Columbus, OH*

Tie Dye With Coffee Filters 3+

Materials paper
scissors
coffee filters
liquid watercolors
eyedroppers
small roller

What to do 1. When you have a few extra moments on a rainy day, cut out T-shirt shapes from paper. Place a coffee filter over the top of a paper shirt.
2. Using an eyedropper, the children drop different colors of liquid watercolors over the filter, and take a small roller and roll over the filter.

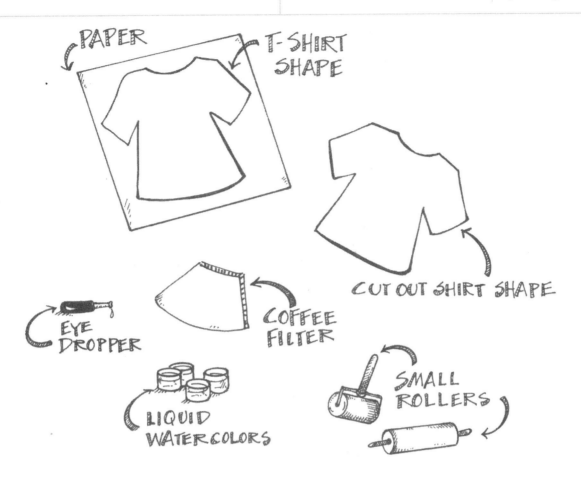

PAPER

T-SHIRT SHAPE

CUT OUT SHIRT SHAPE

EYE DROPPER

COFFEE FILTER

LIQUID WATERCOLORS

SMALL ROLLERS

3. Then they can place the filter on another part of the T-shirt and do the same thing again. These shirts dry quickly.
4. Use the filters again and make butterflies out of them. See how colorful the butterflies are!

★ *Cookie Zingarelli, Columbus, OH*

Rainy Day Activities

3+

Materials   scented markers

What to do
1. To fill a few spare moments on rainy days, keep scented markers and only let children use them on rainy days. This makes rainy days special.
2. Also, read *Little Cloud* by Eric Carle, using a homemade flannel board set.

★ *Audrey Kanoff, Allentown, PA*

Raindrop Art

3+

Materials
paper plates (not Styrofoam)
food coloring

What to do
1. This is a great spare time activity to do on a day with light rain.
2. Give each child a paper plate. Let them put a few drops of food coloring on their plates. (This works best when you use a few different colors.)
3. Go outside and have the children hold the plates flat in the rain. The raindrops will hit the food coloring and splash them across the plate, making pretty works of rainy day art. Lay flat to dry.
4. Leave plates as is, or have the children enhance their artwork by drawing on them or adding glitter to them.
5. This activity is inexpensive, and the children enjoy playing in the rain and creating the artwork.

★ *Rikki Deal, Beggs, OK*

Picture-Song Storybooks

3+

Materials
picture-song storybook

What to do
1. Plan ahead for rainy days and "hard" days when you are low on energy or when children can't seem to focus.
2. When you have a few extra moments, select a song storybook to read to the children. This always seems to generate interesting conversation.
3. Following are several selections that you might enjoy. You may want to buy or make your own recording of the song on a cassette to accompany the book.

By Pam Adams
◆ *Old MacDonald Had a Farm*
◆ *There Was an Old Lady Who Swallowed a Fly*
◆ *There Were Ten in a Bed*
◆ *This Is the House That Jack Built*
◆ *This Old Man*

By John Langstaff
- *Frog Went A-Courtin'*
- *Oh, A-Hunting We Will Go*
- *Over in the Meadow*

By Peter Spier
- *The Erie Canal*
- *The Fox Went Out on a Chilly Night*
- *London Bridge Is Falling Down*
- *The Star-Spangled Banner*

By Iza Trapani
- *How Much Is That Doggie in the Window?*
- *I'm a Little Teapot*
- *The Itsy Bitsy Spider*
- *Mary Had a Little Lamb*
- *Oh Where, Oh Where Has My Little Dog Gone?*
- *Row, Row, Row Your Boat*
- *Shoo Fly!*
- *Twinkle, Twinkle, Little Star*

By Nadine Westcott
- *Eensy-Weensy Spider*
- *I've Been Working on the Railroad*
- *Mary Had a Little Lamb*
- *Miss Mary Mack: A Hand-Clapping Rhyme*
- *Peanut Butter and Jelly: A Play Rhyme*
- *House That Jack Built*
- *Skip to My Lou*
- *There's a Hole in My Bucket*
- *Yankee Doodle*

Picture-song storybooks by other authors

Fiddle-I-Fee by Melissa Sweet
Five Little Pumpkins by Iris Van Rynbach
Going to the Zoo by Tom Paxton
Hush, Little Baby by Margot Zemach
It's Raining, It's Pouring by Kin Eagle
Mama Don't Allow by Thacher Hurd
Roll Over! A Counting Song by Merle Peek

 *Jackie Wright, Enid, OK*

Raffi's Rainy Day Songs

3+

Materials   "Songs-to-Read" books and cassettes by Raffi (see list below)

What to do
1. During a few extra moments on a rainy day, select a song to read for your group. This always seems to generate interesting conversation.
2. Raffi has several songs to read that you might enjoy.

- ◆ *Baby Beluga*
- ◆ *Down by the Bay*
- ◆ *Everything Grows*
- ◆ *Five Little Ducks*
- ◆ *Like Me and You*
- ◆ *One Light, One Sun*
- ◆ *Rise and Shine*
- ◆ *Shake My Sillies Out*
- ◆ *Tingalayo*
- ◆ *This Little Light of Mine*
- ◆ *The Wheels on the Bus*

★ *Jackie Wright, Enid, OK*

Rain Songs

3+

Materials   none

What to do   Use this collection of rain songs whenever you need to fill a few spare moments on a rainy day.

It's Raining, It's Pouring
It's raining, it's pouring
The old man is snoring.
He bumped his head,
And went to bed,
And couldn't get up in the morning.

Rain, Rain, Go Away

Rain, rain, go away
Come again another day.
We want to go outside and play.

Sprinkle, Sprinkle, Rain, Rain, Rain (Tune: "Twinkle, Twinkle, Little Star")

Sprinkle, sprinkle, rain, rain, rain
Keeps us here inside again.
We'll find lots of things to do.
A little rain is good for you.
Sprinkle, sprinkle, rain, rain, rain
Keeps us here inside again.

(continued on the next page)

Rainy Day Ideas

Itsy Bitsy Spider
The itsy bitsy spider
Went up the water spout.
Down came the rain
And washed the spider out.
Out came the sun
And dried up all the rain.
And the itsy bitsy spider
Went up the spout again.

There's a Little Rainstorm (Tune: "I'm a Little Teapot")
There's a little rainstorm right outside,
Into our room we go to hide.
Watch out of the window while you play.
We'll go outside when the rain goes away.
There's a little rainstorm right outside,
Into our room we go to hide.

Rain, Rain, Rain (Tune: "Three Blind Mice")
Rain, rain, rain
Rain, rain, rain
Falling down
All around.
It's raining here and it's raining there.
It's raining, raining everywhere.
Did you ever see such a sight in your life
As rain, rain, rain?

More to do   **Art**: Make rain paintings. On a rainy day, place thick, glossy paint paper on a flat surface and sprinkle several colors of powdered tempera paint on it. Put it outside in the rain for a while. Carefully lift the rain painting and hang it to dry.
Literacy: Create Rainy Day Books. Ask the children to draw illustrations for one of the songs listed above. Print the words to the song under the pictures. Create a front and back cover and bind the pages together. Do the same for other songs.

Related books   *And It Rained* by Ellen Raskin
Bringing the Rain to Kapiti Plain by Verna Aardema
Come On, Rain! by Karen Hesse
In the Rain With Baby Duck by Amy Hest
It's a Shame About the Rain by Barbara Shook Hazen
It's Raining, Said John Twaining by N.M. Bodecker
Listen to the Rain by Bill Martin, Jr. and John Archambault

The GIANT Encyclopedia of Transition Activities

Mushroom in the Rain by Mirra Ginsburg
Rain Drop Splash by Alvin Tresselt
Rain Makes Applesauce by Julian Scheer and Marvin Bileck
Rain Rain Rivers by Uri Shulevitz
Rain Talk by Mary Serfozo
That Sky, That Rain by Carolyn Otto
The Rain Came Down by David Shannon
The Rain Door by Russell Hoban
The Rainbabies by Laura Krauss Melmed
We Hate Rain! by James Stevenson
When the Rain Stops by Sheila Cole
Where Does the Butterfly Go When It Rains? by May Garelick

★ *Virginia Jean Herrod, Columbia, SC*

Basket Bounce

3+

Materials
6" or 8" bouncing ball
wastebasket
masking tape

What to do
1. When the children have energy to burn on a rainy day, play this game.
2. Make a start line with tape about 6 to 8 feet from an empty wastebasket.
3. Challenge the players to throw the ball so that it bounces once and lands in the wastebasket. Allow three throws for each turn.
4. Change the start line to make the game easier or more difficult.

More to do
You can also play this game as a relay race.

★ *Susan A. Sharkey, La Mesa, CA*

Rainy Day Obstacles

3+

Materials   gross motor materials (balls, jump rope, hoops, and so on)
masking tape
tables and other ordinary classroom furniture

What to do
1. Use this activity as a transition from one inside activity to another when you are stuck inside due to weather. It will help settle the children.
2. Prepare an obstacle course in the classroom while the children are busy at free play or other activities. Enlist the children's help and ideas as you create the course.
3. Obstacle course possibilities include using tape to give the children direction or creating a route using tables and chairs as tunnels and hoops to hop into.

More to do   **Gross Motor:** Use this activity to assess children's gross motor abilities.

★ *Ann Kelly, Johnstown, PA*

A House Is a House for Me

4+

Materials   *A House Is a House for Me* by Mary Ann Hoberman
paper
pencil

What to do
1. Read the book aloud on several different occasions until the children are familiar with it.
2. When you have a few extra moments on a rainy day, invite the children to name items or animals and their homes.
3. Write them down on paper.
4. Help the children write a new poem, similar to the one in the book, about the things they suggested.

An apple is a home for a worm,
A hive is a home for a bee,
A hutch is a home for a rabbit,
And a house is a house for me.

5. See how many verses you can write.
6. Make a class book with your new verses. Let the children illustrate their ideas. Keep the book in your reading area for all to enjoy.

Jackie Wright, Enid, OK

Visualization Treasures

4+

Materials
heavy paper
scissors
markers, colored pencils, crayons
art materials

What to do
1. Cut out large magnifying glass shapes from heavy paper.
2. When the children have spare time inside because of inclement weather, have them stretch out on their backs and look through the magnifying glasses. Ask them to pretend to see treasures they would like to collect if they were outside.

(continued on the next page)

3. Ask the children to draw their treasures on the glasses if they wish to. Or they can design their own treasures on the glasses.

More to do   The next nice day, children can look for "treasures" outside. Encourage them to see how many they can collect and compare it with their drawings or designs.

★ *Eileen Lucas, Halifax, Nova Scotia, Canada*

Going to Sleep   3+

Materials   none

What to do   1. To help children transition to nap time, sing this song to the tune of "My Bonnie Lies Over the Ocean."

My arms are going to sleep now.
My arms are going to sleep.
My arms are going to sleep now.
My arms are going to sleep.
Go to sleep, close your eyes,
Go to sleep.
Sleep, sleep, and sleep.

2. Substitute different body parts.

★ *Jackie Wright, Enid, OK*

Nap Transitions

3+

What to do   Some young children are outgrowing their nap, but still need a quiet time during the day to decompress and relax. If you have a non-sleeper, or a child who is waking up before the others, provide one of the following ideas:

- A "journal" that the child can quietly write or draw in
- A basket of books for her to look at
- A shoebox of quiet toys, games, or puzzles to do at the child's mat

⭐ *Tracie O'Hara, Charlotte, NC*

Nap Time Stories

3+

Materials   none

What to do
1. To help children transition to nap time, gather for story time before naps, after mats are out and toileting is done.
2. Begin a story that includes the children, such as, "As Bear was walking through the woods, he saw Billy and Susie, and they were yawning because they were so sleepy." The children whose names are mentioned in the story (which are the names of the children in the class) should yawn and go lie down on their mat. Continue until all the children are on their mats.
3. Substitute different types of phrases and actions that the children can act out, such as "Two cats named Bobby and Vera were taking catnaps in the sun."
4. As the children move to their mats, continue telling the story in a slow, monotone voice. Don't get the children excited, but hold their attention so that they listen until they fall asleep.
5. After some practice, you may want to tape your stories for use by substitutes, or you may want to write them down later.
6. Try asking children for story ideas before nap time so they will listen for their ideas in your story.

Related songs   *Quiet Times* album by Hap Palmer

⭐ *Linda Ford, Sacramento, CA*

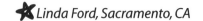

Quiet as a Crab

3+

Materials
nap time mats
CD player or cassette player
new-age CD or cassette (preferably with ocean sound)

What to do
1. This is a great activity to prepare children for nap time.
2. Have the children lay out their mats and sit on the carpet. Play a new-age CD or tape as background music.
3. In a soothing voice tell this original story. Have the children act it out, moving from the carpet to their mats, and preparing to rest.

It's summer and you are crabs on the beach. You've been busy all morning roaming the rocky shores scavenging for food to eat. You climbed rocks and dug into the sand. Now all your limbs are weary. Slowly crawl to your resting place (mat) and take a deep slow breath in, then out. Stretch out your tired claws (arms). Your claws helped you gather food and are now tired. After you've stretched out your claws, bring them in close to your soft belly to rest. Stretch out your legs. They were busy all morning scurrying over rocks. After you've stretched them out, pull them into you shell to rest.

The sun shines on you. You are warm and dry and comfy in your shell. The waves wash the shore over and over again. It is a calm sound, like music to your ears. You close your eyes and dream of finding more tasty treasures after you wake up.

More to do
Movement: When the children get up from their rest time, encourage them to scurry around the room like crabs looking for a new shell.
Science: Read and learn about how hermit crabs live and move.

Related books
Is This a House for Hermit Crab? by Megan McDonald
What Lives in a Shell? by Kathleen Weidner Zoehfeld

⭐ *Monica Hay Cook, Tucson, AZ*

Rag Doll

3+

What to do

1. When preparing for rest time, help children relax by acting like "rag dolls." As they stand by their mats, help them pretend they are rag dolls.
2. Say, "You have no bones to hold you up straight. Your heads drop forward. (They bend their heads down.) Your backs are soft. (They bend forward from the waist.) Your legs bend. (They bend their knees so they are now crouching on their mats.) You are soft all over. (They stretch out on the mats.) If you lift your arms or legs, and let go, they drop." Move among the mats, lifting arms and legs, noting if they fall and showing children who are relaxed.
3. Now all the rag dolls are ready to rest!
4. In the winter months, children can pretend to be snowmen melting into a big puddle on their mats.
5. Try sprinkling "fairy dust" to cast a "spell" on the resting children. Once the imaginary dust is sprinkled, they are very still.

⭐ *Mary Jo Shannon, Roanoke, VA*

See the Sleeping _____

3+

Materials   none

What to do

1. Use this activity when children need to prepare for rest or nap time, or when they get restless in circle.
2. Chant the words on the following page and have the children act out the parts of the animals.
3. Ask the children if they can pretend to snore softly so you know they are sleeping.
4. Choose another animal and sing the song again.

SLEEPING KITTENS

(continued on the next page)

See the little kittens sleeping 'till it's nearly noon.
Come, let us wake them with this merry little tune.
See the little kittens sleeping 'till it's nearly noon.
Come, let us wake them with this merry little tune.
Oh! How still. Are they ill?
Wake up, little kittens, (the children pretend to wake up and quietly
*   cry like little kittens)*
Meow, meow, meow,
Wake up little kittens,
Meow, meow, meow.

★ *Cookie Zingarelli, Columbus, OH*

Sleep Tight

3+

Materials   none

What to do   To help children transition to nap time, sing the following to the tune of "Goodnight, Sweetheart."

Sleep tight, children, well it's time for nap,
Da, da, da, da.
Sleep tight, children, well it's time for nap,
Da, da, da, da.
I hate to say it, but you really must rest,
Sleep tight, children, sleep tight.

★ *Jackie Wright, Enid, OK*

Time for Quiet Time

Materials   none

What to do
1. The first time through this song, sing or chant it in your normal voice. Each repetition thereafter, sing it in a softer voice.
2. Prolong the first syllable of the word "quiet" in the first two lines. Extend it a bit longer in the third line. Then, put an emphasis on the second syllable of the word "today" in the last line.
3. This helps bring the children together so you can lead them into the rest or nap area.

   Time for qu-i-i-i-et time,
   Time for qu-i-i-i-et time,
   Time for qu-i-i-i-et time today.
   (repeat)

More to do   Use the same rhythmic pattern and apply it to various aspects of your curriculum or day. An example would be to replace "quiet" with "circle."

★ *Steve Rubin, Waldorf, MD*

The Sticker Fairy

Materials   stickers

What to do
1. As the children transition to nap time, quietly motivate them to rest by telling them that the "sticker fairy" passes out stickers when children fall asleep.
2. Carefully and quietly place stickers on children's hands after they fall asleep.
3. Be sure to give stickers to children who may not be sleeping but are resting quietly.

(continued on the next page)

More to do   **Math:** Have blank sticker charts ready for all the children. Ask the children to add their stickers to their chart each day. Use these charts for math activities, counting, sorting stickers, and other appropriate activities.

⭐ *Ann Kelly, Johnstown, PA*

The Sun Is Sleeping

3+

Materials   large piece of yellow paper
scissors
large piece of white paper
black marker
glue or glue stick
hole punch
string

STRING

HOLE

YELLOW CIRCLE

CLOSED EYES (OTHER SIDE TOO)

TWO LARGE CLOUDS

What to do   1. Cut out a large circle from the yellow paper. This will be the "sun."
2. Cut out two large clouds from the white paper.
3. Draw closed eyes in front and back of the sun.
4. Glue the clouds onto the sun so that only the upper part of the sun is visible.
5. Punch a hole in the sun and attach a piece of string.
6. Hang it in a semi-darkened room.
7. Turn on soft low music and tell the children that they are resting with the sun.

⭐ *Ingelore Mix, Gainesville, VA*

Dinosaur Dreams

3+

Materials   *How Do Dinosaurs Say Goodnight?* by Jane Yolen
CD and player, or cassette tape and player

What to do
1. To help children transition to nap time, talk about their goodnight rituals. Do they brush their teeth? Read a story?
2. Introduce the book by Jane Yolen. Show the children the cover. Ask the children how they think dinosaurs say goodnight. Read the story.
3. Ask the children to pretend to be dinosaurs. Play music and walk around like big dinosaurs. Ask them to lie down and pretend to sleep when the music stops. When it starts, they may get up and walk around again.
4. Each time the "dinosaurs" are sleeping, tap one or two children on the shoulder and dismiss them to wash their hands or go to the nap area.

More to do   **Art**: Make "window dinosaurs" with contact paper. Cut out a stencil of a dinosaur large enough to fit on an 8 ½" x 11" page. Cut a piece of contact paper the same size for each child and put it on the table sticky side up. Invite the children to cover the contact paper with green items, such as tissue paper, feathers, sequins, beads, and so on. Make sure there are open spots on the paper, too. When finished, place a clean sheet of contact paper on top to seal the items. Use the stencil to cut the dinosaur shape. Hang them in the window.

(continued on the next page)

Fingerplays, Songs, and Rhymes: Use dinosaur stick puppets or act out this favorite rhyme with a little twist:

There were ten in the bed and the BIG one said, "Roll over, roll over."
They all rolled over and one fell out...

Science: Make "dinosaur eggs." Buy small plastic dinosaurs, enough for the whole class. Put each in a small wax-coated paper cup. Fill each cup to the top with Plaster of Paris. Let them harden for one day, then tear off the paper cups and let them dry completely. Don't be concerned that it is not exactly egg-shaped, and if a bit of dinosaur is sticking out, tell the children their egg is starting to "hatch." Give the children the eggs, plastic bags, and various items to make nests, such as rocks, yarn, straw, and sand. Invite each child to choose an egg and make a nest by putting items in the plastic bag. Put the egg in the bag with a note and send it home. In the note, invite parents to help hatch the egg by tapping it gently with a hammer. If they are very careful, the plaster will stay in large pieces and leave the impression of the dinosaur. This can lead to a discussion on fossils. You may also dictate a story about the dinosaur. What is her name? What does she eat?

Related books *How Do Dinosaurs Get Well Soon?* by Jane Yolen
How Do Dinosaurs Learn to Read? by Jane Yolen
How Do Dinosaurs Clean Their Rooms? by Jane Yolen

★ *Sue Fleischmann, Sussex, WI*

Sleep Sack

3+

Materials large sack or bag
quiet materials, such as books, portable music player with a lullaby cassette, stuffed animals, puzzles, a writing box, and journals

What to do 1. Put the quiet materials in a large sack or bag.
2. To help children relax, let them choose an item from the Sleep Sack.

Related book *A Nap in a Lap* by Sarah Wilson

★ *Ann Kelly, Johnstown, PA*

Listen to the Seashell

Materials seashell (from a beach or purchased)

What to do
1. Show the shell to the children. Explain that they will hear sounds in the shell.
2. Ask them to think about what they might hear in the shell. Some ideas might include waves, fish bubbles, submarines, and mermaids.
3. When all the children are settled in their sleeping cots, tell them that they will get a chance to hear the sounds. Explain that you will have a turn first, and then everyone will get a turn.
4. The children listen to the shell, tell the group what they heard, and then close their eyes and wait until everyone has had a turn.

More to do If your center or school is near a beach, take the children on a field trip to collect their own special seashell.

✷ *Eileen Lucas, Halifax, Nova Scotia, Canada*

When I Was a Child...

3+

Materials none

What to do
1. Tell the children you are going to tell them a story about when you were a child.
2. Say, "Before I begin the story, everyone has to relax and get comfortable. I am going to show you how. Close your eyes, stop talking, and listen to what I say. I am going to tell you which part of your body to relax. Just think of that body part, move it a little, and it will relax."

(continued on the next page)

3. Say the following very slowly. "Relax your nose, lips, shoulders, arms, and fingers. Remember to keep your eyes closed. Now relax your belly, bottom, legs, and feet. And now your toes, wiggle them and relax. Keep your eyes closed and I'm going to tell you my story. You can ask questions about the story after naptime. Sweet dreams."

4. Begin telling a story about your childhood. Most children do not make it through the whole story and want it finished the next day. Some want the story told over and over. Children will be eager to ask their questions when they wake up, so be ready with the answers.

   Author's Note: I try to tell stories that relate to things that may be unfamiliar, such as having no running water, phone, or bathroom in the house and what my family did instead.

More to do   Use this relaxation technique when children are frustrated and need time to unwind, or if you need extra quiet time during a hectic day.

This is also a great activity to learn the parts of the body and to discuss body parts.

⭐ *Eileen Lucas, Halifax, Nova Scotia, Canada*

Put Your Shoes On   3+

Materials   none

What to do   Sing this little song after nap time to encourage the desired behavior.

Put Your Shoes On (Tune: "She'll Be Coming 'Round the Mountain")
Oh, it's time to put your shoes on, girls and boys.
It's time to put your shoes on, girls and boys.
Oh, it's time to put your shoes on.
Oh, it's time to put your shoes on.
Oh, it's time to put your shoes on, girls and boys.

⭐ *Jackie Wright, Enid, OK*

Read Aloud

`4+`

Materials   chapter book appropriate for young children

What to do
1. After the children are settled, read to them from a chapter book. Remember that you are trying to put the children to sleep, so don't read with drama or excitement. This works best when you read in a monotone voice.
2. If at all possible, choose a book without pictures, or make a practice of showing the children the pictures **before** you start reading! (If the children find out later that there are pictures, they won't be happy!)
3. Good choices include Beverly Cleary books, Laura Ingalls Wilder books, *Black Stallion* books, Anna Sewell's *Black Beauty* and even *The Hobbit*! If you read *A Cricket in Times Square* by George Selden, it's fun to play some of the music mentioned in the book!

★ *Linda Ford, Sacramento, CA*

Sweet Dreams Book

`4+`

Materials   pieces of white felt or flannel cloth (6" x 6")
markers/paint
magazine pictures
glue
hole punch
pipe cleaners or twist ties

What to do
1. Help the children make their own Sweet Dreams book that includes things they would love to dream about.
2. Tell them they can paint or use markers to draw pictures or glue magazine pictures onto white felt or cloth pages. Let them decide how many pages to put in their books. They may have a lot of things to dream about or just a few!

(continued on the next page)

3. When their pictures are complete, help them punch three holes in each piece of cloth using a hole punch. Bind the pages together using pipe cleaners or twist ties.

   Safety Note: Be careful of the sharp ends of the pipe cleaners and twist ties.

4. The children will have a keepsake that they can bring to nap time. The book will help them relax and soothe them for sleep.

More to do   **Home-to-School Connection:** This can be a great parent/child home project. Send materials home so the child can make a Sweet Dreams book at home with the support of her family. Family photos, which are familiar to the child and add extra comfort, can be part of a Sweet Dreams book.

Eileen Lucas, Halifax, Nova Scotia, Canada

Snack Time Sing-Along Song   3+

Materials   none

What to do   When the children are in the midst of cleaning up for snack time, washing hands, or sitting at the table waiting for the food to be passed out, lead them in this song to the tune of "Yankee Doodle."

I have a stomach getting hungry,
I have two hands to wash and dry.
I have two eyes to see our plate of snacks,
With some great new foods to try.
Sometimes they have a very smooth taste,
Sometimes we eat them with a crunch!
But every time they pass the plate,
I'm glad I was so hungry.
We love to get new snacks to munch.

Related books   *Bread and Jam for Frances* by Russell Hoban
Green Eggs and Ham by Dr. Seuss
Where the Wild Things Are by Maurice Sendak

Susan Oldham Hill, Lakeland, FL

All Sit Down

3+

Materials   none

What to do   To transition children to snack or lunch, sing this song to the tune of "Love Somebody (Yes, I Do)."

Are you ready to sit down?
Are you ready to sit down?
Are you ready to sit down?
We won't begin snack until you all sit down.

★ *Jackie Wright, Enid, OK*

Snack Time Song

3+

Materials   none

What to do   To transition children to snack, sing the following to the tune of "Jingle Bells."

Tap your toes,
Shake your hands,
Turn yourself around,
We're ready now for our snack time,
So won't you please sit down?

★ *Jackie Wright, Enid, OK*

Are You Hungry?

3+

Materials   none

What to do   To transition children to snack or lunch, sing this song to the tune of "Frère Jacques."

> Are you hungry?
> Are you hungry?
> Yes I am, yes I am.
> You may munch now,
> You may crunch now,
> Munch and crunch!
> Munch and crunch!

★ *Kaethe Lewandowski, Centreville, VA*

Are You Ready?

3+

Materials   none

What to do   To transition children to snack, sing the following to the tune of "Frère Jacques."

> Are you ready, are you ready,
> For snack time, for snack time?
> Quietly wash your hands now, quietly wash your hands now,
> Then sit down, then sit down.

> Are you ready, are you ready,
> For snack time, for snack time?
> (Child's name) wash your hands now, (child's name) wash your hands now,
> Then sit down, then sit down.

★ *Jackie Wright, Enid, OK*

Breakfast Break

3+

Materials   none

What to do

1. Allowing children to be as independent as possible during breakfast time can make transition times easier for all. Follow this routine to help the children take control and take care of themselves.
2. Wipe the tables beforehand with a solution of bleach and water. Arrange the needed plates, cups, and utensils in a buffet style on a side table.
3. Let them get their own plates, cups, and utensils and choose a place to sit at the table. Place the food on the table in small bowls with serving spoons.
4. Let the children serve themselves from the small bowls and pour their own juice or milk from a child-sized pitcher.
5. When done eating, the children should clean up their own places and scrape their plates into a garbage can or designated container.
6. If the routine is well established and organized, then the transition times before and after meals will be very smooth.
7. Follow the same routine at snack time. Modify the routine to meet your program's individual needs.

Related books   *Breakfast Time, Ernest and Celestine* by Gabrielle Vincent
Breakfast With My Father by Ron Roy
The Cow Is Mooing Anyhow by Laura Geringer
Good Morning, Let's Eat! by Karin Luisa Badt
Mr. MacGregor's Breakfast Egg by Elizabeth MacDonald
Pancakes for Breakfast by Tomie dePaola
Pancakes, Pancakes by Eric Carle
Pizza for Breakfast by Maryann Kovalski
We're Making Breakfast for Mother by Shirley Neitzel

Related song   **The Breakfast Song** by Virginia Jean Herrod
(Tune: "Mary Had a Little Lamb")
Breakfast time is really neat
Wash your hands and have a seat.
Pour some juice into your cup
Serve yourself and eat it up.
Clean your place when you are done
Breakfast time is really fun.

 *Virginia Jean Herrod, Columbia, SC*

Healthy Food Fun

3+

Materials   healthy foods

What to do
1. To get ready for snack time, sing the following song, or ask the children what their favorite healthy food is. Sing the song to the tune of "London Bridge":

   Good food helps us grow up strong,
   Grow up strong, grow up strong.
   Good food helps us grow up strong, I like _____.

2. Choose one child at a time to name a healthy food he likes. After he has named a food, he may go wash his hands for snack. Continue until everyone has named a food.
3. Serve some of the children's favorite fruits or vegetables for snack. Ask parents to bring in their child's favorite healthy food to share.

★ *Deborah Litfin, Forest Hills, NY*

What's for Lunch?

3+

Materials   8 ½" x 11" poster board
pictures of food from magazines, or markers
glue

What to do
1. Cut poster board in half. On each piece, glue or draw a picture of a food that is served in your school lunch program.
2. Each morning, hold up the food that will be served that day and chant:

   Today is Monday,
   Today is Monday,
   Monday macaroni,
   All you hungry children, come and have some lunch!

(continued on the next page)

3. Before snack or lunch time each day, show the food card and repeat the previous day's menu by holding up that picture, too.

Today is Tuesday,
Today is Tuesday,
Tuesday tuna sandwich,
Monday macaroni,
All you hungry children, come and have some lunch!

★ *Barbara Saul, Eureka, CA*

Table Setting

3+

Materials
paper for placemats
markers
plates, napkins, and silverware
glasses
containers

What to do

1. On each piece of paper (placemat), trace around a plate, glass, napkin, and silverware. Laminate for durability.
2. Place plates, napkins, silverware, and glasses on a shelf or in the center of the table. The children can help carry small serving dishes and other additional items to the tables.
3. After children have washed their hands, encourage them to take a placemat and corresponding items to set their own table space.
4. After the meal provide labeled containers and a small bucket of water and washcloths for each child to clean up his own space.
5. If desired, let children create their own placemats to use daily.
6. Transition activities such as this provide you with the time to prepare food without the children having to sit and wait.

★ *Lauri Robinson, Big Lake, MN*

Table for Two

3+

Materials   small table large enough for two children
inexpensive lace tablecloth or lace material

What to do

1. At lunchtime set up a "table for two" with a lace tablecloth. Make this a special event each day by choosing two children to have lunch together at this special table.
2. To make sure everyone gets a turn regularly, write each child's name on a tongue depressor and keep them in a can. As you choose children each day, remove their tongue depressors and attach them together with a rubber band until all have had a turn. Then start over.
3. This is a nice way to help a child who may be having a bad day. It may perk him up to sit at this table with a special friend in quieter environment.

★ *Gail Morris, Kemah, TX*

It's Time to Wash Our Hands

3+

Materials   none

What to do   A great way to help children wash their hands and make sure they're clean for snack is to sing this song. Sing it to the tune of "The Farmer in the Dell."

It's time to wash our hands,
It's time to wash our hands,
Because we want clean hands,
It's time to wash our hands.

★ *Cookie Zingarelli, Columbus, OH*

Getting Ready for Snack

3+

Materials   none

What to do   Get ready for snack or lunch by singing this song to the tune of "She'll Be Comin' 'Round the Mountain."

Oh we'll all wash our hands, yes we will.
Oh we'll all wash our hands, yes we will.
Oh we'll all wash our hands,
Oh we'll all wash our hands,
Oh we'll all wash our hands, yes we will.

Oh, we will dry our hands, yes we will.
Oh, we will dry our hands, yes we will.
Oh, we will dry our hands,
Oh, we will dry our hands,
Oh, we will dry our hands, yes we will.

Oh, we will sit down for snack time, yes we will.
Oh, we will sit down for snack time, yes we will.
Oh, we will sit down for snack time,
Oh, we will sit down for snack time,
Oh, we will sit down for snack time, yes we will.

Oh, we will use our best manners, yes we will.
Oh, we will use our best manners, yes we will.
Oh, we will use our best manners,
Oh, we will use our best manners,
Oh, we will use our best manners, yes we will.

Jackie Wright, Enid, OK

Soap Dispenser

3+

Materials   liquid soap pump

What to do

1. One of the hardest transitions during the day is when children are waiting in line to wash their hands before snack or lunch.
2. Assign a daily "soap dispenser." This child's job is to take the liquid soap dispenser and pump one squirt into each child's hand as they wait in line. (This also prevents waste of the soap.)
3. As an added manners lesson, when the soap dispenser puts the soap into a child's hand, the child must say, "Thank you" and the dispenser must say, "You're welcome."
4. The children are occupied rubbing the soap into their hands and are ready to wash and rinse their hands when they reach the sink.

⭐ *Wanda Guidroz, Santa Fe, TX*

Edible Ladybugs

3+

Materials   strawberry cream cheese or yogurt
red jam/jelly or pink icing
round crackers or cookies
plastic knives
paper plates
raisins

(continued on the next page)

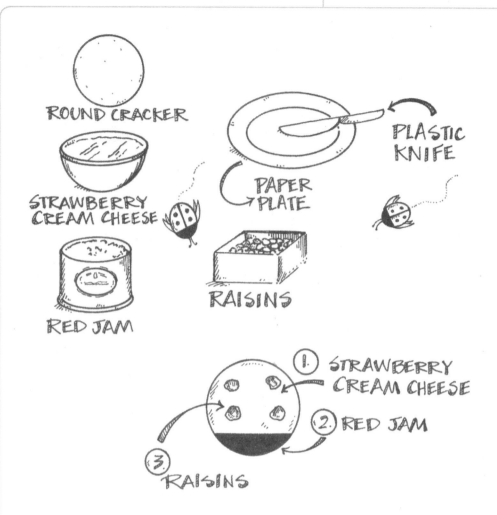

What to do

1. Transition two or three children to the snack table at a time.
2. Encourage them to make "ladybugs" by spreading cream cheese or jam over the cracker or cookie, and then placing raisins on top for the ladybug's black spots.
3. Let all the children make their ladybugs before they eat their snack.

More to do

Books: Fill the book center with pictures of and books about ladybugs, such as *Busy Bugs Little Ladybugs* by Modern Publishing, *Ladybugs: Red, Fiery, and Bright* by Mia Posada, and *Five Little Ladybugs* by Karen Henley.

Outdoors: Go outside on a ladybug hunt. Use magnifying glasses to get a better look. Encourage the children to count how many ladybugs they see, remember the number, and record it when you return to the classroom. Tally them for a total.

★ *Barb Lindsay, Mason City, IA*

Frozen Bananas

3+

Materials   bananas (one for every two children)
Popsicle sticks
plastic wrap

What to do
1. This is a favorite snack for children, and it's nutritious! Eating the frozen bananas is great way to interest children in snack time, and help them eat slowly.
2. Peel the bananas and cut them in half.
3. Insert a Popsicle stick in each half and wrap in clear plastic wrap.
4. Freeze until solid. Do not keep frozen longer than a week.

★ *Mary Jo Shannon, Roanoke, VA*

Birds in the Wilderness

3+

Materials   none

What to do
1. Encourage the children to wait until everyone is seated before they begin eating. This is difficult for hungry children. This song helps make this routine more enjoyable.
2. Sing this song to the tune of "Old Gray Mare."

Here we sit like birds in the wilderness,
Birds in the wilderness, birds in the wilderness,
Here we sit like birds in the wilderness,
Waiting to be fed.
Waiting to be fed (children tilt their heads back like baby birds waiting to be fed, and smack their lips)
Waiting to be fed (repeat above).
Here we sit like birds in the wilderness,
Waiting to be fed.

(continued on the next page)

Related books   *Birds* by Susan Kuchalla
Birds Eat and Eat and Eat by Roma Gans
Feathers for Lunch by Lois Ehlert
What Makes a Bird a Bird? by Mary Garelick

Related song   "Birds" by Hap Palmer

Lunch Box Duty

4+

Materials   lunch boxes or lunch bags

What to do
1. Gather the children's lunches as they come into the classroom in the morning. Assign a child to be "lunch person."
2. Right before lunch, when everyone is hungry and restless, the lunch person calls out names and hands out lunch boxes or bags.
3. Children will quiet down to hear their names.
4. They pick up their lunches and line up, one by one, to proceed to the lunch table or cafeteria.
5. At the beginning of the year, young children need help identifying the owners of the lunches. They will learn quickly. This transition increases children's observation skills and introduces the beginning skills of speaking before a group.

Related books   *Arthur's Back to School Day* by Lillian Hoban
Lunch by Denise Fleming

⭐ *Diane L. Shatto, Kansas City, MO*

Name Cards

4+

Materials
poster board or card stock
laminator
markers

What to do
1. Laminate a piece of poster board or card stock and cut out a rectangle for each child.
2. Write each child's name on a rectangle with permanent ink. This can be done before or after laminating them.
3. Use these cards as place cards at lunch and snack time.
4. This is a great way to mix up the children at lunch and snack time so they can get to know all their classmates. It also serves as name recognition practice.
5. At midyear, write the children's last names on the back of their card and put them on the table with the last name facing up. This will help the children recognize their last names.

★ *Gail Morris, Kemah, TX*

Napkin Folding

4+

Materials
paper towels

What to do
1. Give each child a paper towel to use for snack time.
2. Encourage the children to fold their paper towel to make a shape or design.
3. Let them share what they made and how they made it.
4. Talk about shapes in their environment and encourage them to imitate the shapes using their paper towels or other materials.

Related book
The Shape of Me and Other Stuff by Dr. Seuss

★ *Monica Hay Cook, Tucson, AZ*

Snack Time Math

4+

Materials   art supplies
                  snack items

What to do

1. Turn everyday routines into meaningful one-to-one correspondence activities by following these steps.
2. Identify a routine where counting is involved. For example, at snack time, each child at a table needs a napkin. Choose a child from the table to be in charge of distributing them.
3. Model for the class how to count how many napkins will be needed by touching the back of each chair where a child is sitting, and counting out loud.
4. Ask the children to tell you how many napkins are needed. Slowly count them out one by one and give them to the child. If the child has counted incorrectly, do not correct him right away; instead, see if he can realize his mistake as he passes out the napkins.
5. This can be a brainstorming activity for the children. Why are there napkins left over? Why were there not enough napkins? How many more or less do you need?

More to do   Use this idea whenever you need to pass out an item. Make sure everyone has an opportunity to count.

Related book   *The Doorbell Rang* by Pat Hutchins

★ *Iris Rothstein, New Hyde Park, NY*

Two Snacks Is Twice the Fun! 4+

Materials   two snack foods that are similar

What to do
1. Show the children two similar snacks, such as pretzel sticks and round pretzels, plain crackers and cheese crackers, or large and small goldfish crackers.
2. Transition to snack by asking each child tell something that is similar or different about the items.
3. Serve the snacks and let them have a taste comparison.
4. Encourage them to use the two snacks to make a pattern on their napkin.

More to do   **Math:** Encourage them to put the snacks on their napkins in pairs and count by twos. If they have one left over, they have an odd number. If they have none left over, they have an even number.

★ *Sandra Gratias, Perkasie, PA*

Shapes and Colors 4+

Materials   poster board in a variety of colors
scissors
black marker

What to do
1. Cut out large 15" diameter shapes from poster board. Use a different color for each shape.
2. Cut out small 4" diameter shapes from poster board. Use the same color poster board for the same, but smaller shapes. For example, a large red square and small red square, large white circle and small white circle, and so on.
3. On each shape write the name of the color on one side and the name of the shape on the other side.

(continued on the next page)

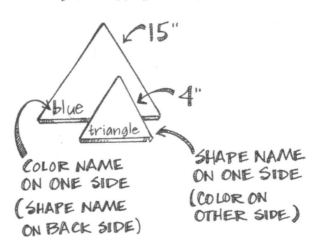

4. When it is time for snack, place one large shape at each table.
5. Call each child by name, hand him a shape, and ask him to identify either the shape or the color.
6. You can also hand out the large shape to children to determine the helpers for the day. For example, whoever has the large square is the cup helper, the large circle is the napkin helper, and so on.

More to do   **Art:** Encourage the children to use a variety of shapes to make "shape people."

Related books   *Shapes* by Guy Smalley
Shapes, Shapes, Shapes by Tana Hoban

⭐ *Sandy L. Scott, Vancouver, WA*

Snack Bucket

4+

Materials   can or cylinder-shaped box
pictures or words related to food
glue
spring-type clothespins (one for each child)
markers

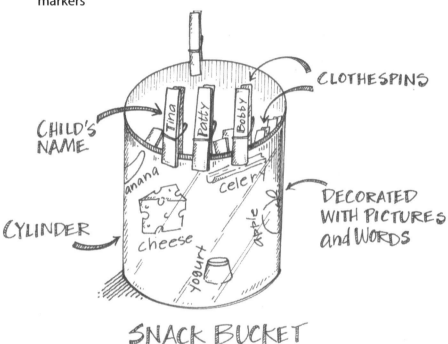

CLOTHESPINS
CHILD'S NAME
CYLINDER
DECORATED WITH PICTURES and WORDS
Tina
Patty
Bobby
anana
celery
cheese
yogurt
apple

SNACK BUCKET

What to do   1. This activity works well in classrooms where children serve themselves their own snacks.

2. Decorate a can or cylinder-shaped box with pictures of words related to food. Put the can in the middle of the snack table.

3. Write each child's name on a clothespin. Clip the clothespins to the side of the can so that the names face out and go around the top of the can.

4. As the children are eating their snack, ask them to find their clothespin and deposit it into the can. This is great for name recognition and for the teacher to know at a glance who has and has not had snack.

5. If parents provide snack, make sure they know the children serve themselves snack so they can send in easy-to-serve snacks.

6. For snacks that are not already in individual bags, use coffee filters. The children can put one serving on a filter and munch away.

7. This is a great way to create independence and self-help skills in children.

⭐ *Gail Morris, Kemah, TX*

Tasting Booklet

4

Materials   9" x 12" construction paper
stickers or rubber stamp with ink pad

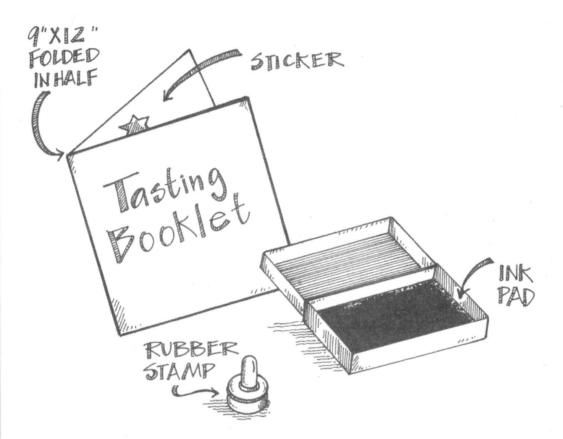

9" X 12" FOLDED IN HALF

STICKER

Tasting Booklet

INK PAD

RUBBER STAMP

What to do
1. To foster good nutrition, give each child a "Tasting Booklet" at the beginning of the year.
2. Fold construction paper in half to make the books.
3. Each time the children taste or eat a new nutritious food prepared by the class, they add a stamp or sticker to their tasting book. Good ideas are vegetables with dip, pumpkin muffins, and fruit salad.
4. Since many children are very particular about what they eat, make sure to give them recognition even when they just taste a new food. The extra recognition encourages reluctant children to try new foods as they learn what is nutritious.

★ *Christine Maiorano, Duxbury, MA*

What Kind of Super-Duper Sandwich?

4+

Materials none

What to do
1. When children are waiting for their lunch, ask them these silly questions to make the time go faster. "What kind of super-duper sandwich would you make for a monkey?" (or dog, rabbit, bird, and so on)
2. Ask them, "What kind of super-duper sandwich would you like to eat?"
3. Use the opportunity to talk about food and nutrition and healthy things to put on a sandwich.

More to do **Science:** Explore different kinds of animals and what they eat.

★ *Amelia K. Griffin, Pontypool, Ontario, Canada*

Lunch Time Foods

4+

Materials
popcorn (unpopped and popped)
pizza dough (raw and baked)
egg (cooked)
spaghetti noodles (uncooked and cooked)
butter (solid and melted)

What to do
1. While waiting for lunch or snack, talk about how cooking changes food. Ask the children to think of foods that change after they've been cooked.
2. Tell the children that they are going to pretend to be different kinds of food. First they will be uncooked food, and then they will become a cooked food.
3. Encourage them to act like an uncooked spaghetti noodle and stand straight. Then they can be a cooked noodle. Demonstrate what this might look like.

(continued on the next page)

4. Show them a variety of cooked and uncooked foods, such as popcorn, pizza dough, and butter.

More to do **Health:** Discuss good nutrition and how it helps the body grow.

Related books *Curious George Bakes a Cake* by Margaret and H.A. Rey
Pete's a Pizza by William Steig
The Popcorn Book by Tomie dePaola
Stone Soup by Ann McGovern
Vegetable Soup by Jeanne Modesitt

Monica Hay Cook, Tucson, AZ

I Can Can

3+

Materials   decorative can or container
small pieces of paper or 3" x 5" index cards cut into fourths
pen or pencil

What to do
1. Write, "I can" on the outside of the can or container.
2. When you have a spare moment, take one child to the can and ask her to add her latest accomplishments to the can.
3. The child can write on the paper, or dictate to you. This is a positive and encouraging activity in which all the children can make a contribution. Examples of accomplishments include, "I can skip," "I can sing a song," "I can read a story to my friend," "I can make my bed," "I can button my coat all by myself," "I can tie my shoe," and "I can print my name."

More to do
Literacy: Focus on the printed word, writing down their words as the children speak. Repeat what you have written down, and then have them say the words with you as you point to each word. This is a good time for those who can print to do so by themselves.

⭐ *Judy Fujawa, The Villages, FL*

Classroom Poster

3+

Materials   computer with color printer, or markers
8 ½" x 11" poster board
laminator (optional)

What to do
1. A transition to begin the school year is to start off by making a poster with your classroom rules on it.

(continued on the next page)

2. You can make an acrostic poem by writing a word vertically such as "team" and writing a rule that begins with each letter of the word. The lines should explain the behavior you expect from the children in the classroom. For example:

Talk using an inside voice.
Each child should do his or her best.
Ask questions politely.
Manners are important.

3. Print out and laminate, if desired.
4. Tell the children how important it is to work as a team. When you have a few spare moments, review the poster with them and tell them that each line begins with a letter of the word "team." Display the poster throughout the year.

⭐ *Jackie Wright, Enid, OK*

Fostering Friendship

3+

Materials   none

What to do

1. Use the transition to snack (or meal time) or when preparing to go home at the end of the day to foster friendship between class members.
2. Ask each child to bring someone else's lunch box, school bag, or coat when it's time for everyone to get organized. Each child helps another get ready.
3. Comment on how happy it makes us feel when we help someone else instead of just doing things for ourselves.
4. Continue the discussion by asking children what other helpful acts they could do for their classmates. Write a list of the children's ideas and post it in the room, or send it home as part of a newsletter. Older children can write the ideas down themselves.

More to do   **Home-to-School Connection:** Ask children what helpful acts they do at home for their parents and/or siblings. Make charts of household tasks children can do to send home. Parents can give children positive feedback by sending notes to the teacher about what their children are doing at home.

⭐ *Elisheva Leah Nadler, Jerusalem, Israel*

Add It to the "Great Vine!"

3+

Materials

brown paper bags
green construction paper
scissors
tape

What to do

1. Twist brown bags together to make a long "vine."
2. Cut out grape leaves from green construction paper.
3. Attach the vine and leaves to the wall with tape.
4. Encourage the children to do good deeds for others. When you have a moment in between activities, highlight what they have done by writing down their good deeds on the grape leaves and adding them on the "Great Vine."
5. Play the song, "I Heard It Through the Grapevine" and make this a musical experience that the children will enjoy. Their good deeds will multiply and, so will the "Great Vine!"

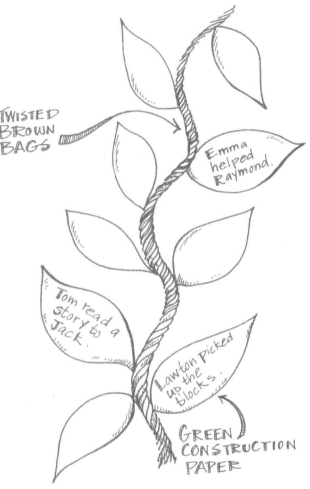

⭐ *Judy Fujawa, The Villages, FL*

Good Deed Apple

Materials

construction paper in red, white, and brown
apple template for tracing
glue
pencils
scissors

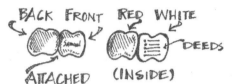

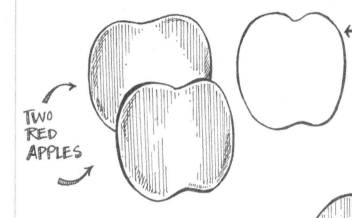

ONE WHITE APPLE

TWO RED APPLES

○ FIVE
○ BROWN
○ SEEDS
○
○

INSIDE WHITE GLUED to RED (RED ON BACK)

Samuel

FRONT

CHILD'S NAME

GOOD DEEDS GO INSIDE WITH SEEDS

What to do

1. Help each child trace and cut out two red apples and one white apple.
2. Help them glue the white apple to one of the red apples. Glue just the top edge of the other red apple to the white side of the two glued-together apples to make a card that opens up to show the white.
3. Help the child write her name on the front.
4. When you have a few moments, take one child's apple and ask the child to tell you one thing that she has done to help another child that day.
5. This activity promotes self-worth and responsibility.

More to do

Home-to-School Connection: Send the apple home with instructions for the children to do at least five good deeds, and to glue one brown seed to the apple for each good deed done.

⭐ *Marjorie Slyhoff, Perkasie, PA*

Good Graffiti

3+

Materials   large sheet of butcher paper
tape
markers or crayons

What to do
1. Attach a large sheet of butcher paper to the wall.
2. Introduce the children to the concept of "Good Graffiti" at a large group time.
3. Talk about graffiti and define it for the group. Tell them that in the classroom the only graffiti permitted is "Good Graffiti." Good graffiti is something that makes another person feel good.
4. When children have a moment or two in between activities, encourage them to go to the Good Graffiti paper and write or dictate something nice (a compliment) about a friend, the class, a family member, or someone else who is special to them.
5. This activity is great to use as children enter in the morning or depart at the end of the day.

Related book   *The Brand New Kid* by Katherine Couric

⭐ *Ann Kelly, Johnstown PA*

Say Something Nice

3+

Materials   none

What to do
1. When you have a few moments at circle or group time, create a loving, caring atmosphere with this activity.
2. Sit on the floor in a circle and start the activity by turning to your left and saying your name, the child's name, and something nice about the child.
3. Continue until it's time for the next activity or everyone has had a turn. End with a group hug.

⭐ *Jodi Sykes, Lake Worth, FL*

Friendship Quilt

3+

Materials
6" squares of drawing paper
large roll of contact paper
2" wide fabric strips

What to do
1. This is the perfect activity for children to do when they are waiting for the next activity to begin.
2. Have each child draw a picture on a square of drawing paper.
3. When all the children have created a picture, assemble a "quilt" by sticking the pictures onto contact paper into a quilt pattern with alternate strips of fabric or paper.
4. With a class of 12, there would be three rows across and four rows down. The contact paper holds it together so it can be displayed on a wall of the classroom.
5. If a roll of contact paper is not available, tape together sheets of sticky paper to achieve the desired size.

Christine Maiorano, Duxbury, MA

Who Am I?

3+

Materials
unbreakable mirror (optional)

What to do
1. Use the following transition activity when you are working on self-concept themes.
2. Have children transition from one activity to another by naming various descriptors about the children. For example, say, "If you have brown hair and blue eyes, go line up."
3. At the beginning of the year, start with only one descriptor, for example, blond hair. When the children are comfortable with one descriptor, use two or more descriptors, for example, blond hair, brown eyes, and glasses.
4. For older children, use descriptors that relate to their names. For example, say, "If your name starts with the letter 'B'…"

5. If working on specific skills, use those descriptors. For example, "If you live at…"

Related books *Is This You?* by Ruth Krauss and Crockett Johnson
Two Eyes, a Nose and a Mouth by Roberta Grobel Intrater

⭐ *Sandra Suffoletto Ryan, Buffalo, NY*

Whose Family? `3+`

Materials one small photo of each child's parent(s) or guardian(s)
card stock
glue sticks
scissors
laminator or clear contact paper

What to do

1. Glue the photo of each child's parent(s) or guardian(s) to a piece of card stock paper. Trim around the photo, leaving a small margin of white showing. Laminate or cover the photo with clear contact paper for durability.
2. When you have a few minutes, take out the cards for a quick game. Hold up one card and ask, "Whose family is this?"
3. Give the children time to answer. Let them guess if they want.
4. Undoubtedly, the child whose family photo you are holding will acknowledge that it is her family.
5. If time allows, continue until you have shown all the family photos.

More to do

Games: Glue a small photo of each child (same size as the adult photos) to a piece of card stock. Trim in the same manner as you did the adult photo. Cover with adhesive paper or laminate. Use the two photos in a matching memory game. Mix up all the photos and lay them face down on a table. Let the children take turns turning the photos over until they find a match of a child and adult(s). Be aware that some children will be upset if somebody else finds their match, so be ready to deal with that situation if it occurs. One possible solution is to agree in advance that each child will only keep their matched set. If they find another match, they can simply turn the cards back over on the table.

(continued on the next page)

Related books   *All Alone With Daddy* by Joan Fassler
Dad and Me in the Morning by Patricia Lakin
I Got a Family by Melrose Cooper
I Love My Family by Wade Hudson
Just Like Daddy by Frank Asch
Lots of Moms by Shelley Rotner
Me and My Family Tree by Joan Sweeney
Mommy Far, Mommy Near: An Adoption Story by Carol Antoinette Peacock
Mommy, Daddy, Me by Lyn Littlefield Hoopes
One Dad, Two Dads, Brown Dads, Blue Dads by Johnny Valentine
Poinsettia and Her Family by Felicia Bond
Room for a Stepdaddy by Jean Thor Cook
Waiting for Mom by Linda Wagner Tyler

★ *Virginia Jean Herrod, Columbia, SC*

Island Time

3+

Materials   rug remnant, 5' x 5'
sharp scissors (adult only)
comfortable child-size chair,
   such as a beanbag chair
portable CD player
earphones
basket
books

What to do

1. Cut the rug into a freeform island shape. Place in an isolated corner. Add a chair, books, basket, CDs, and CD player. Add a beach scene to the wall or a palm tree photo to enhance the environment.
2. When a child needs quiet time to calm down, call it "Island Time." The child may read or listen to music on the earphones until she is ready to join the group.
3. Children may elect to go to the "island" if they are upset, or you may suggest they go.
4. If desired, add a sand kitchen timer or lava timer for children to redirect their focus. Also, a photo album filled with calming or happy pictures changes moods fast!

★ *Susan R. Forbes, Daytona Beach, FL*

S-T-O-P

3+

Materials   none

What to do   1. Any time you have a few extra moments during the day, talk to the children about how they feel when someone pushes, hits, or says something mean to them.
2. Tell the children that when this happens, the first thing they can do is stop, hold up their hand like a stop sign, and say, "Stop!" Demonstrate how to do this.
3. Hold your hand as a sign for "Stop!" and teach the following song to the tune of "If You're Happy and You Know It."

   If somebody _____, tell them "stop."
   If somebody _____, tell them "stop."
   If you want to be a friend,
   Then being mean should end.
   If somebody _____, tell them "stop."

4. Verse options include if someone pushes you, hits you, says mean words, or any other bothersome or troublesome behavior.
5. Talk about other situations that might arise, such as on the bus or school van, or at home.

Related books *Froggy Goes to School* by Jonathan London
If You Take a Mouse to School by Laura Joffe Numeroff
Little Critter: Just a School Project by Mercer Mayer
Max and Ruby Play School by Rosemary Wells
Spot Goes to School by Eric Hill

⭐ Sue Fleischmann, Sussex, WI

Time Capsule Envelope

3+

Materials
9" x 12" envelopes
questionnaires (see suggested questions below)
children's drawings
small photos of children or pictures from home

What to do
1. At the beginning of the school year, complete this activity over a period of time using children's waiting time or any extra moments in the day.
2. Help each child answer the questions below. (Add your own questions.)
3. Place each child's questionnaire in the envelope with her drawings and photo.
4. Write the child's name and address on front of envelope.
5. At the end of the year (or the end of two years or however long the children are with you) check the validity of the address and mail the letters to the children at home. They love getting mail!

Questionnaire Questions
1. What is your favorite food?
2. What is your favorite color?
3. Who is your best friend?
4. What is your favorite book?
5. What is your favorite game?
6. What did you do last weekend?
7. What is your favorite celebration and why?
8. What is the funniest thing you ever saw?
9. Draw your favorite clothes to wear.
10. Draw your favorite animal.

★ *Amelia K. Griffin, Pontypool, Ontario, Canada*

Interviews

4+

Materials socks
glue
foam shapes, glitter, rhinestones

What to do

1. Tell the children they will be making pretend microphones out of a sock.
2. Give each child a sock. Encourage them to glue decorations to their socks.
3. When the socks have dried, the children take turns putting them on their hands.
4. Discuss what an interview is. Have the children take turns being an interviewer and being interviewed.
5. The children ask each other interview questions. Sample interview questions include:

   ◆ If you could be any animal, what would you most like to be? Why?
   ◆ If you could change any rule, what rule would you change?
   ◆ If you could have one new thing, what would it be?
   ◆ What would you most like to be when you grow up?
   ◆ What is your favorite sport?
   ◆ What activity do you most like to do with your family?
   ◆ What are you really good at?

6. Conduct interviews with children any time during the day to ease transitions, fill a few extra moments, help children wait patiently, or give a child extra attention.

More to do **Language:** After some practice, children can interview family members and others in the school.

★ *Monica Hay Cook, Tucson, AZ*

Take a Seat

3+

Materials none

What to do
1. When you want the children to get ready for Story Time, sing the following to the tune of "If You're Happy and You Know It." Here are the words and accompanying actions for the song.
2. Start with "If you're ready for a story, clap your hands..." while children are busy throughout the classroom. Add "If you're ready for a story, move your feet..." as they move to story area. Finish with "If you're ready for a story, take at seat…"

Related books *Clap Hands* by Helen Oxenbury
Clap Your Hands by Lorinda Bryan Cauley
My Hands by Aliki

★ *Christina Chilcote, New Freedom, PA*

It's Story Time

3+

Materials none

What to do
1. To prepare the group for story time sing the following to the tune of "Polly Wolly Doodle."

   Oh, if you want to hear a story now,
   This is what I need you to do.
   You've got to sit right down on the rug
   For story time today.
   Turn on your ears, turn on your ears,

Turn on your ears to hear what I say.
For I'm goin' to start to read (have the book in your hand)
When I open up the book (show the cover of the book)
'Cause it's story time! HOORAY!

2. As soon as you open up the book, it is a signal that it is your turn to talk.

⭐ *Jackie Wright, Enid, OK*

Time to Sit Down

3+

Materials   none

What to do
1. To let the children know that story time is about to begin and that it's time to sit down, sing the following to the tune of "Frère Jacques."

    Time to sit down, time to sit down,
    Everyone, everyone.
    It is time for story, it is time for story,
    Everyone, everyone.

2. Instead of "story" substitute "lunch" or any other time during the day, or use individual children's names instead of saying "everyone."

⭐ *Jackie Wright, Enid, OK*

If You're Ready for a Story

3+

Materials   none

What to do

1. As children are gathering for story time, sing the following to the tune of "If You're Happy and You Know It."

   If you're ready for a story, sit on the rug,
   If you're ready for a story, sit on the rug,
   If you're ready for a story, check your hands and then your feet.
   If you're ready for a story, sit on the rug.

2. Change "sit on the rug" to fit your situation—come sit down, find a chair, and so on.

⭐ *Jackie Wright, Enid, OK*

Talking Stick

3+

Materials   talking stick

What to do

1. To help children quiet down and make the transition to story time, show them a "talking stick."
   Author's Note: I was lucky to have a real talking stick given to me by one of the members of my native band.

2. Just before story time, explain to the children that long ago the native people used talking sticks when they met in groups for discussions. The only one allowed to speak in the group was the one holding the stick. When that person was finished speaking, he passed it to the next person who had something to share.

3. Ask the children who would like to try it. Most children (even the reluctant speakers) will want to use it.

More to do   **Art:** After you try the talking stick during story time, let the children know that they can decorate their own stick to take home. Tell them that traditional talking sticks are decorated with stories that were passed on to families by means of drawings and carvings. They can make drawings that represent their own stories.

★ *Eileen Lucas, Halifax, Nova Scotia, Canada*

A Bounty of Books

3+

Materials   multiple copies of a book

What to do
1. Gather the children for story time. Put out multiple copies of the book you want to read.
2. As the children transition to the story area, they can explore the book you will be sharing with the group. This gives them an opportunity to linger over the pages and enjoy the book more closely.
3. Look for books that have editions in other languages, such as Spanish. Parents who speak other languages can enjoy these books with their children.
4. During story time, read from your copy (ideally a "big book") while the children look at theirs. Shop online or at yard sales or secondhand stores for discount books that you can buy in bulk.
5. If possible, gather multiple copies of the same story told in different ways, such as "Cinderella," "Goldilocks and the Three Bears," and "The Mitten."

Related books   *Chicka Chicka Boom Boom* by Bill Martin, Jr.
The Little Mouse, the Red Ripe Strawberry, and the Big Hungry Bear by Don and Audrey Wood
Seven Little Rabbits by John Becker

★ *Linda Ford, Sacramento, CA*

Story Sounds

3+

Materials   none

What to do
1. As a general rule, using a very animated, child-like voice appeals to children. Have fun reading stories to children, and make sound effects as well.
2. When a child's attention begins to drift, remember to be animated. You can try speaking in a whisper, which children will often stop to listen closely to.
3. Use facial expressions to the point of overdoing it, or ask the children questions while you read, such as, "What do you think will happen next?"
4. Involve the children in stories. Eric Carle's books are great for this because of the repetition that allows children to join in on the storytelling.

★ *Deborah R. Gallagher, Littleton, NH*

Flexible Straw Puppet

3+

Materials
paper
scissors
bits of colored or silver paper
markers
glue
flexible straw
sticky tape

DETAIL ADDED WITH PAINT and PENS

PAPER CUT-OUT ATTACHED to BENT PART

BENT PART

BITS of PAPER

What to do
1. Make a puppet to attract the children's attention during story time.
2. Cut out a puppet shape from construction paper. Color and decorate it.
3. Bend the straw.
4. Use the sticky tape to attach the puppet shape to the shorter part of the straw, so that you have the longer part to hold.

More to do   **Art:** Encourage the children to make their own puppets.
Dramatic Play and **Language:** Suggest that the children make up simple stories using the characters.

★ *Jane Moran, Stockport, United Kingdom*

Calling All Book Lovers   3+

Materials   new book and paper large enough to wrap around the cover of a book
chalkboard and chalk

What to do   Following are some ideas to use to grab children's attention when introducing a book or story.

◆ When introducing a new book, put a wrapper around the book jacket to hide the picture and title. Give children clues about the story and let them guess the plot or characters before you uncover and read it.

◆ Tell a story by drawing simple stick figures and other outlines on a chalkboard. This new storytelling technique will intrigue them. For example, for "Goldilocks and the Three Bears," draw three faces of varying size for the three bears, simple half circles for bowls, lowercase "h"-shaped chairs, and so on. Erase characters and shapes as they appear and disappear in the story.

◆ Let them participate in stories by repeating a gesture, sound, word, or phrase that occurs often in the narration. Give individual children actions or sounds to make every time their particular character appears in the story. They have to pay attention so they don't miss their cue.

◆ Tell a familiar story with mistakes that the children can correct. This is a good way to introduce opposites or rhyming words.

◆ Fill a bag with props appropriate to the story and pull them out as the story progresses.

More to do   **Art:** Let the children make masks of the story characters.

(continued on the next page)

Dramatic Play: After a progressive story that introduces many characters to solve a problem, let the children re-enact the plot.

More Dramatic Play: Retell a familiar story by introducing dolls or stuffed animals to be the characters in the story, and let the children, alone or in pairs, find other props to use in the story.

Language: Let children make up alternate endings to a story. This works well with "The Gingerbread Boy" (so he isn't eaten) and "The Little Red Hen" (so other animals can eat the bread, too).

⭐ *Sandra Gratias, Perkasie, PA*

Story Time Present

3+

Materials   book
wrapped gift boxes or gift bags

What to do
1. To grab the children's attention, introduce a story by saying, "Here is a present. It says it is for this class. I wonder what it is."
2. Have the children guess what might be in the box. When using a gift box, wrap the top and bottom of the box separately and just lift the lid so you can reuse the box at a later time. (The story time book will be in the box.)
3. Now you have the children's attention and interest. When reading the story, read with enthusiasm.
4. Another way to grab children's attention is to wear a silly hat. This can be your Story Hat. This will keep the children's attention.

More to do   Wear something to represent the story—a red cape or hood for "Little Red Riding Hood," rabbit ears when reading a rabbit story, and so on. Use your imagination and be creative. The more fun you have, the more interesting it will be for the children.

⭐ *Phyllis Esch, Export, PA*

Let's Tell a Story

3+

Materials   none

What to do
1. When you have a few minutes at the beginning of story time or before the next activity, say the first line of a familiar story, or make up the beginning of an imaginary story, and have each child add a line.
2. Do this activity during story times. Stop reading a story in the middle and ask the children to create their own endings.

⭐ *Michelle Barnea, Millburn, NJ*

Author and Illustrator

3+

Materials   none

What to do
1. Sing this simple song at circle or story time when you have a few extra minute to fill. It will teach the children the difference between an author and an illustrator.
2. Sing the following to the tune of "The Farmer in the Dell."

The author writes the story.
The author writes the story.
The illustrator draws the pictures
To make the book complete.

⭐ *Jackie Wright, Enid, OK*

Class Book Reader

3+

Materials

stapler
picture of each child and teacher and a group picture
laminator or clear contact paper

What to do

1. Use this class version of *Brown Bear, Brown Bear, What Do You See?* by Bill Martin, Jr. as a way to fill extra time.

2. At my school, each class is named after an animal. If your class is "The Seals," for example, title the class book *Green Seal, Green Seal, Who Do You See?*

3. On the first page, glue a picture of the teachers. For example, "Green seal, green seal, who do you see? I see Mrs. Wanda looking at me." The teacher's picture is under the words. The next page will have a child's picture and state, for example, "Mrs. Wanda, Mrs. Wanda, who do you see? I see Lynn looking at me." Lynn's picture would be under the words. The very last page will have the last child's name from the previous page, for example, "Austin, Austin, who do you see? I see my Seal Class looking at me!" with a class picture to end the book.

4. Start the year by reading this book to the children, but it may became so popular, that you might want to create a new job: during transition times, one child a day is allowed to read the book to the class.

   Author's Note: The children will memorize this book and read it along with the reader. I ended up laminating this book several times during the year, because it got so much use. But the children never got tired of it!

Wanda Guidroz, Santa Fe, TX

Goodnight Moon

Materials
Goodnight Moon by Margaret Wise Brown
felt in a variety of colors
scissors
flannel board

What to do
1. Use this activity to fill extra time as children are gathering for story time.
2. Cut out pieces of felt in the shapes and colors of the objects mentioned in *Goodnight Moon*.
3. Read the book with the children several times until they are very familiar with it, and you know it well enough to tell it on the flannel board.
4. Tell the story without the book, using a flannel board and the cut pieces of felt. The children can follow along and will learn to add the felt pieces themselves.

Karyn F. Everham, Fort Myers, FL

I CAN Tell a Story

Materials
pieces of paper
pen or pencil
large see-through plastic container
film canisters

What to do
1. Write story starters on pieces of paper. Examples include:

   - Once upon a time…
   - A long time ago…
   - Remember when…
   - The last time I…
   - In my dream…
   - A scary thing happened…
   - On my vacation…
   - When my grandparents came…
   - My favorite hero…
   - When I was two….

(continued on the next page)

2. Put one piece of paper in each film canister, and put all the film canisters in a large see-through plastic container.
3. When you are waiting for everyone to gather for story time, ask one child to pull a film canister out of the container. Remove the rolled-up paper, with the story starter printed on it. Read the story starter, and give that child a chance to tell a short story using the story starter.

⭐ *Judy Fujawa, The Villages, FL*

Puppet Theater

3+

Materials
large cereal box
scissors
glue
paint and paintbrush
decorations

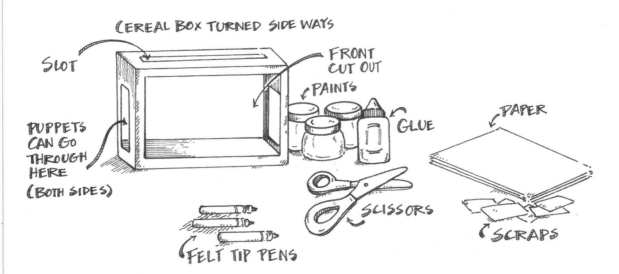

CEREAL BOX TURNED SIDE WAYS
SLOT
FRONT CUT OUT
PAINTS
GLUE
PAPER
PUPPETS CAN GO THROUGH HERE (BOTH SIDES)
SCISSORS
SCRAPS
FELT TIP PENS

What to do
1. Make a simple puppet stage that children can use while they wait for story time to begin.
2. Turn the box sideways like a television screen and cut a rectangle shape from the front of the box.
3. Cut about half of the sides out so that puppets can be put in through the holes.
4. Cut a slot into the top for puppets to hang through.

5. Make thick paint with a bit of liquid soap and use it to paint the box inside and out.

6. When the paint is dry, add any decorations.

More to do **Dramatic Play:** Encourage children to use the puppet stage to put on plays that they make up.

More Story Time: Make simple puppet characters from books or stories that the children enjoy and then act out the story in the theater. Children's favorite stories are a good starting point or traditional tales like "The Three Little Pigs."

Related books *Goodnight Moon* by Margaret Wise Brown
The Rainbow Fish by Marcus Pfister
The Very Hungry Caterpillar by Eric Carle
We're Going on a Bear Hunt by Michael Rosen
Where the Wild Things Are by Maurice Sendak

Jane Moran, Stockport, United Kingdom

Read Me a Story

3+

Materials books (see lists below)

What to do
1. Reading to children can be the most rewarding activity you do in any given day. However, reading to children in a large group setting can lead to discipline problems as you try to keep a large group of wiggly bodies quiet and still through a whole story.

2. Try the following story time ideas to fill a few extra moments.

3. Make a cozy corner that is designated just for reading. Pile several large pillows on a small rug in a corner of the room. Add a small quilt or afghan or two. Place a large bucket with several favorite books in it nearby. Use this area to read to small groups (two or three) of children. Cuddle up together! It's definitely a warm and fuzzy time!

4. Place books in smaller containers around the room. Use fancy buckets or wicker baskets. When a child asks you to read one of the books, just plop right down where you are and read, read, read!

5. Place books related to the different interest centers right in the interest centers, and then read to children right there in the center.

(continued on the next page)

Story Time

Books for the Art Center
All the Colors of the Earth by Shelia Hamanaka
The Art Lesson by Tomie dePaola
An Artist by M.B. Goffstein
Beginning to Learn About: Colors by Richard L. Allington
Draw Me a Star by Eric Carle
I Spy: An Alphabet in Art by Lucy Micklethwait
Painted Dreams by Karen Lynn Williams
Willy's Pictures by Anthony Browne
The Young Artist by Thomas Locker

Books for the Block Center
Block Book by Susan Arkin Couture
Building by Elisha Cooper
Changes, Changes by Pat Hutchins
The Line Up Book by Marisabina Russo
Listen to a Shape by Marcia Brown
Roberto, the Insect Architect by Nina Laden

Books for the Dramatic Play Center
Family Farm by Thomas Locker
I Go With My Family to Grandma's by Riki Levinson
I Love My Family by Wade Hudson
Poinsettia and Her Family by Felicia Bond
Pretend You're a Cat by Jean Marzollo

Books for the Manipulatives Center
Panda's New Toy by Joyce Dunbar
Leo Cockroach: Toy Tester by Kevin O'Malley
Mr. Fong's Toy Shop by Leo Politi

Books for the Music Center
Be-Bop-A-Do-Walk by Sheila Hamanaka
Ben's Trumpet by Rachel Isadora
The Little Brass Band by Margaret Wise Brown
Can You Dance, Dalila? by Virginia Kroll
Dancin' in the Kitchen by Frank P. Christian
Gabriella's Song by Candace Fleming
Geraldine the Music Mouse by Leo Lionni
Grandpa's Song by Tony Johnston
In the Time of the Drums by Kim Siegelson
The Maestro Plays by Bill Martin, Jr.
Mama Rocks, Papa Sings by Nancy Van Laan
Max Found Two Sticks by Brian Pinkney

Music, Music for Everyone by Vera B. Williams
Noah's Square Dance by Rick Walton
The Piano Man by Deborah Chocolate
Snake Alley Band by Elizabeth Nygaard
Thump, Thump, Rat-A-Tat-Tat by Gene Baer
Willie Blows a Mean Horn by Ianthe Thomas

Books for the Reading Center
At the Library by Christine Loomis
How My Library Grew: By Dinah by Martha Alexander
I Took My Frog to the Library by Eric A. Kimmel
The Ink Drinker by Eric Sanvoisin
The Library by Sarah Stewart
Stella Louella's Runaway Book by Lisa Campbell Ernst
Tomas and the Library Lady by Pat Mora

Books for the Science Center
I Know How We Fight Germs by Kate Rowan
Rocks in His Head by Carol Otis Hurst
The Science Book of the Senses by Neil Ardley
Tadpoles by Betsy James
Water Dance by Thomas Locker

Books for the Woodworking Center
Fix It by David McPhail
Grandpa's Hammer by Ronald Kidd

★ *Virginia Jean Herrod, Columbia, SC*

Song Books

Materials   children's books of illustrated songs
basket or tub

What to do
1. Collect children's books that illustrate songs. Book suggestions include:

   Down by the Bay (and other books) by Raffi
   Mary Wore Her Red Dress and Henry Wore His Green Sneakers by Merle Peek
   Miss Mary Mack by Mary Ann Hoberman
   The Lady With the Alligator Purse (and other books) by Nadine Bernard Westcott

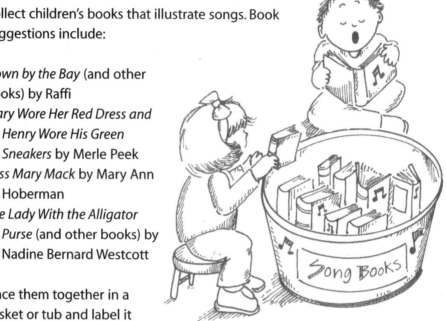

2. Place them together in a basket or tub and label it "Song Books." You might want to draw musical notes on the label to make it clear for children to choose and return the books to the tub. You could also make a sticker with a musical note on it to put on each book to help them return it there.
3. These books are great to grab during a transition time or waiting period. Pick out a book, or ask a child to choose one from the song book tub.
4. Hold the book as you all sing, or pick a child as a "song leader" to hold the book as you all sing it together.
   Author's Note: Song books make great pre-reading books because they are easier to memorize.

⭐ *Laura Durbrow, Lake Oswego, OR*

Spend Some Time With The Cat in the Hat

3+

Materials
The Cat in the Hat by Dr. Seuss
stuffed Cat in the Hat (optional)

What to do
Provide books and props, such as *The Cat in the Hat* by Dr. Seuss and a stuffed version of the cat in the hat, for children to read and play with when they have a few moments before story time, when they need to calm down, or other times during the day.

More to do
Home-to-School Connection: Each week, select a different child to take a book bag home for the weekend. (Each book bag contains a book, one or two props related to the book, and a journal.) Encourage the children to include the stuffed character in as many activities as they can. Ask parents to read the book to their child, and write about the family's weekend adventures in the provided journal. Be sure to read the journal out loud to the class each Monday. You can have more than one book bag circulating through the class. Use different books and characters, such as *If You Give a Pig a Pancake* by Laura Joffe Numeroff, *Brown Bear, Brown Bear, What Do You See?* by Bill Martin, Jr., or any of the *Clifford* books. Use any book that you can pair with a stuffed animal.

★ *Carla LeMasters, Bartonville, IL*

Acting Out

3+

Materials   children's books

What to do
1. At the end of story time, read a book that invites children to act out character roles.
2. Ask the children which character they would like to be as they move to the next activity. For example, one child may choose to move like the purple cat in *Brown Bear, Brown Bear, What Do You See?* on his way to wash his hands for lunch.

Related books   *Brown Bear, Brown Bear, What Do You See?* by Bill Martin, Jr.
The Gingerbread Man by Eric A. Kimmel
Hey! Get Off Our Train by John Burningham
A House for Hermit Crab by Eric Carle
I Wish That I Had Duck Feet by Theo LeSieg
The Mitten by Alvin Tresselt
Mushroom in the Rain by Mirra Ginsburg
Panda Bear, Panda Bear, What Do You See? by Bill Martin, Jr.
Parade by Donald Crews
Polar Bear, Polar Bear, What Do You Hear? by Bill Martin, Jr.
The Wedding Procession of the Rag Doll and the Broom Handle and Who Was In It by Carl Sandburg

★ Laura Durbrow, Lake Oswego, OR

A Mystery Story

4+

Materials   an interesting box or trunk
decorations for the box or trunk
books
props and hats to match books

What to do
1. Use this activity as a transition to story time.
2. Decorate the box or trunk so it looks interesting to the children.
3. Choose a book for a group read.
4. Fill the "mystery box" with props that will enhance the storytelling.
5. If possible, find or create a hat or prop that matches the story and will lure the children to story time.
6. Wear the hat or hold the prop as you bring the mystery box to story time and call the children to story time.

More to do
Language and Literacy: Use the mystery box as a language extender. Put a mystery item inside and give clues or have the children ask questions until they can guess what the item might be.

⭐ *Ann Kelly, Johnston, PA*

What Do You See?

4+

Materials
Brown Bear, Brown Bear, What Do You See? by Bill Martin, Jr.
9" x 12" picture cards of animals of different kinds

What to do
1. Use this activity when you want to prepare children for story time.
2. Read the book to the children so they are very familiar with the rhythm of the story. You can also put a copy of the book in the book area for them to read on their own.
3. As the children come to the whole group area, set out a group of five animal picture cards on the rug or chalk rail so they can see the pictures easily.
4. Ask one child to choose a card, stand in front of the group, and say, "Brown giraffe (or whatever animal card he chooses), brown giraffe, what do you see?"
5. The next child selects another animal card and answers, "I see a gray snake looking at me."
6. The whole group then asks, "Gray snake, gray snake, what do you see?" Another child would choose a new card and answer, "I see a green parrot looking at me."
7. Repeat this as long as time permits.

(continued on the next page)

8. Modify the cards to match any theme, such as community helpers, musical instruments, holiday items, or any other topic.

More to do Repeat the activity with photo cards of the children.
Math: Try the same approach with shape cards in various colors.

⭐ *Susan Oldham Hill, Lakeland, FL*

From Start to Finish

4+

Materials sets of story sequence cards (5 cards per story)

What to do
1. While the children are waiting for story time, put a set of story cards in random order on the rug or chalk rail so all of the children can see the cards.
2. Ask the children to think of which picture comes first in the story while their friends are finishing their activities and coming to the rug.
3. When almost all of them have joined the group, ask one child to find the first picture of the story and put it all the way on the left of the group of cards.
4. Continue with another child until the story is in the correct order from left to right.
5. Ask a child to tell the story from start to finish. Repeat with another set of cards as time allows.
   Tip: For self-checking, number the cards on the back.
6. If desired, collect groups of story cards that focus on unit themes, such as seeds, weather, and holidays, to match the theme you are teaching.
7. As the children become comfortable with five-card stories, find stories with more cards.

More to do **Art:** Invite the children to illustrate a story they like using four to six different pictures. Mount the drawings on cards to use for the sequencing activity.
Math: For math skills, order five pictures of triangles from smallest to largest.

⭐ *Susan Oldham Hill, Lakeland, FL*

Mama Don't Allow

4+

Materials *Mama Don't Allow* by Thacher Hurd

What to do
1. To get the children ready for story time or put them in a lively musical mood read *Mama Don't Allow*. Follow the reading with the song found in the back cover of the book.
2. Teach the children how to "play" air instruments to accompany the song. Start with instruments found in the book, such as a guitar, trumpet, drum, and saxophone. Then try others, such as the piano, harmonica, and fiddle.
3. Sing the song, improvise verses, and "play" instruments of choice when you and the children have a spare moment to fill.

★ *Karyn F. Everham, Fort Myers, FL*

Queen Forgetta Boutit and Concepts of Print

4+

Materials crown
big book of pictures with large print

What to do
1. Capture the children's attention at story time by putting on a crown and introducing yourself as Queen (or King) Forgetta Boutit.
2. Tell the children that you are forgetful and need their help remembering how to read the book. (This works best with a book that is familiar to the children.)
3. Show the children the back cover and ask them where you should start reading. Allow the children to direct you to the front cover.
4. While you read the book, make mistakes and allow the children to correct you. Turn the book upside down, read text right to left, read text top to bottom, and begin reading from the middle of a sentence.

(continued on the next page)

More to do

Social Development: Have Queen or King Forgetta Boutit help the children review classroom procedures, such as cleanup, recess, snack, and so on.

Related books   *Edward and the Pirates* by David McPhail
The Library Dragon by Carmen Agra Deedy
Wings: A Tale of Two Chickens by James Marshall

★ *Cassandra Reigel Whetstone, San Jose, CA*

Story Leader

4+

Materials   tape recorder
picture book with matching cassette

What to do
1. When you are in between activities, and are busy helping one group, another group can listen to a book with a "story leader."
2. Give one child a picture book with the cassette that tells the story and has turn-the-page signals.
3. The child (the story leader) holds up the book and the children listen to the cassette as he turns the pages.
4. Place the book and cassette in a large zipper-closure baggie for children to use themselves at free choice time.
   Note: Make your own cassettes by recording yourself reading a book.

Related books   *Chicka Chicka Boom Boom* by Bill Martin, Jr. and John Archambault
Dinofours (series of books) by Steve Metzger
Love You Forever by Robert N. Munsch

★ *Laura Durbrow, Lake Oswego, OR*

Children's Book Index

1 Is One by Tasha Tudor, 57, 399

1, 2, 3 to the Zoo by Eric Carle, 317

26 Letters and 99 Cents by Tana Hoban, 238

70 Wonderful Word-Family Poems by Jennifer Wilen & Beth Handa, 132

A

A My Name Is Alice by Jane Bayer, 26, 171, 254

ABC, A Family Alphabet Book by Bobbie Combs, 274

Abuela by Arthur Dorros, 76

Aesop's Fables by Aesop, 298

Albert's Alphabet by Leslie Tryon, 238

Alexander and the Terrible, Horrible, No Good, Very Bad Day by Judith Viorst, 92

Alistair in Outer Space by Marilyn Sadler, 322

All Alone With Daddy by Joan Fassler, 454

All in a Day by Mitsumasa Anno, 285

All the Colors of the Earth by Shelia Hamanaka, 470

Alligator Shoes by Arthur Dorros, 247

Alpha Bugs by David A. Carter, 25

The Alphabet Room by Sarah Pinto, 274

The Amazing Bone by William Steig, 227

Amelia Bedelia by Peggy Parish, 56

Amelia Bedelia Helps Out by Peggy Parish, 145

And It Rained by Ellen Raskin, 410

Angry Arthur by Hiawyn Oram, 92

Anna Banana and Me by Lenore Blegvad, 26

Anna's Goodbye Apron by Julie Brillhart, 167

Anno's Alphabet by Mitsumaso Anno, 238

The Art Lesson by Tomie dePaola, 113, 470

Arthur's Back to School Day by Lillian Hoban, 438

An Artist by M.B. Goffstein, 470

Ashanti to Zulu by Margaret Musgrove, 324

At the Library by Christine Loomis, 471

B

Baby Beluga by Raffi, 408

The Backward Day by Ruth Krauss, 285

A Bad Case of Stripes by David Shannon, 58

Barn Cat by Carol Saul, 323

Bat Loves the Night by Nicola Davies, 125

Bats and Their Homes by Deborah Chase Gibson, 125

Bears in Pairs by Niki Yektai, 258

The Beaver at Long Pond by Lindsay Barrett George, 238

Be-Bop-A-Do-Walk by Sheila Hamanaka, 470

Beginning to Learn About: Colors by Richard L. Allington, 470

Ben's Trumpet by Rachel Isadora, 470

The Berenstain Bears and the Messy Room by Stan & Jan Berenstain, 163

The Best Mother Goose Ever! by Richard Scarry, 219

The Best Time of Day by Valerie Flournoy, 285

Big and Little by Margaret Miller, 72

The Big Book of Trains by Christine Heap, 393

Birds by Susan Kuchalla, 438

Birds Eat and Eat and Eat by Roma Gans, 438

Birthday Bugs by David A. Carter, 63

Birthday Monsters! by Sandra Boynton, 63

Biscuit Finds a Friend by Alyssa Satin Capucilli, 177

Black and White Rabbit's ABC by Alan Baker, 239

Black Beauty by Anna Sewell, 425

Black Cat by Christopher Myers, 192

Black Like Kyra, White Like Me by Judith Vigna, 26

Black Mother Goose Book by Elizabeth M. Oliver, 219

Black Stallion books by Walter Farley, 425

Black, White, Just Right! by Marguerite Davol, 250

Block Book by Susan Arkin Couture, 470

Blueberries for Sal by Robert McCloskey, 295

The Book of Kids Songs by Nancy & John Cassidy, 334

Boot Weather by Judith Vigna, 390

Boxes! Boxes! by Leonard Everett Fishers, 44

A Boy Named Giotto by Paolo Guarnieri, 26

The Boy Who Was Followed Home by Margaret Mahey, 220

The Brand New Kid by Katie Couric, 451

Bread and Jam for Frances by Russell Hoban, 427

Breakfast Time, Ernest and Celestine by Gabrielle Vincent, 430

Breakfast With My Father by Ron Roy, 430

Bringing the Rain to Kapiti Plain by Verna Aardema, 410

Brown Bear, Brown Bear, What Do You See? by Bill Martin, Jr., 57–58, 466, 473–475

The Bubble Factory by Tomie dePaola, 29

Buckaroo Baby by Libby Ellis, 368

Buggy Bear Cleans Up by Robert Kraus, 142, 148

Bugs! Bugs! Bugs! by Bob Barner, 181

Building by Elisha Cooper, 470

Bumble B. Bear Cleans Up by Stephen Cosgrove, 142, 148

Buster Loves Buttons! by Fran Manushkin, 272

Busy Bugs: Little Ladybugs by Modern Publishing, 436

The Button Box by Margaret S. Reid, 247

Buttons by Brock Cole, 272

Index

C

Can You Dance, Dalila? by Virginia Kroll, 470

Caps for Sale by Esphyr Slobodkina, 114

The Car Trip by Helen Oxenbury, 320

Career Day by Anne Rockwell, 38

Carl Goes to Daycare by Alexandra Day, 284–285

The Cat in the Hat by Dr. Seuss, 473

Cat Is Sleepy by Satoshi Kitamura, 192

Cat Up a Tree by Ann Hassett, 192

The Cat Who Loved to Sing by Nonny Hogrogian, 235

The Chalk Doll by Charlotte Pomerantz, 108

Changes, Changes by Pat Hutchins, 470

Chicka Chicka Boom Boom by Bill Martin, Jr., 66, 239, 274, 324, 461, 478

Chicken Soup With Rice by Maurice Sendak, 352

Chrysanthemum by Kevin Henkes, 171

Cinderella by various authors, 461

Clap Hands by Helen Oxenbury, 458

Clap Your Hands by Lorinda Bryan Cauley, 458

Clean Your Room, Harvey Moon! by Pat Cummings, 152

Clean-Up Day by Kate Duke, 142, 148

Clifford books by Norman Bridwell, 473

Clifford's Birthday Party by Norman Bridwell, 63

Clifford's Spring Clean-Up by Norman Bridwell, 142, 148

The Color Box by Dayle Ann Dodds, 44

Color Dance by Ann Jonas, 199

Color Zoo by Lois Ehlert, 317

Come On, Rain! by Karen Hesse, 356, 410

Community Helpers From A to Z by Bobbie Kalman & Niki Walker, 38

Corduroy by Don Freeman, 257

Count and See by Tana Hoban, 399

Counting Kisses: A Kiss and Read Book by Karen Katz, 330

The Cow Is Mooing Anyhow by Laura Geringer, 430

Cowboy Bunnies by Christine Loomis, 368

Cowboys Can Do Amazing Things, Too! by Kelly Stuart, 368

The Crayon Box That Talked by Shane Derolf, 260

A Cricket in Times Square by George Selden, 425

Curious George ABC by H.A. Rey, 239

Curious George Bakes a Cake by Margret & H.A. Rey, 446

Curious George by H.A. & Margret Rey, 171

D

Dad and Me in the Morning by Patricia Lakin, 454

Daddies Are for Catching Fireflies by Harriet Ziefert, 225

Dancin' in the Kitchen by Frank P. Christian, 470

The Day the Teacher Went Bananas by James Howe, 280

Did You Carry the Flag Today, Charley? by Rebecca Caudill, 91

Digby and Kate and the Beautiful Day by Barbara Baker, 285

Dinofours series by Steve Metzger, 478

Do Baby Bears Sit in Chairs? by Ethel Kessler, 258

Do You Want to Be My Friend? by Eric Carle, 177, 346

Don't Open This Box by James Razzi, 44

The Doorbell Rang by Pat Hutchins, 233, 440

Down by the Bay by Henrick Drescher, 377

Down by the Bay by Raffi, 408, 472

Dr. Seuss's ABC by Dr. Seuss, 269

Draw Me a Star by Eric Carle, 470

Dustin's Big School Day by Alden R. Carter, 285

E

Edward and the Pirates by David McPhail, 478

Eensy-Weensy Spider by Nadine Bernard Westcott, 407

Elmer by David McKee, 337

The Erie Canal by Peter Spier, 407

Ethan's Favorite Teacher by Hila Colman, 280

Everett Anderson's Friend by Lucille Clifton, 346

Everybody Wins by Jeffrey Sobel, 173

Everything Grows by Raffi, 408

F

Family Farm by Thomas Locker, 470

Farm Alphabet Book by Jane Miller, 239

Farm Friends Clean Up by Cristina Garelli, 142, 148

Feathers for Lunch by Lois Ehlert, 438

Fiddle-I-Fee by Melissa Sweet, 407

First Comes Spring by Anne F. Rockwell, 390

The First Song Ever Sung by Laura Krauss Melmed, 235

Fish Eyes: A Book You Can Count On by Lois Ehlert, 330

Five Little Ducks by Raffi, 408

Five Little Ladybugs by Karen Henley, 436

Five Little Pumpkins by Iris Van Rynbach, 407

Fix It by David McPhail, 471

Floppity Pup Cleans Up by Lois Keffer & Kenneth Spingler, 142, 148

A Fly Went By by Mike McClintock, 55

Flying by Donald Crews, 364

Follow Me! by Nancy Tafuri, 220

Forecast by Malcolm Hall, 390

The Fox Went Out on a Chilly Night by Peter Spier, 407

Foxie the Singing Dog by Ingrid D'Aulaire, 235

Freight Train by Donald Crews, 24, 326

A Friend Is Someone Who Likes You by Joan Walsh Anglund, 346

Friends at School by Rochelle Bunnett, 284

Frog and Toad Together by Arnold Lobel, 24

Frog Went A-Courtin' by John Langstaff, 407

The Frog Who Wanted to Be a Singer by Linda Goss, 235

A Frog's Body by Joanna Cole, 194

Froggy Goes to School by Jonathan London, 455

From Head to Toe by Eric Carle, 364, 370

G

Gabriella's Song by Candace Fleming, 235, 470

Georgia Music by Helen V. Griffith, 376

Geraldine, the Music Mouse by Leo Lionni, 376, 470

Ginger Jumps by Lisa Campbell Ernst, 309

The Gingerbread Man by Eric A. Kimmel, 474

Going to the Zoo by Tom Paxton, 407

The Golden Goose by L. Leslie Brooke, 64

Goldilocks and the Three Bears by Jan Brett, 64

Goldilocks and the Three Bears by various authors, 461

Good Morning, Let's Eat! by Karin Luisa Badt, 430

Good Night, Gorilla by Peggy Rathman, 317

Goodbye Geese by Nancy White Carlstrom, 167

Goodbye House by Frank Asch, 92

Goodbye Little Bird by Mischa Damjan, 167

The Goodbye Painting by Linda Berman, 167

Goodnight Moon by Margaret Wise Brown, 467, 469

Grandpa's Hammer by Ronald Kidd, 471

Grandpa's Song by Tony Johnston, 470

Green Eggs and Ham by Dr. Seuss, 427

Growing Colors by Bruce McMillan, 332

H

Half a Button by Lyn Littlefield Hoopes, 272

Handtalk Zoo by George Ancona & Mary Beth Miller, 86

Happy Birthday to You! by Dr. Seuss, 63

Happy Birthday, Moon by Frank Asch, 63

Here Are My Hands by Bill Martin, Jr., 117

Herman the Helper by Robert Kraus, 145

Hey! Get Off Our Train by John Burningham, 474

Hired Help for a Rabbit by Judy Delton, 145

The Hobbit by J.R.R. Tolkien, 425

The Honeybee and the Robber by Eric Carle, 25

Hooray for Me! by Remy Charlip, 118

Hop Jump by Ellen Stoll Walsh, 309

Hop on Pop by Dr. Seuss, 309, 344

A House for a Hermit Crab by Eric Carle, 474

A House Is a House for Me by Mary Ann Hoberman, 412

House That Jack Built by Nadine Bernard Westcott, 407

How Do Dinosaurs Clean Their Rooms? by Jane Yolen, 422

How Do Dinosaurs Get Well Soon? by Jane Yolen, 422

How Do Dinosaurs Learn to Read? by Jane Yolen, 422

How Do Dinosaurs Say Goodnight? by Jane Yolen, 421

How Do You Say It Today, Jesse Bear? by Nancy White Carlstrom, 232

How Much Is That Doggie in the Window? by Iza Trapani, 407

How My Library Grew: By Dinah by Martha Alexander, 471

How to Hide a Butterfly and Other Insects by Ruth Heller, 181

Humpty Dumpty and Other Nursery Rhymes by Lucy Cousins, 64

Hurry Up! by Bernette Ford, 284

Hush, Little Baby by Margot Zemach, 407

I

I Can Tell By Touching by Carolyn Otto, 224

I Go With My Family to Grandma's by Riki Levinson, 470

I Got a Family by Melrose Cooper, 454

I Hate Goodbyes! by Kathleen Szaj, 167

I Know How We Fight Germs by Kate Rowan, 471

I Like Your Buttons! by Sarah Marwil Lamstein, 272

I Love My Family by Wade Hudson, 454

I Read Signs by Tana Hoban, 320

I Spy: An Alphabet in Art by Lucy Micklethwait, 470

I Took My Frog to the Library by Eric A. Kimmel, 471

I Want to Be an Astronaut by Byron Barton, 363

I Wish That I Had Duck Feet by Theo LeSieg, 474

I'll Teach My Dog a Lot of Words by Michael Frith, 381

I'm a Little Teapot by Iza Trapani, 407

I've Been Working on the Railroad by Nadine Bernard Westcott, 407

If Animals Could Talk by Don Dentinger, 32

If You Give a Moose a Muffin by Laura Joffe Numeroff, 334

If You Give a Mouse a Cookie by Laura Joffe Numeroff, 24, 233

If You Give a Pig a Pancake by Laura Joffe Numeroff, 473

If You Take a Mouse to School by Laura Joffe Numeroff, 455

In All Kinds of Weather, Kids Make Music! by Lynn Kleiner, 380

In the Rain With Baby Duck by Amy Hest, 410

In the Time of the Drums by Kim Siegelson, 470

Incredible Indoor Games Book: One Hundred Sixty Group Projects, Games, and Activities by Bob Gregson, 173

The Ink Drinker by Eric Snavoisin, 471

Inside a Zoo in the City by Alyssa Satin Capucilli, 317

Ira Says Goodbye by Bernard Waber, 167

Is It Red? Is It Yellow? Is It Blue? by Tana Hoban, 199

Is This a House for Hermit Crab? by Megan McDonald, 416

Index

Is This You? by Ruth Krauss & Crockett Johnson, 453

It's a Shame About the Rain by Barbara Shook Hazen, 410

It's Hard to Share My Teacher by Joan Singleton Prestine, 280

It's Raining, It's Pouring by Kin Eagle, 407

It's Raining, Said John Twaining by N.M. Bodecker, 410

The Itsy Bitsy Spider by Iza Trapani, 407

J

Jack, Skinny Bones, and the Golden Pancake by Marie-Clare Helldorfer, 227

Jamal's Busy Day by Wade Hudson, 285

Jambo Means Hello by Muriel J. Feelings, 324

Jobs People Do by Christopher Maynard, 38

Jonathan Cleaned Up—Then He Heard a Sound by Robert Munsch, 152

Julius, the Baby of the World by Kevin Henkes, 254

Jump, Frog, Jump! by Robert Kalan, 194, 309

Just Another Ordinary Day by Rod Clement, 285

Just Like Daddy by Frank Asch, 454

Just Me by Marie Hall Ets, 27, 254

Just My Friend and Me by Mercer Mayer, 177

Just You and Me by Sam McBratney, 27

K

Kindergarten ABC by Jacqueline Rogers, 307

The Kissing Hand by Audrey Penn, 198

Kitten Care for Children by Grace & Gordon McHattie, 381

Knots on a Counting Rope by Bill Martin, Jr., & John Archambault, 76

L

The Lady With the Alligator Purse by Nadine Bernard Westcott, 472

Ladybugs: Red, Fiery, and Bright by Mia Posada, 436

Leo Cockroach: Toy Tester by Kevin O'Malley, 470

Let's Pretend by Rose Greydanus, 184

A Letter to Amy by Ezra Jack Keats, 169

The Library Dragon by Carmen Agra Deedy, 478

The Library by Sarah Stewart, 471

Like Me and You by Raffi, 408

Lilly's Purple Plastic Purse by Kevin Henkes, 92

The Line Up Book by Marisabina Russo, 253, 302, 470

Listen to a Shape by Marcia Brown, 470

Listen to the Rain by Bill Martin, Jr., & John Archambault, 410

Little Blue and Little Yellow by Leo Lionni, 24, 57–58, 332

The Little Brass Band by Margaret Wise Brown, 470

Little Cloud by Eric Carle, 405

Little Critter: Just a School Project by Mercer Mayer, 455

The Little Engine That Could by Watty Piper, 24, 36, 326

The Little Mouse, the Red Ripe Strawberry, and the Big Hungry Bear by Don & Audrey Wood, 461

Lizards, Frogs and Polliwogs by Douglas Florian, 132

London Bridge Is Falling Down by Peter Spier, 407

A Long Long Song by Etienne Delessert, 235

Lots of Moms by Shelley Rotner, 454

Louie by Ezra Jack Keats, 334

Love You Forever by Robert N. Munsch, 478

Luap by June Rachuy Brindel, 250

Lucy and Tom's Day by Shirley Hughes, 285

Lunch by Denise Fleming, 438

M

The Maestro Plays by Bill Martin, Jr., 470

The Magic School Bus by Joanna Cole, 175

Maisy's Train by Lucy Cousins, 393

Maisy Cleans Up by Lucy Cousins, 142, 148

Make Friends, Zachary! by Muriel Blaustein, 346

Mama Don't Allow by Thacher Hurd, 407, 477

Mama Rocks, Papa Sings by Nancy Van Laan, 235, 470

Mary Had a Little Lamb by Iza Trapani, 407

Mary Had a Little Lamb by Nadine Bernard Westcott, 407

Mary Wore Her Red Dress and Henry Wore His Green Sneakers by Merle Peek, 472

Max and Ruby Play School by Rosemary Wells, 455

Max Cleans Up by Rosemary Wells, 142, 148

Max Found Two Sticks by Brian Pinkney, 470

May I Bring a Friend? by Beatrice Schenk de Regniers, 346

Me & Neesie by Eloise Greenfield, 27

Me and My Family Tree by Joan Sweeney, 454

Me First by Helen Lester, 27

Meet M & M by Pat Ross, 27

The Memory Box by Mary Bahr, 44

Millions of Cats by Wanda Gag, 192

Mirandy and Brother Wind by Patricia C. McKissack, 367

Miss Bindergarten Gets Ready for Kindergarten by Joseph Slate, 307

Miss Mary Mack by Mary Ann Hoberman, 472

Miss Mary Mack: A Hand-Clapping Rhyme by Nadine Bernard Westcott, 407

Miss Nelson Is Missing! by Harry G. Allard, 280

The Mitten by Alvin Tresselt, 474

The Mitten by Jan Brett, 461

Mommy Far, Mommy Near: An Adoption Story by Carol Antoinette Peacock, 454

Mommy, Daddy, Me by Lyn Littlefield Hoopes, 454

Moog-Moog, Space Barber by Mark Teague, 363

Mother Goose by various authors, 226

Mouse Around by Pat Schories, 184

Mouse Count by Ellen Stoll Walsh, 24

Mouse Paint by Ellen Stoll Walsh, 24, 199

Mouse's First Day of School by Lauren Thompson, 198

Mr. Fong's Toy Shop by Leo Politi, 470

Mr. MacGregor's Breakfast Egg by Elizabeth MacDonald, 430

Mushroom in the Rain by Mirra Ginsburg, 411, 474

The Music in Derrick's Head by Gwendoline Battle-Lavert, 376

Music, Music for Everyone by Vera B. Williams, 471

My Crayons Talk by Patricia Hubbard, 199

My Father's Hands by Joanne Ryder, 117

My Favorite Things by Richard Rogers, 69

My First Day at Nursery School by Becky Edwards, 198

My Five Senses by Aliki, 224, 257, 336

My Friends by Taro Gomi, 346

My Hands by Aliki, 458

My Mama Sings by Jeanne Whitehouse Peterson, 235

My Two Hands/My Two Feet by Rick Walton, 117

My Very First Mother Goose by Iona Archibald Opie, 219

N

A Nap in a Lap by Sarah Wilson, 422

The Night Before Kindergarten by Natasha Wing, 307

No, David! by David Shannon, 91

Noah's Square Dance by Rick Walton, 471

Norma Jean, Jumping Bean by Joanna Cole, 309, 314

O

Officer Buckle and Gloria by Petty Rathmann, 92

Oh Where, Oh Where Has My Little Dog Gone? by Iza Trapani, 407

Oh' A-Hunting We Will Go by John Langstaff, 407

Old MacDonald Had a Farm by Pam Adams, 406

Olivia Counts by Ian Falconer, 323, 330

On Market Street by Anita & Arnold Lobel, 324

One Dad, Two Dads, Brown Dads, Blue Dads by Johnny Valentine, 454

One Fine Day by Molly Bang, 285

One Fish, Two Fish, Red Fish, Blue Fish by Dr. Seuss, 295

One Hot Summer Day by Nina Crews, 390

One Light, One Sun by Raffi, 408

One Minute Stories by Shari Lewis, 298

One Smiling Grandma: A Caribbean Counting Book by Ann Marie Linden, 76

One, Two, Three, Jump! by Penelope Lively, 309

Over in the Meadow by John Langstaff, 407

Owl Moon by Jane Yolen, 48

P

Pages of Music by Tony Johnston, 376

Painted Dreams by Karen Lynn Williams, 470

Pancakes for Breakfast by Tomie dePaola, 430

Pancakes, Crackers, and Pizza: A Book of Shapes by Marjorie Eberts & Margaret Gisler, 223

Pancakes, Pancakes by Eric Carle, 430

Panda Bear, Panda Bear, What Do You See? by Bill Martin, Jr., 474

Panda's New Toy by Joyce Dunbar, 470

Parade Day: Marching Through the Calendar Year by Bob Barner, 102

Peanut Butter and Jelly: A Play Rhyme by Nadine Bernard Westcott, 407

People on the Move by Pierre De Hugo, 154

Pete's a Pizza by William Steig, 446

The Piano Man by Deborah Chocolate, 471

A Piece of the Wind and Other Stories to Tell by Ruthilde Kronberg & Patricia McKissack, 298

Pizza for Breakfast by Maryann Kovalski, 430

Planting a Rainbow by Lois Ehlert, 332

Play With Me by Marie Hall Ets, 27

A Pocket Full of Kisses by Audrey Penn, 198

Poinsettia and Her Family by Felicia Bond, 454, 470

Polar Bear, Polar Bear, What Do You Hear? by Bill Martin, Jr., 382

The Popcorn Book by Tomie dePaola, 311, 446

Popcorn by Alex Moran, 311

Pretend You're a Cat by Jean Marzollo, 470

R

Raggedy Ann: A Thank You, Please, and I Love You Book by Norah Smaridge, 294

Rain by Peter Spier, 356

Rain by Robert Kalan, 367

The Rain Came Down by David Shannon, 411

The Rain Door by Russell Hoban, 411

Rain Drop Splash by Alvin Tresselt, 411

Rain Makes Applesauce by Julian Scheer & Marvin Bileck, 411

Rain Rain Rivers by Uri Shulevitz, 411

Rain Talk by Mary Serfozo, 411

The Rainbabies by Laura Krauss Melmed, 411

The Rainbow Fish by Marcus Pfister, 469

A Rainbow of Friends by P.K. Hallinan, 250, 346

The Random House Book of Poetry for Children by Jack Prelutsky, 69

The Real Mother Goose by Blanche Fisher Wright, 102, 219

Red Bear by Bodel Rikys, 199

Index

Red Leaf, Yellow Leaf by Lois Ehlert, 190, 195

Red, Blue, Yellow Shoe by Tana Hoban, 199

Regards to the Man in the Moon by Ezra Jack Keats, 363

Ricardo's Day by George Ancona, 284

Rise and Shine by Raffi, 408

Roberto, the Insect Architect by Nina Laden, 470

Rocks in His Head by Carol Otis Hurst, 471

Roll Over! A Counting Song by Merle Peek, 407

Room for a Stepdaddy by Jean Thor Cook, 454

Roses Sing on New Snow by Paul Yee, 235

Row, Row, Row Your Boat by Iza Trapani, 407

Ruby Mae Has Something to Say by David Small, 232

Ruby the Copycat by Peggy Rathmann, 118

S

Sail Away by Donald Crews, 390

Sam and Gus Light Up the Night by P.D. Eastman, 225

School Bus by Donald Crews, 175

School Days by B.G. Hennessy, 285

The Science Book of the Senses by Neil Ardley, 471

The Scrambled States of America by Laurie Keller, 273

Seven Little Rabbits by John Becker, 461

Shake My Sillies Out by Raffi, 377, 408

The Shape of Me and Other Stuff by Dr. Seuss, 27, 439

Shape Space by Cathryn Falwell, 44

Shapes by Guy Smalley, 442

Shapes, Shapes, Shapes by Tana Hoban, 442

Shoo Fly! by Iza Trapani, 407

Shy Little Moth by Elizabeth Lawrence, 129

Sing a Song of Popcorn by Beatrice Shenk De Regniers, 311

Sing, Pierrot, Sing by Tomie dePaola, 235

Skip to My Lou by Nadine Bernard Westcott, 407

Skip to My Lou by Robert Quakenbush, 309

Sleep Tight, Little Mouse by Mary Morgan, 184

Snake Alley Band by Elizabeth Nygaard, 471

Snowflake Bently by Jacqueline Briggs Martin, 356

The Snowman by Raymond Briggs, 356

The Snowy Day by Ezra Jack Keats, 169, 356, 359

Song and Dance Man by Karen Ackerman, 235

Sophie and Jack Help Out by Judy Taylor, 145

Sorting by Henry Pluchrose, 247

Spider on the Floor by Raffi, 377

Spot Goes to School by Eric Hill, 455

The Star-Spangled Banner by Peter Spier, 407

Stella Louella's Runaway Book by Lisa Campbell Ernst, 471

Stellaluna by Janell Cannon, 125

Stone Soup by Ann McGovern, 446

The Story of Clocks and Calendars: Marking a Millennium by Betsy Maestro, 102

A Summertime Song by Irene Haas, 235

The Sun's Day by Mordicai Gerstein, 285

Sunshine Makes the Seasons by Franklyn M. Branley, 403

Sunshine on My Shoulders adapted by Christopher Canyon, 377

Surprise Box by Nicki Weiss, 44

Swimmy by Leo Lionni, 364

T

Tadpoles by Betsy James, 471

Teacher's Pet by Miska Miles, 280

Teddy Bears 1 to 10 by Susanna Gretz, 258

The Teeny Tiny Teacher by Stephanie Calmenson, 280

Ten Minutes 'Til Bedtime by Peggy Rathmann, 47

That Sky, That Rain by Carolyn Otto, 411

There Was an Old Lady Who Swallowed a Fly by Pam Adams, 406

There Were Ten in the Bed by Pam Adams, 406

There's a Hole in My Bucket by Nadine Bernard Westcott, 407

There's a Wocket in My Pocket! by Dr. Seuss, 344

Think of Something Quiet by Clare Cherry, 173

This Is My Body by Gina & Mercer Mayer, 369

This Is the House That Jack Built by Pam Adams, 406

This Little Light of Mine by Raffi, 408

This Old Man by Pam Adams, 406

Thumbelina by Hans Christian Anderson, 228

Thump, Thump, Rat-a-Tat-Tat by Gene Baer, 369, 471

Thunderstorm! by Nathaniel Tripp, 390

Tingalayo by Raffi, 408

To Hilda for Helping by Margot Zemach, 145

Today I Feel Silly: And Other Moods That Make My Day by Jamie Lee Curtis, 92

Tracy's Mess by Elise Petersen, 163

Trains by Byron Barton, 326, 393

A Tree Is Nice by Janice May Udry, 195

Twinkle, Twinkle, Little Star by Iza Trapani, 407

Two Eyes, a Nose, and a Mouth by Roberta Grobel Intrater, 453

Two Good Friends by Judy Delton, 346

Two Tiny Mice by Alan Baker, 184

V

Vegetable Soup by Jeanne Modesitt, 446

The Very Hungry Caterpillar by Eric Carle, 84, 181, 242, 469

The Very Lonely Firefly by Eric Carle, 224

The Very Quiet Cricket by Eric Carle, 242

A Very Special Friend by Dorothy Hoffman Levi, 86

Victoria's ABC Adventure by Cathy Warren, 239

W

Wacky Flips: Counting Critters by Peggy Tagel, 323

Wacky Wild Animals by Angie Sage, 32

Wait and See by Robert Munsch, 34

Waiting for Mom by Linda Wagner Tyler, 34, 454

Waiting for Mr. Goose by Laurie Lears, 34

Waiting for the Evening Star by Rosemary Wells, 34

Waiting to Sing by Howard Kaplan, 235

Walk the Dog by Bob Barner, 270

Water Dance by Thomas Locker, 471

We Are Best Friends by Aliki, 346

We Hate Rain! by James Stevenson, 411

We're Going on a Bear Hunt by Michael Rosen, 469

We're Making Breakfast for Mother by Shirley Neitzel, 430

Weather Words and What They Mean by Gail Gibbons, 403

The Wedding Procession of the Rag Doll and the Broom Handle and Who Was In It by Carl Sandburg, 474

Wee Sing Animals, Animals, Animals by Pamela Conn Beall, 154

What Am I? by N.N. Charles, 250

What Do I Say? by Norma Simon, 232

What Is Your Language? by Debra Leventhal, 76

What Lives in a Shell? by Kathleen Weidner Zoehfeld, 416

What Makes a Bird a Bird? by Mary Garelick, 438

What Will the Weather Be? by Lynda DeWitt, 403

The Wheels on the Bus by Paul O. Zelinsky, 175

The Wheels on the Bus by Raffi, 408

When I Cross the Street by Dorthy Chlad, 320

When Sophie Gets Angry—Really, Really Angry… by Molly Bang, 92

When the Rain Stops by Sheila Cole, 411

When the Teddy Bears Came by Martin Waddell, 258

Where Are Maisy's Friends? by Lucy Cousins, 177

Where Does the Butterfly Go When It Rains? by May Garelick, 181, 411

Where Does the Teacher Live? by Paula Kurzband Feder, 280

Where the Wild Things Are by Maurice Sendak, 427, 469

Which Is Willy? by Robert Bright, 250

Who Said Red? by Mary Serfozo, 58, 199

Why Do Leaves Change Color? by Chris Arvetis & Carole Palmer, 191

Why Do Leaves Change Color? by Betsy Maestro, 190, 195

Wilbur Waits by Victoria Sherrow, 34

A Wild Cowboy by Dana Kessimakis Smith, 368

Willie Blows a Mean Horn by Ianthe Thomas, 471

Willy's Pictures by Anthony Browne, 470

Wings: A Tale of Two Chickens by James Marshall, 478

Winnie the Pooh and the Blustery Day by Teddy Slater et al., 398

Words in Our Hands by Ada B. Litchfield, 86

Y

Yankee Doodle by Nadine Bernard Westcott, 407

You Can't Taste a Pickle With Your Ear by Harriet Ziefert, 336

The Young Artist by Thomas Locker, 470

Z

Zoo Do's and Don'ts by Todd Parr, 317

Song Index

"1, 2, Come Here to Me," 118
"1-2-3, to the Chairs, Please," 187
"5 Is Such a Pretty Number," 295

A
"ABC Rock" by Greg & Steve, 238
"All Sit Down," 428
"Alligator Pie" by Dennis Lee, 200
"Alphabet Song," 238, 371
"Alphardy" by Dr. Jean, 238
"The Ants Go Marching," 222
"Anytime Rhyming Song," 54
"Are You Hungry?" 429
"Are You Ready?" 52, 429
"Author and Illustrator," 465
"Autumn Leaves," 190

B
"Baby Beluga" by Raffi, 408
"Be a Friend," 176
"B-I-N-G-O," 207, 296
"Birds" by Hap Palmer, 438
"Birthday Boy or Girl," 343–344
"Boom Chica Boom" by Dr. Jean, 238
"Bored? No Way!" 195
"Breakfast Song," 430

C
"Catch a Bubble," 118–119
"Chicken Dance" by Greg & Steve, 307
"The Children Are Smiling Now," by Mary Brehm, 123
"Children, Children, Jump Up and Down," 328–329
"Choose a Friend," 346
"A Circle Is a Shape," 223
"Class Song," 209
"Clean Up the Room," 142
"Cleanup Chant," 143
"Cleanup Song," 278
"Cleanup Song" by Diane Weiss, 193
"Cleanup Theme Song," 143
"Come and Join Me," 52
"Come Form a Line," 396

D
"Days of the Week," 210
"Departure Song," by Diane Weiss, 165–166
"Dinosaurs, They Had Fun," 246
"Down by the Bay" by Raffi, 408, 472
"Down by the Station," 36

E
"Everything Grows" by Raffi, 408
"Exercise Song," 308

F
"The Farmer in the Dell," 295
"Field Trip Song," 342
"Find Your Mat," 376
"Five Little Ducks" by Raffi, 408
"Five More Minutes," 19, 188
"Five Speckled Frogs," 193–194
"Follow the Leader," 200, 220
"Free Play," 196
"The Freeze" by Greg & Steve, 372

G
"Galloping," 313
"Good Food Helps Us Grow Up Strong," 431
"Good Morning," 88
"Goodbye Everybody," 166
"Goodbye Song," 168, 197
"Goodbye, Little Friend," 167
"Goodnight Song," 197
"The Grand Old Duke of York," 216

H
"Hanging Out the Linen Clothes" by Ruth C. Seeger, 159
"Heigh Ho, Heigh Ho," 385, 397
"Hello, Hello, Hello," 85–86
"Hello, How Are You?" 82–83
"Hello Song," 197
"Here Sits a Monkey" by Raffi, 170
"Here We Go 'Round the Mulberry Bush," 314
"Here We Sit Like Birds in the Wilderness," 437
"The Hokey Pokey," 222
"Hurry, Hurry, Beat the Timer," 151

I
"I Am Special," 213
"I Am Walking," 302
"I Can't Find the Cheese Again," 234
"I Heard It Through the Grapevine," 449
"I Know an Old Lady," 345
"I Wiggle, I Wiggle, My Fingers," 200
"I'll Be Cleanin' Up the Classroom," 144
"I'll See You Tuesday," 165
"I'm a Cowpoke on My Horse," 367
"I'm a Little Firefly," 225
"I'm a Little Sweeper," 144
"I'm Glad I'm Me," 250
"I'm Glad You Came to School," 83
"I'm Ready to Learn," 198
"I've Been Workin' on the Railroad," 36
"If You're Happy and You Know It," 140
"If You're Listening," 224
"If You're Name Is …" 347
"If You're Ready for a Story," 458, 460
"If You're Ready to Go Outside," 221
"If Your Name Starts With," 65
"Interruption Song," 338
"It's Raining, It's Pouring," 408
"It's Story Time," 458–459
"It's Time for Show and Tell," 341
"It's Time to Clean Up," 189
"It's Time to Come to Circle," 327–328
"It's Time to Put the Toys Away," 141
"It's Time to Say Goodbye," 168
"It's Time to Wash Our Hands," 433
"Itsy, Bitsy Spider," 410

J
"Janie Had a Little Shoe," 234
"Johnny Works With One Hammer," 216–217

L
"The Lady With the Alligator Purse," 472
"Let's Go Outside," 390
"Like Me and You" by Raffi, 408
"Little Buttons Song," 272
"Little Red Caboose," 387

M

"Make a Circle," 328
"Marching Around the Alphabet" by Hap Palmer, 238
"Mary Wore Her Red Dress and Henry Wore His Green Sneakers," 472
"Merrily We Hop Along," 219
"Michael, Row Your Boat Ashore," 378
"Miss Mary Mack," 472
"My Arms Are Going to Sleep Now," 414

N

"Nursery Rhymes Are Lots of Fun," 228–231

O

"Oh, Come on Children," 397
"Oh, Do You Know What Time It Is?" 47
"Oh, I Wish That I Could See a Clean Classroom," 140
"Oh, We'll All Wash Our Hands," 434
"Old MacDonald Had a Farm," 153," 296, 345
"On a Bright and Sunny Day," 145
"On the Floor," 146
"One Light, One Sun" by Raffi, 408

P

"Parachute-Pokey," 373
"Pick Up Your Work," 147
"Picking Up," 148
"Pickup Song," 146
"Please Quiet Down" 205
"Popcorn" by Greg & Steve, 372
"Pull a Name," 34
"Push the Wheelbarrow," 236

"Put Your Shoes On," 424
"Put Your Work Away," 147

Q

"Quiet, Shh," 121

R

"Rain, Rain, Go Away," 409
"Rain, Rain, Rain," 410
"Rhyme Time" by Greg & Steve, 344
"Rig a Jig Jig," 244
"Right and Left," 215
"Rise and Shine" by Raffi, 408

S

"The School Bus Goes," 200
"Sensory Song," 232
"Shake My Sillies Out" by Raffi, 408
"She'll Be Coming 'Round the Corner," 372–373
"S-I-N-G-O," 235
"Sleep Tight," 418
"Snack Time Sing-Along," 427
"Snack Time Song," 428
"Somebody's Wearing Red," 198
"Spelling Numbers," 241
"Sprinkle, Sprinkle, Little Rain," 234
"Sprinkle, Sprinkle, Rain, Rain, Rain," 409
"Stop!" 53
"S-T-O-P," 455

T

"Ten Little Teddy Bears," 258
"Ten More Minutes Left to Play," 149
"Thank You," 151
"There's a Little Rainstorm," 410
"This Is the Way We Clean Our Room," 149

"This Is the Way We Wash Our Clothes," 159
"This Little Light of Mine" by Raffi, 408
"Thumbelina," 228
"Time for Art," 104
"Time for Circle," 331
"Time for Quiet Time," 419
"Time to Sit Down," 459
"Tingalayo" by Raffi, 408
"Try to Whisper," 49
"Twinkle, Twinkle, Little Star," 322

W

"Walk to Group Time," 327
"Walking Feet," 377
"We Are Cleaning," 341
"We Are Going to Clean Up," 150
"We Are Walking," 340
"We Know How to Get in Line," 201
"We Will All Clean Up Our Work," 141
"We're Glad You're Here," 217
"What Are You Wearing?" by Hap Palmer, 67
"What Will You Do When You Go Outside?" 388
"Wheelbarrow," 236
"The Wheels on the Bus," 24, 278, 296, 381
"The Wheels on the Bus" by Raffi, 408
"When I Shake Your Hand," 338
"When Johnny Comes Marching Home," 222
"The Wiggle Song," 222

Z

"Zip-a-Dee-Doo-Dah!" 150

Index

A

Acetate, 403
Acrylic paint, 304
Airplanes, 184
Alike and different, 72
Alphabet cards, 247, 255, 268
Aluminum foil, 259
American sign language, 85–86, 301
Animals, 44, 90, 380–381, 384, 445, 475
    classroom pets, 45, 90
    farm, 295
    pictures, 266
    stuffed, 62, 181, 318, 334, 336, 345, 350, 389, 422, 464, 473
Anytime ideas, 19–80
    3+, 19–55
    4+, 56–75
    5+, 77–80
Aprons, 38, 55, 248
Arrivals, 81–102
    3+, 81–96
    4+, 97–102
Art activities, 27–28, 31, 35, 79, 102–115, 154, 178, 181, 190, 225, 246, 253–254, 295, 390, 394, 402–406, 410, 413–414, 421, 442, 461, 463, 476
    3+, 103–111
    4+, 112–114
    5+, 115
    aprons, 402
    books, 470
    materials, 112, 413, 440
Attention grabbers, 116–139
    3+, 116–133
    4+, 134–139

B

Bags, 422
    decorative, 350
    drawstring, 143
    fabric, 335
    gift, 69, 464
    grocery, 292, 449
    lunch, 438
    paper, 66, 335, 350, 367
    plastic, 132, 335, 422
    sandwich, 41
    squishy, 41
    transition, 25
    zippered plastic, 41, 249, 258, 271, 296, 303, 359
Balance beams, 309, 321
Balloons, 373
Balls, 179, 223, 318, 347, 387, 411–412
    golf, 350
    Koosh, 171
    Nerf, 171
    rubber, 388
Bananas, 437
Bandanas, 265
Baskets, 24, 69, 214, 156, 158–159, 259, 310, 415, 454, 469, 472
Bead maze games, 158
Beads, 114, 421
Beanbag chairs, 454
Beanbags, 62, 318
Beeswax, 357
Beginning school, 81–82
Bells, 126–127, 134, 176, 276, 300, 365, 391
    cowbell, 365
    dinner, 137
    hand, 15
    jingle, 375
Bicycle horns, 365
Bingo markers, 98, 393
Binoculars, 259
Birthdays, 62–63, 305, 343
    hats, 62, 305
Blackboards. *See* Chalkboards
Blindfolds, 32
Blocks, 223, 350, 276, 388, 400
    books, 470
    stuffed, 178
Blueprint paper, 107
Boats, 292
Book pockets, 94
Books, 24, 223, 415, 422, 454, 461, 463–464, 469, 474
    about birds, 245
    homemade, 26, 64, 178, 241, 285, 344, 347, 353, 410, 412–413, 425–426, 444, 466
    picture, 477–478
    picture-song, 406–407, 472
    pop-up, 25
    rhyming, 55
Bottle caps, 258
Bowls, 39
Boxes, 33, 44, 77, 173, 248, 264, 312, 323, 350, 474
    after five, 173
    busy, 41
    cereal, 468
    cylinder, 443
    file card, 211
    gift, 464
    jewelry, 69, 299
    lids, 258, 399
    lost and found, 38
    music, 299
    my own, 43, 184
    packing, 132
    plastic, 38, 173
    shoeboxes, 62, 132, 399, 415
    small, 41, 43
    tissue, 332
    writing, 422
Brads, 28, 70, 74, 255, 261, 266
Breakfast, 430
Broom handles, 367
Bubble solution, 29, 118
Buckets, 385–386, 394
Buses, 174, 184
Busy boxes, 41
Butcher paper, 59, 108, 451
Butter, 445
Buttons, 257, 271, 293

C

Calculator paper, 96
Calendars, 101–102, 109, 352, 358
    numbers, 352
Cameras, 26, 63, 294, 280, 284, 290–291, 392
    digital, 26, 249, 281, 284
Candles, 87
Cans, 80, 130, 443, 447
    coffee, 130
    nut, 359
    potato chip, 359
    soup, 80
Capes, 464
Card stock, 20, 26, 30, 70, 74, 92, 101, 210, 249, 255, 261, 266, 269–270, 283, 291, 293, 361, 390, 439, 453
Cardboard, 41, 60, 77, 290, 304, 383, 392

Cards, 362
  alphabet, 247, 255, 268
  color, 58, 255
  file, 54, 314
  greeting, 109
  index, 33, 41, 55, 66, 68, 69, 113,
    191, 211, 214, 274, 285,
    296–297, 447
  name, 274, 361, 439
  note, 81, 211
  number, 255, 398
  picture, 127, 475
  postcards, 278
  shape, 255
  story sequence, 476
  word, 273–274
Carpet squares, 29, 78, 310, 334, 350
Cars, 184
Cartons, 310
Cassette tapes, 91, 297, 350, 406, 421,
  478
Castanets, 375
Catalogs, 270
Cattails, 403
CD players, 151, 155, 297, 330, 333,
  369–370, 374, 832, 395, 416, 421,
  454
CDs, 297, 322, 421
Cereal boxes, 468
Chairs, 78, 157, 174, 363, 454
Chalk, 106–107, 136, 248, 97,
  393–394, 463
Chalkboards, 51, 66, 97, 136, 248, 463
  homemade, 107
  paint, 107
Chants. See Rhymes/chants
Chapter books, 425
Chart paper, 68, 97, 177, 299, 358
Chart stands, 177
Charting, 162, 243, 269, 420
Charts, 87
  flip, 282
  song, 377
  sticker, 420
  word, 51
Cheese crackers, 441
Chimes, 126
Choices, 156
Circle patterns, 370

Circle time, 65, 157, 325–362
  3+, 325–348
  4+, 349–361
  5+, 361–362
Classroom pets, 45, 90
Classroom visitors, 207
Cleanup, 140–163, 288, 305
  3+, 140–160
  4+, 160–163
Clip art, 284
Clipboards, 107
Clocks, 281
  chiming, 47
  wall, 49
Clotheslines, 172
Clothespins, 159, 280, 287, 443
Cloths, 46
Coffee cans, 130
Coffee filters, 404, 443
Coins, 359
Collages, 35, 190, 403
  materials, 43
Color cards, 58, 255
Colored pencils, 133, 139, 360, 413
Colored tape, 316, 322
Colorform sets, 25
Colors, 31, 35, 57–58, 72–73, 105, 111,
  134, 198–199, 255, 295, 301, 305,
  310, 319–320, 332, 360, 384,
  404–406, 441–442
Computers, 103, 210, 249, 274, 279,
  284, 289, 297, 343, 447
Conductor's hats, 36, 133
Construction paper, 21, 31, 35–36,
  63, 80, 96, 98, 103, 112, 159, 194,
  225, 270, 281, 285, 317, 319, 332,
  351, 370, 384, 444, 449–450
Contact paper, 30, 99, 253, 263, 291,
  317, 322–323, 384, 421, 452–453,
  466
Containers, 69, 77, 93, 156, 261, 263,
  268–270, 310, 350, 358, 361, 398,
  402, 447, 467
  plastic, 130, 293, 312
Cookie cutters, 90, 350
Cookies, 243, 295, 435
Cooking activities, 243, 295
Cooking oil, 90
Cooking pots, 351
Cords, 107
Costumes, 401

Cotton balls, 60, 404
Counting activities, 31, 39, 48, 50–51,
  57, 60–61, 84, 138, 162, 225, 242,
  255, 301, 312, 314, 323, 330, 344,
  359–360, 393, 398–399, 420, 440
Cowbells, 365
Cowboy hats, 376
Crackers, 435, 441
Craft glue, 115
Craft sticks, 34, 40, 100, 183, 437
Crawl tunnels, 309
Crayons, 43, 57, 59, 79, 99–100, 103,
  105–106, 109, 113, 157, 177, 274,
  298, 319, 323, 350, 353, 360, 393,
  413, 451
Cream cheese, 435
Cream of tartar, 90
Crepe paper, 398
Critical thinking, 250
Crowns, 401, 477
Cultural diversity, 76, 83, 85–86, 88,
  120, 168–169, 185, 301, 339, 374
Cups, 430
  measuring, 90
  paper, 114
  plastic, 41, 271
  wax-coated, 422
Cutting boards, 39

D

Dancing, 368, 371, 378–379, 383
Date stamps, 103
Decision making, 79
Decorations, 468, 474
Departure time, 164–179
  3+, 164–173
  4+, 174–178
  5+, 179
Developmental levels
  3-year-olds, 14
  4-year-olds, 15
  5-year-olds, 15
  6-year-olds, 15
Digital cameras, 26, 249, 281, 284
Dimes, 359
Dinner bells, 137
Dinosaurs, 421–422
  counters, 246
  plastic, 422
Dip, 444
Dog biscuits, 227

Index

Dolls, 389, 464
    clothing, 389
    paper, 390
Double-sided tape, 286
Dramatic play, 45, 180–186, 315, 368, 388, 401
    3+, 180–183
    4+, 183–185
    5+, 186, 463–464, 469, 474
    books, 470
Drawing paper, 103, 105, 109, 353, 360, 452
Dress-up clothes, 401
Dresses, 401
Driftwood, 106
Drinking glasses, 61
Drinking straws, 61
    flexible, 462
Dry-erase
    boards, 51
    pens, 99
Duct tape, 287, 359
Duffle bags, 25
Dump trucks, 162

E

Earphones, 454
Easel paper, 110, 248
Easels, 106, 110, 113, 190, 248, 283, 292, 358
Eating utensils, 430, 432
Eggs, 445
Electrical tape, 253, 290
Ellison punch machines, 41
Emotions, 92–93
Envelopes, 81, 247, 456
Erasers, 107
Etch-a-Sketches, 25, 43, 158
Eyedroppers, 404
Eye-hand coordination, 312, 359–360, 394, 411

F

Fabric, 194
    bags, 335
    drawstring bags, 132
    squares, 310
    strips, 452
Fairy dust, 417

Families, 453–454
    home-to-school connections, 69, 86, 177, 251, 281, 285, 426, 448, 450, 473
    partnering with, 295
Farm animal play pieces, 259
Feathers, 114, 373, 421
Felt, 77, 425, 467
    letters, 274
Fences, 312
Fidgety toys, 357
Field trips, 175, 342
    to kindergarten, 307
    to the beach, 423
File card boxes, 211
File cards, 54, 314
Film, 280, 290–291
    canisters, 467
    X-ray, 186
Fine motor skills, 27, 59–61, 78, 97–99, 102–115, 157, 191, 254, 274, 359–361, 390, 402–406, 413–414, 421, 439, 442, 461, 463, 476
Finger puppets, 162, 242
Fingerpaint, 253
Fingerplays
    "Autumn Leaves," 191
    "Eensy Weensy Spider," THE 202
    "Five Little Beavers," 237–238
    "Five Little Monkeys," 212
    "Fly Away, All," 194–195
    "Grandma's Glasses," 213, 296
    "I Have Five Fingers," 295
    "Open, Shut Them," 204, 296
    "Ten in the Bed," 422
    "Two Little Blackbirds," 211
    "Where Is Thumbkin?" 212, 296
    "Whoops, Johnny!" 218
Flannel, 425
Flannel board, 182, 225, 286, 405, 467
Flashlights, 224, 315
Flip charts, 282
Floor puzzles, 260
Flour, 90
Flowers, 350
Foam
    board, 21, 304
    cores, 358
    fun, 77
    pieces, 373
    shapes, 457

Foghorns, 137
Folders, 248
Food coloring, 41, 90, 406
Forms, 279
Friendship, 448, 452
Fruit salad, 444

G

Games, 41, 243–274, 415
    3+, 243–254
    4+, 255–272
    5+, 272–274
    Alike and Different, 72
    Alphabet Riddles, 274
    Around the Room, 255
    Basket Bounce, 411
    Bead Maze, 158
    Beginning Sounds Wheel Game, 255
    Birds Fly, 244–245
    Button Math, 271–272
    Button, Button, 257
    Chairs for Bears, 258
    Clap the Parts, 245
    Cookie Jar Name Game, 243
    Copy Me, 365
    Dinosaur Game, 246
    Duck, Duck, Goose, 296, 314
    Find a Match, 272–273
    The Freeze, 372
    Freeze Tag, 155
    Go-Togethers, 270
    Guess What's Missing, 296
    Hot Potato, 296
    Hula Hoop Sort, 246–247
    I Spy, 154, 259, 296
    If You're Happy, 140
    Letter Game, 247
    Listening Game, 263
    Match the Photo, 248
    matching, 453
    memory, 453
    Mirrors and Shadows, 315
    Mother, May I? 155, 296, 314
    Musical Circles, 370–371
    My Name Starts With …, 268
    Name It, 248
    Nursery Rhyme Riddles, 269
    Officer, Where Is My Child? 250
    Opposite Game, 266
    Pass It On, 259–260

Pass Some Love, 245
Popcorn Name Game, 243
Red Light, Green Light, 155, 296
Red Light, Yellow Light, Green
    Light, 391
Relay Race, 388
Remote Control, 268
Rhyming Game, 261
Rhyming Wheel, 70–71
Rig a Jig Jig, 244
Robot Says, 174
Roll the Ball, 348
Scavenger Hunt, 223
Sight Word Wheel Game,
    261–262
Simon Says, 314
Target Toss, 394
    travel, 25
Twenty Questions, 264
Watch Me! 375
Weather Charades, 263–264
What Am I? 270
What If …? 265
What's Missing? 265
Who Am I Thinking Of? 254
Whose Feet? 266
General tips, 275–307
    3+, 275–303
    4+, 304–307
Gift bags, 69, 464
Gift boxes, 464
Glitter, 98, 131, 225, 406, 457
Gloves, 38, 242, 350, 384, 401
Glue, 28, 33, 35–36, 43, 70, 74, 80, 98,
    100, 109, 114, 183, 255, 261, 263,
    266, 270, 280–281, 290–291, 390,
    392, 420, 425, 431, 443, 450, 457,
    462, 468
    craft, 34, 40, 100, 103
    guns, 107, 115, 258, 271, 290
    PVA, 131
    sticks, 26, 249, 279, 284–285, 420,
    453
Goldfish crackers, 441
Golf balls, 350
Graph mats, 259
Graphing activities, 63, 96, 355
Greeting cards, 109
Grocery bags, 292, 449
Grocery carts, 353

Gross motor skills, 27, 54, 62, 126,
    155, 180, 192, 201, 207, 219–220,
    222, 235, 306, 308–324, 337, 388,
    412, 416
    3+, 308–319, 363–381
    4+, 319–323, 382–383
    5+, 324
Guitars, 377

H

Hair gel, 41
Hand
    bells, 155
    drums, 130
    puppets, 165
    signs, 335
    washing, 160, 433–435
Handkerchiefs, 36, 265
Hats, 38, 401, 474
    birthday, 62, 305
    conductor 36, 133
    cowboy, 376
    crowns, 401, 477
    sailor caps, 139
    thinking caps, 114
    visors, 305
Headbands, 194
Hermit crabs, 416
Hole punches, 26, 55, 59, 96, 163,
    270, 285, 293, 297, 420, 425
Holidays, 404
Home-to-school connections, 69, 86,
    177, 251, 281, 285, 426, 448, 450,
    473
Hooks, 281, 283
Hula hoops, 246, 322, 412

I

Ice cream tubs, 312
    lids, 271
Ice cubes, 259
Icicle ornaments, 182
Icing, 435
Index cards, 33, 41, 55, 66, 68, 69, 113,
    191, 211, 214, 274, 285, 296–297,
    447
Individuality, 15
Inkpads, 41, 444
Interviews, 457

J

Jacks, 25
Jam, 435
Jewelry, 401
    boxes, 69, 299
Jigsaw puzzles, 303
Jingle bells, 375
Journals, 415, 422
Juice cartons, 251
Jump ropes, 412
Jungle gyms, 321

K

Key chain rings, 55
Keys, 350
Kitchen timers, 151, 454
Knives, 359
    plastic, 435
Koosh balls, 171

L

Labels, 34, 94, 103, 131, 245
Lace tablecloths, 433
Ladles, 331
Laminate, 20–21, 30–31, 60, 69, 74,
    94, 99, 104, 133, 139, 163, 210,
    261, 263, 269–270, 274, 282, 285,
    290, 355, 358–359, 370, 384, 392,
    439, 447, 453, 466
Language skills, 50, 54, 76–77, 84–86,
    93, 111, 113, 134, 219, 253–254,
    299, 301, 339, 403, 457, 463–464,
    475
Leaves, 190
Legos, 25
Letters, 43, 65, 247, 255, 264,
    268–269, 273–274, 301, 306–307,
    324, 351, 360, 384, 400, 452
    cards, 66
    magnetic, 274
    stamps, 274
    stencils, 23
Lids
    box, 258, 264, 399
    ice cream tub, 271
    plastic, 271
    yogurt container, 271
Life vests, 292
Light switches, 127
Limericks, 239–240

Index

Lining up, 30–31, 33, 48, 61–62, 76, 119, 201, 203, 253, 278, 301, 384–387, 392, 395–396, 398–399
Liquid soap, 345, 402, 435, 469
Liquid starch, 98
Liquid watercolors, 90, 404
Listening skills, 48–49, 50, 136–138, 224, 263
Literacy activities, 41, 65–66, 67–69, 73–74, 77–78, 81, 93, 95, 97–99, 108, 111, 136, 171, 247, 253, 264, 268–270, 280, 285, 299, 331, 347, 351, 354, 359–362, 377, 410, 443, 447, 472, 475
Loose-leaf rings, 55
Lost and found, 38
Lunch. *See* Snack/lunch

M

Magazines, 54, 109, 270, 284, 425, 431
Magic
 boards, 25
 wands, 46, 401
Magnetic boards, 94
Magnetic letters, 274
Magnetic stripping, 290
Magnetic tape, 94
Magnifying glasses, 259, 350, 413
Mailing labels, 94
Manipulatives, 41
 books, 470
Manners, 449–450
Map pins, 96
Maps, 350
Marbles, 126
Markers, 23, 26, 28, 30, 40, 43, 60, 66–68, 74, 80, 93–94, 96, 98, 100–101, 104, 106, 108–109, 113–114, 133–136, 139, 159, 177, 183, 186, 237, 248, 251, 255, 261, 269–270, 281, 283–284, 286–287, 289, 293, 298, 303, 319–320, 323, 325, 332, 343, 353, 355, 358, 360, 362, 384, 413, 420, 425, 431–432, 439, 441, 443, 447, 451, 462
 multi-colored, 177
 permanent, 38, 69, 184, 249, 303, 322, 350
 scented, 405
 washable, 228, 242

Masking tape, 41, 105, 251, 280, 287, 312, 350, 393, 411–412
 blue, 322
Masks, 175, 463
Matching activities, 33, 58, 72–73, 112, 248, 272–273, 453
Math activities, 31, 33, 35, 39, 48, 50–51, 57, 60–61, 63, 66, 84, 96, 112, 138, 162, 185, 225, 241–243, 246, 253, 255, 269, 271–272, 281, 285, 301, 312, 314, 323, 330, 352, 359–361, 366, 382, 393, 398–399, 420, 440–441, 476
Matte board, 399
Me puzzles, 249
Measuring
 activities, 39, 90, 185, 312
 cups, 90
 spoons, 90
Memory skills, 67, 453
Microphones, 339
Milk
 cartons, 251
 crates, 322
 jugs, 23
Mineral oil, 39
Mirrors, 315, 379, 452
Modeling clay, 98
Money, 359–360
Mosaic tiles, 41
Muffins, 444
Music boxes, 299
Music/movement activities, 55, 61, 130, 159, 164, 222, 235, 275, 295, 331, 363–383
 3+, 363–381
 4+, 382–383
 books, 470–471
Musical instruments, 61, 127, 139, 372, 375–378, 380–382

N

Name cards, 274, 361, 439
Nap time, 414–426
 3+, 414–424
 4+, 425–426
Napkins, 329, 432
Nature, 263–264, 355–356, 358–359, 363, 367, 380, 389, 398
Necklaces, 350, 401
Nerf balls, 171
Newspaper, 178, 312, 323

Nickels, 359
Note cards, 81, 211
Notepads, 54
Numbers, 43, 60–61, 66, 241–242, 253, 255, 269, 271–272, 295, 352, 361, 398–400
 cards, 255, 398
Nursery rhymes, 64, 214, 219, 226, 228, 255, 269
 "Little Jack Horner," 64
 "One Potato, Two Potato," 214
 "One, Two, Buckle My Shoe," 50
Nut cans, 359
Nutrition, 352, 431, 444–446

O

Oak tag, 54
Odd and even, 441
One-to-one correspondence, 31, 398–399
Opposites, 78–79, 120, 266
Outdoor activities, 29, 48, 126, 296, 312, 321, 366, 380, 383, 384–400, 406, 410, 436
 3+, 384–397
 4+, 398–400

P

Packing boxes, 132
Packing materials, 251, 404
Pails. *See* Buckets
Paint shirts, 292
Paint, 40, 43, 106, 110, 114, 190, 425, 468, 469
 acrylic, 304
 chalkboard, 107
 finger, 253
 poster, 402
 tempera, 403, 410
Paintbrushes, 106–107, 110, 394, 402, 468
Palettes, 402
Paper, 34, 41, 65, 69, 79, 93, 98, 106, 109, 113, 115, 157, 183, 237, 245, 251, 253, 272, 289, 292, 295, 320, 323, 325, 354, 379, 393, 403–404, 412, 420, 432, 447, 462–463, 467
 art, 64
 bags, 66, 335, 350, 367
 grocery, 292, 449
 lunch, 438
 blueprint, 107

butcher, 59, 108, 451
calculator, 96
card stock, 20, 26, 30, 70, 74, 92,
    101, 210, 249, 255, 261, 266,
    269–270, 283, 291, 293, 361,
    390, 439, 453
chart, 68, 97, 177, 299, 358
construction, 21, 31, 35–36, 63,
    80, 96, 98, 103, 112, 159, 194,
    225, 270, 281, 285, 317, 319,
    332, 351, 370, 384, 444,
    449–450
contact, 30, 99, 253, 263, 291, 317,
    322–323, 384, 421, 452–453,
    466
crepe, 398
cups, 114, 422
dolls, 390
drawing, 103, 105, 109, 353, 360,
    451
easel, 110, 248
fasteners, 101
glossy, 410
heavy, 20, 298, 413
newspaper, 178, 312, 323
pads, 43
plates, 100, 246, 406, 435
tissue, 98, 268, 421
towels, 160, 439
typing, 279
waxed, 225
wrapping, 44, 62, 264
Parachutes, 373
Partners, 32
Party favor games, 158
Paste, 285
Patterning, 35, 50, 315, 319–320,
    365–366, 382, 391
Pencils, 43, 54, 77, 98, 106, 109, 115,
    211, 272, 286–287, 353, 359, 383,
    412, 447, 450, 467
    colored, 133, 139, 360, 413
Pens, 33, 54, 92, 97, 106, 109, 131,
    134, 211, 242, 272, 289, 291,
    296–297, 353, 447, 467
    dry-erase, 99
    Sharpie, 305
Pepper shakers, 131
Permanent markers, 69, 184, 249,
    303, 322, 350

Pet
    food, 90
    supplies, 90
    toys, 380
Photo albums, 454
Photocopiers, 279, 285, 291, 33, 99,
    109
Photos. See Pictures
Picture cards, 127, 475
Pictures, 33, 54, 70, 74, 82, 87, 94, 109,
    115, 163, 169, 174, 180, 182, 245,
    248, 255, 261, 263, 266, 274, 279,
    281, 284, 291, 298, 347, 349, 358,
    363, 390, 395, 398, 425, 431, 443,
    453–454, 456, 466, 476
Pillows, 38, 78, 469
Pine trees, 182
Pinecones, 403
Pipe cleaners, 425
Pitchers, 430
Pizza dough, 445
Place mats, 432
Plants, 46
Plaster of Paris, 422
Plastic, 403
    aprons, 292
    bags, 132, 335, 422
        sandwich, 41
        zippered, 41, 249, 258, 271,
            296, 303, 359
    boxes, 38, 173
    containers, 130, 293, 312
    cups, 41, 271
    dinosaurs, 422
    hooks, 281
    jars, 34
    knives, 435
    lids, 271
    needles, 59
    sleeves, 178
    snowflakes, 182
    spoons, 41
    wrap, 437
Plates, 430, 432
    paper, 100, 246, 406, 435
Play people, 184
Playdough, 43, 90, 274
    recipe, 90
    tools, 90
Pocket charts, 20, 66, 68, 92, 210, 274,
    358, 362

Poker chips, 393
Pompoms, 114, 171
Popcorn, 445
Pops, 345
Popsicle sticks. See Craft sticks
Pop-up books, 25
Postcards, 278
Poster board, 19–20, 60, 67, 70, 74,
    93, 104, 133–135, 139, 210, 255,
    261, 263, 266, 274, 280, 284–287,
    325, 343, 431, 439, 441, 447
Poster paints, 402
Potato chip cans, 359
Printers, 210, 249, 274, 284, 343, 390,
    447
Pumpkin muffins, 444
Puppet theater, 468–469
Puppets, 91, 126, 128–129, 132, 166,
    168, 175, 182, 187, 214, 300, 334,
    350, 462, 468–469
    finger, 162, 242
    hand, 165
    stick, 225
    straw, 462
Purses, 401
Puzzles, 41, 157, 303, 415, 422
    flannel board, 286
    floor, 260
    homemade, 41, 59–60, 359
    me, 249
    pieces, 404
PVA glue, 131

Q
Quarters, 359
Questionnaires, 456
Quilts, 469

R
Rabbit ears, 464
Railroad board, 28
Rain barrels, 386
Rain sticks, 131, 375
Rainy day ideas, 393, 401–414
    3+, 401–412
    4+, 412–414
Raisins, 435
Reading center, 471
Recipes
    edible ladybugs, 435–436
    frozen bananas, 437
    playdough, 90

Index

Recorded music, 151, 155, 235, 297, 330, 333, 368–371, 374, 377, 382, 395–396, 416, 421–422
  American Folks Songs for Children by Ruth C. Seeger, 159
  Corner Grocery Store by Raffi, 170
  Greg & Steve CDs, 372
  John Philip Sousa marches, 372
  Keep on Singing and Dancing by Dr. Jean, 238
  Learning Basic Skills Through Music by Hap Palmer, 238
  Quiet Times by Hap Palmer, 415
  Sing to Learn by Dr. Jean, 238
  Songs to Read by Raffi, 408
  We All Live Together (Vol. 1) by Greg & Steve, 238
  We All Live Together (Vol. 2) by Greg & Steve, 197
Remote controls, 268
Rhinestones, 457
Rhymes/chants, 54, 68–69, 70–71, 135, 172, 261, 344, 395, 422
  "1, 2, 3, 4," 325
  "1, 2, I Love You," 325
  "A Dot," 105
  "A Knocking at the Door," 206
  "A Smile," 20
  "Alphabet Soup," 351
  "Apples, Pears, Peaches, Plums," 343
  "Bendable Me," 207
  "Birthdays, Birthdays," 63
  "Button, Button," 257
  "Can You?" by Barbara Saul, 208
  "Cats" by Barbara Saul, 192
  "A Cocky Cucumber Named Billy" by Penni L. Smith, 239
  "Doggie, Doggie, How Quiet Are We?" 128
  "Doggy, Doggy, Where's Your Bone?" 227
  "Eeny, Meeny, Miney, Moe," 231
  "Elephant, Elephant, in the Zoo," 316–317
  "Elevator" by Mary Jo Shannon, 313
  "Eyes Are Watching," 116
  "Five Little Fireflies," 225
  "Five Little Snakes," 209–210
  "Get on Board, Little Children," 326

"Get Ready," 117
"Give Me One!" 116
"Going Outside," 385
"Good Manner" by Mary Brehm, 294
"Hands Go Up," 196
"Hands Up High," 203
"Hello! Hello!" 339
"Hello, Everybody," 84
"House Is a House," A 413
"I Say Day," 120
"It Might Be You," 121
"Left and Right," 340
"Line Up," 119
"The Listening Position," 205–206
"Look at Me!" 203
"Lucky Leprechaun" by Barbara Saul, 164
"More Friends," 329
"Move, Chucka-Lucka-Lucka," 379
"A Nincompoop Called Nurp" by Pennie L. Smith, 240
"One Elephant," 337
"One, Two, Three, Eyes on Me," 122
"Pay Attention," 122
"Peanut Butter March," 395
"Pizza Pizzazz," 199
"Point," 117
"Popcorn" by MaryAnn F. Kohl, 311
"Potatoes and Carrots," 331
"Roll the Ball," 348
"See the Little Kittens," 418
"Sneaky Black Cat," 201
"Someone Just Like Me," 73
"There Once Was a Bee Named Bo" by Penni L. Smith, 240
"There Once Was a Candle Named Max" by Penni L. Smith, 240
"There Once Was a Ghost Named Boo" by Penni L. Smith, 239
"There Was a Girl Named Heather" by Penni L. Smith, 240
"There Was a Princess Named Dee" by Penni L. Smith, 239
"There Was a Robot Named Hymie" by Penni L. Smith, 240

"Time to Leave," 169
  "Today Is Monday," 431
  "Tool Rap," 135–136
  "Washing Hands," 345
  "What's That Sound Coming From the Barn?" 355
  "Who Stole the Cookie From the Cookie Jar," 233, 243
  "Wiggle Your Nose," 218–219
  "Willaby Wallaby," 336
Rhythm activities, 50, 331, 333, 365–366, 375–376, 382–383
Ribbons, 293, 309
Rings, 401
Rocks, 259, 334, 422
Rollers, 404
Rolling pins, 403
Room arrangement, 14
Rope, 159, 302
Routine, 14
Rubber balls, 388
Rubber bands, 297, 399
Rubber stamps, 41, 105, 164, 444
Rugs, 322, 454, 469
Rulers, 101, 183, 185

S

Safety glasses, 40, 292
Safety notes, 426
Safety pins, 163, 272
Sailor caps, 139
Salt, 90
Sand, 422
  play, 386, 399
  timers, 454
  tools, 386
Sand/water table, 23, 292
Sandpaper, 39–40
Scarves, 350, 372–373
Scatter rugs, 322
Scented markers, 405
Schedules, 14
Science activities, 32, 61, 106, 100–101, 154, 186, 263–264, 336, 355–356, 363, 367, 379–381, 394, 398, 403, 416, 422, 445–446
  books, 471
Scissors, 20–21, 23, 28, 30–31, 35–36, 59–60, 66, 70, 74, 77, 93, 96, 104, 112, 133–135, 139, 159, 172, 183, 210, 214, 249, 251, 253, 255, 261, 266, 269–270, 274, 280–281,

286–287, 290–291, 304, 312, 317, 319, 322–323, 358–359, 370, 383, 384, 398–399, 404, 413, 420, 441, 449–450, 453–454, 462, 467–468

Seashells, 423

Second language, 76, 83, 85–86, 88, 120, 168–169, 301, 339

Self-esteem, 447, 450

Self-managing props, 292

Sensory cues, 17

Sentence strips, 362

Sequencing, 61, 285, 476

Sequins, 421

Shadows, 315

Shampoo bottles, 126

Shamrocks, 164

Shapes, 35, 43, 66, 69, 95, 223, 255, 281, 358, 384, 399–400, 439, 441–442
    cards, 255

Sharpie pens, 305

Shawls, 401

Shellac, 403

Ships, 184

Shoeboxes, 62, 132, 399, 415

Shoelaces, 383

Shoes, 347, 350, 401

Shovels, 385–386

Shower curtains, 184

Sign-in sheets, 99

Signs
    5 more minutes, 19
    open/closed, 20

Silly putty, 259

Silverware. See Eating utensils

Skirts, 401

Slinkies®, 25, 158

Snack/lunch, 427–446
    3+, 427–438
    4+, 438–446
    breakfast, 430

Soap dispensers, 435

Social studies, 38

Social/emotional development, 185, 251, 270–273, 346, 378–379, 387–399, 439, 447–456, 460–461, 478

Socks, 457

Song charts, 377

Songs, 422
    puppet, 334
    routine, 297
    silly, 200, 234–235

Sorting
    activities, 33, 35, 39, 112, 246, 420
    bears, 43, 258

Soup
    cans, 80
    tureens, 331

Spaghetti, 445

Special days, 295, 305

Spiral notebooks, 97

Sponges, 106, 164, 394

Spoons, 61
    measuring, 90
    plastic, 41
    wooden, 130

Spray bottles, 46

Stamp pads. See Inkpads

Stamps, 81
    date, 103
    rubber, 41, 105, 164, 444

Staplers, 59, 100, 103, 194, 298, 466

Stick horses, 367

Stick puppets, 225

Sticker charts, 420

Sticker photos, 63

Stickers, 26, 34, 62, 253, 293, 419, 444
    dot, 222
    letters, 274
    numbers, 271

Sticky notes, 54

Sticky tac, 403

Stories, 226
    fairytales, 298
    quiet, 415
    transition, 298–299
    "The Billy Goats Gruff," 307
    "The Gingerbread Boy," 464
    "Goldilocks," 296
    "The Little Red Hen," 464
    "Little Red Riding Hood," 64, 296, 464
    "Quiet as a Crab," 416
    "The Three Bears," 64, 296
    "The Three Little Pigs," 64, 296, 307, 469

Story sequence cards, 476

Story time, 182, 235, 225–226, 241, 251, 295, 457–478
    3+, 458–474
    4+, 457, 474–478

Storytelling, 298, 350, 423–424, 463, 465, 467–468

Straw puppets, 462

Straw, 422

String, 19, 163, 297, 380, 420

Stuffed animals, 62, 181, 318, 334, 336, 345, 350, 389, 422, 464, 473

Stuffed blocks, 178

Styrofoam packing pieces, 404

Substitute teachers, 279–280

Sugar shakers, 131

Suitcases, 349

Sunglasses, 350

T

Table setting, 432

Tablecloths, 433

Tables, 157, 412
    sand/water, 23, 292
    small, 433

Tagboard, 94

Talking sticks, 460–461

Tambourines, 375, 378

Tape, 62, 94, 251, 264, 309, 320, 323, 332, 390, 403, 449, 451, 462
    colored, 316, 322
    double-sided, 286
    duct, 287, 359
    electrical, 253, 290
    magnetic, 94
    masking, 41, 105, 251, 280, 287, 312, 322, 350, 393, 411–412

Tape measures, 185

Tape players, 33, 91, 137, 141, 155, 297, 330, 369–370, 374, 382, 395, 406, 416, 421–422, 478

Teddy bear counters, 393

Telephones, 126, 350

Tempera paint, 403
    powdered, 410

Templates, 450

Textures, 259–260, 335–336

Three-ring binders, 279

Tickets, 397

Tic-tac-toe, 25

Time, 134, 188, 280–281

Tissue boxes, 332

Index

Tissue paper, 98, 268, 421
Toilet paper tubes, 403
Tongue depressors. *See* Craft sticks
Tops, 25, 158
Toys
 barns, 355
 fidgety, 357
 outside, 385
 quiet, 415
 small, 265
 table, 156
 transition, 157
Trains, 184, 392–393
 patterns, 281
 whistles, 36, 137, 365, 392
Transition cubes, 251
Transitions
 substitute teachers, 279–280
 to kindergarten, 306–307
 to preschool, 278
Transparency sheets, 115, 186
Trashcans, 411, 430
Travel games, 25
Trucks, 385
Trunks, 474
Tubs, 472
 ice cream, 312
Typewriters, 279
Typing paper, 279

V

Vegetables, 444
Velcro, 21, 31, 77, 107, 248, 304
Venetian blinds, 59
Videos
 "Yoga Kids" by Marcia Wenig, 375
Vinyl pads, 334
Visors, 305
Visual development, 138, 259
Vygotsky, Lev, 260

W

Waiting, 34, 47, 49, 72–76, 80, 437
Wands, 46, 401
Washable markers, 228, 242
Water, 46, 61, 90, 394
Water buckets, 394
Wax paper, 225
Weather, 355–356, 358–359, 367, 389, 402–403
Weaving, 27
Websites, 245, 274
Wedding veils, 401
Whistles, 350, 391
 train, 36, 137, 365, 392
Whiteboard, 136, 248
Wiggle eyes, 332
Window blind strips, 59
Windows, 402
Wind-up toys, 158
Wood, 21, 39–40, 309

Wooden
 bowls, 39
 shapes, 41
 spoons, 130
Woodworking center books, 471
Word
 cards, 273–274
 charts, 51
Workbenches, 292
Wrapping paper, 44, 62, 264
Writing
 activities, 34, 41, 78, 97–99, 233, 274, 361, 361, 447
 boxes, 422

X

X-ray films, 186
Xylophones, 61, 127, 371, 382

Y

Yardsticks, 287
Yarn, 26–28, 59, 61, 98, 159, 270, 281, 285, 292–293, 422
Yoga, 374–375
Yogurt, 435
 container lids, 271

Z

Zippered plastic bags, 41, 249, 258, 271, 296, 303, 359